Laughter and Ridicule

Theory, Culture & Society

Theory, Culture & Society caters for the resurgence of interest in culture within contemporary social science and the humanities. Building on the heritage of classical social theory, the book series examines ways in which this tradition has been reshaped by a new generation of theorists. It also publishes theoretically informed analyses of everyday life, popular culture, and new intellectual movements.

EDITOR: Mike Featherstone, *Nottingham Trent University*

SERIES EDITORIAL BOARD
Roy Boyne, *University of Durham*
Mike Hepworth, *University of Aberdeen*
Scott Lash, *Goldsmiths College, University of London*
Roland Robertson, *University of Aberdeen*
Bryan S. Turner, *University of Singapore*

THE TCS CENTRE
The *Theory, Culture & Society* book series, the journals *Theory, Culture & Society* and *Body & Society*, and related conference, seminar and postgraduate programmes operate from the TCS Centre at Nottingham Trent University. For further details of the TCS Centre's activities please contact:

Centre Administrator
The TCS Centre, Room 175
Faculty of Humanities
Nottingham Trent University
Clifton Lane, Nottingham, NG11 8NS, UK
e-mail: tcs@ntu.ac.uk
web: http://tcs.ntu.ac.uk

Recent volumes include:

Sex and Manners
Cas Wouters

The Body in Culture, Technology and Society
Chris Shilling

Globalization and Belonging
Mike Savage, Gaynor Bagnall and Brian Longhurst

Bootlegging
Lee Marshall

Laughter and Ridicule

Towards a Social Critique of Humour

Michael Billig

SAGE Publications

London ● Thousand Oaks ● New Delhi

© 2005 Michael Billig

First published 2005

Published in association with Theory, Culture & Society, Nottingham Trent University

SAGE Publications Ltd
1 Oliver's Yard
55 City Road
London EC1Y 1SP

SAGE Publications Inc
2455 Teller Road
Thousand Oaks, California 91320

SAGE Publications India Pvt Ltd
B-42 Panchsheel Enclave
Post Box 4109
New Delhi – 100 017

British Library Cataloguing in Publication data

A catalogue record for this book is available from the British Library

ISBN 1 4129 0250 9
ISBN 1 4129 1143 5

Library of Congress Control Number: 2004099514

Printed and bound in Great Britain by Athenaeum Press, Gateshead
Printed on paper from sustainable resources

Contents

Acknowledgements

A book on humour should have been enjoyable to write. For some reason, it did not turn out that way. In fact, there have been many days when I wished I'd undertaken a less ostensibly pleasant task. So, I am grateful for friends and colleagues who have given encouragement. I am particularly grateful to those who have read drafts of chapters: Steve Brown, Mike Gane, Dave Middleton, Yair Neuman, Thomas Scheff, and John Shotter. And thanks too to Susan Dunsmore for making the copy-editing such fun.

I feel particularly fortunate to work in the Department of Social Sciences at Loughborough University. It has provided a happy home for me, being surrounded by colleagues who are willing to discuss ideas and to laugh at the world. Once again, I should pay tribute to Peter Golding who has unselfishly managed to protect the department against the demoralizing pressures undermining so much British academic life.

Finally, of course, I would like to thank my family – to Sheila and to our children Daniel, Becky, Rachel and Benjamin. A conventional sense of humour often calls for an element of malice. Certainly the children and I have teased, mocked and laughed at each other in the ways that families do. But over the years, Sheila, like her mother before her, has demonstrated that there are far more important, far more serious virtues than the ability to make jokes. So this book is dedicated to Sheila and to the memory of her mother.

1

Introduction

The idea of a critical approach to humour sounds somewhat sinister. It suggests bossiness or craziness. Either way, the prospect is not pleasant. Bossy critics would dictate what we should and should not be laughing at. The image of the crazy critic is more disturbing. Fierce-eyed and serious to the point of derangement, the crazy critic would be warning us against the dangers of laughing at all. An admission must be made right at the outset. In terms of these two possibilities, the present investigation tends towards craziness rather than bossiness.

Of course, the temptations of bossiness will not be resisted. One of the compensatory pleasures of being an academic is to act as a bossy know-all in front of minuscule audiences. Nevertheless, the present inquiry sets out on the way to craziness. To be more precise, the aim is to go beyond the partial critique of humour that the bossy critic provides. Critical bossiness is a familiar characteristic of the high-minded writer. A seriousness of purpose demands judgements. If comedy is the topic, then the bossy critic aims to raise the level of laughter. There is a left-wing version of such bossiness, telling us that we should not laugh at jokes suspected of national, ethnic or sexist prejudices. Bossy critics may also disparage the comedies that the big entertainment companies offer and that many of their readers might readily enjoy. The message is that we should smarten up the quality of our laughter. We will be told to look elsewhere for our humour: maybe to obscure alternative comedians, or to the great comic literature of the past, such as *Don Quixote* or *Tristam Shandy*, that is little read today; or perhaps we will be recommended the unsuspected wit of difficult critics.

Bossy critics, whatever might be their particular recommendations, accept the common-sense dictum that laughter is good. Their mission is to improve that goodness. There is another critical direction. Rather than criticizing some types of humour as inappropriate, and commending others for meeting the requisite standards, it is possible to call into question laughter's assumed goodness. This is the path to craziness. How in all sanity can one criticize the precious gift of humour? Everybody knows that laughter is better than misery. To be anti-laughter, surely, is just plain ridiculous.

The social critic should not worry too much about the accusation of craziness or ridiculousness. One of the tasks of social critique is to question what passes for common sense. In so doing, the social critic may well fall foul of common sense's own criteria for what is sensible and what is not. This was well recognized by those sceptical Marxist philosophers of the Frankfurt School, who in the 1930s created the idea of the critical social theory. They were aware that social critique must attempt to get beyond what is generally thought to be sensible, in order to understand the ideological basis of that sensibleness. So it is with a critical approach to humour. This involves critically examining common-sense views about humour, calling into question beliefs that are taken to be self-evidently true. A critical approach to humour, therefore, takes as its object common-sense assumptions about humour's desirability, rather than the actual enjoyment of humour. Seen from this perspective, the craziness is perhaps not quite so crazy.

Common-sense beliefs about humour are not straightforward. We may assert that 'it is good to laugh' and, when we do so, we may believe that we are uttering something so evidently banal that it requires no further justification. However, beliefs about humour's goodness do not stand outside of history. What seems natural and so full of common sense in one era will appear strange in another. That is why the analysis of common sense needs a historical dimension. As will be seen, today's beliefs about humour are not so obviously true that they transcend the pattern of history.

There is another reason why our common-sense beliefs are not straightforward. They are open to the possibility of self-deception. Since laughter is held to be such a good thing, we want to believe that we possess a 'good' sense of humour in all aspects of the term. In consequence, we may ignore the more problematic aspects of the funniness that we enjoy with family and friends or as part of a mass audience of strangers. If this collective laughter has a shameful, darker side, then there is much that we may wish to hide from ourselves. Because the task of critique is to question common-sense beliefs, it must also ask what, if anything, such beliefs overlook and even conceal from the believers themselves.

The search for what is neglected will be one of the main themes of the present inquiry. It will be argued that humour is central to social life, but not in the way that we might wish for; nor in the way that much popular and academic writing on the topic suggests. It is easy to praise humour for bringing people together in moments of pure, creative enjoyment. But it is not those sorts of moments that constitute the social core of humour, but, instead, it is the darker, less easily admired practice of ridicule. This argument builds upon the insights of Bergson and Freud. It suggests that ridicule lies at the core of social life, for the possibility of ridicule ensures that members of society routinely comply with the customs and habits of their social milieu. Of course, humour can be rebellious, kicking against the dictates of social life. But social theorists have often concentrated on the rebellious aspect to the exclusion of the disciplinary aspects. Those who are motivated to believe in the goodness and creativity of laughter's rebelliousness turn their heads from the more problematic aspects of ridicule.

A few preliminary words are necessary in order to clarify what is and what is not being attempted here. The intention is not to construct a full-blown, complete theory that aims to explain every occurrence of humour. The sub-title stresses that the inquiry is hoping to move *toward* a critical theory, not that it has succeeded in producing one. There is preliminary work to be done, in questioning current theoretical assumptions about the intrinsic goodness of humour. Of course, the movement *toward* is also a movement *away from*. If the present work moves toward a critique that places ridicule at the centre of social life and that locates humour in the operations of social power, then it moves away from more good-natured, even sentimental, theories of humour. It is the good-natured theories that currently predominate. Accordingly, the present analysis is an argument against such theories. It does not attempt to provide carefully crafted definitions that will enable each incident of funniness to be duly categorized and inserted into a systematic theoretical catalogue. Readers, therefore, should not expect to find clear ways to distinguish wit from irony, or satire from pantomime, benevolent humour from malevolent humour, and so on. Nor should they expect a new methodology that would enable researchers to work towards such clarity of definition.

Robert Provine, in his interesting book *Laughter*, recommends that a scientific approach, based on observation and experimentation, should be adopted when studying laughter. In an early chapter, Provine describes the 'road not taken' by his book (2000: 11f.). Basically, Provine's untaken road is that of philosophy. He believes that there has been too much speculation and insufficient experimentation in the area of humour: 'Much of the literature about laughter is still mired in its prescientific phase where logic and anecdote, not empirical data, reign.' Provine includes both Bergson and Freud as pre-scientific investigators who would have done well to have risen from their respective 'philosophical armchairs' (ibid.: 11).

The road not taken by Provine is, in essence, the road that is taken here. In the social sciences, there are dangers in accumulating data for its own sake. The result can be confusion, as the details of data overwhelm the broader pattern. Sometimes what is required is the simplicity of a theory that does not seek to cover everything. Instead, it aims for an ordering of ideas that will attempt to distinguish the primary from the secondary. In so doing, it seeks to direct attention to phenomena that might otherwise escape attention.

In one important respect empiricists such as Provine are correct. Social theory should not be constructed purely from theoretical ideas. Theories should serve to illuminate the phenomena rather than vice versa. Therefore, theorists should try to make themselves aware of the relevant findings. Cultural theorists today sometimes ignore the sort of evidence that Provine recommends, especially when it comes to the study of psychology. A facility with Freudian theory – or an ability to juggle Lacan's concepts – is no substitute for knowing about psychological and sociological investigations. On the other hand, knowledge of empirical investigations on its own is insufficient for a critical inquiry. As will be suggested, academic psychologists, in designing their studies and interpreting their results, often make use of the very common-sense assumptions about humour's goodness that need to be critically questioned. So, the critical approach to humour must also include a critique of existing approaches and theories.

There is another reason why the approach should not be narrowly empirical. Investigators in the current academic climate often feel pressured to choose a particular area of study in which to become an expert. There are signs that humour is becoming a specialist field, displaying the conventional signs of successful expansion. There is a technical journal devoted to academic studies of humour. International congresses are regularly organized for humour researchers. Postgraduates are conducting doctoral research in the subject, and then entering academic life as trained experts in humour-studies. They will be teaching specialist courses, guiding a future generation in the use of relevant methodologies. So, the academic world is producing a small but growing number of humour-experts.

In these circumstances, it is good to remember the wise words of the radical critic C.L.R. James. He prefaced his book on the history of cricket with an epigram adapted from Rudyard Kipling: 'What do they know of cricket who only cricket know?' (James, 1964: 11). His point was that cricket experts, who supposedly know about the game but who have not studied social and political history, do not properly understand the game. When they watch a match, there is so much they cannot notice. The specialist, who principally knows but one subject area, does not properly know that area. It is the same with humour. To understand the social and psychological significance of humour, one needs more than a knowledge of the specialist research. One must seek to understand the seriousness of social life and, for that, one needs more than knowledge of humour.

Anton Zijderveld (1982) proposed that the world of comedy in premodern times represented the reversal of the ordinary, serious world. To understand this reversed world, one has to know about the world that is being reversed. So, Zijderveld needed to draw on his considerable knowledge of mediaeval and modern social life, in order to formulate his view of the comic. Similarly, Michael Mulkay (1988) has argued that the world of humour cannot stand apart from the world of seriousness. Before he turned his attention to humour, Mulkay had spent considerable time analyzing the sociology of the serious world, principally looking at science and its claims to knowledge. Peter Berger (1997) is another sociologist, who after years of studying the construction of social life, has been able to write with great insight about humour. As will be seen, the past theorists of humour, including Bergson and Freud, have historically been notable theorists of seriousness. What can they know of humour, who only humour know?

The maxim can, however, be reversed to show the importance of studying humour. What can they know of seriousness, who only seriousness know? There are good reasons for claiming that an understanding of humour is necessary for understanding serious social life. Certainly, today humour is a significant force within mass culture. The entertainment industry invests billions of dollars to try to make us laugh again and again, night after night. Arguably, contemporary culture cannot be understood without understanding how and why powerful economic forces are devoted to laughter. There is a further, more general reason to connect humour with seriousness. And this forms the basis of the present book's argument. The key question is not why present conditions have produced such an industry of humour, but why humour is to be found universally in all cultures. In answer to this question, it will be suggested that humour plays a central, necessary part in social life. It is not an extra but enjoyable adornment, like an embroidered pattern on a garment designed to keep out the cold. It is central to social life. Without the possibility of laughter, serious social life could not be sustained. And this is not necessarily a happy thought to those who only want to know of humour's joys.

Overview of the book

The book is divided into two parts. There is a historical part that reviews the main theories of the past, placing particular emphasis on the theoretical treatment of ridicule down the ages. Then comes the theoretical part of the book, arguing that ridicule plays a central, but often overlooked, disciplinary role in social life. In some respects, the historical chapters aim to trace the origins of ideas that are outlined in the second part.

Before the historical section, however, comes a chapter to argue why a critical approach to humour is required. Chapter 2 looks at the widespread positive evaluation of humour in today's popular and academic psychology. This positive evaluation is part of a wider outlook that is here called 'ideological positivism'. Since it is common-sense to be positive, the task of criticism is to become negative – or at least to draw attention to the negatives that are overlooked by the positive common sense. In the case of humour, this means drawing attention to the importance of ridicule, which is the great neglected negative in the psychological theories of ideological positivism. In the rush to sentimentalize the supposed goodness of humour, such theories overlook, and even repress, the negatives. Chapter 2 discusses how they do so and why this is not ideologically haphazard.

From there it is back into the past. As the theorists of the Frankfurt School realized, ideological critique should have a historical dimension, especially if it lacks clear convictions about the shape of the future. There are two related reasons why critique should look beyond the present. First, it is necessary to see where the ideas of today's common sense have come from. Second, in taking a historical perspective, a critical analysis aims to do more than just look at the past. It seeks to undermine the assumption that our common sense is a 'natural' perspective that is universally sensible. What seems obvious to us might have appeared strange, perhaps even deeply immoral, in other times. History can encourage us to distance ourselves from our own times, thereby providing a means to help resist ideological positivism's good sense.

Chapters 3, 4 and 5 examine in turn the three great theoretical traditions for understanding humour: the theories of superiority, incongruity and release. Each of these theories is examined in its historical and theoretical context. This means that the theories are not broken down into a set of separate hypotheses that are evaluated separately in terms of the modern evidence. Instead, the theories are set within their contexts, for these classic theories belonged to, and took their meaning from, wider currents of philosophy, aesthetics and politics.

Historically, the first of these theories is that of superiority, some of whose ideas can be traced back to ancient times. Sometimes the superiority theorists have been seen as enemies of laughter. This makes their ideas out of tune with the mood of today. Certainly, some thinkers, who are classed as superiority theorists, did not treat ridicule as the negative that it has become in ideological positivism. In the seventeenth century Thomas Hobbes formulated the most famous of all theories of superiority. Like its classical forebears, Hobbes's theory of humour was much more than a technical hypothesis about the causes of laughter. It was part of a fearful vision of society that emerged from the cruel times of the English revolution.

By contrast, the theories of incongruity, formulated in the following century, represented a gentlemanly reaction of taste and reason against Hobbes. Class, gender and the dreams of amiable reasonableness belong to the story of this theory. In this context, the issue of ridicule became a troubling one, foreshadowing modern theoretical dilemmas. However much the gentlemanly theorists kept trying to downgrade the importance of Hobbes's vision, back came the problem of ridicule. Why do we have the faculty of ridicule and what purposes might it serve?

The problem of ridicule was reformulated in the nineteenth century with the relief theories of Bain and Spencer. These theories are to be understood as belonging to the Darwinian revolution of the Victorian era. Both Spencer and Bain sought a scientific understanding of humour that would be based on biology. However, the biology in question was not just biological. It incorporated a wider view of human nature and the development of human society. Again, much more was at stake in the analysis of laughter than an entertaining intellectual problem.

If these classic theories of humour were more than just theories of humour, then so also were the great contributions of Bergson and Freud, which are examined respectively in Chapters 6 and 7. Their particular theories of humour are to be appreciated in relation to their wider *œuvre* and this, in turn, is related to a wider context. From Bergson come several important ideas for understanding humour: such as its disciplinary role, its cruelty and the idea that humour may fulfil a social function. Freud teaches that the social world makes demands on its members and that humour becomes a way of evading those demands, at least momentarily. Above all, Freud conveys the message that one should distrust humour: our laughter is not necessarily an honest reflection of the soul. Yet, curiously, Freud's own analysis contains its own evasions and omissions. These are taken as further evidence that the disciplinary functions of humour are both socially important and also matters of evasion.

A word of caution should be made about Part I. It comprises historical analyses rather than a history of humour. Completeness is not to be expected. Some theorists, such as Hobbes, Locke, the Earl of Shaftesbury, Bain and Spencer feature prominently. Others such as Kant, Kierkegaard and Descartes are ignored. English and Scottish writers are given more space than French or German theorists, at least until one gets to Bergson and Freud. A proper history of theories of humour would not be so cavalier with the inclusions and exclusions.

The aim of these chapters, however, is not just historical. Theoretical considerations are never far away. First, there is the general point to make: theories of humour are theories of more than humour. Second, the theories are examined in relation to their strengths and weaknesses, especially in relation to the issue of ridicule. In classical theories, ridicule did not pose the moral problem that it does today. But the issue of ridicule becomes a contested matter with the development of incongruity theories in the eighteenth century, which laid down the basis for many of today's modern psychological approaches. Third, the emphasis is on discussing some of the intellectual origins of modern ideas. Thus, the idea of a social function is traced to Herbert Spencer, who, interestingly, did not specifically use it in his theory of humour. That was left to Bergson. In such discussions, the historical analyses reach toward the views that are presented in Part II.

If theories of humour often take their meaning from wider ideological issues and if ideologies contain significant absences, then the discussion of past theories should be searching for significant absences as well as for significant presences. For instance, Bergson is the modern theorist who, above all other, pointed to the cruelty of humour and to its disciplinary function. Yet he shied away from considering the implications of these insights for understanding human nature. Freud might have provided the theoretical resources for analyzing why people should deceive themselves about the nature of their humour. Nevertheless, he shows a surprising innocence – even traces of denial – when he analyzes the jokes that give him pleasure. It is as if he cannot bear to be too harsh on the seemingly innocent world of fun. There are parallels with the ideological positivism of today.

Readers, who are impatient with the past and who wish to extract efficiently the nub of the present argument, might be advised to go straight from Chapter 2 to Part II, where the main theoretical arguments are to be found. Chapter 8 considers the relations between laughter and humour. The emphasis is on the social and rhetorical nature of laughter. Rhetorically, the positive can only have meaning in relation to the possibility of the negative. It is claimed that laughter is meaningful in human interaction because there exists the possibility of its opposite, namely, 'unlaughter'. This means that we can use laughter as an expression of approval because we possess the rhetorical means to display disapproval. Philosophers have called humans 'the laughing animal'. But we are the laughing animal only because we are also the unlaughing one.

The main argument for the social importance of ridicule comes in Chapter 9. A theoretical distinction is made between humour's rebellious and disciplinary functions, although, in practice it may be difficult to distinguish between the two. The difficulty arises, not because of a weakness of theory, but because humour can be an inherently controversial matter. One person's harmless bit of teasing will be another's cruelty. In this chapter, the dialectic between seriousness and humour shifts to the study of seriousness – or at least to the serious function of humour. This brings the argument to some of the central issues of serious social theory, namely, to the nature of the social order and its power over social actors.

It is suggested that social theorists have had difficulty explaining how social life maintains its hold over social actors. Even Freud did not really manage to explain this. Erving Goffman came close with his theory of social embarrassment. However, there is a significant gap in Goffman's theory. And this gap mirrors the general gap in optimistic theories of humour. Goffman does not say from where the fear of embarrassment derives its social power. It is suggested that it comes from ridicule, both socially and developmentally. Consequently, ridicule lies at the heart of social life. This is not a conclusion to be expected from the optimistic theories of ideological positivism.

Two caveats should be made. First, the theoretical ideas, which are presented in the Part II, examine the general links between social order and humour. It is not intended to evaluate the role of humour in contemporary culture, but to explore why humour is to be found universally in all cultures. If these ideas have any merit, then hopefully they will help to contribute to an understanding of current conditions. This possibility is very briefly touched on in the final concluding chapter. But no systematic analysis of the state of contemporary humour is provided here. That is a task for others. This is, as it were, a preliminary analysis that seeks to understand humour in terms of general, rather than particular, features.

The second caveat is that readers should not expect to be amused. The topic may be humour, but a critical approach encourages serious treatment. The historical analyses suggest that only in modern times do analysts of humour regularly include jokes in order to amuse their readers and to display their own good-heartedness. Older works on humour give little space, if any, to the joke. The critic, who wishes to stand aside from current assumptions, should resist the pressure to become a joke-teller. Indeed, the critic needs to question seriously the force of that pressure. Seriousness and humour, however, do not divide themselves into two totally distinct opposites. Irony can be a useful rhetorical means for standing aside and for seeking the distance that critique requires. But irony is not the same as telling jokes.

There are few jokes *qua* jokes in the present work, except as occasional illustrations of more general points. As Freud realized, personal and intellectual preferences become indissolubly intertwined in the matter of humour. So a personal statement is in order. I must admit that I do not particularly care for jokes as such. I certainly have great difficulty remembering them. Mostly they disappear from conscious memory the moment after the punch-line has been delivered. Consequently, readers who might expect a loving compilation and analysis of jokes, in the style of the recent book by the philosopher Ted Cohen (2001), will be disappointed. So will those friends and colleagues, who, having heard that I was writing a book on humour, passed on jokes that they were certain I would appreciate and would wish to include.

What is intriguing is that colleagues and friends have presumed that I would be celebrating humour. The presumption says much about the current positive view of humour. However, a critique cannot be a celebration. In some quarters of contemporary politics, it is asserted that 'if you are not with us, then you're against us'. If this assertion were translated from serious political issues to ideas about humour, then the present work would certainly not be on the side of those who wholeheartedly praise the virtues of humour. The celebrants may see this book as being anti-humour. And why not be anti-humour? There are worse crimes.

2

A Critique of Positive Humour

It might be thought that the critique of humour could best be accomplished scientifically. One might compare common-sense beliefs with the most recent scientific evidence, in order to discover whether common sense rests upon assumptions that succeed in meeting the relevant empirical tests. Experimental psychology might be especially useful for helping to distinguish between the myth and reality of human laughter, its causes and its effects. This may be true up to a point. But beyond that point, which cannot be determined in advance, it is liable to be misleading. An essential part of critical theory, and possibly one of its important aspects, has been to look critically at the theories of experts, in order to see how these theories have reproduced wider assumptions of common sense. This means that the critic has to be cautious about accepting social scientific theories at face value. They, too, are located within history and are marked by ideological currents.

This chapter will concentrate on examining current psychological ideas about humour. It will be argued that psychological analyses have incorporated common-sense values and common-sense omissions. To sustain this argument, the chapter will examine several different types of psychological writing about humour. These include popular self-help psychology, professional psychotherapy and academic theories of humour. The argument will be that an ideological pattern can be detected across these different genres. Humour is seen in terms of 'positives' and 'negatives', and psychological writers emphasize the 'positives'. The less pleasant faces of humour – its so-called negatives – tend to be pushed aside. In some cases, this neglect is so striking that one might even talk of 'textual repression'.

This pattern is part of a more general perspective, in which the 'positives' of life are to be stressed. This is 'ideological positivism' that represents an optimistic, can-do outlook in a society that offers its inhabitants the dream of constant, positively productive pleasures. The cruelties of this social order are overlooked, as if there is an imperative to wish away negatives. The critical philosopher, Herbert Marcuse, in a postscript to his book *Eros and Civilisation*, delivered a ferocious critique of neo-Freudians, including his former colleague the psychologist, Erich Fromm. Marcuse claimed that Fromm's later work had lost its critical edge and that psychology amounted to little more than platitudinous advice. The message of the neo-Freudians, and especially that of Fromm, was, according to Marcuse, 'tantamount to the conformist slogan "Accentuate the positive"' (1972: 174).

Marcuse's point was that psychological advice to 'accentuate the positive' was deeply ideological. The neo-Freudians had jettisoned the more disturbing aspects of Freudian theory, including the idea that all societies demand a certain amount of repression. Instead, there was a superficial, soothing optimism. The advice to 'accentuate the positive' was telling people to make the most of things, to cope with dissatisfactions that might not be their own making. It was commending the individual to adapt to social conditions, rather than seek to change conditions that should not be adapted to. In this way, the neo-Freudians, according to Marcuse, were themselves eliminating the 'negatives' from Freudian theory in order to construct a positive, but deceptive, view of the world. In these conditions, social critique needed to proceed along the negative path.

A similar pattern of accentuating positives and eliminating negatives can be seen in the contemporary psychology of humour, no matter whether this is the psychology of popular writers, academics or professional psychotherapists. The negatives of ridicule, sarcasm and mockery seem to be eliminated in a view that positively praises the warm-heartedness of humour. Where positive thinking appears as plain common sense, then the critic must aim for negativity.

Freud in his book on *Jokes and their Relation to the Unconscious* ([1905] 1991) recounts the story of Heine on his deathbed. A priest told the dying writer that he hoped God would forgive him for his sins. Heine replied that, of course, God would forgive him for *'c'est son métier'* – it's his job (ibid.: 160). So, the job of the critical theorist is to be negative, to be critical. Even when the topic is humour, the job must be done. Don't expect the critic to dispense happy smiles and sensitive reassurance. The critic has to examine the idea that the world might be changed by warm-heartedness, lots of hugging and a little more laughter. However, the demands of negativity do not exclude the possibility of humour. There still remain the pleasures of ridicule, especially those that might offend the ideology of being positive, just as they remained with Heine in his final moments.

A good sense of humour

It is easy to claim that possessing a sense of humour is nowadays deemed desirable. To say that someone has no sense of humour is to utter a criticism. It may not be the worst criticism that can be offered. Being cruel, heartless and immoral will probably be taken as a more severe condemnation. But lacking a sense of humour is up there among the modern undesirables. Daniel Wickberg (1998), in his excellent history of the concept of a sense of humour, draws attention to the moral dimension. If a person is said not to possess a sense of humour, this means more than that they might be boring company: it suggests that they lack a vital human quality.

Evidence suggests that people today consider a sense of humour to be an important factor in selecting sexual partners. A public opinion survey in Britain indicated that 94 per cent of females and 92 per cent of males would prefer their partner to be humorous rather than serious (*Observer Magazine*, 26 October 2003). A glance at the personal advertisements in newspapers would confirm the desirability of a sense of humour. One study of personal ads in American newspapers claimed that one in eight of those seeking a partner either mentioned their own sense of humour or declared this to be a trait they wished to find in their prospective partner (Provine, 2000). Often the advertisers, who are being charged per word, economize by using conventional abbreviations. Having described their own qualities, the advertisers might declare that they WLTM (would like to meet) someone with GSOH (a good sense of humour). The very abbreviation indicates that a 'good sense of humour' is being treated as a readily understood commodity (Coupland, 1996). In the context of the personal advertisements, this quality is not reversible, for it has no equally desirable opposite. Some advertisers might claim to enjoy 'country-living' or 'quiet nights in'. Other advertisers might prefer opposites such as 'the city-life' or 'exciting nights out'. By contrast, GSOH has no valued opposite. No-one WLTM that loving special person with NSOH (no sense of humour). The latter abbreviation does not exist. In seeking to attract others, people will no more declare themselves to be humourless than claim to be selfish, insensitive or criminally insane.

It was not ever thus. As Wickberg stresses, the concept of 'a sense of humour' has a short history, at least in its contemporary sense. It started to be used during the 1840s and only by the 1870s was it being used in its modern sense to denote the 'altogether familiar notion of the sense of humour as a personality characteristic' (1998: 18). The emergence of this notion was linked to a broader change in thinking about the person. People were no longer being considered principally in terms of social position or physiological make-up. Instead, they were being conceived as autonomous individuals, possessing enduring characteristics of individuality.

The idea of people having individual personalities seems 'natural' to us. We possess and regularly use a wide vocabulary to express personality. We act as if this vocabulary and the concepts that it denotes always existed – as if the world always contained introverts and extraverts, depressives, compulsives, easy-going types, and so on. A glance at old texts will show the absence of this vocabulary of personality in other times. In the Hebrew Bible, the nature of persons is revealed through their actions. There is no attempt to describe the actors with ready labels that constitute a typology of inner lives. Moses, for instance, is not described as possessing a particular personality-type or even a range of personality characteristics. He is not specifically categorized as hard-working, socially concerned, brave, intelligent, serious, let alone introvert, inner-directed or positively orientated, etc. The original text does not heap personal adjectives upon its characters to make them appear as recognizable characters, except in one significant passage. As Moses went up Mount Sinai for the second time, bearing this time two hewn stones upon which the commandments were to be re-written, the Deity is said to have passed before him, proclaiming: 'The Lord, the Lord, mighty, merciful and gracious, long-suffering and abundant in goodness and truth ...' (Exodus, 34: 6). No human character in the text receives or describes themselves with such an adjectival list of traits. This is something reserved for the Deity, occurring in a moment that transcends ordinary human life.

As regards 'sense of humour', the Bible pays no attention to such a characteristic *qua* characteristic. It appears neither in the Deity's self-description nor in the descriptions of the human actors. Later Talmudic tales tell of the Deity searching for a people willing to receive the Law. These tales might take the form 'Merciful and long-suffering God WLTM a special people with a view to a long-term relationship'. Neither the special people nor the Deity are specifically said to require GSOH – although, as Theodor Reik noted, within Jewish folklore their relationship came to be characterized in terms of humour (Reik, 1962). In the biblical text, the patriarchs and other central characters do not seem to laugh much. If Moses and Aaron, after a hard day of tramping through the desert, relaxed in the evenings swapping anecdotes and laughing together, we do not hear of this. One would like to think they did. Or at least, a modern reader might like to think so. But we belong to a society in which fun has become an imperative and humour is seen as a necessary quality for being fully human.

The conditions of modern life are different from other ages with respect to humour. No longer is it necessary to wait for carnival time to engage in socially sanctioned fun. Comedy, just like warm water, is constantly on tap in contemporary affluent society. This comedy comes in numerous varieties, making carnival a vast, constant and profitable business, not a brief, intermittent release from a life of toil. The entertainment industry invests mightily to ensure the regular amusement of all. The television companies compete with each other to offer the most laugh-filled entertainment. The advertisers who interrupt the programmes will frequently attempt to capture attention with humour. There are specialist television channels devoted to providing nothing but comedy shows all and every day. In Britain, comedy is the most successful genre of film, outstripping action and drama movies (The *Guardian*, 6 June 2003). Each social group, which is identified as a profitable market, has comedies targeted to suit their tastes. Even the most powerful potentates of the past did not have at their command so many and so varied offerings of amusement as are available now to the ordinary citizen of Western society. No-one is expected to like every comic show, film or magazine. But everyone is expected to have some favourites. To remain unamused by the never-ending programme of comic opportunity would indicate a personal failing or a clinical condition.

As Daniel Wickberg suggests, the past seems like a foreign country, especially in relation to its views about humour. His excellent history makes it unnecessary here to recount how the modern notion of a sense of humour developed. The purpose here is to use the past in order to make the present seem, at least momentarily, somewhat foreign. Some brief examples will help to reinforce the idea that what might have once seemed 'natural' now seems ridiculous – just as our common sense might seem ridiculous to past and future times.

In 1877, the Victorian novelist George Meredith delivered a lecture on 'The idea of comedy' at the London Institution. This lecture was published in a literary magazine in the same year, and then was republished in book form in 1897. Meredith's lecture may have been given just when the notion of a 'sense of humour' was becoming a desirable human quality. However, he began his talk as if comedy were a matter of controversy. In outlining his argument he attacked the 'agelasts', who never laughed. He attributed the term to Rabelais, who had in earlier years battled against laughter's enemies. According to Meredith, the agelasts still existed as immovable forces, glowering over the social life of the times: 'The old grey boulder-stone that has finished its peregrination from the rock to the valley, is as easily to be set rolling up again as these men laughing' (1897: 9). The 'agelasts' typically went further than not laughing – they despised laughter. So, they were better described as 'misogelasts', a word that Meredith coined.

The term 'agelast' has even less currency today than in Meredith's day. His neologism 'misogelast' has failed to make the *Oxford English Dictionary*. These terms have not been usurped by zippier synonyms, but they have disappeared. Modern writers on humour have little need for them. Analysts of humour no longer have to justify their endeavours by claiming to be battling against recognizable figures who refuse to laugh or who disdain the comic. No-one today wishes to be thought a misogelast, and certainly not to acquire one as a partner. There is no general common sense of seriousness to refute.

Those figures, whom Meredith might have had in mind as he used the words 'agelast' and 'misogelast', seem distant absurdities. In the eighteenth century, Lord Chesterfield advised his son that a proper gentleman should avoid laughing. A smile might be an appropriate reaction to tasteful wit, but full-bodied laughter was the sort of coarse behaviour to be expected only of the lower orders. Today, no-one would bother to refute these ideas.

Some 150 years before Chesterfield, Francis Bacon was writing in his essay 'On Discourse' that certain matters should be exempt from jest, 'namely, religion, matters of state, great persons, any man's present business of importance' ([1625] 1902: 102). Bacon's protected topics comprise just the things that nowadays seem to be proper targets for humour. How ludicrous of the man, who was to become Lord Chancellor, to declare that important personages and great matters of state should be above jest. Again, it is so easy to mock, that such mockery is unfair. In this case, the possibility of mockery has been increased by omitting the final item in Bacon's list of things to be exempted from humour: 'any case that deserveth pity' (ibid.: 102). That final item today does not make for a good punch-line.

The examples of Chesterfield and Bacon show the link between common sense and laughter. We do not have to pause to assess Chesterfield's advice. Quote his remark to an audience nowadays – whether academics, students or people of sound sense – and they, as likely as not, will react immediately with a smile that ridicules what is beyond common sense. As Poinsinet de Sivry wrote in the seventeenth century, 'the eruption of laughter is too quick for anyone to attribute its cause to the slow processes of judgement' (quoted in Piddington, 1933: 176). The superior smile of ridicule is a constantly loaded weapon designed to repel any challenge to common sense. For this reason, the critical social theorist should be wary of that smile, which can easily be turned upon the very notion of social critique.

Being seriously humorous

In an age when a sense of humour is regarded as being self-evidently desirable, serious writers on humour face a dilemma. Whatever they do can be taken as evidence of their unfitness for the task. The very task of analysis seems antithetical to humour, as Michael Mulkay (1988) points out in his thoughtful book on humour. Even if their topic is humour, social analysts must operate primarily within the realm of seriousness. However, if one gets too serious about humour, then one can easily end up as a figure of ridicule – the earnest academic who simply didn't get the joke and is therefore unfit to study the topic. On the other hand, a jokey piece of social science, whatever its topic, cannot be trusted as a serious contribution. The French philosopher Dugas began his book on the psychology of laughter by expressing concern that because reflection kills laughter, it would therefore be impossible to find laughter's causes (1902: 1–2). Freud was so struck by the irony of the remark that he quoted it in his *Jokes and their Relation to the Unconscious* ([1905] 1991: 197–8).

When a sense of humour is obligatory, the serious analyst is faced by the old rhetorical problem of *ethos*: how to present oneself as a suitable person, in this case as a person equipped to write seriously about the nature of humour? The issue was different before the possession of a sense of humour became a necessary quality. Many of the historical writers to be discussed in later chapters did not go out of their way to present themselves as great lovers of the comic. Some, such as Schopenhauer and Spencer, reveal themselves to be particularly bereft of humour. Others, like Hobbes, seem to have been known for their wit, but kept all sense of fun from their writings about laughter. Only with Freud, do we find a major, serious writer on humour, sharing his humour with his readers. However, Freud's case was somewhat curious for he was suggesting that humour could hide some nasty little secrets.

In earlier times theorists of humour did not feel compelled to display their personal sense of humour as a warrant for their expertise to write on the topic. In the eighteenth century, the approach of the Scottish philosopher and poet, James Beattie, was typical. At the start of his *Essay on Laughter*, Beattie justified his choice of topic, using a cautious double-negative. He wrote that laughter distinguishes 'Man from the inferior animals' and, therefore 'must be allowed to be not unworthy of the philosopher's notice' (1779: 299). What Beattie omits in his prefatory justification is significant. He does not say that he personally is not unworthy for the task of analyzing humour because he was not unprone to joking. Like other writers on the topic in the eighteenth century, Beattie's task is to present humour as worthy of serious attention. For this, he needed to demonstrate his own seriousness of purpose, not his capacity for laughter.

Today, by contrast, serious writers on humour, often aided by their publishers, engage in the self-presentation of their own humorous character. This is particularly true of popular psychology books that are aimed at a wide non-academic readership and which promote laughter as a means to improve the quality of their readers' lives. Such books constitute a sub-type within the overall genre of self-help psychology. Their titles are designed to catch attention, while lengthy subtitles inform potential readers of the help that is on offer: *A Laughing Place: The Art and Psychology of Positive Humor in Love and Adversity* (Hageseth, 1988); *Relax – You May Only Have a Few Minutes Left: Using the Power of Humour to Overcome Stress in Life and Work* (LaRoche, 1998); *The Healing Power: Techniques for Getting Through Loss, Setbacks, Upsets, Disappointments, Difficulties, Trials, Tribulations and All That Not-So-Funny Stuff* (Klein, 1989); *The Courage to Laugh: Humour, Hope, and Healing in the Face of Death and Dying* (Klein, 1998); *Serious Laughter: Live a Happier, Healthier, More Productive Life* (Conte, 1998); *Becoming a Humour Being: The Power to Choose a Better Way* (Rizzo, 2000).

The writers of these books are required to present themselves as serious fun-guys. Who would wish to purchase a book recommending the life-enhancing positives of laughter, if the author were obviously a pompously unfunny professor? On the other hand, the message that humour is a means for living better must not be seen as a joke. Credentials of humour and seriousness must be displayed, if the author is to achieve the desired *ethos*.

Allan Klein, in *The Courage to Laugh* calls himself a 'jollytologist' – a term that captures the ambivalence of the writer's rhetorical dilemma: the last three syllables suggest a seriousness of purpose, whilst the first two denote folksy fun. Klein begins with a personal account. His career as a jollytologist started after the death of his wife. His sense of humour helped him cope with the loss: 'As you will see in the numerous heart-warming and often hilarious stories in this book that it helped others, too, to bear the unbearable' (Klein, 1998: 5). In this way, the reader of those early pages is introduced to Klein as a caring man with a sense of humour and professional qualifications: he has serious advice to offer, the personal experience of grief to share and, most importantly, funny stories to tell. The back cover of Klein's earlier *The Healing Power of Humour* (1989) advertises the book to be 'brimming with pointed humorous anecdotes and learn-to-laugh techniques'. The prospective reader is to be enticed not just by the prospect of wisdom and therapy but also by fun.

Christian Hageseth III, in common with Allan Klein, possesses medical qualifications that are clearly displayed on the front cover of *A Laughing Place* (1988). The blurb on the back cover describes the author as a qualified psychiatrist, popular speaker and innovative humour-theorist. It adds: 'He has been described as funny and the "most normal shrink" ever to escape a consulting room.' The description appears alongside a picture of the author which shows him without tie or jacket and catches his face suitably in mid-smile. Early in the text, the author presents his credentials for possessing a sense of humour. In the acknowledgements, he praises the good humour of his father, brother and sister: 'together we shared some wonderful laughter' (ibid.: 9). Then there are his children – 'sharing laughter with them has been a joy' (ibid.: 10). Finally, and predictably, there is the humour-theorist's wife, the person 'who has opened my being so fully that my creativity could sing' (ibid.: 10). That's not a joke. It's a boast, wrapped up as a loving tribute by a man who claims to know the value of sharing.

The first chapter of *A Laughing Place* presents the author as fun guy, able to give and take a joke. Hageseth tells of the time when he was about to give a public televised lecture on humour. In the men's room, just before the start of the lecture, he realizes that his trouser-fly is broken. It cannot be closed. He borrows some safety pins; goes on stage ten minutes late; and begins his talk by saying that his fly just broke. His assistant points to the pins. The audience laughs. The television captures the moment. The author has a story with which to begin his book. Not only can he draw the moral that humour helps you through life's adversities, but the author shows how he personally can turn embarrassment into laughter. The story is designed to amuse the reader – more wonderful laughter to be shared.

The presentation of self as having a sense of humour is not confined to the popular self-help genre. It can be found in more academic writings. Professional psychologists, who use humour as a therapeutic tool, will often display their own appreciation of humour, when writing academically about the benefits of their method. William Fry has been one of the leading advocates of the use of humour in therapy. In the preface to the *Handbook of Humour and Psychotherapy*, which he edited with Waleed Salameh, Fry offers a brief biographical sketch. He tells how as a young man he was 'a somewhat silly person' (1987: xiv). When he began his professional career as a clinical psychiatric therapist, he tried to overcome this silliness by utter professional seriousness. However, as he grew older, he realized the silliness of this seriousness. He returned to the silliness of his youth, introducing humour into psychotherapy. The implication is that seriousness is as ridiculous as silliness is serious.

The contributors to the *Handbook* and to the later *Advances in Humour and Psychotherapy* (Fry and Salameh, 1993) were encouraged to give examples of how humour could assist therapy. In doing so, some of the authors make direct claims about their appreciation of humour. For instance, Schimel declares that 'my use of humour, I believe, is inherent in my makeup and my capacity to recognize the absurdity in many of life's contretemps' (1993: 49). More often the laughter-therapist's sense of humour is displayed within examples rather than being overtly claimed. In these examples, the therapists recount how patients had laughed at their jokes and how they, in return, had appreciated the wit of their patients.

Practising therapists, who advocate that their fellow professionals use humour, have a need to demonstrate their own possession of the requisite skills. Academic researchers and theorists have no such obligations. There is no more reason why academic psychologists investigating the subject of humour should feel obliged to affirm their sense of humour than an expert on the psychology of crime should claim proficiency at shop-lifting. Nevertheless the affirmations are frequently made, whether explicitly or implicitly.

Gruner (1997), in his psychological investigation of humour, goes out of his way to include lists of jokes. One or two jokes might fulfil a theoretical point, but a whole page suggests a wish to amuse. Herbert Lefcourt's *Humour: The Psychology of Living Buoyantly* (2001) is instructive and will be discussed in more detail later. Lefcourt is a distinguished social psychologist with a long track record of investigating personality. His book is firmly based within academic, quantitative research in psychology. Its sub-title might echo the language of the self-help genre but neither the word 'buoyantly' nor the general concept of 'buoyancy' figure largely in his substantive theoretical framework.

In his preface, Lefcourt pays tribute to his family: 'Humour and laughter filled the milieu in which I grew up' (ibid.: v). He comments that 'mine was a childhood punctuated with laughter' (ibid.: vi). The preface then links the personal with the professional: humour is not only a topic worthy of study, 'but it is also an intrinsically attractive subject because of the amusement we can find in the studies we do and the stories we tell' (ibid.: vii). His opening chapter, like Hageseth's, recounts a personal story of using humour. Lefcourt gives 'my personal odyssey' to humour research. He tells of his father who liked to joke even in grim circumstances – mothers tend to figure less prominently in these tributes by male humour theorists. At his father's funeral, Lefcourt and the other mourners jested in the way that his father would have enjoyed. He comments that 'the relatives revelled in that good humour so that everyone left the ceremonies with better feelings towards each other' (ibid.: 6). It is a story to fit Allan Klein's stock of 'hilarious, heart-warming' anecdotes about humour and adversity. It is a happy-ending anecdote.

Lefcourt's book closes with yet another personal anecdote. He tells of a vacation in the tropics of Australia with wife, son, daughter-in-law and three-year-old grandchild. They were camping in oppressive temperatures, amidst flies and defecating birds. His son at one moment utters a humorous, zany remark. That one remark induced 'a wonderful feeling of closeness with my son, to whom I'll always be grateful' – the little joke enhanced 'the pleasure of our time together, leaving us feeling healthier and happier' (ibid.: 172).

It is not just psychologists and those searching for partners through the personal columns who are keen to affirm themselves as having good senses of humour. Other academics writing on humour can show the same tendency, which is well promoted by their publishers. Peter Berger's superb sociological study *Redeeming Laughter* (1997) positions itself as more than just a serious analysis produced by a serious academic. In his preface, Berger assures readers that his treatise is not a 'jokebook' but adds that 'I very much hope that readers will occasionally laugh' (ibid.: x). James Beattie did not have to advertise to readers that his volume was not a joke-book. He certainly did not hope that they would laugh.

Like Lefcourt, Berger cites the influence of his father, 'an inveterate teller of jokes' who encouraged the infant Berger to follow suit (1997: x). He also gives credit to his oldest friend who, Berger says, has endured his jokes for years. The book proper begins with a short four-page Prologue. In the course of this Prologue, Berger manages to tell four jokes. The book's back cover carries a recommendation from a distinguished political scientist who asserts: 'Of all the people I know, Peter Berger tells the best jokes.' The recommendation concludes that *Redeeming Laughter* not only analyzes the position of the comic in life but 'also includes some great jokes'.

No-one could have complimented James Beattie for including great jokes in his analysis of laughter. In those times, a different sense of personal propriety and self-presentation obtained. We do not know whether Beattie laughed off embarrassing incidents. Philosophers did not then share their trouser problems with readers. Neither warm-hearted family moments, nor the sort of tragic circumstances that marked Beattie's family life in the years following the *Essay on Laughter*, were the business of strangers. When the essay was republished later, Beattie did not add footnotes to say that laughter had enabled him to deal with his wife's insanity and the deaths of his sons. While Beattie sought to present himself to his readers as a detached, rational observer, today's writers show their good intentions by presenting anecdotes with happy endings and expressing gratitude for their laughter-filled beginnings. Such analysts of humour do not distance themselves from the topic that they are studying: they position themselves on the side of humour. If there are hidden secrets within laughter, then these analyses come with outward signs of complicity.

Accentuating the positives

The authors' prefaces at the start of the books about humour and the promotional blurbs on the back covers do not prove that the general value for humour is affecting the substantive work. It is necessary to look at what comes between preface and back cover. As a first step this will involve looking at the language that today's theorists typically use when discussing humour. The language of 'positives' and 'negatives' features prominently, as theories follow the common-place dictum of 'accentuating the positives and eliminating the negatives'. This dictum is more than just good sense, for, as Marcuse argued, it is highly ideological. If this ideological viewpoint can be called 'positivism', then this is 'ideological', rather than 'logical', positivism.

The words 'positive' and 'negative' deserve special attention, for writers on the psychology of humour slip easily into using them. This is true whether the writer be a popular, academic or clinical psychologist. A few illustrative examples can be given. Salameh, one of the editors of *Advances in Humour and Psychotherapy*, writes about the growing acceptance of using humour in psychotherapy. According to Salameh, humour is becoming recognized by patients, as well as by therapists, 'as a welcome and positive modality' (1993: xxxii). Other contributors to the volume amplify the point. Gerald Amada, a psychotherapist who specializes in working with students, writes of 'the positive experience' of hearing a good joke (1993: 158). One contributor writes that laughter blocks 'negative emotion' (Surkis, 1993: 126) and another claims that 'the judicious use of humour' can aid the development of 'a positive atmosphere' during therapy (Heuscher, 1993: 218).

In these and other instances the writers do not define what is 'positive' and what is 'negative', for they assume that the words are readily understood. A positive experience is something good while 'negative emotions' are bad emotions that should be eliminated. The use of 'positive' and 'negative' semantically avoids the moralistic baggage of 'good' and 'bad'. A 'negative emotion' seems to denote something more objective than a 'bad' or 'evil' emotion. Its negativity does not depend on the personal moral preferences of the observer. The rhetoric implies, but does not specifically assert, that the positivity and negativity of emotions are just as objectively founded as the positivity and negativity of electrical currents.

The language of positives appears across the genres of psychological writing. It is prominent in Hageseth's popular work for developing 'positive humour' which provides readers with exercises to help them 'transform humour into a positive and helpful skill' (1988: 22). Positive humour has much to offer the individual, for it reduces 'stress and enhances communication' and 'the use of positive humour favours mental and physical health' (ibid.: 22). The confidence of the statements conveys a sense of objectivity. The positiveness of positive humour is assumed to exist out-there in the world, rather than reflecting the subjective preferences of the writer.

Our world, according to Hageseth, suffers from a lack of positive humour: 'I wish leaders of the world would learn and practice positive humour' (ibid.: 24). Recognizing the limitations of his own situation, Hageseth adds that: 'I don't have much influence on world leaders' but 'I do know how to help individuals change' (ibid.: 24). Maybe the way to change the world is 'by teaching one individual at a time' (ibid.: 24). Perhaps his readers might care to 'join together for a form of humour support group' (ibid.: 141). Should they do so, they should read the footnotes carefully because the term 'humour support group' is trademarked (ibid.: 45n). If professional psychologists are to change the world by humour, they will need to be protected by the serious laws of copyright.

Positivism can be found in Lefcourt's academic book on *Humour* (2001). According to Lefcourt, the study of humour belongs to that part of psychology that is concerned with investigating 'positive processes', particularly the study of 'positive affect' (ibid.: 168). Along with the popular writers, Lefcourt stresses the benefits of humour for coping with problems and for overcoming stress. Lefcourt outlines studies that show how humour can help 'individuals maintain positive affect during encounters with negative events' (ibid.: 120). He describes how psychologists have correlated respondents' sense of humour with their responses on the Positive Life Event scale and also with their responses on the positive affect subscale of the Positive and Negative Affect Schedule (PANAS). The results, according to Lefcourt, show that persons who appreciate humour were 'likely to derive positive affect from their positive experiences' (ibid.: 120). In other words, the positives match up, if you positively appreciate humour.

The case of humour and health is interesting. The popular writers have no hesitation in declaring that humour has positive effects. Hageseth asserts that 'beyond merely protecting you from illness, positive humour enhances wellness' (1988: 22). In *The Healing Power of Humour*, Klein proclaims medical and scientific research to have proved that a sense of humour and a 'positive attitude' will help withstand physical disorders (1989: 8). The back cover of the book declares that 'science has proved, although we knew it all along, that humour is our best medicine'. Actually, the scientific studies are by no means so clear. One recent review of the relevant evidence failed to find any firm evidence that humour improves health. Its author concludes that 'despite the popularity of the idea that humour and laughter have significant health benefits, the current empirical evidence is generally weak and inconclusive' (Martin, 2001: 516). This is supported by another recent study that found that 'overall a better sense of humour is not particularly related to higher levels of health' (Boyle and Joss-Reid, 2004: 62).

Yet, there is pressure to believe in the positive benefits of humour. Robert Provine, who is sceptical about the medicinal value of laughter, writes of the widespread publicity given to three small-scale studies purportedly showing that humour increases the power of the immune system. All three studies were methodologically flawed and were only published as abstracts and not as full reports (see also Martin, 2001). Despite this, they have been cited as established fact. According to Provine, 'it's sobering to realise that these three abstracts are the basis of much of the folklore about laughter's positive effects on immune function' (2000: 198). Provine recounts how the media has often approached him to comment on the relationship between laughter and health. His message that there was little evidence to suggest that laughter actually improves health was not what the media wanted to hear. As he puts it, his views were 'as welcome as a skunk at a picnic' (ibid.: 190).

Here we are clearly in the realm of ideology. There is a cultural climate that wants to believe in the positive powers of laughter. This message is more readily spread than that of scepticism. In the process of mass dissemination, ambiguous scientific evidence is transformed both literally and figuratively into 'positive' findings. However, one should beware of insisting upon a distinction between science and ideology, at least in relation to this sort of psychology. As will be seen, the ideology of positivism reaches into central areas of academic psychology, which pride themselves on being scientific.

Eliminating the negatives

However, there is a cloud in the blue skies of the positive world. Not all the positives in the universe may be in alignment. Some negatives may possibly have positive outcomes and vice versa. It is unrealistically optimistic to presume otherwise. This constitutes a general problem for ideological positivism. With respect to humour, there is the specific problem of ridicule. One might wish to put humour on the side of the positives. But ridicule, as a form of humour, is associated with many of the things that psychologists would prefer to classify as negative. It can demean, cause suffering to and humiliate its victims. How can such cruelty be numbered among life's positives? The short answer would be to divide the category of humour into positives and negatives, into good and bad humour. Then ridicule, along with sarcasm and the laughter of bigotry, can be classified on the bad, negative side.

For the social theorist, any such division into positive and negative humour would require justification. By contrast, popular psychologists are little troubled by the demands of theory. Their business is not to provide rigorous definitions or to root distinctions in tight theoretical structures. They are generally working with the values of common sense, not against them. They point the finger, smile with approval or frown sternly, justifying themselves with the shared values of common-sense.

Hageseth does not treat humour as an undifferentiated positive, for 'it is necessary to distinguish positive (loving, healing) humour from negative (aggressive destructive) humour' (1988: 12). Positive humour, he suggests, is associated with optimism, while 'pessimism in humour is expressed as irony, satire, sarcasm, or put-down ethnic humour' (ibid.: 60). The distinction between positive and negative humour is asserted, rather than treated as something problematic. As might be expected, Hageseth suggests that positive humour accumulates more positives: 'health, wellness and productivity are all enhanced by use of positive humour'. Negative humour 'causes harm'; but positive humour 'will promote love, healing and creativity' (ibid.: 24). It seems so sensible, so reassuringly familiar. So does the moral that Hageseth draws from his distinction: 'You can learn the difference and then accentuate the positive and eliminate the negative' (ibid.: 22).

The distinction between positive and negative forms of humour is by no means confined to popular writers of psychology. Academic researchers of the highest quality in their field tread the same path. Lefcourt, for instance, distinguishes 'positive humour' that 'encourages group solidarity' from 'negative or aggressive humour that separates, divides and excludes' (2001: 72). He comments that this is 'perhaps the weightiest dimension on which humour may be evaluated' (ibid.: 72). Despite its supposed weight, Lefcourt does not elaborate on this distinction. In fact, he moves almost casually into a further distinction – that between 'genuinely funny humour' and 'hostile humour' (ibid.: 72). This further distinction implies that ridicule and mockery, even if they provoke laughter, cannot be genuinely funny.

Lefcourt had previously made this assumption when he suggested that 'genuinely funny' jokes do not depend on 'disparagement' (ibid.: 63). This distinction between ridicule and what is 'genuinely funny' would appear to be a moral one, rather than a psychological one. Lefcourt is not denying that some people – perhaps even many people – might find hostile humour funny. He is denying that this sort of humour, however much it is enjoyed by people, should properly be accorded the title of 'humour'. In the context of academic writing, the distinction has to be made quickly and casually, despite being admittedly weighty. Too much analytic attention would bring up problems in establishing a firm theoretical basis by which the genuinely funny can be distinguished from the apparently funny.

The problem is not confined to psychologists. The sociologist Peter Berger claims that when humour functions 'sociopositively', it brings groups together; however, it can have 'socionegative aspects' when it divides people (1997: 57). Berger then goes on to suggest that sociopositive humour can help people recover from illness. But not all humour might be so health-giving: 'There is unhealthy laughter, presumably associated with socionegative humour' (ibid.: 59). Berger's presumption is revealing. It accords with Hageseth's far less sophisticated distinction between positive and negative humour, and also with Lefcourt's distinction between genuinely funny humour and hostile humour. In all these cases there is a distinction between good, positive humour and bad, negative humour. Then there is the presumption that positive humour will produce positive outcomes such as good health, while negative laughter will lead to negative outcomes. In Lefcourt's case the presumption has a further protective refinement. He implies that negative humour does not share the characteristics of humour, and, thus, should not properly be called humour.

The dark cloud is dispelled by asserting that positive and negative humour are totally different phenomena and that they produce very different effects. Ridicule cannot bring positive benefits because it is not proper humour, however much enjoyment ridicule brings to those who practise it. If one tells the ridiculers that their mirth is not genuinely funny, they may just redouble their mocking laughter. Perhaps, one day a psychologist will conduct a methodologically sound study to show that such redoubled laughter is injurious to the immune system.

Nevertheless, the chances are not great that a psychologist would undertake such a project. The pattern of empirical research on humour is not random. Some topics, such as the potential positive benefits of humour, seem to attract more attention than others. In *Humour*, Lefcourt includes a comparatively short section on 'Cruel and Hostile Humour' (2001: 64–72). Lefcourt introduces the section thus: 'Although hostility and aggression have been major topics of interest in psychology, aggressive or hostile humour has not been investigated extensively' (ibid.: 64). He does not comment on this imbalance, let alone try to explain it.

In the context of positivism, the lack of research on hostile or negative humour cannot be considered fortuitous. It fits an ideological pattern that accentuates the positives of humour and downplays the negatives. Would any researcher wish to gain a reputation for trying to show that the humour in general has negative effects? Imagine the case of a researcher who is professionally devoted to demonstrating the Positive Life Benefits that can accrue from enjoying the humour of ridicule. The invitations to address international symposia would soon dry up. Suspicions of sexism, homophobia and racism would circulate. It is much safer to be positive about positive humour.

Downplaying humour's negatives is not confined to the choice of research programmes in psychology. It is reflected rhetorically in the writings of academic and professional psychologists. The stress is on the positives, while the negatives tend to be mentioned almost in a cursory way, with the result that the rhetorical balance between positives and negatives falls firmly in favour of the former.

The contributions to *Advances in Humour and Psychotherapy* all follow the same basic structure, as do the chapters in the earlier volume *Handbook of Humour and Psychotherapy*. There is a section on 'Technique', where the writers outline their clinical techniques for using humour in psychotherapy. This is followed by 'Pertinent Uses' in which the writers discuss how and when humour can be used successfully. Often this is continued in the next section, 'Clinical Presentation', as the writers draw on examples from their own practice. The examples tell of successful cases, where improvements have followed humorous exchanges. The anecdotes have happy endings, with smiles all round.

The format does not provide for sections on 'Impertinent' or 'Inappropriate Uses'. The issue of inappropriate humour is not completely ignored. Typically, it is taken into account, sometimes only by implication, only then to be passed over. Nearly all the authors state that it is important for psychotherapists to use humour appropriately. For instance, it is claimed that humour 'when used wisely ... can enrich patients' lives and facilitate the psychotherapeutic process' (Mosak and Maniacci, 1993: 16). This implies that humour can be used inappropriately or unwisely. No examples of unwise humour in the psychotherapeutic context are provided.

Michael Maher is more specific than most of the other contributors about the dangers of using humour. He would not recommend using humour with patients with fragile egos. He states that 'humour, when used callously, or at the expense of someone else, will have no useful value' (1993: 90). He offers no examples to justify this. His case histories in 'Pertinent Uses' all describe the use of appropriate humour (i.e. humour that does not ridicule). In these stories humour leads to successful, positive outcomes.

One contributor recounts an incident when he as a therapist made a joke, which almost produced an unhappy outcome. It was, in his words, a 'near "fatal" incident'. He was treating a patient, who used to apologize compulsively for her imagined mistakes. As he was seeing her out after a therapeutic session, she made more apologies 'in the most friendly and protracted way'. The therapist then made 'a seemingly equally friendly, "teasing" remark to the effect that I might consider forgiving her in a few years' (Heuscher, 1993: 222). The patient was angered by the remark, but fortunately she was able to speak later about this anger. The result was that 'we had a chance to explore together her compulsive apologising and its negative effect upon most of her human relationships' (ibid.: 222). In this way, the 'near fatal' story too has a happy ending.

The telling of Heuscher's story is interesting. Negatives are transmuted into positives. Anger is turned into successful psychotherapeutic treatment. The anger, however, is one-sided. The therapist does not describe his remark as mockery, driven by resentment against the patient, although it seems that the patient received it as such. He calls his remark friendly and teasing. The word 'teasing' is so much gentler than 'ridicule' or 'mockery' (Terasahjo and Salmivalli, 2003). A 'friendly tease' seems to deny hostility, callousness or negative feelings. The rhetoric of description can be used to dissipate the negatives, like an air-spray freshening up a bathroom.

This rhetorical move will be encountered on other occasions. It can be called, for the sake of convenience, the 'Tease-Spray'. Just squirt on your own humorous talk, and all you will notice is your own good nature: other nasty, critical names will become undetectable. The spray comes in handy sizes with a range of other soothing epithets. There is, for instance, a 'Just Joking' spray. There are also specialist academic versions to be sprayed on human nature as a whole. Athena Du Pré, in *Humour and the Healing Arts*, has a subsection on the Disparagement Theory of humour. Like Lefcourt's analogous section, Du Pré's is brief – it is less than a page. She suggests that 'liberation' might be a better word than 'disparagement' to describe this form of humour (1998: 56). Squirt, squirt to make humour come up smelling fresh and friendly.

There is, however, no need to use the rhetorical sprays if only seemingly positive uses of humour are mentioned. The psychotherapists in *Advances in Humour and Psychotherapy*, as well as those in *Handbook of Humour and Psychotherapy*, concede that humour can be inappropriately used. However, they only provide examples of their own appropriate usage. We hear of patients whose problems are relieved by humour: even the 'near-fatal' joke fits this pattern. There are no stories with unhappy endings, where the patient storms away from the joking psychotherapist, never to return – or where humour in therapy leads to deteriorating conditions. Of course, it might be unreasonable to expect psychotherapists to write lengthily about their own failures. Too much is at stake for them, especially when contributing to a volume that is partisan in its advocacy of the use of humour in psychotherapy. Patients are not the only ones who have fragile egos.

The almost elimination of negatives appears in other academic writing, where the author has no personal stake in justifying the use of humour. Du Pré's *Humour and the Healing Arts* investigates the use of humour in health settings. By analyzing recorded conversations, she shows how patients and care-givers can use humour to achieve a variety of ends, such as minimizing embarrassment, displaying empathy and compassion, providing mutual identification, facilitating communication, etc. Detailed transcripts of recorded examples illustrate all these positives. Almost at the end of her book, Du Pré includes a chapter entitled 'A Few Cautions' in which she offers some words about 'the potentially negative effects of humour' (ibid.: 186). 'A few' is no underestimate. The chapter is only three pages long. Significantly, it contains no examples from her data. Only common-sense generalities remain: health professional should avoid sarcastic, mocking and degrading humour; caregivers should be sensitive, etc. Any negatives that she might have collected in her research have been textually eliminated. Theoretically, 'disparagement' has already been re-sprayed as 'liberation'.

Lefcourt provides a remarkable example of the way that the negatives can be textually overlooked. In an early chapter of *Humour* Lefcourt describes how he introduces students to the topic of humour. He asks students in class to recount funny events that occurred in their lives. He presents at length one such story told by a Canadian student. It concerns a family gathering to celebrate Christmas not long after a tragedy. The mood is sombre and strained, quite unlike their normal Christmas celebrations. The student tells how his cousin's new fiancé, who is meeting the wider family for the first time, then tells a risqué joke. The punch-line involves the young man pulling down his trousers. Everyone looks alarmed until the old grandmother starts chuckling. Then the others laugh. Lefcourt points to the story's salient features that he discusses with students. These include the issues of tension-release, the personality of joke-tellers, the incongruity of respectable elderly relatives and the cheeky young man, the way humour can bring people together etc. The story, thus, emerges as one that demonstrates the positive functions of humour.

But something glaring is omitted: the nature of the joke itself. Although Lefcourt discusses the positive functions of the joke, he does not draw attention to the fact that the joke is an ethnic one. 'How does a Newfie pull up his socks?' the young man had asked before pulling down his trousers and pretending to pull up his socks. The family is collectively mocking the supposed stupidity of people from Newfoundland. Lefcourt's omission is all the more surprising because in a short section on 'Cruel and Hostile Humour' he discusses ethnic jokes. Lefcourt suggests that demeaning ethnic stereotypes can be reinforced by jokes. Not only this, he specifically mentions 'Newfie' jokes, citing a couple of studies that examine these types of jokes. He writes that Newfoundlanders are the victims of 'Newfie' jokes in Canada, because they are a 'vulnerable group' whose education and literacy levels are lower than those in other Canadian provinces (2001: 68). Thus, 'Newfie' jokes reinforce the demeaning stereotype of Newfoundlanders and contribute to their vulnerability.

Lefcourt does not connect his own example of a 'Newfie' joke with this later discussion of cruel humour. The two are kept entirely separate. When the Christmas story is told in the early chapter, the joke is not identified as a 'Newfie' joke. Only the positive consequences are discussed. The later discussion, which considers the negative consequences of negative humour, does not discuss the supposed positive outcomes of the earlier example. Here, the possible positive benefits of telling 'Newfie' jokes, that have been discussed earlier, are omitted. One can understand repression to be a form of motivated but unconscious forgetting or avoidance (Billig, 1999). If so, Lefcourt's separation of the positives and negatives can be seen as a form of 'textual repression'. This does not mean that Lefcourt is deliberately hiding something. But, in writing about the family incident, he follows a pattern of thinking that overlooks matters that would be uncomfortable to notice.

Nor is the overlooking a personal one. Lefcourt is describing his discussions with students. One might imagine the whole group, laughing at the joke as the story is told and then collectively discussing the positive benefits in the ways that Lefcourt describes. In so doing, they would be collectively forgetting the nature of the joke, not as a matter of conscious intent but as a reaction that resembles a habit. These routines of noticing and not noticing are patterns of ideology. By such differentials of attention, ideology can collectively reproduce a form of repression, in which the positives are stressed and the negatives are eliminated from awareness. Thus, the common-sense maxim is proven by common experience.

A positive psychology

Recently in the United States a number of academic psychologists have been developing an approach that they have described as 'Positive Psychology'. It has the support of some well-known empirical psychologists. Martin Seligman, during his year as president of the American Psychological Association (APA) in 1998, specifically promoted Positive Psychology. He has established a group of like-minded distinguished psychologists to form the Positive Psychology Network. In 2000 Seligman and Mihaly Csikszentmihalyi jointly edited a special issue of the APA's journal, *American Psychologist*, devoted to Positive Psychology.

According to Seligman, psychology traditionally has concentrated upon 'negative processes', such as mental illness, prejudice or other social problems. Psychologists hoped that their research would contribute to the elimination of these negative phenomena. As an example of such negative psychology, Seligman cited his own notable work on depression as a form of 'learned helplessness'. Seligman had not merely sought to understand the causes of depression but, through that understanding, he sought to develop a behavioural programme that would cure the learned helplessness of depression. In this way, negative psychology seeks to eliminate its topics. By contrast, Positive Psychology deals with positive processes, looking at health rather than illness, psychological strength rather than weakness and so on (see, for instance, Seligman and Csikszentmihalyi, 2000; Seligman, 2002a, 2002b). Positive psychologists hope that understanding will enable us to increase these positive phenomena. Humour finds its place among the positives. One of the first tasks of the Positive Psychology Network group was to draw up a taxonomy of positive human strengths. 'Humor/playfulness' was listed under the heading of 'Relational and Civic Strengths' (Seligman, 2002b).

Positive Psychology proposes that positive psychological states tend to produce positive outcomes, including physical well-being (Salovey et al., 2000) and longer life (Danner et al., 2001). Barbara Fredrickson has been developing a model of emotions, in order to show 'the life-enhancing effects of positive emotions' (2003: 330). In her article 'Cultivating positive emotions to optimize health and well-being' she argues that positive emotions function differently than negative ones (Fredrickson, 1998). Negative emotions, such as fear and anger, narrow the focus of the individual. Positive emotions, by contrast, 'broaden-and-build'. Fredrickson cites the positive emotions of joy, interest and contentment. These broaden the individual's momentary thoughts and actions, providing ways for the individual to develop long-term positive meaning in their lives. Laughter and humour are to be found among the positive emotions because they tap into the broadening effects of joy and they help build 'bonds and coping resources' (Fredrickson, 2000: 16). Thus, people who are amused by a film in experimental circumstances will show broadening patterns of thinking (Fredrickson and Branigan, 2005). The theory asserts that people who regularly experience positive emotions are lifted on an 'upward spiral' of positive psychological growth (Fredrickson, 2003; Fredrickson and Joiner, 2002).

It should be noted that Fredrickson's broaden-and-build theory, like Seligman's taxonomy, does not identify positive emotions by their tendency to produce positive outcomes. Otherwise, the theory would be circular. Positive psychologists claim that empirical findings show positive emotions to produce positive outcomes, just as Lefcourt cites empirical findings to claim that a sense of humour has positive outcomes. However, Fredrickson does not specify the criteria by which joy, contentment, amusement and interest are classified as positive emotions, while fear, anger and aggression are negative ones. A recent study has added sexual desire to the list of positive emotions (Fredrickson et al., 2003). The accusation that Marcuse levelled against Fromm remains relevant. Fromm had claimed to distinguish between productive and destructive, or positive and negative, personalities. The distinction, according to Marcuse, was 'not derived from any theoretical principle, but simply taken from the prevalent ideology' (1972: 174). Thus, common sense tells us that joy is good, while aggression is not. Humour is good; anger is bad.

Fredrickson does not explore possibilities that threaten the image of a possible harmony between positives. She does not discuss, for example, the hypothetical example of a racist, murderous political movement that might promise its supporters the positive emotion of 'strength through joy'. The promise might be met as supporters experience inner joy – or feel good about themselves – as they broaden and build the politics of hatred. Perhaps if such an example had been considered, there would have been the necessity to distinguish between 'genuine positive joy' and 'negative joy', just as Lefcourt separated the humour of ridicule from the 'genuinely funny'.

Positive Psychology involves more than a dispassionate theory about the ways that different emotions might function. It incorporates a belief that the positives of the world can and should be brought into alignment. In this regard, Positive Psychology does not itself stand apart from the phenomena that it seeks to study objectively. It aims to promote, or 'broaden-and-build', the positives of life, just as the old negative psychology aimed to eliminate the negatives from human conduct. As Fredrickson writes, 'to harness the power of positive psychology, we need to understand how and why "goodness" matters' (2003: 330). To this end, Positive Psychology encourages a positive psychology of optimism.

The idea of optimism figures large in Positive Psychology. Seligman has switched the focus of his research from attempting to prevent 'learned helplessness' to teaching a 'learned optimism' that, he claims, will promote psychological health (Seligman, 1990). Studies have been conducted to show that being optimistic can lead to positive outcomes (e.g., Carver et al., 2003; Peterson, 2000). It is claimed that there is a link between enjoying humour and being hopeful (Vilaythong et al., 2003). Fredrickson (2000) reviews evidence to suggest that optimistic individuals will experience positive emotions. Following Seligman, she advocates that people should be helped to find positive meaning in their lives so that they can practise 'positive reappraisal'. This means that they acquire the ability to reframe 'adverse events in a positive light' (ibid.: 14). Even unrealistic optimism, or possessing 'positive illusions', is said to be psychologically beneficial (Taylor, 1991; Taylor and Brown, 1994). Thus, it is better to be optimistic than realistic.

Humour can play its part in this life-enhancing, optimistically positive outlook. Athena Du Pré, in her study of humour in medical settings, writes that care-givers can show compassion by using humour 'to actively promote a positive mind-set' (1998: 138–9). The popular writers, such as Klein and Hageseth would concur: being positively cheerful, being humorous will help to see you through the negatives. Hageseth specifically relates positive humour to optimism: 'Positive humour requires optimism' while pessimism in humour is expressed as irony, satire, sarcasm, or put-down ethnic humour' (1988: 60). Again, the positives and negatives are neatly stacked in different piles.

In talking of a 'mind-set' or sense of optimism, the psychologists are talking about something that is more than momentary. It reflects a whole way of experiencing the world and its vicissitudes. Gerald Amada, in writing of the 'positive' effect of humour in therapy, claims that humour 'reflects an attitude and a way of being' (1993: 160). Stephen Sultanoff makes a similar point when writing the 'President's Column' in the journal *Therapeutic Humor*, which is published by the American Association for Therapeutic Humor. He claims that 'our use of therapeutic humour is not an isolated moment in time' but it is 'a lifestyle or perhaps a philosophy of life' (1999: 2). Similarly, having a positive outlook is more than a way of reacting to incidents – it is a way of *being* a positive person.

One might speculate why Positive Psychology has emerged as an academic movement at the time and place it has. Seligman specifically located Positive Psychology in the United States of the new millennium. He wrote that 'the nation – wealthy, at peace and stable – provides a world historical opportunity' that can be realised by moving from the negative to the positive (Seligman and Csikszentmihalyi, 2000). One might note how the description of Positive Psychology's background uses positive, or uncritical, terms. The society is described in terms of wealth, peace and stability. It is presented as a context in which one can reasonably feel joy and contentment, not anger and discontent. It is as if the positive outer world has been successfully established, and now all that is required is for the inner world to be aligned with the positive conditions of social reality.

Seligman's comments about the background to Positive Psychology were written before the terrorist attack on the New York World Trade Center in 2001, and the subsequent American invasions of Afghanistan and Iraq. The political background may no longer look so peaceful, as the US government has committed itself to a global war against terror. In these non-peaceful circumstances, the theorists of positive psychology see enhanced benefits for being positive. It is suggested that people in New York were better able to cope with the terrorist crisis if they were able to experience positive emotions and to think positive thoughts (Fredrickson et al., 2003). As Fredrickson (2003) writes, in times of adversity it is important to cultivate positive emotions by 'finding positive meaning'. She goes on to say: 'you can find benefits in a grim world ... by focusing on the newfound strength and resolve within yourself and others' (ibid.: 335).

The origins of 'positive thinking' as a popular ideology of self-help have a longer history than academic Positive Psychology. It is now over fifty years since Norman Vincent Peale originally published his *Power of Positive Thinking* (1996b), which was to sell more than 40 million copies and be translated into over twenty languages. In that book and in later works, Peale offered a combination of uplifting anecdotes and moralizing. His basic message was that if you think positively, you will not be a failure. Positive thinking held out the twin promises of economic success and psychological fulfilment. People who fail in life are not defeated because of the outward situation but because there is 'something amiss' inwardly (*You Can If You Think You Can*, 1987: 9). There was one type of person 'who has what it takes' and who 'by God's help' is equal to all of life's challenges – 'the tough-minded optimist' (*Tough-Minded Optimist*, 1996a: viii). Marcuse slyly drew a parallel between Peale and the style of the neo-Freudians. He criticized Fromm and other Freudian revisionists for discarding philosophical thinking and replacing it with the style of the sermon or the social worker. Fromm's later way of writing, Marcuse continued, evokes 'the Power of Positive Thinking to which the revisionist critique succumbs' (1972: 181).

Peale's inspirational message was simultaneously optimistic and deeply conservative. It emphasized the power of the individual to succeed or fail. Excuses will not wash. In *Six Attitudes for Winners*, Peale proclaims that 'no problem is too great to solve' (1990: 5). The message is outwardly democratic: you don't need inborn talent or inherited position to be a success. Everyone can be a winner – the losers have only brought it on themselves. This appears as harsh a message as can be found in Samuel Smiles's classic *Self-Help* (1882), which was such a success in capitalism's Victorian heyday. In effect, Peale, like Smiles, was assuring people that capitalism does not create necessary suffering. The poor and the vulnerable are not victims of a system that demands losers if it is to have winners. Instead, the unsuccessful are the instruments of their own distress. They too could have succeeded had they applied themselves to positive thinking. In a brilliant analysis of political thinking about poverty, Murray Edelman (1977) showed that in contemporary ideology the language of blame need not be heartless, for it can, and typically does, co-exist with sympathy. We can reassure ourselves that we sympathize with the poor, while simultaneously blaming them. The latter thought neutralizes any sense of commitment to changing matters.

In the positivism of late capitalism, a number of psychological themes are prominent. Many observers have noted that capitalism in its late, or post-industrial, phase differs from its earlier forms, and poses different problems for its inhabitants. Today's constant processes of change have created conditions where people no longer have secure places in the social world and thereby no longer possess secure identities. Unlike their grandparents or great-grandparents, the adults of today are not constrained by strict codes about how genders, classes and individuals should behave. The lifetime guarantees of work and relationships are gone. Males no longer expect to have both a job and a wife for life; nor conversely are women conditioned to expect to stand by an economically productive man. The only constant seems to be the continual flux.

In these circumstances, men and women are continually having to create and recreate their own selves, negotiating what in previous generations might have been taken for granted (e.g., Bauman, 1995; Beck, 1992; Gergen, 1991; Giddens, 1991). If the creation of identity is the project for the individual, then, according to today's self-help message, positive identities and positive selves should be the target of all. Experiencing positive emotions and eliminating negative emotions are not sufficient in themselves. One has to *be* as much as *do*. Therefore, the task is to become the sort of person who appreciates joy, contentment and the rest – in short, each person has the duty to become a positive person, no matter what sort of identities they are creating for themselves.

Psychology is catching this mood. Psychological writers not only claim to provide the techniques for accentuating the positives but they celebrate the 'mind-set' of positivity in itself. They teach how to *be* positive. Humour has its place within this general pattern of psychological positivity. Again and again, it is emphasized that humour has positive benefits. It can achieve wellness, creativity, adaptability, and so on. It can aid productivity as a tool of management (e.g., Barsoux, 1993; Morreall, 1997). The authors of the self-help books are serious in their promotion of humour. But it is not enough to *use* humour positively from time to time: one has to *be* someone with a good sense of humour.

Individualism remains constant as a conservative force within ideological positivism, whether it is the earlier hard-nosed positivism of Peale or the smiling positivism of late capitalism. Marcuse was accusing Fromm and other neo-Freudians of advocating a philosophy that conservatively sought to patch up the damaged individual, rather than trying to change the society that was damaging the individual. Within ideological positivism, the blame for failure and the credit for success are placed on the individual, rather than on the social processes that create the individual. Critics today have noted how the advice 'be positive' can become oppressive. For instance, women cancer patients may blame themselves if they fail to maintain the positive outlook that is demanded of them (Kitzinger, 2000; Wilkinson and Kitzinger, 2000). As such, positivism can be experienced as an intolerant imperative. It continually sets examinations that all apparently can pass. Those who fail have only themselves to blame for inner weakness, negative mind-set and meagre production of smiles.

The conservative implications are perhaps clearer in the popular writers. According to Hageseth, if positive humour is to change the world, it will do so by changing individuals first, one by one. Social change is put to one side as individuals try to acquire the correctly positive mind-set. Professional therapists and trade-marked support groups are on hand to give succour. The positive mind-set is not directed to social change but to inner change. To be positive, the individual has to learn to adapt positively to life's negatives. In the words of Klein, the individual learns to bear the unbearables of life. This itself is positive reappraisal: the unbearables, by definition, are no longer unbearable. Everything in the world becomes bearable, if only we can learn to reframe negatives into positives. It is our own mind-sets that need be changed. Humour is a useful tool. It is a part of the positive mind-set. This is the way that ideological positivism looks out cheerfully upon a world of potential positives. It sets an example to us all.

In these circumstances, the critic has to take the path of negativity – or what appears as negativity from the perspective of the prevailing positivism. This means resisting the power of positive thinking, its optimism and cheerful humour. The negatives have to be rescued from amnesia. Marcuse claimed that neo-Freudians were wishing away the disturbing implications of Freudian theory, eliminating the negative force of destructiveness from their theories. So it is with ridicule which ideological positivism optimistically treats as the unfortunate by-product of an insufficiently positive character. The critic, by contrast, should be prepared to take the idea of ridicule seriously. Perhaps ridicule is deeply, even necessarily, rooted in social processes rather than being a character trait that can be reversed by learned optimism.

To consider these possibilities – to take seriously what might be laughed away – the critic cannot just focus on positivism and its sunny-side-up psychology. The critic must go back in time, to put positivism in context. Past theories of humour and their treatment of ridicule must also be examined, in order to make our present homely assumptions appear momentarily foreign. In doing this, the critic of humour must expect to be criticized for being unhelpful, humourless or, worse still, negative. *C'est son métier.*

I
Historical Aspects

3

Superiority Theories
Hobbes and Other Misogelasts

If a critical view of humour is to question positive assumptions, then it cannot merely smirk at laughter's supposed enemies. The critic needs to take seriously the views of those whom George Meredith dismissed as the 'miso-gelasts' or the so-called haters of laughter. Merely to mock the misogelasts would be tantamount to accepting uncritically the assumption that laughter is self-evidently desirable. Therefore this chapter discusses out-of-fashion misogelastic theories. The term 'misogelast' is a handy concept, but, as will be seen, it is a simplification. In the main, the so-called misogelasts did not formulate a complete hatred of laughter, rather, they expressed a wish to reduce the amount of frivolity in the cause of a serious philosophy or theology.

Taking misogelast theories seriously means discarding a particularly seductive assumption. It is easy to believe that today we have greater insights into human nature in general, and laughter in particular, than earlier thinkers did. Because we have to hand the accumulated evidence of psychology, sociology and anthropology, we can notice things about human behaviour that might have been overlooked in previous times. In some cases this is undoubtedly correct: recording devices, for instance, permit a far more detailed investigation of the use of laughter in conversation than was ever possible previously. Confidence in our better self-knowledge coincides with living in an age that values humour as something desirable in itself. The seductive assumption is to connect these two beliefs, by assuming that the growth of knowledge about humour is related to our growing appreciation of humour's worth. Thus, we might suppose that earlier thinkers, who distrusted laughter, were merely displaying their ignorance of the human condition.

It is too simple to suppose that the thinkers of past ages were hampered by an ignorance that has today shrunk into manageable proportions – as if human history is the story of the onward march of self-understanding and laughter. We, too, have our ideological preferences and blind spots as we look at human nature. Ideological positivism, with its optimistic good-heart-edness, leads to patterns of denial and not noticing in relation to humour. Even psychologists do not want to notice their own 'negatives'. Self-deceit is not the result of weak individual personalities, but it operates in conform-ity with ideological imperatives.

Misogelastic views are valuable in that they can provide a mirror of contemporary attitudes, reflecting back the positives as negative and vice versa. In general, misogelasts did not share a desire to sentimentalize laughter, nor did they proclaim their own credentials as possessors of life-enhancing senses of humour. Consequently, misogelasts often had less ideological need to deny what must be hidden today, although they might have had other secrets to conceal from themselves. As will be seen, disciplinary ridicule could be openly admitted and even praised in ways that are uncomfortable today.

But there is more. Misogelastic theories have also provided the ground-work for present understandings. This is true particularly of Thomas Hobbes, who produced the greatest misogelastic theory of them all. Hobbes prepared the way in two ways. First, his views on humour provoked a reaction in succeeding generations of theorists who produced the sort of amiable, optimistic views of humour that are the forerunners of modern approaches. Second, Hobbes's own insights, with their mixture of profundity, fear and exaggeration, prepared the way for Freudian views that place self-deceit at the core of human activity, including humorous activity.

In this, there is more than the movement of theory and counter-theory. Any such movement takes place against a backdrop of wider political and social happenings. Yet the backdrop is more than mere backdrop. Theories of laughter express the moral, aesthetic and political themes of their times. As such, philosophies of humour belong to wider patterns of laughter and disapproval, protestation and disavowal, as well as a complex dialectic of discipline and rebellion.

Distrust and degradation

It has become customary to categorize intellectual theories of humour into three major types: the superiority theories, the incongruity theories and the release theories. Sometimes the superiority theories are known as degradation theories. Those who use this three-fold classification normally place the theories in a historical order with the superiority theories coming first. John Morreall (1983, 1987), reviewing the history of philosophies of humour, counts both Plato and Aristotle as adherents of the superiority theory. Morreall claims that the superiority theory 'held the field for over two thousand years' until the formation of incongruity theories (1983: 4). Simon Critchley also claims that the superiority theory originated in ancient Greek philosophy. He comments: 'it is the superiority theory that dominates the philosophical tradition until the eighteenth century' (2002: 3). Incongruity theory, which put an end to this dominance, will be discussed in the following chapter. Then, after the incongruity theories of the eighteenth century, came the release theories.

Actually, Critchley and Morreall somewhat exaggerate the dominance of the superiority theory. It is too simple to say that this particular theory dominated 'the field' or the philosophical tradition until the eighteenth century. The theory in its earliest forms was not really a theory. Neither Plato nor Aristotle described their views on humour as 'theories'. They produced somewhat scattered observations when discussing broader issues such as education, rhetoric and social morality. Moreover, these observations cannot be said to have dominated 'the field', for no field existed as such. Laughter was not a specialist topic to be taught in classical and mediaeval curricula. Nor was it an issue that greatly caught the attention of philosophers before the seventeenth and eighteenth centuries.

It was only with the development of modern psychological thinking that one really finds 'theories of laughter' and a specialist field. Hobbes can fairly be called the first such theorist, presenting his views on laughter as part of a systematic account of human motives. Even he did not claim that his views amounted to a 'theory of laughter'. When later writers objected to Hobbes's account, they often described it as the 'superiority theory' of laughter. They did this to distinguish Hobbes's position from their own. In this way, the superiority theory, far from dominating competing theories for centuries, only properly became known as such when it was under challenge.

That being said, the term 'superiority theory' is a useful term, especially when trying to distinguish between different approaches to humour. So, niceties about the exact suitability of the label will be put aside. Using the conventional terminology, one can go along with analysts such as Critchley and Morreall in claiming that the superiority/degradation theory is the oldest of the three types of theory. It is also the one that is the most out of tune with the optimism of positive psychology. The superiority theory is basically a theory of mockery, for it suggests that laughter results from disparaging or degrading others. James Sully, an early British psychologist whose *Essay on Laughter* was published in 1902, described the superiority theory as proposing that 'the function of laughter is to accompany and give voice to what may be called the derogatory impulse in man, his tendency to look out for and to rejoice over what is mean and undignified' (ibid.: 119–20).

Theorists today often treat the superiority theory with suspicion because it suggests that laughter is less than wholesome. John Morreall notes that superiority theory depicts laughter to be fundamentally scornful. As a result, the theory views humour as a 'nasty business' and makes 'humour ethically suspect' (1987: 3). According to Athena Du Pré, the theory of superiority asserts that 'laughter is a triumphant response to the denigration of objects, concepts, or persons unaffiliated with the self' (1998: 56). As mentioned in Chapter 2, she suggests that the theory is misnamed. She claims that 'phenomenological analysis' shows that people do not feel a sense of superiority when they laugh and so *liberation* may be a better word than *superiority*.

However, superiority theory should not be resprayed with a more user-friendly nomenclature. The theory addresses aspects of humour that may lie at the root of social order in the form of disciplinary humour. For this reason, superiority theory, which seems so out of tune with ideological positivism, may offer clues about the maintenance of power, order and ideological self-deception, as well as discouraging the unquestioning acceptance of laughter's goodness.

Platonic roots

The superiority theory emerged in social conditions very different from those of today. It is common now to point to the crudity of much humour in former times. In less enlightened times delight was taken in the suffering of others. The physically afflicted were mocked in ways that are now distasteful. Robert Provine makes the point that 'as we grapple with Hobbes and his predecessors concerning their view of laughter as derisive, it is help-ful to remember that we are looking back to times when "good taste", "good manners" and "good form" were based on standards that were very different from today's' (2000: 14). The superiority theory, Provine continues, came from times when 'even torture and executions were public events often conducted in a carnival atmosphere complete with snacks and refreshments' (ibid.: 14–15).

All this is true, but it oversimplifies the superiority theory by depicting it as a crude theory fit only for crude times. Certainly, Plato and Aristotle were arguing against laughter in ways that seem unfamiliar today. Yet, even today, when humour is considered self-evidently desirable, there are still types of humour that are censured. Not all laughter is considered benefi-cially positive. The laughter of mockery is one of the negatives. Where Plato and Aristotle differ from modern sensibilities is that they contended that there was too much laughter in the world. But their aim was not to reduce the laughter of mockery. If they distinguished 'good' laughter from 'bad' laughter, then they did not necessarily assume that ridicule was unambigu-ously bad. In fact, the laughter of mockery was, under certain circumstances, one of the types of laughter to be encouraged.

In the Platonic dialogue *Philebus*, Socrates voices his suspicion of laugh-ter. When we enjoy comedies, he tells Protarchus, our souls combine pleas-ure and pain. We delight in laughing at those who have misplaced views of themselves. We laugh at those who think they are richer, wiser or more handsome than they actually are. As Socrates noted, we find such ignorance funny and, thus, there is malice in amusement. In arguing thus, Socrates was going along with the basic assumptions of a superiority theory of humour and was questioning the motives behind laughter. Peter Berger points to an underlying implication of this passage in *Philebus*: 'Since malice is hardly an admirable quality, this also raises an ethical issue: Is there something repre-hensible about comic laughter?' (1997; 18).

Socrates was also questioning the morality of laughter in another respect. He was linking it to untruth. 'Ignorance was an evil', he asserted. Since we take pleasure in ignorance, laughing at 'the false conceits of our friends', then we are taking pleasure in evil (*Philebus*, 1925 edn: 337). For Socrates, ignorance was no laughing matter. Socrates could have gone on to suggest that such laughter of mockery was actually on the side of truth. It was serv-ing to discipline erroneous belief. People would be discouraged from think-ing that they are better than they are, if they expected to be mocked for doing so. Socrates could have said this, but he did not.

As is well known, Plato expressed his own views about the ideal state through the mouth of Socrates. In a famous passage in *The Republic*, Socrates briefly discusses how laughter can be used to bring order. The ideal state was to be a hierarchical community run by philosopher-princes, who, in their dedication to the pursuit of truth, would brook no opposition. This state would not be a fun-filled place. Much care would be spent in educating the future guardians to assume their serious duties. Self-control was to be the watch-word: 'the pleasures of eating, drinking and sex' would need to be disciplined. It was unlikely that the masses would be able to show the sort of self-control expected of the guardians. So, the masses should show 'obedience to their rulers', who would be obliged to ensure that their inferiors did not step out of line. Laughter was one of the pleasures to be tightly controlled, particularly the sort of impertinent laughter that mocks authority. Thus, 'impertinences of the rank and file against those in authority' would be firmly prohibited (*The Republic*, 1974 edn: 145).

The drive against laughter went further than stopping the lower ranks from mocking their betters. Too much frivolity would be undesirable for the higher ranks: 'We don't want our guardians to be too fond of laughter,' comments Adeimantus to the evident approval of Socrates (ibid.: 144). The young should not be exposed to texts that portray 'reputable characters being overcome by laughter'. The rulers of the state should prevent their young charges from reading about the gods laughing helplessly. 'We can't allow it,' agrees Socrates (ibid.: 144). So censorship would be necessary to curtail laughter in the ideal republic.

Grim it sounds. So different from today's descriptions of the ideal life, in which one smiles through troubles and laughs positively in happy empathy with others. But one should note the qualification in Plato's criticism of laughter. He did not say that the guardians should never laugh – only that we don't want them to be 'too fond' of laughter. It would be permissible to laugh in certain circumstances. Socrates claimed that romantic poetry was particularly unhealthy, especially when poets went on about men sighing and lamenting. He did not want the muscular young guardians behaving like that. He offered some examples of unsuitable romantic poetry and then commented to Adeimantus: 'If our young men listen to passages like these seriously and don't laugh at them as unworthy, they are hardly likely to think this sort of conduct as unworthy of them as men' (ibid.: 143). Not only should the guardians mock that which deserved to be mocked, but they should also teach the young to do so. In short, the guardians of state could and should laugh in the serious interests of morality, truth and discipline.

There is a paradox. Plato is often portrayed as the arch-misogelast, seeking to reduce laughter in the ideal state. Yet, more than any other philosopher, Plato's writings contain comic moments. He wrote playlets, not abstract, dry treatises. He presents Socrates talking with friends and fellow philosophers. They do not always discuss the big issues with high-minded seriousness. They can argue, grumble and mock with most unguardian-like liveliness. And Plato can mock with sly malice. In the *Meno*, Socrates ridicules Anytus who is convinced of the immorality of non-Athenian sophists. Socrates leads him on. Has any Sophist done you personal harm? No, I don't have anything to do with them. So you don't know any? Heavens no, and I don't want to ever, replies Anytus, seemingly oblivious to the ridiculousness of his prejudices (Plato, 1982 edn: 147).

One thing is clear. Socrates and Plato did not approve of carnivalesque humour whereby the lower orders might mock philosophical notions of truth and beauty. Most definitely this sort of laughter, which Socrates knew only too well from personal experience, was to be discouraged. Aristophanes mocked him and other philosophers on the stage. In the *The Clouds*, Socrates, the master of the high philosophical ideas, is portrayed as a comic figure. A student tells in one scene that he had heard Socrates discussing with Chaerephon how a flea could jump. Just then a flea had jumped on to Socrates's bald patch. Later that night, the great man was investigating the moon, staring up at it with open mouth. And then, says the student, a gecko on the roof crapped onto him. Ha-ha-ha. The audiences loved it – mocking the superior philosopher (Aristophanes, 1973: 4.1:1).

Socrates didn't appreciate the low fun. He sought to rise above it. According to Diogenes Laertius, he was a man 'able to look down upon any who mocked him' (1972, XI: 27). Looking down on the mocker involves more than just greeting the mockery with straight-faced disapproval. A sense of superiority must be communicated, so that the mocker is seen to be inferior in the eyes of the mocked. So Socrates demonstrated that he looked down on the theatre-goers who laughed at Aristophanes's parodies. He even went to the theatre to do so. The audiences needed to be set proper examples.

Socrates conversed with Anytus, even as he ridiculed his views. They are social equals who could talk, even banter, together. But others lived beyond the boundaries of equal dialogue. The most famous passage in the *Meno* has Socrates bending down in the sand, drawing triangles and squares to show that knowledge is innate. He quizzes a slave boy about the lengths of lines and by clever questioning leads the boy to state the correct length of a diagonal through a square. In talking to the slave boy, Socrates uses no pleasantries. He doesn't joke with him. He just asks his questions: 'Now, boy, do you know a square is a figure like this?' (Plato, 1982 edn: 130). Socrates speaks about the boy as if he were just an object: 'Observe, Meno, the stage he has reached on the path to recollection' (ibid.: 135). When Socrates has finished his demonstration, the boy is neither thanked, nor bade goodbye. His usefulness over, he ceases to exist in the dialogue.

A rigid sense of class permeates both the society in which Socrates was living and the ideal society that he envisaged. If there were too much idle mockery in the former, then in the latter it would be eliminated. The well-bred, free-born members would learn to respect their moral superiors and to control their laughter. As for the slaves, it would be better if they also showed discipline and respect. They would probably have to be compelled to do so. Their humour was below respectability. The free-born did not jest with them. They gave orders, asked questions and expected immediate obedience.

Perhaps the poor in their hovels mocked posh-spoken, bald-headed philosophers. Maybe the slave boy recounted to his friends with much mocking laughter how Socrates had bent down to draw his lines; how he had asked his silly questions and then beamed smugly at Meno. No matter. Socrates would not have been bothered by such mockery. It was routine to look down on a slave. To look down on an accomplished comic poet, who won applause from fashionable theatre-goers, now that was a harder accomplishment. Platonic notions of comedy, malice and superiority were worked out against a background of hierarchy and discipline. Sections of the free-born struggled to look down mockingly on each other. At the same time, they seriously looked down upon those who seemed unquestionably inferior – too inferior to ridicule in good taste.

Aristotle and more superiority

Aristotle's views on laughter were less trenchant than those of Plato. Aristotle provided no blueprint for a future state that would patrol its members' desires, thoughts and reading habits. He was more concerned with correcting the manners and politics of the present. Nevertheless, Aristotle's views about humour contain some similarities to Plato's assumptions about the need to restrict the wrong sort of laughter.

Like Plato, Aristotle linked laughter to degradation, as well as providing a defence of the usefulness of ridicule. In *The Poetics*, he made a number of remarks that have led later commentators to classify him as a superiority theorist. In discussing the nature of comedy, he claimed that in comedies people are normally depicted as 'worse than the average and the comic is a sub-species of the ugly' (1963 edn: 10). Ridiculousness, then, may be 'defined as a mistake or deformity which produces no pain or deformity to others' (ibid.: 11). Sully cites this passage as evidence of Aristotle's belief in the superiority theory, adding that 'of an adequate theory of the subject there is here, of course, hardly a pretence' (1902: 120). Berger (1997) also cites the passage to show Aristotle as a superiority theorist. In Berger's view, Aristotle recognizes that comedy, in contrast to tragedy, permits us to contemplate the discrepant aspects of life 'in a painless manner' (ibid.: 18).

When Aristotle referred to the absence of pain in comedy, he was not thinking of the pain suffered by the object of mockery but by the mockers. The audience of a tragedy shares the pain of its characters. By contrast, the audience of a comedy laughs, not cries, when a character falls over or suffers a misfortune. In his very brief remarks, Aristotle was noting something that Henri Bergson over two thousand years later would call the temporary anaesthesia of the heart. It is easy to see why the remarks in *Poetics* make it easy to class Aristotle as a superiority theorist. If comic figures are depicted as ugly or deformed, then the average audience can feel superior to these below average figures of fun.

There is another aspect to Aristotle's views on humour. In his *Rhetoric* Aristotle examined the persuasiveness of different rhetorical ploys. He includes a brief passage to suggest that ridicule can be persuasively useful. He quotes with approval Gorgias's maxim that 'we ought to worst our opponent's earnest with mockery, and his mockery with earnest' (*Rhetoric*, 1909 edn: 197). Gorgias's formula, of course, offers no guarantee of rhetorical success. Bishop Whately was to point out many years later that our ridicule can always be countered by a further bout of earnestness from our opponent and vice versa (1860: 147f.). Having quoted Gorgias, Aristotle added a significant word of caution. Not all types of humour were equally suitable. Some forms 'befit a free man and others do not' and one should take care to choose the appropriate sort of humour (*Rhetoric*: 1909 edn: 197). The free man should use irony and eschew buffoonery.

This passage encapsulates the central dilemma of classical rhetoric. Rhetoricians taught the arts of public persuasion. Gorgias, whom Aristotle was quoting, was well-known for his boast that he could teach anyone to argue convincingly, even to make a weak argument appear more persuasive than a stronger one. It was a claim that outraged Socrates and/or Plato, who claimed that rhetoricians were merely manipulative tricksters. For their part, the rhetoricians such as Gorgias did not like to think of themselves in this way. They claimed to have a higher calling. Typically they would say that they instructed their students in the most moral and aesthetic ways of speaking. Plato, in the guise of Socrates, was to lambaste the rhetoricians again and again for trying to have it both ways: either they were concerned with swaying an audience or they were concerned with truth. There was no middle ground.

Aristotle's comment on humour in *Rhetoric* was offering a piece of pragmatic advice for influencing an audience. If the rival is too earnest, then try humour. This is the way to persuade. Then Aristotle switches from the pragmatic to the aesthetic. He reminds free-born orators that they should conform to the standards of humour required by gentlemen of good social standing – no buffoonery, please. Winning the argument at all costs is not what counts, but the speaker should maintain standards of taste and class. However, there is a problem: audiences might want a bit of buffoonery, especially at the expense of a seriously boring rival. They might not appreciate high-minded irony. Then, the pragmatic and aesthetic would stand in conflict. The orator would have to choose between being a hard-nosed professional persuader, who takes the low route to persuasion, or a being gentleman of superior taste, who might be oratorically ineffective. However, Aristotle does not pose the dilemma. He does not even draw attention to it. He writes as if there were harmony between the pragmatic and the aesthetic, between the useful and the tasteful. Roman writers on rhetoric such as Cicero and Quintillian were to do much the same.

Aristotle discussed the issue of humour and good taste in *The Nicomachean Ethics* (1926, Book IV, Chapter 8). There were those 'buffoons or vulgar fellows' who laugh too much and who 'are more concerned to raise a laugh than to keep within the bounds of decorum and avoid giving pain to the object of their raillery' (1926, edn: 245). By the same token, there are those who never say anything funny and 'take offence at those that do' (ibid.: 247). Aristotle, as typified by his approach to morality, sought the middle path between the laughing buffoons and the morose misogelasts. He recommended 'the middle disposition' of those who would show wit, not buffoonery, and would say only 'the sort of things that are suitable to a virtuous man and a gentleman' (ibid.: 247). The gentleman would know when not to make a hurtful sally and when levity would be appropriate. Although Aristotle presents gentlemanly wit as the middle path, it is clear that his real target was buffoonery. Misogelasts were comparatively unimportant, while Athenian gentlemen were generally showing far too much buffoonery: 'As matter for ridicule is always ready to hand, and as most men are only too fond of fun and raillery, even buffoons are called witty and pass for clever fellows' (ibid.: 247).

Aristotle does not specify what exactly distinguished buffoonery from wit, although he does say that the witty gentleman will respect propriety, show tact and prefer innuendo to obscenity. One presumes that the virtuous woman will show even greater propriety, laughing with even less frequency. Aristotle linked wit with irony in the *Rhetoric*, but he did not develop this theme in *The Nicomachean Ethics*. However, he linked buffoonery with mockery. He argued that since raillery was a form of vilification and since some forms of vilification were against the law, then perhaps some forms of mockery should also be against the law (ibid.: 249). Maybe Aristotle was joking. He might have been displaying the irony of a free-born gentleman, having a dig at Plato. We cannot tell at this distance, for gentlemanly wit aimed to be so much subtler than knock-about, drop-your-trousers buffoonery.

Ridicule and social hierarchy

Aristotle's critique of buffoonery was not directed against the lower orders of society. He took it for granted that their manners, behaviour and humour would be crude. But, he was bothered that free-born gentlemen, even those of his acquaintance, were letting the social order down by their buffoonery. Here lies another difference from today's ideology of laughter. Today's theorists might distinguish between good (positive) laughter and bad (negative) laughter. They would also resonate to Aristotle's claim that the bad laughter might harm its victims. However, modern theorists of humour do not attribute the good laughter to a particular social class, such as free-born Athenians, thereby dismissing by implication the humour of socially inferior groups. Today the gift of humour must not be restricted to one class, nation or gender: in theory, positive humour belongs to everyone.

The comparison between Ancient Athens and contemporary society is not between a social order of hierarchy and that of equality. It is between a society in which hierarchy is clear and one in which the hierarchy must appear as if it is egalitarian. In Ancient Athens a free-born member of the elite would not be embarrassed by looking down upon the unedifying manners of the mass. Today, the value of equality creates ideological dilemmas in conditions of inequality (Billig et al., 1988). Codes of informality permeate formal life. Meno and Socrates could give clear commands to the boy, summoning him and dismissing him with a curtness that would be out of place now. Complex norms of politeness have to be followed. 'So sorry to bother you, but I wonder if you wouldn't mind coming over here to help us out for a moment', the modern Meno might say, using the indirect syntax of contemporary politeness and implying that the social underling might have a choice in the matter (Brown and Levinson, 1987).

In these conditions, humour might have a pragmatic function that is less necessary in openly hierarchical conditions. Aristotle's writings on the usefulness of humour are largely confined to the situation of formal, competitive rhetoric. He does not discuss the functions of humour for team-bonding or improving the morale of servants. Today, management experts recommend that managers use humour in their dealings with those they have to manage (e.g., Barsoux, 1993; Caudron, 1992). Humour has become a routine means of accomplishing discipline. Janet Holmes (2000) has studied the use of joking in the work-place and has identified hierarchical patterns of humour. Humour often flows downwards, as superiors make jokes to inferiors, rather than vice versa. In Holmes's words, this type of humour can be 'repressive'. Managers will often phrase commands jokingly, especially using irony to do so, although different work-places may have their different practices of joking (Holmes and Marra, 2002).

In one recorded example, a manager says to her assistant, who is chatting with a secretary, 'OK, Marion, I'm afraid serious affairs of state will have to wait, we have some trivial issues needing our attention' (Holmes, 2000: 172). Marion understands the irony. She recognizes that her boss intends the opposite of what she literally says, for that is how irony works in conversation (Kotthoff, 2003). The manager conveys that the talk of the underlings is trivial and that her own business is serious. She could not have said that directly without the risk of causing offence. So she inverts the ascription of the adjectives, knowing that the inversion will be recognized. The recipient of the remark recognizes that her own conversation is, in the eyes of her superior, the trivial one – although the manager leaves open the ambiguous possibility that in a higher scheme of things work might be less important than social conversation. But in the here and now, where jobs have to be done and money earned, the indirect ironic statement is an order. Marion is being summoned just as Meno summoned the slave boy. She too must obey.

But Marion has to do something more than the slave boy did. She has to laugh, as if to show that she is enjoying the summons. The laughter and the obedience are connected. She probably appreciates having a 'boss' with whom she can have a laugh. It adds to the good atmosphere of work. Marion would also be aware that, if her supervisor were chatting with another supervisor, she as a mere 'assistant' would not be permitted to interrupt with an identical, ironical remark. She could not tell her boss that her serious affairs of state will have to wait. Thus, the language of informality, the first-name terms, the sharing of laughter, the obligation to joke, do not do away with hierarchies of power but they do help to reproduce them.

One might speculate that in Ancient Greece superiors felt far less need to use the indirect codes of disciplinary humour: they could utter their commands with a directness that is considered misplaced today. That is speculation. We do not have the necessary direct evidence. Plato's dialogues are dramatic fictions, not transcriptions of recorded conversations. However, the superiority theories of Plato and Aristotle are suggestive. In their assumptions, we catch glimpses of past customs of humour. We see 'buffoons', showing their lack of taste, by laughing crudely at the ugly and the misshapen. We see gentlemen scorning this crude humour, preferring detached irony. As Jan Swearingen (1991) has argued, irony in the ancient world was the humour of the established, male order.

This superiority was not a sudden feeling that wells up, when a comic sight is viewed – when, for instance, a particularly ugly figure is chanced upon or when someone else fails to meet a minor code of conduct. This superiority is more deep-seated. It is a form of life. The Athenian gentleman, making his ironic reflections in a limited democracy that permitted slavery and excluded the women from public life, would be confident that he was superior from the moment of birth. These early superiority theories, falling short as they do in explaining the psychology of laughter, nevertheless succeed in illustrating how humour was bound up with an ideology of order, taste and superiority.

Assorted misogelasts

It was not just in Ancient Greece that philosophers might have sought to reduce the volume of laughter. Throughout Western history until modern times, misogelasts can be spotted warning that the laughter of their fellows was offensive to morality, etiquette or the heavens. In Roman times, the stoics were particularly severe on frivolity. Epictetus warned aspiring philosophers to avoid 'vulgar entertainments'. Good taste dictated an economy of laughter: 'Let not your laughter be much, nor on many occasions, nor profuse' (*Moral Discourses*, 1910 edn: 267). In conversation, one should avoid trying to excite laughter for its own sake 'for this is a slippery point that may throw you into vulgar manners' (ibid.: 268). One might note the careful qualification. The criticism that there is too much laughter permits the possibility that some laughter is permissible, at least if it serves higher purposes. Stoics, who deprived themselves of so much bodily pleasure, might still enjoy the occasional delights of haughty ridicule.

The problem was not laughter as such, and certainly not ridicule *per se*, but coarse laughter and crude mockery. Mikhail Bakhtin suggested that the 'great and diverse world' of ridicule continued in an unbroken tradition from the ancient world through to the carnivals of the mediaeval period

(1981: 52). Official texts, religious practices and high philosophy were all bawdily mocked by the masses. The high-minded, of course, hit back, not just with disdainful condemnation of the ridiculers. In this matter, the Christian theologians of the Middle Ages continued the traditions of Plato and Epictetus, as they snootily looked down upon the continuing counter-tradition of carnival.

Within Christianity there has been a long tradition of 'grim theologians', who, according to Berger (1997), have set their face against the redemptive power of laughter. Part of the problem, Berger suggests, is the lack of references in the ancient holy texts to good-natured open laughter. Screech in his scholarly *Laughter at the Foot of the Cross* (1997) discusses the mediaeval Christian approach to humour. What was at stake was fiercer than good manners or tasteful philosophy: it was the possibility of divine retribution. Most Christian theologians before the age of Erasmus, and many afterwards, were convinced that God preferred his creatures to be serious of mind and disciplined of body. The vulgar carnivals of the peasantry risked divine disapproval on both counts.

Again, laughter was to be limited, even policed, but not abolished utterly. There were approved ways of laughing, although the slots for appropriate laughter in the calendar of the faithful should not be too numerous. Theologians, both Christian and Jewish, often cited the biblical story of Abraham and Sarah being told by an angel that they would have a son despite their advanced years. Both, according to the biblical text, greeted the news with laughter. Theologians have frequently distinguished between the approved laughter of the husband and the disapproved chortles of his wife. Abraham's laughter was said to be joyous, while Sarah, who well knew the state of her aged body, mocked the idea that she might give birth. Ridiculing God was most certainly not advisable, particularly on the part of woman. The gentle, joyous and essentially restrained laughter of the pious was the model. The problem with Sarah's laughter was not that it was the laughter of mockery but that the butt of this female laughter was God – although there is also a Jewish rabbinic tradition that Sarah was laughing at Abraham, deriding him for being too old to fulfil his requisite husbandly duties.

Despite the Hebrew Bible not being a laugh-filled text, quotes could be provided to suggest that God in heaven would occasionally break into a laugh, particularly the laugh of mockery. The second psalm describes God observing the vain talk of idolaters: 'He who sits in heaven will laugh, the Lord will mock them' (Psalms, 2: iv). The Supreme Being would, it seems, enjoy the cruel pleasures of ridicule, especially when the idolaters get their come-uppance. In the Talmud, one Rabbi explains the verse in the second psalm by saying it refers to the final destruction of God's enemies. Only on that day God will 'truly laugh' (Feuer, 1977: 68). True laughter, thus, is not something humanly cosy.

Christian grimness certainly did not die out with the waning of the Middle Ages. It experienced a new political and spiritual boost with Puritanism, although, as Berger (1997) points out, Martin Luther possessed a fierce, even bawdy, sense of humour. His rhetoric was hardly restrained and derision was part of his theology. According to Screech (1997), Luther interpreted the Latin text of Galatians to suggest that Jesus was answering his accusers with 'derisive mocking laughter'; and Luther used this interpretation to further his own campaign that the papacy 'merited the omnipotent and divine derision of God' (ibid.: 55).

Bawdy though Luther may have been, some of his successors advocated a far more restrained type of piety that curtailed the redemptive qualities of laughter, whether derisive or not. The spirit of Puritanism lived on long beyond the heights of its political power in the seventeenth century. Its supporters continued to criticize the manners of their times, being particularly offended by the freeness of the laughter that they could hear all around them. A typical example, that well exemplifies the later sanctimonious spirit of serious Puritanism, comes in a book written in the mid-nineteenth century by George Winfred Hervey, an American low churchman.

Hervey's volumes sold well in the States, where pious congregants in small isolated towns required guidance about suitably Christian deportment. In *The Rhetoric of Conversation*, Hervey instructed his readers how to converse appropriately. He found the manners of his time troublesome, for there was much too much levity. The old Puritans might have displayed an austerity that was a bit too demanding, but, comments Hervey, one could not doubt their sincerity. Now it had all gone too far in the opposite direction for 'we have in general backslidden into levity and frivolousness' (1854: 258). Hervey saw too much idle laughter and 'incessant efforts to amuse' (ibid.: 260). Gentle joyousness was appropriate but (and a 'but' typically follows any such concession to enjoyment) 'it is scarcely worth while to say that boisterous laughter does not comport with Christian gravity' (ibid.: 267). Hervey did not approve of joking with servants: 'We must address them in a firm yet mild tone' (ibid.: 38). Seriousness was the order of the day.

A broad pattern of belief can be outlined, linking this latter-day Puritanism with Aristotle and Plato. First, there is the advocacy of a serious mode of life, whether the life of the Platonic guardian, the Stoic philosopher or pious Christian. Although seriousness is valued over fun, laughter is not proscribed as such. What matters is the purpose to which laughter is put. Because so much of humanity laughs at the wrong sorts of things – and seems to delight in unseemly bawdiness – the scope of laughter has to be limited. Purposeless laughter – or laughter for its own sake – is condemned. But laughter in the service of righteousness, including the laughter of ridicule, can be appropriate. In the hands of the pious and the stoically righteous, the time for seriousness expands, while the time for laughter is correspondingly contracted. Self-righteous laughter, which ridicules the unfaithful, might not sound pleasant to the outsider. But laughter it is.

In the main, misogelasts have been more concerned to criticize laughter than to understand its causes. They might cite inferior breeding, weakness of character, or the hand of Satan. But they tend not to augment their critiques with detailed psychological explanations. An opposition to purposeless laughter does not in itself entail support for a superiority theory. Nevertheless, worthy critics were placing the laughter of others under psychological suspicion. Sometimes they would come close to the tenets of superiority theories. Hervey wrote: 'Were we to analyse the habitual laugher, I am afraid we should find him chiefly composed of vanity, scorn and dissimulation' (1854: 267).

Had Hervey read secular texts more widely, he would have been able to find support for his diagnosis. But, of course, Hervey would not have wished to have backslidden by giving too much credence to ideas originating outside the spirit and traditions of Puritanism. He felt little need to supplement his criticisms of laughter with deeper psychological analyses. He already knew what would be the results of such analyses. Anyway, there was much more urgent work at hand. Whenever he heard the tones of vain laughter in conversation, he would be reminded of the urgency of his calling. Fortunately, as his book makes clear, daily life was providing regular enough reminders.

Thomas Hobbes and the suspicion of laughter

The theory of superiority is principally associated with Thomas Hobbes, the seventeenth-century English philosopher from Malmesbury in Wiltshire. His ideas on laughter justify being called a 'theory', for they form part of a wider psychological account of human nature. Hobbes's theory of laughter is especially interesting because it puts ridicule at the psychological core of humour. In one important respect, Hobbes's theory departs from previous approaches to laughter. Plato, the Stoics and Christian theologians might have sought to limit laughter, but they left just enough theoretical space to justify, and indeed to celebrate, certain sorts of laughter, albeit the sort of laughter that served disciplinary functions in the cause of seriousness. Hobbes, by contrast, pursued a single psychological idea that put all laughter under suspicion. Hobbes was not devising a theory of humour for its own sake, but his view of laughter was part of a suspicious theory of human passions. In their turn, these general suspicions reflected the circumstances in which Hobbes lived.

Hobbes proposed that human laughter is elicited by a feeling of superiority. We see the deformed or the weak; we feel superior to them; and so we laugh. Aristotle had said much the same in *Poetics*. Whereas Aristotle was attempting to describe what humans laugh at, Hobbes was attempting to explain why they did so. He outlined his views on human psychology in *Human Nature*, which was written in 1640. Hobbes begins his account of the human condition with a description of how the senses form conceptions. At all times he stresses the relations between ideas and bodily feelings. Our conceptions 'are nothing really, but motion in some internal substance of the head' (1999 edn: 43). These motions proceed to the heart where they produce either feelings of pleasure or pain. Pleasure induces us to draw near to the thing that has provoked the feeling, while pain induces us to 'retire from the thing that displeaseth' (ibid.: 43). In arguing thus, Hobbes was outlining an early utilitarian, materialist psychology according to which the organism is driven by bodily impulses to maximize pleasure and to minimize pain.

Such a materialist psychology tends towards a cynical view of humans and their motives. It suggests that our displays of morality grow out of selfish motives to gain pleasure and to avoid pain. Hobbes's conception of human nature was particularly shocking in the fervid religious atmosphere of mid-seventeenth-century England. Hobbes was portraying Man, supposedly created in God's image, as a material creature with selfish bodily appetites. Worse still, he was detailing how the moral beliefs of humankind were really only expressions of selfish, material desire.

There is no such thing as absolute goodness, writes Hobbes in *Human Nature*, but 'every man, for his own part, calleth that which pleaseth, and is delightful to himself "good"' (1999: 44). Hobbes subjected one after another of the various high-minded virtues to the same treatment. To accord someone 'honour' is merely to acknowledge their power over us; 'repentance' is realizing that the course we have taken will not bring us what we had hoped; 'pity' for another is based on imagining a similar calamity happening to ourselves; and so on. Each time an apparently unselfish motive, that seems to reflect the general goodness of humans, is revealed to be at root selfish. Most dangerous of all, Hobbes subjected belief in God to the same debunking treatment: 'Even the goodness which we attribute to God Almighty, is his goodness to us' (ibid.: 44).

Hobbes compares human life to a race in which humans can be supposed to have 'no other goal, nor no other garland, but being foremost' (ibid.: 59). Accordingly, life was a competitive game, in which all, by nature, wish to jostle to achieve their own individual advantage. Laughter finds its place in this catalogue of selfishness and competition. Hobbes asserts that the passion, of which laughter is the sign, is one 'that hath no name'. No-one had accurately described exactly what we experience when we laugh. It was too simple to say that the passion consists of wit and that it resides 'in the jest', for 'men laugh at mischances and indecencies, wherein there lieth no wit nor jest at all' (ibid.: 54). Also what we laugh at must be new and unexpected, for we cease to laugh at things when they grow 'stale or usual'. Hobbes claimed that people above all laugh 'at the infirmities of others wherewith their own abilities are set off and illustrated' or at jests whose wit 'always consisteth in the elegant discovering and conveying to our minds some absurdity of another' (ibid.: 54).

In psychological terms, Hobbes was proposing a motivational theory of laughter, based upon perceptual and cognitive premises. He assumed that we see, or hear about, the misfortunes or deformities of another. This triggers off a cognitive comparison with our own selves. This comparison then produces a feeling of superiority, which is a pleasant experience and which provokes the reaction of laughter.

Hobbes conceded that we can laugh at ourselves sometimes, but he did not see this as contradicting his basic premise that laughter is based on a comparative judgement of our own superiority. He treated self-mockery as being essentially the same process as laughing at others. We tend to laugh at our former infirmities, comparing these with our present superiority. We do not laugh at our present selves in the way that others might laugh at us, because 'men take heinously to be laughed at or derided' (ibid.: 54). Thus, Hobbes proceeded to his conclusion which has been much quoted over the years: 'I may therefore conclude, that the passion of laughter is nothing else but a sudden glory arising from sudden conception of some eminency in ourselves, by comparison with the infirmities of others, or with our own formerly' (ibid.: 54–5).

Hobbes puts ridicule at the centre of humour and thereby questions the goodness of laughter. He is telling us to look behind the smiles and the jests. If we do so, then we will see something not too pleasant. Hobbes did not ignore the social aspects of laughter, but he conceived these as secondary. When one person laughs in company, then others will be jealous. They overcome this jealousy by joining in the laughter: 'laughing to one's self putteth all the rest to a jealousy and examination of themselves' (ibid.: 55). Thus, the communality of laughter derives from the self-interested pleasure of ridiculing the weakness of others and it is that latter pleasure which is the primary one.

Hobbes's description of laughter was brief, somewhat brutish and certainly nasty in its implications. In *Human Nature* he did not discuss apparent counter-examples, except to say in general terms that 'laughter without offence must be at absurdities and infirmities abstracted from details' (ibid.: 55). Unlike Aristotle, Plato, Christian theologians and others who were offended by raucous laughter, Hobbes was not distinguishing between good and bad laughter, high-class and low-class humour, positive or negative wit. He was proposing a theory of ridicule that would democratically place all types of humour under suspicion. His phrasing was confident and unqualified. Laughter was 'nothing else' but sudden glory, just as goodness was nothing else but self-interest. He was leaving no room for exceptions.

The obvious weakness of Hobbes's theory is closely allied to its strength. Hobbes was presenting a bold and clear statement, without variety, nuance and difficult cases. As later critics were to point out, not all types of wit necessarily involve finding some absurdity in another. One might think of word-play or puns as victimless humour, although, as some observers have suggested, the realm of victimless wit may not be quite so large and untroubled as some of Hobbes's later critics liked to think (Norrick, 2003). By the same token, Hobbes's treatment of the social aspects of laughter is unsatisfactory. The model is essentially individualist: one person laughs and then others, out of a fear of jealousy, join in. The model ignores that laughter can be spontaneously social and that it rarely occurs when the individual is alone. In this regard, Hobbes only sees laughter as the outward and essentially meaningless manifestation of an inner emotional state: he does not see laughter as meaningful, rhetorical communication.

Unlike most modern writers on humour, Hobbes did not feel obliged to include jokes or anecdotes in order to display his own love of mirth. That would have contradicted his purpose. Like his misogelastic forebears, Hobbes was not seeking to increase laughter. He concluded his discussion of laughter in *Human Nature* with the comment that 'it is vain glory, and an argument of little worth, to think the infirmities of another, sufficient matter for his triumph' (1999: 55). He went on to describe 'levity' as a 'defect of the mind' (ibid.: 62). He picked up these themes in his great work *Leviathan*, where he claimed that it was a mark of small minds to laugh greatly. Such people are constantly deriving pleasure from the defects of others. In doing so, they reveal their weakness for they 'are forced to keep themselves in their own favour, by observing the imperfections of other men' (1996 edn: 43). It was much better to compare oneself with one's moral and intellectual betters.

Apparently Hobbes was a ready wit in private company. John Aubrey, in the notes that he compiled for an intended biography, described Hobbes as being marvellous in his ability to offer witty, unrancorous replies in conversation (1999: 237–8). Aubrey also notes that Hobbes was much baited by the so-called wits at the court of Charles II. When Hobbes came to the court, the King would exclaim 'Here comes the bear to be baited!' In old age, according to Aubrey, Hobbes was completely bald. He used to sit and study bare-headed: 'His greatest trouble was to keep the flies from pitching on the baldness' (ibid.: 239). As Aristophanes had recognized, there is comedy in the sight of fleas or flies landing on a philosopher's bald head. The great mind is helpless inside its awkward head. Unphilosophical onlookers can smile.

Suspicious life and times

Hobbes's account of laughter belonged to a political argument. *Human Nature* was the first half of Hobbes's manuscript *Elements of Law, Natural and Politic*. The second part, *De Corpore Politico*, specifically addressed the problems of civil society and government. Hobbes was to rework the same elements of psychology and politics into *Leviathan*. Hobbes argued that humans could not be trusted to control their selfish instincts. Our passions, if left unchecked, would threaten any social order. Humans, therefore, need external controls in order to prevent their selfishly destructive urges from running riot. The comments on laughter fit this sombre, fearful picture. The apparently innocent joy of laughter is not so innocent. It indicates an unpleasant feeling that strikes at social relations. A society filled with laughter would not be a happy place. It would be a place of mockery where each is trying to outdo everyone else in the competitive game of life – a place where human bears are baited unmercifully.

Hobbes was living in dangerously violent times. He had completed the manuscript of *Human Nature* and had begun to circulate it privately just before the outbreak of the English Civil War. He feared the zeal of the Puritan revolutionaries, who certainly would not appreciate his materialist analyses of religious belief and goodness. People were being burnt to death for lesser theological errors. Hobbes fled to France, where he lived in comparative safety during the war and the subsequent Cromwellian republic. Even in France, he was not above suspicion. Some French Catholics suspected Hobbes of holding anti-Catholic views, just as English Puritans had thought him to be dangerously papish. After the restoration of the monarchy, Hobbes returned to England. He had good relations with Charles II, the new king. In fact, he had tutored him while they were both in France. Despite this, the dangers continued. There were mutterings from some bishops, who were suggesting that Hobbes should be burnt as a heretic.

Hobbes's view of human nature represented a curious mixture of bold cynicism and fear. He cynically claimed that self-interest lay behind most human conduct, including laughter. Yet, he was no psychological free-marketeer, trusting individuals to judge their own best interests. The state of nature was dangerous. Humans needed to make a compact to respect authority. Religion and kings were useful devices for establishing the social order that could control the anti-social instincts of humans. His justifications for the institutions of authority and for religion were pragmatic rather than intrinsically respectful. We need religious authority, not because of the majesty of God, but because authority is good for us. No wonder some of the bishops muttered, wishing to light a fire beneath the tethered old bear.

Hobbes had good reason to fear the extremes of religious passions. The third Earl of Shaftesbury, who was to criticize Hobbes's general view of human nature some 50 years later and whose grandfather was politically active in Hobbes's day, understood how the events of the age had affected the philosopher. Shaftesbury wrote that 'the fright he took upon the sight of the governing powers, who unjustly assumed the authority of the people, gave him an abhorrence of all popular government and of the very notion of liberty itself' (1999 edn: 42). Hobbes's account of human nature contained one particular omission which was dangerous in those times, but which brings a modern freshness to his psychology. Passions were explained downwards in terms of bodily states, not upwards in terms of divine powers. This very materialist explanation of human motives offers little space for the actions of the divine.

Hobbes did not criticize laughter specifically on religious, aesthetic or even political grounds. His argument was that laughter reflects the sort of base, selfish motives that need to be disciplined. Whether or not God is offended by the sounds of boisterousness is irrelevant to his argument. Or, rather, God comes in to serve human needs. People require an authority to check their passions. A belief in a strict religious authority will serve the purpose well. Thus, God is useful as a belief. Supporters of Cromwell, who were trying to found the state upon the principles of true, pious belief, were hardly likely to look favourably on a philosophy that gave God the supporting philosophical role of being useful.

Later writers on the issue of humour would claim that Hobbes exaggerated the role of superiority. They would provide examples of humour that did not seem to fit his model. Hobbes had said that we experience superiority when we laugh, but his critics would cite their own laughter and declare that they personally experienced no such sense of superiority when they laughed. Francis Hutcheson was particularly scathing on this score in his *Thoughts on Laughter* (1758). He wrote that philosophers such as Hobbes rush to their closets 'to spin out some fine conjectures about the principles of our actions, which no mortal is conscious of in himself during the action'. The apparent feeling of superiority, according to Hutcheson, 'seldom arises in our minds in the hurry of a cheerful conversation among friends, where there is often an high mutual esteem'. Indeed, continued Hutcheson, the pleasure that we supposedly take from the misfortunes of others 'must indeed be a secret one, so very secret, that many a compassionate heart was never conscious of it' (1758: 17). Hutcheson's argument has a modern feel. Ideological positivists too claim that they feel no superiority to others when they laugh. As mentioned in the previous chapter, Athena Du Pré (1998) suggested that the superiority theory should be relabelled because people report no feelings of superiority when they laugh.

The comments of the critics suggest that the experience of laughter is, and should be, straightforward. We laugh openly and we experience our feelings openly. So to confirm or disconfirm Hobbes we need only check our own reactions. Few would wish to admit that their laughter is based on the cruel, unsociable feeling of superiority that Hobbes claimed to have exposed. Hobbes did not develop a psychology of self-deception, but the arguments of his psychology were pointing towards the need to understand the nature of self-deception. Hobbes was claiming that we call selfish motives by noble altruistic names. By doing so, we individually and collectively conceal the nature of our desires from ourselves. Thus, we delude ourselves daily. If we report no feeling of superiority when we laugh, then this is to be expected, just as we report no experience of selfishness when we claim to be morally good.

Hobbes had no readily available psychology of self-deception that he could use to argue that his critics were not pointing to flaws in his own arguments but to flaws in human nature. There would not be a systematic psychology of self-deception for another two and a half centuries, when Freud formulated his psychoanalytic theory. In many respects, there are parallels between Hobbes and Freud. Like Freud, Hobbes was proposing a psychology of suspicion. Both thinkers were saying in effect: don't accept what people tell you about their desires, look for the inadmissible motives. Hobbes's comments about the desire for pleasure and the avoidance of pain were to be reflected in Freud's work, particularly in his later metapyschological writings such as *Beyond the Pleasure Principle*. And, of course, Freud was to suggest that humour is fuelled by less than worthy feelings and that the quality of wit could not, of itself, account for the volume of people's laughter.

In their visions of society, both Hobbes and Freud were convinced that there was a fundamental conflict between individual desire and social order. Humans were selfish but needed to live socially. If egoistic desires were not curtailed, social order would collapse. Thus, both thinkers distrusted the anti-social force of passion. Hobbes's *Leviathan* and Freud's *Civilization and its Discontents* were addressed to this problem. Hobbes believed external political force was required to police selfish individual passion, because people could not be trusted to control themselves. Freud, on the other hand, believed in the power of rational self-knowledge and self-discipline. Neither Hobbes nor Freud, however, developed their theories of humour in order to suggest that laughter might play a role in exerting disciplinary force over potentially disruptive desires. Both saw laughter as a potentially rebellious element, with Freud, unlike Hobbes, seeing the benefits of diverting dangerous psychological motives into the pleasures of humour.

There are further parallels between Hobbes and Freud, linking their common vision of social order to similar experiences. Both men knew dangerous circumstances and had good reason to fear mass passions. Hobbes saw established monarchical power overthrown by waves of popular religious fanaticism. Freud witnessed the success of Nazism and the popularity of its anti-Semitic message. Both Freud and Hobbes fled their homelands in fear of these new popular movements, aware that they risked death had they stayed. Freud fled to England, which he could think of as a secure land. By contrast, Hobbes had to travel in the other direction across the Channel to find his safety. Hobbes was to return to the country of his birth, but Freud died in exile.

Of course, Freud's psychology was much more complex than Hobbes's, being more attuned to the subtle ambiguities of human conduct. In Hobbes's hands, but not in Freud's, all humour stands ostensibly condemned. Even the Puritans, who knew that God would occasionally smile with triumph, and that Abraham laughed in a divinely approved way, were not so severe on humour. They could justify their own occasional laughter, as they claimed to carry out God's work without compromise. But that was part of the problem. Hobbes had ample reason to distrust the laughter of Puritans.

4

Incongruity Theories and Gentlemanly Laughter

Incongruity theories represent the second major tradition for understanding humour. The basic approach was developed in the eighteenth century as a reaction against Hobbes's view of laughter. Instead of seeking the origins of laughter within the motives of the person who laughs, incongruity theories have sought to identify those incongruous features of the world that provoke laughter. In doing this, the theory took a decisive step towards rescuing laughter from suspicion and laying the foundations for modern approaches to studying humour. Indeed, it has been claimed that incongruity theories in one form or another continue to dominate psychological research into humour (Raskin, 1985). Peter Berger comments that 'there is widespread agreement that a sense of humour leads above all to a perception of *incongruence* or *incongruity*' (1997: 208, emphasis in original).

Although this chapter will discuss the emergence of incongruity theories in the eighteenth century, there will be no attempt to provide an exhaustive history. The discussion will mainly concentrate on English and Scottish theorists. In eighteenth-century Britain major philosophers and literary figures took the topics of humour and laughter seriously. In many respects this was the golden age for the philosophy of humour. The topic attained a greater philosophical importance than previously, and, arguably, more so than it would in the future. It would be wrong to suggest that only British philosophers were speculating about humour at this time. Kant had important observations to make in his *Critique of Judgement*. In the early nineteenth century Schopenhauer produced an influential version of the incongruity theory. Whereas the present discussion will pass over Kant, we will take a brief trip across the Channel to comment upon Schopenhauer. The opportunity is too good to miss, for Schopenhauer's treatment of humour demonstrates how low assumptions can be found in an apparently lofty philosophy.

The metaphor of height is appropriate. The ancestors of today's professional theorists of incongruity were doing more than constructing an interesting psychology of laughter. The eighteenth-century thinkers did not inhabit a world of pure thought, divorced from the social superiorities and inferiorities of their times. Like Aristotle, the British philosophers of laughter in the eighteenth century typically sought to distinguish the peaks of gentlemanly wit from the depths of coarse laughter. Matters of morality, politics and aesthetics affected their speculations about laughter.

The negatives that ideological positivism might wish away theoretically have a habit of returning. So it was in the eighteenth century. Philosophers may have sought to restore the good name of laughter after Hobbes's accusations, but the spirit of Hobbes was not easily dismissed. As will be seen, the problem of ridicule haunted the image of gentlemanly wit. On occasions, the theorists of incongruity, particularly the Earl of Shaftesbury, confronted their Hobbesian daemon. When they did so, they can be seen to be grappling with the notion that the laughter of mockery might serve disciplinary purposes in the cause of good taste, social propriety and God.

Coffee, cocoa and wit

The British incongruity theorists of the eighteenth century lived in different political circumstances from Hobbes. Two revolutions and one monarchical restoration separated them from the time when the gloomy sage of Malmesbury first formulated his idea that laughter was nothing more than a sudden feeling of superiority. Hobbes had been writing on the eve of the great Puritan Revolution that would institute England's only period of republicanism. That was a time of fearful austerity. Hobbes felt able to return to England with the Restoration of the monarchy. The High Church was back in power, and the misogelastic Puritans were in retreat. The upper classes could pursue pleasure fearlessly. In the London theatres the fashion was for bawdy comedies. But this was not the context for the theories of incongruity. Another revolution had to occur.

This was the Glorious Revolution or *coup d'état* of 1688. James II, suspected of Catholic and despotic tendencies, was replaced by the joint rule of William and Mary. The new monarchs owed their position to Parliament, which was not in the mood to surrender its newly gained powers. John Locke was the philosophical architect of this second revolution. His theory of knowledge was provocatively democratic. The mind is a blank sheet at birth. All knowledge is built upon perceptions. No god has implanted innate qualities of kingship within the regal brain. Thus, infant monarchs are as ignorant as their lowest subjects. It is only a social contract, or mutual agreement, that joins together the citizens of society. If monarchs fail to fulfil their obligations – by giving themselves up to frivolous, perfumed pleasures, or by encouraging inappropriately Roman forms of worship – then the citizenry was justified in dissolving the social contract. They would then be free to negotiate a new social contract with a more suitable monarch.

This new democratic philosophy, which in practice only permitted a very small percentage of the population to exercise the right of social contract, was very different from Hobbes's dour image of the polity. Humans were not depicted as being driven by dangerous, selfish passions that needed constant, strict disciplining. Locke's philosophy trusted the people, at least in theory, to be rational. They were perceivers of the world, receiving clear and distinct ideas from their senses. This move from a suspicious psychology of emotions towards a trusting psychology of cognition, was reflected not just in the differences between Hobbes's and Locke's respective images of the polity. It also led, as will be seen, to very different views of humour.

Hobbes's account of human nature seemed altogether foreign to many living a hundred years later in Britain. The Scottish philosopher, Francis Hutcheson, the author of *Thoughts on Laughter*, was professor at Glasgow University from 1729 until his death in 1746. In his *System of Moral Philosophy*, Hutcheson wrote that if the human constitution were entirely selfish, as Hobbes had alleged, then 'human life would be quite different from what we feel every day, *a joyless, loveless, cold, sullen state of cunning and suspicion*' (Vol. 1: 88–9, emphasis in original). Hutcheson took it for granted that life was not so joyless and filled with suspicion as Hobbes had depicted. However, Hobbes's psychology might have been appropriate for a previous time, when the citizens of Britain distrusted their neighbours and when political authorities imposed order with grim brutality. Hutcheson and his contemporaries did not daily fear the whispered word or the undisciplined laugh as Hobbes had done.

It was not merely politics that had changed, but so materially had the lives of the middle to upper ranks of society. With world trade, colonization and profits from slavery came national wealth and exotic luxuries, such as silks, spices and tobacco, not to mention new woods, vegetables and dyes. The import of coffee and chocolate had an important impact on social life. In the metropolitan centres, coffee-houses and cocoa-houses were established. These were very different from the traditional ale-houses of the rough working man. They were places in which gentlemen could meet to take the new beverages and to discuss agreeably the latest art, commerce and politics. The more intellectually minded also established scientific and philosophical clubs. This was an age of sociability and conversation, rather than dour devotion.

These new types of meeting places were neither totally public nor private spaces. New codes of manners were required for conversations whose content, location and manner seemed completely novel. The problem was not confined to the clubs and coffee-houses of England. New codes were required for the salons being developed in France and elsewhere in Europe (Burke, 1993). Laughter became a practical problem. The devotees of the salons and the coffee-houses needed to determine what was the appropriate sort of laughter that would encourage conviviality without being raucously lower class.

A preoccupation with wit, taste and social rank can be seen in the writings of Joseph Addison, the great commentator and promoter of the coffee-house culture in Britain. *The Spectator*, the magazine that Addison and Richard Steele founded, was directed at the new audience of coffee-house readers. Its authors claimed to be spectators observing a cast of characters in their favourite London coffee-houses. In one of the early issues Addison praised the new clubs whose members were motivated by 'a love of society' and came together 'to relax themselves from the business of the day by an innocent and cheerful conversation' (*The Spectator*, 9; Addison, 1965 edn: 42).

But how cheerful should the cheerful conversation be? That was the question. Throughout the ages, the ablest philosophers have addressed the pressing practical problems of their day. So in the eighteenth century, literati and philosophers discoursed on the nature of wit, addressing similar issues that Aristotle had discussed in *The Nicomachean Ethics*, when he advocated a tasteful middle way between buffoonery and moroseness. The philosophers discussed these issues in their own philosophical clubs. Some of the foremost philosophers of Scotland formed the Wise Club in Aberdeen in 1758. On the second and fourth Wednesday of each month, they gathered in a tavern to dine and discuss philosophy, followed by 'a slight and unexpensive collation' (Forbes, 1824: 16). Within this convivial atmosphere, they would talk *inter alia* about the philosophy of conviviality. James Beattie presented early drafts of his *Essay on Laughter* to the Wise Club, and George Campbell did likewise with his *Philosophy of Rhetoric*, which contained extended discussions of wit and humour.

There is little reason to accept at face value the claims of coffee-house regulars that their places of meeting were filled with constant wit of a superior quality. As always, participants are apt to exaggerate the wittiness of themselves and the company they keep. James Boswell's *London Journal* provides glimpses of the wit to be enjoyed in fashionable coffee-houses. His favourite place was Child's in the courtyard of St Pauls. It was, according to Boswell, a place that was 'dusky, warm and comfortable' (1950 edn: 74). Boswell provided snippets from his Saturday visits. He recounted a dialogue about the literary critic Joseph Wharton. One speaker reported Wharton's view that the poet Thomson possessed 'great force'. Another speaker replies, 'He has great faults.' The first repeats himself, 'Ay, but great force, too.' To which the other responds: 'I have eaten beefsteaks with him.' A third speaker pipes up: 'So have I' (1 January 1763, Boswell, 1950 edn: 115). This was the only exchange that Boswell noted from that particular visit. One must presume that the rest of the morning's talk was even less witty. To be fair, the diarist had other things on his mind that day. He left Child's to visit his friend Mrs Louisa Lewis, hoping to persuade her this time to share his ardour.

Many of the writers who discoursed on the nature of humour in the eighteenth century were Scotsmen. Some of the most creative heirs of Locke were to be found north of the border, Hume being only the famous example. Beattie and Campbell have already been mentioned. In the course of this chapter, there will be occasion to quote other Scottish literary critics and philosophers such as Lord Kames, Dugald Stewart, David Hartley and Francis Hutcheson. In part, this reflects the power of the Scottish Enlightenment, as Edinburgh, not to mention Aberdeen, vied with London as a centre for arts, science and philosophy. There were also particular circumstances in Scotland making the topics of talk and laughter especially propitious.

The Act of Union, linking Scotland with England and Wales, was passed in 1707. Many of the Scottish educated classes saw this as opportunity for playing a wider stage (Colley, 1992). This entailed taking up the language of the English. James Beattie, poet and Professor of Philosophy at Aberdeen, wrote in his essay about laughter that among his compatriots 'the learned and polite' had for the most part abandoned their Scottish language and had 'adopted the English in its stead' (1779: 382). This preference was, he suggested, 'justly due to the superior genius of that noble language, and the natural effect of the present constitution of Great Britain' (ibid.: 382). The intellectual figures of the Scottish Enlightenment, like their English counterparts, were enjoying new forms of assembly in which to discuss their ideas. In addition, the Scottish thinkers were doing this in a language, which their grandparents, if not their parents, would scarce have used. Those grandparents would have been the inheritors of sterner and more taciturn ways, which, as Adam Ferguson described in his *Essay on the History of Civil Society*, were already disappearing. They might well have looked askance at their grandsons who discussed humour so seriously and at such length.

The dilemma for the gentlemen of the clubs and coffee-houses, and also for ladies who partook of dinner-table conversations and acted as society hostesses, was how to appear to be congenial but not indecorous, witty but not unseemly, serious but not overly earnest. 'Amiable humour' was a moral matter and moderation was to be the key (see Tave, 1960, for an excellent historical account). Incongruity theory developed against this background. Its proponents wished to dissociate themselves from Puritan zealots, who took a miserly view of laughter. They also rejected the old-fashioned noblemen such as the Earl of Chesterfield or Lord Monboddo, who believed that it was unbecoming for the well-bred aristocrat to laugh overmuch. Lord Monboddo, who passed much of his time in virtual social exclusion on his remote Scottish estate, had little need for the new metropolitan manners as he took lonely pride in ancestral gloom. On the other hand, the new laughter theorists of the coffee-house had little time for the bawdy hedonism of the Restoration period. In the mid-eighteenth century Lord Kames, who was a Scottish judge as well as aesthetic philosopher, wrote that 'the licentious court of Charles II, amongst its many disorders engendered a pest, the virulence of which subsists to this day' (*Elements of Criticism*, 1854 edn: 36).

So the path to gentlemanly wit lay between over-asceticism and hedonism. It should lead neither to the pleasures of the uncouth masses nor to those of the idle aristocracy. The middle way to wit, which Aristotle had recommended, had to be rediscovered. It was as much a matter of class and gender as philosophy. Being witty in the appropriate manner was a serious matter – serious enough for philosophical attention.

Locke and incongruity

To begin with, a matter of terminology needs attention. The word 'humour' has changed its meaning in the past two hundred years. It is now a general term describing a wide variety of things that supposedly make people laugh. In the eighteenth century it had a much more restricted meaning. Writers conventionally treated wit and humour as distinctly different phenomena. Wit involved playing with ideas or words, whereas humour occurred when the object of the laughter was a person. The word 'humour' derived from the psychological terminology of the age. The 'humours' were the bodily fluids whose admixtures supposedly provided people with their individual temperaments. A 'humorist' was not originally a comical writer but a person with an extreme character that seemed to comprise a single humour rather than a balance of various humours.

The late seventeenth and early eighteenth centuries saw the development of a popular type of theatrical comedy that featured farcical characters with extreme temperaments. Audiences would laugh at the stock figures, such as the pompous deceived husband, the hypocritical clergyman, the maladroit social climber, and so on. These characters spoke words that were not in themselves witty sayings but which revealed the absurdity of their temperaments. Thus, fun was to be had at the expense of the 'humorists'. As on the stage, so it was in real life. There were people with an oddness of manner that seemed to induce mirth in those around them. As Aristotle had written, people laugh at those who are below average in their characteristics. In time, the word 'humorist' came to describe the creative writers who invented comic 'humorous' characters.

Modern readers should be aware that eighteenth-century theorists viewed 'wit' and 'humour' as distinctly different phenomena. Wit referred to clever verbal sayings, whereas 'humour' denoted a laughable character. If eighteenth-century writers wanted to describe the general category of things that might provoke laughter, they would tend to use 'the ridiculous' or 'the ludicrous', both terms then conveying a wider sense than they do now. This needs to be borne in mind in the following discussion. The present analysis will use the word 'humour' in its modern, general sense, but, of course, in quotations from eighteenth-century writers the word has a more specific meaning, for which modern English provides no really adequate synonym.

In its origins, incongruity theory was a theory of wit rather than 'humour', although it came to be applied, often rather awkwardly, to what was then called 'humour'. Incongruity theory looked at laughter's cognitive processes, rather than its emotional dynamics. This is clear in a passage, in which Locke discussed wit in his great *An Essay Concerning Human Understanding*, published in 1690. Although Locke's discussion was brief and tangential to his main epistemological themes, it came to be much cited by the British writers on laughter in the next century.

In Book Two of the *Essay*, Locke discussed the perceptual basis of knowledge. The mind, having received clear and distinct impressions, must be able to make judgements on what it perceives. It must be able to compare present impressions with past memories in order to discern whether present perceptions resemble or differ from past ones. Locke was arguing that any true judgement depends on the '*clear discerning faculty* of the mind where it perceives *two* ideas to be the same, or different' (ibid.: 123, emphasis in original). Appearance of similitude can be misleading, if there really are differences between two ideas. Thus, careful judgement consists 'in separating carefully, one from another, *ideas* wherein can be found the least difference, thereby to avoid being misled by similitude' (ibid.: 123, emphasis in original).

If judgement involves carefully distinguishing between things that appear to be similar but which are actually different, then wit is based on the reverse process. It brings together ideas that are different in order to treat them as if they were similar. Accordingly, wit operates through 'the assemblage of *ideas*, and putting those together with quickness and variety, wherein can be found any resemblance or congruity, thereby to make up pleasant pictures and agreeable visions in the fancy' (ibid.: 123, emphasis in original). In these respects, wit resembles the poetic use of allusion or metaphor. Locke's brief comparison between wit and judgement comes down heavily on the side of the latter. Wit, like poetic metaphors, might strike 'so lively on the fancy', but when compared with the deeper level of knowledge, it is superficial (ibid.: 124). It succeeds by quickness and fanci-fulness but it does not stand the test of slow, careful judgement. Because wit and judgement are based on differing mental processes, Locke suggested that men 'who have a great deal of wit, and prompt memories, have not always the clearest judgement or deepest reason' (ibid.: 123).

Locke's purpose was to elucidate the basis of clear judgement, rather than to promote the pleasantries of wit. Those who wanted to do the latter could nevertheless take up his basic point. It could be conceded that the amusement of the coffee-house was not to be compared with the serious judgement of the philosopher's study. Yet, wit was not to be dismissed despite its intrinsic imperfections. It took a fine sensibility to notice similar-ities, or congruities, when others could only see differences – even if such similarities strike upon the fancy rather than reflect the minute differences that science was discovering to exist in the material world. Dugald Stewart, in the first volume of his *Elements of the Philosophy of the Human Mind*, first published in 1792, began his sub-section on wit by quoting with approval Locke's definition (1814 edn: 301). Stewart also stressed the role of surprise: the witty person draws together ideas that listeners do not expect. He concluded that 'we consider wit as a sort of feat or trick of intellectual dexterity, analogous, in some respects, to the extraordinary performances of jugglers and rope-dancers' (ibid.: 305). By ending his sub-section with the philosophically surprising connection with rope-dancing, Stewart was demonstrating his own faculty for simultaneous judgement and wit.

At first sight, Locke seems to be advancing a view of wit based upon 'congruity' rather than 'incongruity'. He was claiming that wit comprised of bringing together ideas in which can be found any 'resemblance or congruity'. Yet, Locke's distinction between serious judgement and wit was based on a further assumption. The witty person and the poet draw atten-tion to similarities for the sake of creating a fanciful impression. The simi-larities do not actually exist in nature. By bringing the dissimilarities together, the wit was creating something incongruous. A poet was praised in Samuel Johnson's presence for nurturing his poems as a gardener might. Yes, answered the great wit of England, his poems are like big cucumbers. Johnson was not implying that the poems were actually cucumbers: the similarity was not to be understood literally. The wit consisted of Johnson bringing into congruity two incongruous ideas – the poem and the cucumber. Something ludicrously fanciful – the poem as a cucumber – is created by this witty act of the imagination.

The basic idea of incongruity theory was that two different ideas would be suddenly connected with comic effect. According to Francis Hutcheson in *Thoughts on Laughter* (1758), wit comprised the bringing together of 'images which have contrary additional ideas, as well as some resemblance in the principal idea' (ibid.: 24). Sydney Smith, in his lectures on aesthetics, stressed that the cause of laughter was not the feeling of superiority, as Hobbes had asserted. On the contrary, the 'discriminating cause is *incongruity*, or the conjunction of objects and circumstances not usually combined' (1864 edn: 132). George Campbell in *Philosophy of Rhetoric* (1776) agreed 'incongruous affinity' is the 'proper object of laughter'; wit and humour achieve their aims by connecting objects that are 'apparently the most dissimilar and heterogeneous' (1856 edn: 41–2). Lord Kames, also citing Locke approvingly, proposed a more concise definition of wit: 'A junction of things by distant and fanciful relations, which surprise because they are unexpected' (1854 edn: 185). David Hartley in *Observations on Man* suggested that adult laughter was evinced by surprise arising from 'some more than ordinary degree of contrast or coincidence' ([1749] 1834: 276).

It has been claimed that the first writer actually to use the term 'incongruity' in relation to wit was Mark Akenside (Tave, 1960). Akenside's *The Pleasures of Imagination* achieved great popularity after its initial publication in 1744 and ran to several revised editions. Unlike many of the eighteenth-century writers on laughter, Akenside was not an aristocrat, a churchman or a Scot. He was the son of a Newcastle butcher and became a poet and physician. *Pleasures* was a didactic poem with accompanying philosophical and explanatory notes. As a genre, the didactic poem has long passed out of intellectual fashion. Cultural theorists today would not try to fit their technical terminology into iambic pentameters. In the eighteenth century, however, the didactic poem was considered appropriate for serious arguments. It was especially suited for a treatise on the pleasures of the imagination, in which form might be congruously matched with content.

Akenside linked the laughter of ridicule to the perception of incongruity. In the main body of his poem he wrote:

> Where'er the power of ridicule displays
> Her quaint-ey'd visage, some incongruous form,
> Some stubborn dissonance of things combin'd
> Strikes on the quick observer. (1810 edn: 100)

Akenside expanded on these ideas in his notes, suggesting that 'the incongruous properties may either exist in the objects themselves, or in the apprehension of the person to whom they relate' (ibid.: 151).

Locke had outlined the mental processes of the person who is creating a witty remark. Akenside and others were widening Locke's insight to describe the psychology of the audience. If the witty person suddenly draws attention to incongruities, then auditors might be expected to react with laughter. This extension retains the essential feature of being cognitive rather than emotional. Locke, Akenside, Kames, Stewart et al. were all describing how perception and judgement lead to wit and laughter. It is a bloodless process: stimuli are combined, incongruities perceived. In the early twentieth century, James Sully was to write that the 'distinctive mark' of the incongruity theory was that it did not propose an emotion behind our enjoyment of the ludicrous. Instead, it posits a purely intellectual attitude, 'a modification of thought activity' so that laughter arises from 'our intellectual mechanism' (1902: 125). The shameful feelings that Hobbes had described are absent. The gentleman of wit is quick, clever and cheerful, not a point-scoring bully.

Incongruity and the Heirs of Locke

Locke may have downgraded wit in relation to judgement, but his heirs by stressing the cognitive aspects were preparing the way for a long-lasting rehabilitation of wit. To be witty was to be creative. Many years later, Arthur Koestler (1964) was to stress this in his theory of bisociation, when he proposed a cognitive parallel between wit and scientific creativity. Both bring together disparate, seemingly incongruous ideas. The implication is that it takes mental flexibility to appreciate humour. Those who think in straight lines, doggedly sorting out the world by putting different things into different boxes, will neither show the genuine creativity on which scientific originality depends, nor appreciate wit. A risk – a flight of fancy – is necessary for both. Hans Speier, in an aside that was neither fully serious nor fully flippant, suggested that psychologists will one day devise an experiment to prove that those who are scandalized by poetry and art will regularly miss the point of jokes and have an aversion to puns (Speier, 1998: 1365).

The shift from emotion to cognitive flexibility prepares the way for giving humour a clean bill of health. Jests need carry no Hobbesian health warning if they are clever exercises of the creative intellect, rather than signs of selfish passion. Nowadays, it is common for analysts to claim that jokes involve a cognitive shift (e.g., Mulkay, 1988; Morreall, 1983; Raskin, 1985). Some psychologists have linked the possession of a sense of humour with the ability to shift between different cognitive frameworks (e.g., McGhee, 1983; Lefcourt, 2001). As Oring (1989) notes, the punch-line of a joke must trigger the perception of an incongruity, requiring the listener to make an abrupt cognitive reorganization. The joke seems to be pulling its listeners in one direction. Then all of a sudden the punch-line comes and listeners realize that they have been led into interpreting a word, phrase or scene in the wrong way. The joke-teller is like the magician who fools the audience into thinking that it has seen the ball being placed under a particular cup. They have heard what has been said, but they have been lulled into the wrong interpretative scheme.

Linguists have examined the structure of jokes. Rachel Giora (1991), who situates her work within the tradition of incongruity theories, claims that well-formed jokes convey two incongruous interpretations. When the punch-line is delivered, the recipient has to cancel one interpretation and substitute the 'correct' one (see Vaid et al, 2003, for an experimental demonstration of this process). Giora uses several jokes to illustrate her point. For instance there is the joke about 'obese Max' going into a restaurant and ordering a whole round cake. The waitress brings it to the table and then asks whether she should cut it into four or eight pieces. 'Into four pieces,' replies Max, 'I'm on a diet.' Giora considers alternative wordings. If Max had said 'Into four pieces, so it will be more convenient to eat' the joke would be spoiled: the final constituent, according to Giora, would not then be sufficiently 'distant' from the prototypical interpretation set up by the joke. 'Distant' was the same term used by Kames to describe the elements which wit manages to combine.

In analyzing jokes in this way, Giora and other such linguists are proceeding in a Lockeian direction. Such analysts, equipped with a much more highly sophisticated technical armoury than was available to Locke, are seeking to answer the same basic question as Locke: What mental processes are required to understand – or in Locke's case, to create – a witticism? Many modern analysts such as Giora often deduce the cognitive processes by examining the linguistic structure of the joke. Thus, jokes are said to bring together suddenly two different, incongruous or distant ideas in the punch-line, thereby falling broadly under Locke's historic definition of wit.

The cognitive approach, such as that used by Giora (1991), reduces humour to the bloodless structure of the joke. There is accordingly little attempt to explore the social nature of laughter, for the jokes are abstracted from the social context in which they might be told (see Norrick, 1993 and 2003, for a critical discussion of this abstract approach to joking). This cognitive approach makes no assumptions about the motives for telling a joke, nor about the emotional states of the recipients. Again there is a similarity with Locke. As will be seen in the discussion of the eighteenth-century theorists, when the analysis turns from the supposed purity of wit to the ridicule of 'humour', then the Hobbesian emotions creep back in.

For all the similarities between Locke and the modern cognitivists, there is one great difference that points to the ideological gulf between the eighteenth-century writers and the technical analysts of today. Today's incongruity theorists approach the topic through the analysis of jokes. Giora, in common with other semantic analysts, shows how jokes embody incongruities and divergent cognitions (see also, for example, Attardo, 1993; Attardo and Raskin, 1991; Raskin, 1985, 1998). Other researchers studying the general topic of humour also take 'jokes as the unit of analysis' (e.g., Davies, 1998: 295). In ordinary conversations, joke-telling accounts for only a small proportion of laughter, as compared with spontaneous remarks or anecdotes about amusing real incidents (Norrick, 1993). Yet, studying humour by looking at the formal properties of jokes seems so obviously sensible to the modern analyst that it does not call for any specific justification. Ted Cohen (2001), a philosopher, has written a short book on jokes, which, despite not even being a hundred pages long, manages to present over a hundred and fifty jokes.

It would have been unthinkable for respectable philosophers in the eighteenth century to repeat so many jokes in print. Their discussions on wit contain hardly a joke between them. Locke's passage in *An Essay* may have been too brief for any examples of humour. Kames, Beattie, Hutcheson, Stewart et al., who devoted whole chapters and books to the subject, included no illustrative examples which today would be recognized as jokes. The authors cite illustrious poets and playwrights to make their theoretical points. Shakespeare and Pope were particular favourites, as was Butler's *Hudibras*, especially the passage that described the morning sky turning from black to red 'like a lobster boiled'. There is nothing along the lines: A fat man goes into Child's and asks for a whole cake ...

Jokes are not only absent as examples, but these eighteenth-century works on wit do not even discuss the telling of formal jokes. They discuss anecdotes and *bons mots*, but not jokes *qua* jokes. This absence was to continue for the next century or so. James Sully, whose *Essay on Laughter* (1902) aimed to provide a synoptic account of the topic, omits joke-telling. The presence of jokes in today's analyses and their past absence cannot be explained on the grounds that the joke is a modern invention. Many of today's jokes have long histories. The eighteenth-century writers must have known jokes. Even if they did not tell jokes themselves, they must have been aware that others did. *Joe Miller's Jests*, possibly the most enduringly famous joke-book in the English language, was first published in 1739. Even the title was a joke. The anonymous collection of jokes was being attributed to a lately deceased actor, Joe Miller, who was famous for his lack of humour. So popular was *Joe Miller's Jests* that within a year the book was into its third edition. The eighth edition appeared a mere six years after initial publication. So, when Beattie was preparing his treatise on laughter, he could scarcely have been unaware that one of the best sellers of the times was a compilation of jokes. Yet, he and his fellow theorists of laughter write as if the joke-form did not exist.

The omission is revealing. *Joe Miller's Jests* was lowly stuff. It contained jokes about farting and copulation. Some of the targets of the jokes were notable aristocrats, being depicted in highly indelicate circumstances. How the lower orders must have loved such mockery. But this was not material for a gentleman – and certainly not for a lady. Heaven forfend that a gentleman's wife should encounter such indecorousness within a serious volume designed to enlighten readers about the nature of wit. The churchmen, judges and professors, who were writing on laughter, would not wish it thought that they might have read *Joe Miller's Jests* – not even in the interests of science. There was no science of the scatological in those days. Worthies such as Beattie or Hutcheson had no intention of creating one.

So the eighteenth-century texts on humour have, to the modern eye, a glaring omission. From a theoretical point of view the omission is significant. If scabrous humour becomes invisible, the way is clear to present wit in ways that suggest that all that matters is the cleverness of creating and resolving incongruities. This was not prudery, as it would be in the next century when sanitized versions of *Joe Miller's Jests* were published. This was an issue of class and taste. Beattie and Hutcheson were no fools. They knew the lower orders loved to mock their betters, enjoying jokes about lords and ladies breaking wind or worse. Their own servants probably joked in this way. But this was not wit. It could not be. It was something else, unworthy of philosophical attention. In this regard, the absence of jokes in the eighteenth-century philosophies of laughter – just like their presence in today's analytic texts – reveals much about the ideological contexts in which the analysis of humour occurs. Theories of incongruity, however much they might seem to be dry, impersonal and technical analyses, concern more than the incongruities of cognition. These theories exist within, and take their illustrative meaning from, contexts of class and gender, taste and morality.

Addison and the wit of the coffee-house

The British theorists of the eighteenth century faced a pressing problem of refutation. There was Hobbes to be dealt with. The famous philosopher of the previous century needed to be put into a position of theoretical inferiority. This was not just a task for pure philosophy, but for all those who wanted to provide philosophical justification for the conversations of the coffee-house. Nowhere is this more apparent than in the writings of Joseph Addison, whose irony and comfortably worn learning were to influence the style of English letters for many years to come. Addison made no claims to being an academic philosopher. In *The Spectator*, number 10, he wrote of his ambition to bring philosophy 'out of the closets and libraries and colleges, to dwell in clubs and assemblies, at tea-tables and in coffee-houses' (1965 edn: 44). For that to happen, as Addison appreciated, good humour and wit would need a different philosophical basis than Hobbes had provided.

Two early issues of *The Spectator* discussed the respective views of Locke and Hobbes. Addison's essay on Hobbes appeared in number 47, 24 April 1711. He began by saying that Mr Hobbes in his book *Human Nature* ('which, in my humble opinion, is much the best of all his works') had some 'very curious observations' to make about laughter. A refutation of Hobbes might be expected to follow. But Addison then states that Hobbes's views have much to commend them: 'Everyone laughs at somebody that is in an inferior state of folly to himself.' He gives examples of how 'the common people' of various countries like to laugh at fools. Then there are the practical jokes that people play on April Fools' day, not to mention those who are 'for making April Fools every day of the year'. At this point the essay is reading like a defence of Hobbes. Addison declares: 'That secret elation and pride of heart which is generally called laughter, arises in him from comparing himself with an object below him.'

Into the final paragraph, Addison still seems to be arguing for the Hobbesian line. He mentions that some people are constantly the 'butt' of others' mirth. It is 'impossible for a club or merry meeting to subsist' without some members being exposed to the 'wit and raillery' of others. Surely, this is the spirit of Hobbes transposed to the cheerier atmosphere of the coffee-house – perhaps even Tom's Coffee-House in Covent Garden where, according to the note at the bottom of the paper, copies of *The Spectator* could be purchased. Addison's readers might have smiled in recognition. Their own company, just like the company of the mythic 'Spectator' and his friends, would have had their wits and their butts.

Just when readers might have suspected that they were being carried full-sail out into a choppy Hobbesian sea, Addison wittily turns the argument around in the middle of the final paragraph. Most of the butts of raillery have some oddness of character, comments Addison, the rigging of his thesis still being blown on the Hobbesian course. There is an unexpected change of wind. Some butts, he writes, are men of wit and sense, who can turn the joke upon the rest of the company: 'A stupid butt is only fit for the conversation of ordinary people: Men of wit require one that will give them play.'

There it is. Hobbes is portrayed as a shrewd psychologist, but his ideas only apply to the sort of ordinary people who go to fairs to laugh at a Jack Pudding. Men of quality are different. Their butts are superior types. By the end, the significance of the untranslated epigram from Martial at the head of the piece becomes clear: *Ride si sapis* – 'Laugh if you are wise'. Addison's readers, as they gathered around the latest *Spectator*, will have laughed knowingly and audibly, thereby displaying to their fellows their own breeding, wisdom and classical education. A gentle breeze had brought them back to the warm harbour of the amiable coffee-house.

Less than a month after the essay on Hobbes, Addison was praising Locke in *The Spectator*. He wrote that Locke had produced 'the best and most philosophical account' of wit that he had ever read (1965 edn: 16). Addison was using Locke in order to establish standards for wit. Because he did not want the laughter of the coffee-house to sink to the level of the carnival, Addison was seeking philosophical criteria by which one could judge the goodness of wit. Thus, he sought from Locke a distinction between true and false wit. Addison took Locke's notion that wit was based upon the sudden discovery of resemblance between distant ideas and then he added an extra element. Addison asserted that 'true wit consists in the resemblance of ideas, and false wit in the resemblance of words' (ibid.: 17).

Puns were examples of false wit because they play with resemblances between words and not with the ideas that the words represent. True wit, by contrast, involves ideas and it resembles poetic metaphor. A poet might claim that his love's bosom was not merely as white as snow, but was just as cold. Such a comparison involves seeing resemblances between disparate things: in this case the appearance and temperature of snow and the (European) female bosom. Addison proposed a methodology for distinguishing the true wit of ideas from the inferior wit of words. True wit should stand being translated into a foreign language. If in the course of translation, the wit vanishes, 'you may conclude it to have been a pun' (ibid.: 15).

Later writers were to take up Addison's distinction. Sydney Smith, voicing a similar hostility to puns, declared that the 'wit of language is so miserably inferior to the wit of ideas' (1864 edn: 126–7). Kames was optimistic that the future would be punless. He assented to Locke's belief that philosophy would succeed in reforming language so that clear and distinct labels would be attached to clear and distinct ideas. When 'language is formed into a system', no longer would there be words with double meanings (1854 edn: 189–90). The ground would then be swept from underneath the irritating punsters.

Such authors depict true wit as if it stands free from base motives such as the desire to ridicule. Wit appears as amusing cleverness in a purified form. Yet, the examples show that the purification may not be complete. Did the young woman, whose bosom was wittily being compared with snow, enjoy the incongruity and join with the manly laughter? Why should there be such pleasure in the comparison? Locke had been silent about the origins of the pleasures involved in seeing resemblances between different ideas. All that seemed to matter was the distance between the ideas and the suddenness with which they are conjoined. But are some ideas, or some types of incongruity, more liable to evoke mirth than others? Why the bosom, not the hand, forehead or nose? Why, today, should we laugh at fat Max and not restructure the joke into one about thin Max? And why, in the research report about that joke, should this fictional figure be named with increased politeness and decreased cadence as 'obese Max'? There are stirrings – base stirrings – beneath the world of pure wit.

The return of the refuted

The eighteenth-century theorists of wit had to dispose of Hobbes. His was the brooding presence haunting the vision of laughter's amiability. Addison's solution was to project undesirable emotions onto social inferiors and to acquit true wit of any reproach. Other writers sought the more direct approach of declaring Hobbes to be totally wrong, ridiculing the implausibility of his theory of laughter. Yet, the more he was refuted, the more the Hobbesian themes kept returning, first into discussions of humour, and then into the supposed examples of pure wit. It was a fitting irony. Ridiculing Hobbes was failing to produce a ridicule-free theory of wit.

Many of the eighteenth-century British writers began their discussions of laughter and wit with an attack on Hobbes. This was Francis Hutcheson's strategy in his *Thoughts upon Laughter*, which was originally written as three essays in *The Dublin Journal* in 1726 and was later published as a book. Hutcheson early in his first essay observed with

almost ho-ho-ho jocularity that Mr Hobbes 'very much owes his character of a philosopher to his assuming positive solemn airs, which he uses
most when he going to assert some palpable absurdity' (1758: 2). Beattie,
too, criticized Hobbes in the opening pages of *Essay on Laughter*. He had
a nice put-down: 'The theory of Mr Hobbes would hardly have deserved
notice, if Addison had not spoken of it in the forty-seventh paper of the
Spectator' (1779: 307).

George Campbell's *The Philosophy of Rhetoric* enjoyed a wide readership
for over a hundred years after its original publication in 1776. Aristotle may
have given laughter cursory mention in his *Rhetoric*, but Campbell was
attempting to update the ancient discipline with the principles of Lockeian
psychology. Two of his early chapters were on wit and humour. This enabled
him to mount a lengthy criticism of Hobbes whose views he declared to be
'in some respect partial, and in some respects false' (1856 edn: 51).
Campbell apologised to his readers for giving so much attention to Hobbes,
assuring them that he only did so because it afforded the best means of
presenting 'the radical principles' of his own inquiry (ibid.: 54).

Campbell, Beattie and Hutcheson all appealed to common sense in their
refutation of Hobbes's link between laughter and feelings of superiority.
Hutcheson's argument from experience has already been mentioned in the
previous chapter: we don't feel superior when we laugh, so Hobbes must be
wrong. Hutcheson also noted that gentlemen in their carriages do not spend
their journeys doubled up in laughter, even though they must feel superior
to the ragged beggars that they saw on the way. Beattie noted that if laughter arises from a sense of superiority then 'the wise, the beautiful, the strong,
the healthy, and the rich, must giggle away a great part of their lives' (1779:
310). Campbell had another variant on the same theme: 'It hath been often
remarked of very proud persons that they disdain to laugh, as thinking that
it derogates from their dignity', while 'the merriest people' were to be least
suspected of being 'haughty and contemptuous' (1856 edn: 53–4). All this
showed how wrong Hobbes had been.

But Hobbes could not be wholly dismissed. Contemptuous ridicule
or raillery did occur, although as Campbell stressed 'there may be, and
often is, both contempt without laughter and laughter without
contempt' (ibid.: 52). When Campbell discussed the nature of humour,
as contrasted with wit, it was clear that the Hobbesian elements could
not be kept at bay. Campbell, following the customary terminology of
the eighteenth century, asserted that 'the subject of humour is always
character', particularly the foibles of character, such as 'jealousies, childish fondness, pertness, vanity and self-conceit' (ibid.: 38). Humour
involves laughing at another's weaknesses, and in consequence it 'rarely
fails to have some raillery in it' (ibid.: 47). Therefore, as a rule the laughter of humour 'is, doubtless, accompanied by some degree of contempt'
(ibid.: 51). From starting out to bury Hobbes, Campbell comes around
to something resembling a Hobbesian view of the cruel laughter of
humour.

Hutcheson explained 'the occasion of laughter' in terms of the 'opposition of ideas of dignity and meanness' (1758: 28). He suggested that 'any little accident' that befalls 'a person of great gravity, ability, dignity, is a matter of laughter' (ibid.: 27). It is funny, for instance, when the clothes of a solemn person become besmirched with mud. So too are 'the natural functions' which we try to conceal from sight, when 'they occur to observation in persons of whom we have high ideas' (ibid.: 27). As Hutcheson describes these conjunctions of opposites, one might note how easily the metaphor of height and lowness, superiority and inferiority, suggests itself. It is not any incongruity that produces laughter, but the conjunction of high solemnity with base bodily accidents. It is the image of Hobbes swatting flies on his bald head, or a gecko defecating from a height onto Socrates. Hutcheson implies that there is no feeling of superiority, for those who laugh at a dignified person stumbling do not imagine themselves to be superior to that person. But there is an analogous delight in seeing the superior person being brought down. This is not emotionless. As Sydney Smith was to note in his *lectures on moral philosophy*, 'the incongruities, which excite laughter, generally produce a feeling of contempt for the person at whom we laugh' (1864: 138).

Beattie took up Hutcheson's idea that much humorous laughter is provoked by the conjunction of dignity and meanness. Laughter, he wrote, was elicited by 'two or more inconsistent, unsuitable or incongruous parts or circumstances, considered as united in one complex object or assemblage' (1779: 320). Beattie took the conjunction of dignity and meanness to be an instance of this general principle. Yet, he noted that laughter is particularly liable to ensue when 'things important, serious or great, are ludicrously compared to such as are mean, frivolous, or vulgar' (ibid.: 344). When he illustrates the general principle of incongruity, he comes back time and again to the mixing of the dignified with the mean, which provide 'a copious source of ludicrous combination' (ibid.: 353). Although the basis of laughter lies in the juxtaposition of incongruities, he concedes that 'the joke would be heightened, if there should also happen to be a mixture of meanness and dignity' (ibid.: 331).

Beattie does not specify why the laughter should be heightened in this way. There must be something additional to pure juxtaposition and distance. The conjunction of meanness and dignity, that provokes laughter, operates to drag the dignity down to the level of meanness, rather than elevate the meanness to dignity. Johnson's comparison of a poet's verses with a cucumber mocks the former rather than praises the latter. The juxtaposition finds the superior person, or rather the person with pretensions of superiority, getting their come-uppance. And this is what is found to be funny. It may not be a straightforward feeling of superiority, as Hobbes had supposed, but it is not a simple perception of incongruity.

The implication is that a purely cognitive theory of incongruity is insufficient, for not all incongruities are found to be equally amusing. The distance between the elements and the speed that they are brought together could not explain why the haughty person splashed with mud is so funny. The great artist and caricaturist William Hogarth touched on this matter in his book *The Analysis of Beauty* (1753). He discussed comic effects, but all too briefly, given that he was one of the great comic artists of all time. Hogarth's basic explanation was a variant of the incongruity thesis: 'When improper, or *incompatible* excesses meet, they always excite laughter' (1955 edn: 48, emphasis in original). Hogarth added a visual detail: incompatibilities are especially likely to provoke laughter if they are inelegant, like a fat man wearing a child's clothing at Bartholomew Fair. But not all visual incongruities are risible. When incompatible forms are comprised of elegant, sinuous lines, they do not make us laugh. Artists, when painting heavenly scenes, would depict creatures with infants' heads and duck wings. Viewers do not react with laughter when they see 'these swarms of little inconsistent objects, flying about or perching on the clouds' (ibid.: 50).

Campbell might have conceded that humour involves contempt but he insisted on the purity of wit's motives. Yet, his examples of wit show signs of the spirit of mockery. This was not a personal lapse, for Hutcheson and Beattie use similar examples. As an illustration of wit, Campbell quoted with approval Edward Young's verses ridiculing atheism. He also cited extracts from Alexander Pope's *The Rape of the Lock*, which used the incongruity of heroic language to laugh at the seriousness with which ladies took their toiletry. Again the conjunction of dignity and meanness – or rather, in this case, high language and triviality – was being used for purposes of mockery. Gentlemen could smile as they recognized the lowness of female preoccupations. Hutcheson's examples of wit included Samuel Butler's satires on classical writers such as Homer and Virgil. Hutcheson adds a characteristic swipe at Hobbes: the readers of such verses do not imagine themselves to be superior to Homer and Virgil (1758: 26). Of course they do not. But they may enjoy seeing the great classical figures, to whom reverence is supposedly due, being taken down a notch or two.

Campbell, Hutcheson and Beattie show what amounts to almost wilful blindness in the way they ignore the witty pleasures of ridicule. Campbell provides one of the most striking examples. In criticizing Hobbes, he suggests that contempt can occur without humour. He then cites a passage from Swift's essay on 'Good Manners' to prove the point. Swift was expressing concern lest the legislature outlawed duelling: 'I can discover no political evil in suffering bullies, sharpers, and rakes to rid the world of each other by a method of their own, where the law hath not been able to find an expedient' (quoted by Campbell, 1856 edn: 40). According to Campbell, such a sentiment might express contempt but 'no man who understands English would say it is humorous' (ibid.: 40). Even allowing for the eighteenth-century meaning of 'humour', the observation reveals more about Campbell than Swift. He seems not to appreciate the irony of Swift's prose.

Despite the desire to portray the amiability of wit, mockery keeps intruding on the party. When it does, one can see the much rejected spirit of Hobbes returning. Years later, Freud would say that the repressed returns to haunt the conscious mind, finding particular expression in jokes that we like to think of as being clever and innocent. Theoretically, writers such as Campbell, Beattie and Hutcheson were attempting to push from their texts Hobbesian ideas, which place wit under suspicion. But back come these suspicions, invading the whole territory of humour and stealthily infiltrating the realm of wit. This was the return of the refuted.

Ridicule and reason

Two themes can be distinguished in the incongruity theories of the eighteenth century: the cognitive, psychological theme and a more sociological, aesthetic theme. The psychological theme aims to identify what produces the reaction of laughter. It depicts the individual perceiving an incongruity and responding. The social context of laughter is barely depicted; the real action supposedly is going on within the cognitive processes of the mind that is combining disparate ideas. This is certainly true of Locke's account of wit.

Yet the eighteenth-century British theorists knew that laughter was a social matter as well as a psychological one, for laughter was something that was to be socially shared. As Francis Hutcheson wrote, laughter is 'very contagious' for 'our whole frame is so sociable that one merry countenance may diffuse cheerfulness to many' (1758: 37). The problem was not just to identify the causes of laughter but also to 'consider the effects of laughter, and the ends for which it was implanted in our nature' (ibid.: 35).

In considering the effects of laughter, there was the problem of ridicule. At first sight, ridicule involves the sort of unpleasant feelings that Hobbes had described and that seemed so inimical to good-hearted, tasteful conversation. But, as Addison's essay implied, some sorts of ridicule might be more acceptable than others. As the eighteenth-century writers discussed the social purposes of ridicule, so they moved from psychological considerations to issues that might nowadays be called sociological. In so doing, the British incongruity theorists, unlike many of their modern cognitive descendants, raised issues about the disciplinary functions of ridicule for promoting social congruity. In this respect, the incongruity theories of laughter were always more than just accounts of mirth.

Nowhere is this better seen than in the extraordinary, but unjustly overlooked, writings of Anthony Ashley Cooper, the third Earl of Shaftesbury. In the same year as Addison was writing on Hobbes's theory in *The Spectator*, Shaftesbury published his anthology *Characteristics of Men, Manners, Opinions, Times* (1711). Locke had been his personal tutor, supervising his education. Shaftesbury shared Locke's commitment to reason and liberty, but there was an important philosophical difference between the two. Locke believed that a clear psychology, which analyzed how the mind formed its ideas, was the key to sorting out truth from falsity. Shaftesbury rejected such systematic philosophy. Knowledge was part of social life and, thus, reason depended upon laying down the conditions for reasonable social conduct.

Shaftesbury's *Characteristics* was not philosophy in Locke's sense of systematizing the origins of knowledge. The goal was not to examine how individuals might best order their ideas and perceptions of the external world. Instead, the aim was to see how the community might best order itself and what beliefs were appropriate to the well-ordered community. Shaftesbury presented a view of the world in which morality, politics, taste and reasonable conduct were inseparable. According to Shaftesbury, in moral matters there was little to be gained by 'philosophy or deep specula-tion', for in the main 'it is best to stick with common sense and go no further' (1999 edn: 61). Therefore, the philosopher should look to the *sensus communis*, or the shared common sense of the community, rather than to abstract theorizing.

No other writer in the eighteenth century placed ridicule so much at the heart of social life as did Shaftesbury. In his view, ridicule or raillery was crucial for the maintenance of a reasonable common sense. He saw a connection between mirth, ridicule and liberty. He noted that in his own times the people of Britain enjoyed more liberty than ever before and that never had there been a time when 'folly and extravagance of every kind were more sharply inspected or wittily ridiculed' (ibid.: 8). This was no coincidence: ridicule was a weapon to be used against the sort of dangerous religious enthusiasm that threatened liberty. Unreasonable enthusiasm is preserved by 'solemn sadness' and threatened by ridicule (ibid.: 8). The enthusiasts fear to put their ideas to the test of ridicule and, in consequence, 'gravity is the very essence of imposture' (ibid.: 9). Religious enthusiasm and extremism of any kind seek to constrain the liberty of ridicule and, thereby, to endanger the liberty of thought.

Shaftesbury's defence of ridicule was based on a rhetorical understand-ing of reason. Truth would not be discovered by abstract philosophy but through the rigours of conversation. Ideas, if they had merit, should be able to 'stand the test of ridicule' (ibid.: 8). In this matter, as in other matters, Shaftesbury drew his inspiration from those great thinkers of ancient Greece and Rome, who discussed philosophically important questions through dialogue. The characters of Plato's dialogues would test each other's positions with wit and humour, seeking to arrive at ideas that would with-stand the criticism of ridicule. This was the means by which reason should operate: 'Without wit and humour, reason can hardly have its proof or be distinguished' (ibid.: 35). Scarce has there been a thinker who has invested humour and ridicule with such a mighty task.

The idea that ridicule might be necessary for reason disturbed many of Shaftesbury's contemporaries. He knew that he was liable to be misunder-stood. Ridicule, in the eyes of many, was a nasty, rough business. It denoted the masses at Bartholomew's Fair laughing senselessly at the fat man dressed in the clothes of an infant. Shaftesbury was at pains to stress that he did not have that sort of ridicule in mind. He was not justifying the liberty of the vulgar to mock their betters. A sense of class and gender accompanied his defence of ridicule: 'I am writing to you in defence only of the liberty of the

Club and of that sort of freedom which is taken among gentlemen and friends who know one another perfectly well' (ibid.: 36). His ideal was conversation conducted in gentlemanly spirit and with good taste, where the company would talk 'in a way of pleasantry and mirth' (ibid.: 62). The ideals of the Platonic dialogue and of Aristotle's middle way between vulgarity and moroseness were being translated to the nobleman's table, the gentleman's club and the better sort of coffee-house.

Later eighteenth-century writers on laughter rarely cited Shaftesbury by name. Nevertheless, philosophers such as Beattie, Stewart and Campbell were influenced by his ideas on common sense. For them the defence of common sense was important because it provided a counter to the dangerous scepticism of Hume. Campbell in *The Philosophy of Rhetoric* followed Shaftesbury in distinguishing between high and low forms of ridicule, or between *banter* and *raillery*. A modern reader might presume that *banter* would refer to the friendly, mirth-filled talk, while raillery denoted the crude, crueller forms of ridicule. In the eighteenth century, the words bore different connotations. According to Campbell, *banter* was coarse talk, while *raillery* was 'a finer sort of ridicule' (1856 edn: 48). He could not let the distinction rest without passing social judgement: 'The former prevails most among the lower classes of the people, the latter only among persons of breeding' (ibid.: 48).

Campbell offered no clear and distinct criteria by which banter could be unambiguously distinguished from raillery. Shaftesbury had sufficient insight to know that the division between well-bred and ill-bred forms of ridicule might be problematic: 'Everyone thinks himself well-bred, and the formallest pedant imagines he can rally with a good grace and humour' (ibid.: 31). No member of the gentlemen's club, then, would own up to bantering – all would imagine that their humour was as tastefully witty as Boswell thought the conversations at Child's to be. Banter was what others do; we do raillery. As with modern distinctions between positive (good) humour and negative (bad) humour, when it comes to describing one's own humorous activities, there is plenty of scope for self-justification and self-deception.

Ridicule's objects and purposes

On its own, the theory of incongruity does not explain why the perception of incongruity should be followed by a sense of pleasure and laughter. Locke did not bother to pursue this question. Later British theorists did, especially when, like Hutcheson, they were inquiring into the effects and purposes of laughter rather than into its causes. A modern sociologist would describe this as examining the 'function' of laughter. Hutcheson and his contemporaries did not have this word in their analytic vocabulary. The term 'function', as used in this way, would have to wait for Herbert Spencer in the next century.

There was a wider context to the psychological speculations of the eighteenth-century theorists. The aesthetic climate of the time valued congruity and due proportion, while incongruity was equated with a lack of taste and a lower order of civilization. Shaftesbury expressed this aesthetic clearly. His ideals of art, philosophy and taste were those of ancient Rome and Greece. The educated gentlemen should seek the harmonies of classical art while avoiding 'ill-designed and monstrous figures' associated with the Gothic and the barbarous (1711: 53). Shaftesbury commissioned the artist John Closterman to paint him in the pose of a classical philosopher dressed in a toga (Uglow, 1997: 74).

The well-bred gentleman, who developed a taste for classical harmony and order, would be developing human nature to its full potential. Our minds, according to Shaftesbury, are designed to sense the harmony of things: 'Nothing surely is more strongly imprinted on our minds or more closely interwoven with our souls than the idea or sense of order and proportion' (1711: 273). The moral and aesthetic senses were bound up together. Whether perceiving the characters of others, physical objects or 'musical numbers', the mind naturally perceives the congruities and incongruities, the proportioned and the deformed, with, of course, a preference for harmony and due proportion (ibid.: 172ff.).

The implication is that our senses are aesthetically and morally repelled by incongruity. The sense of ridicule expresses this repulsion. As Shaftesbury wrote in echo of Aristotle, 'nothing is ridiculous except what is deformed, nor is anything proof against raillery except what is handsome and just' (ibid.: 59). Hogarth, in *The Analysis of Beauty*, was to produce a visual version of this idea. The mind finds symmetrical, curving lines beautiful, while angular lines are perceived as ugly. The artist who wishes to produce a comic or grotesque effect, will avoid curves and depict characters with straight lines, for angular figures are apt to be seen as ridiculous. In a similar vein, Lord Kames claimed that humans are 'framed by nature' to be pleased by relations of congruity and propriety and 'to be displeased when we find the opposite relation of incongruity or impropriety' (1854 edn: 165). He asserted that what is beautiful is congruous and, therefore, not one bit ridiculous (ibid.: 184).

This was a confident aesthetic. Congruities were objectively pleasant while incongruities and dissonances were objectively deformed and ridiculous. The implication is that one cannot ridicule what is proportional for it is not ridiculous. Again and again the eighteenth-century writers expressed their confidence in the faculty of ridicule: the faculty will only ridicule that which is actually ridiculous. According to Shaftesbury, 'a man must be soundly ridiculous who, with all the wit imaginable, would go about to ridicule wisdom or laugh at honesty or good manners' (1711: 60). Akenside claimed that we have 'a *natural* sense or feeling of the ridiculous' and we must suppose that the Supreme Being had good reason 'for bestowing it' (1810 edn: 153, emphasis in original). The faculty of ridicule permits us to discover the incongruity between claim and fact, and then urges the mind to reject the claim 'with laughter and contempt' (ibid.: 154). Since this faculty is divinely bestowed, then 'the sense of ridicule always judges right', ridiculing that which deserves to be ridiculed (ibid.: 155).

Dugald Stewart discussed the sense of the ridiculous in *Outlines of Moral Philosophy* (1793). He suggested that 'the natural and proper object of ridicule, is those smaller improprieties in character and manners which do not rouse our feelings of moral indignation, nor impress us with a melancholy view of human depravity' (1808 edn: 160). The sense of ridicule has a beneficial purpose. Because it renders 'the more trifling imperfections ... a source of amusement to their neighbours', the sense of ridicule 'excites the exertions of every individual to correct those imperfections' (ibid.: 160). Although the sense of ridicule might seem a trivial faculty, it is 'one of the most striking characteristics of the human condition' and it has 'an intimate connection with its highest and noblest principles' (ibid.: 161).

Hutcheson similarly identified 'the smaller vices' as the objects of ridicule in his *Thoughts on Laughter* (1758: 51). Such smaller vices are principally comprised of incongruities. The dignified person has a lapse of taste, behaviour or judgement that ill befits their lofty status. This incongruity is perceived by the sense of ridicule and the result is laughter. The implication is that the moral sense, because it judges rightly, operates objectively rather than subjectively, ridiculing just those things that actually *are* improper. The sense of ridicule is dispassionate and serves the purpose of discouraging incongruous behaviour. Hutcheson commented that the smaller vices are 'more effectually corrected by ridicule than by grave admonition' (ibid.: 51). Also, ridicule could temper the sort of dangerous enthusiasms that lead to 'wild apprehensions' (ibid.: 46).

In this way, the sense of ridicule is seen as an essential element for regulating human conduct in accord with the highest standards of morality. Shaftesbury referred to raillery as a 'lenitive remedy against vice, and a kind of specific against superstition and melancholy delusion' (1711: 59). His metaphor was medical: a 'specific' denoted a treatment and 'lenitive remedy' was one that softened the symptoms. In using such a metaphor Shaftesbury was not just alluding to the power of raillery to raise spirits and to test the reasonableness of beliefs. He was referring to its power of deterrence. People will think twice before engaging in vice if they feel they will be mocked. The complete villain is, of course, beyond mockery as is, for very different reasons, the completely honest person. But the person in between, who may be tempted do 'this *little* villainy or commit this *one* treachery' is a ridiculous figure (ibid.: 61). In this case, the prospect of ridicule serves a disciplinary function in the interests of creating the good society.

Such arguments have come a long way from Locke. The perception of incongruity is not a minor cognitive faculty, inferior to the faculty of judgement. It is tied to the moral and aesthetic sense that is so necessary for social life. Moreover, ridicule fulfils a key social role in maintaining morality, taste and good manners. High indignation might be required for major infractions of ethics, but ridicule was required for maintaining those standards of daily behaviour that Shaftesbury believed to be vital for communal living and for the good sense of the *sensus communis*.

In the early years of the nineteenth century, the influence of Shaftesbury and the wider ideology of incongruity theory could be heard in the lectures of Sydney Smith. Again, wit and humour figured prominently in his themes. Both forms of laughter, he argued, were the product of sudden incongruities. The sight of a young man dressed in the garb of an old clergyman is incongruous and 'would make everybody laugh' (1864 edn: 132). So would the sight of a tradesman, ostentatiously dressed in a pea-green coat, slipping gently down into the mud.

Smith then proceeded to the disciplinary effects of laughter. Being laughed at was worse than death for most people. That being so, 'in polished society, the dread of being ridiculous models every word and gesture into propriety' (ibid.: 139). Although not mentioning Shaftesbury by name, or quoting his controversial view that ridicule provided a test of beliefs, Smith sketched out the disciplinary function of ridicule in a way that fitted the third Earl's philosophy of conduct. Ridicule was, according to Smith, 'the great cure of extravagance, folly, and impertinence; it curbs the sallies of eccentricity, it recalls the attention of mankind to the one uniform standard of reason and common sense' (ibid.: 139). Like Shaftesbury before him, Smith was implying that ridicule was not something trivial; nor was it an ethically suspect act. Quite the contrary, it was central to the moral sense of humanity.

From the objectively ridiculous to the relatively ridiculous

Sydney Smith, in claiming that the fear of laughter models every word and gesture into propriety, was not proposing a general law about the way that ridicule can function to enforce group norms. His purposes, like those of Shaftesbury before him, were different from those of modern sociological theorists. Smith was not wishing to construct a general theory about social life, but to promote an objective sense of reasonableness. Smith's phrasing was careful. He did not say that laughter models everyone's words and gestures into propriety. He specifically located the modelling and the propriety within 'polished society'. He then claimed that the fear of laughter also produces 'an exquisite attention to the feelings and opinions of others' (1864: 139). He had in mind the polite circles of Britain, whose members cared to believe that they possessed exquisite sensibilities. Smith was not implying that the members of the lower classes, who regularly served his food, fetched his washing water and polished his boots, would have been capable of such exquisiteness.

Neither Smith nor Shaftesbury was arguing in a relativist, sociological manner, suggesting that all societies use ridicule to establish what they consider to be reasonable and socially acceptable – and, thus, ridicule has a useful function for all social groups, whatever their codes of morality. Ridicule, in Shaftesbury's view, would produce behaviour, which conformed to objective standards of taste and propriety. It would do this because the sense of ridicule – or rather the 'true' sense of ridicule – could only be properly directed against the genuinely ridiculous. Similarly, Smith suggested that the dread of laughter was helping to establish a universal standard of reason and common sense. This was an absolute, universal good sense, which just so happened to coincide with the shared manners of eighteenth-century English gentlemen.

Just as Addison distinguished between true and false wit, so Shaftesbury claimed that there was a true and false raillery: true raillery worked in the service of the good sense, while false raillery did not. The rhetorical move is a familiar one, to be found today in the writings of those who seek to distinguish positive humour from negative humour. A general category of behaviour is championed, whether it be wit, humour or ridicule. Then the undesirable examples are dismissed as not being genuine or 'true' instances of the general category. The rhetorical spray is at work, banishing bad odour from the general category. In this way, Shaftesbury hoped that the category of ridicule, redesigned for his own purposes and class, would come up smelling of rose-water.

According to Shaftesbury, true raillery was completely unlike 'that gross sort of raillery that is so offensive in good company' (1864: 31). There was a world of difference between the raillery of gentlemen, discussing philosophy and art with good-humoured give-and-take, and the raillery of the masses who mocked those very things. Shaftesbury added that it was not possible to describe exactly what constituted the right sort of ridicule: 'To describe true raillery would be as hard a matter, and perhaps as little to the purpose, as to define good breeding' (ibid.: 31). It was unnecessary because any well-bred gentlemen would instantly recognize good manners and true raillery. An ill-bred person would be unaware of their own deficiencies. That was a sign of their lack of breeding.

Unsurprisingly, not everyone accepted Shaftesbury's view. The idea that an earl might possess a superior sense of ridicule was open to ridicule from those who moved in less exalted social circles. This, in essence, was the basis of an attack on Shaftesbury that was published almost forty years after his death. John Brown had been a chaplain to the Bishop of Carlisle, but was drawn to the not so respectable world of the London theatre. He wrote plays and associated with actors and actresses in ways that scandalized many in the Church. In 1751, he published his *Essays on the Characteristics*. The book attracted much attention, being reprinted several times in the first years of its publication.

Brown was writing against the followers of Shaftesbury, especially Akenside, whose *The Pleasures of Imagination* was then enjoying enviable success. Brown described Akenside as one of Shaftesbury's 'most zealous followers' (1751: 88). The main point of Brown's essay was to attack Shaftesbury in a direct and disrespectful manner. Brown's principal argument was a simple one. Shaftesbury had suggested that ridicule, or at least true ridicule, was a means of testing opinions in order to discover the truth. With gusto, Brown sought to show the implausibility of this view.

Ridicule was, Brown argued, a device of rhetoric. Like other rhetorical devices, it could be used to 'befriend either truth or falsehood' (ibid.: 46). All sides in a dispute can use ridicule, 'even the sourness of Puritanism, nay, the sullenness of Quakerism, have sometimes relaxed, and yielded themselves up to the love of joking' (ibid.: 50). Different people will mock each other: 'What is more ridiculous to a beau than a philosopher: to a philosopher than a beau?' (ibid.: 48). Brown took on Shaftesbury's idea that true wit can only be found among men of taste and breeding. Brown conceded that the attention of a country fair might be engaged by the 'coarse pranks of a merry Andrew', but 'the peasant and his Lord are equally susceptible to false impressions' (ibid.: 67).

As for Shaftesbury's notion that one can only laugh at what is truly deformed, Brown commented that 'what is *really* handsome and just, is often rendered false and deformed and thus becomes *actually* contemptible and ridiculous' (ibid.: 56, emphasis in original). The obvious example was Aristophanes ridiculing Socrates. The great philosopher may indeed have been estimable, but he easily became a butt of mockery. Looking about him, Brown declared 'what is high humour at Wapping is rejected as nauseous in the city' (ibid.: 54). If Shaftesbury believed that only the truly ridiculous can be ridiculed, then, commented Brown, 'I should be glad to know where the noble author has conversed' (ibid.: 55).

If all this sounds like a move towards relativism, it was not. Brown was not saying that there is a truth for Wapping and a truth for the city and none can decide between them. He was arguing against the idea that ridicule, as practised in gentlemanly conversation, was the way to discover truth. He declared that 'reason, not ridicule, was the *detector of falsehood*, and the *test of truth*' (ibid.: 41, emphasis in original). He did not say how the truths of reason could be discovered: he merely trusted the sense of reason. His essay was steeped in the assumption that there were clear, unambiguous truths. Right at the beginning, Brown declared himself to be opposing Shaftesbury in the cause of 'Truth and Christianity' (ibid.: ii). He was stirring up the old rumour that Shaftesbury had been a deist, rather than a good Christian.

Brown was a strange man. As a churchman, he may have been appalled by Shaftesbury's beliefs, but Brown himself had difficulty keeping his various church posts. He was known as a swearer and a curser. His theatrical leanings were not considered appropriate to his calling. He may have declared agreement with Shaftesbury's 'frequent recommendations of politeness, cheerfulness and good humour' (ibid.: 5), but in this matter too there was a gap between theory and personal practice. Throughout his life Brown suffered periods of depression, alternating with bouts of sudden frenzy. His friends despaired of him. In 1766 he committed suicide by slitting his throat.

Brown's attack on Shaftesbury touched a popular nerve for a while. It is a reminder that the British incongruity theorists of the eighteenth century did not command universal agreement. They were not a unified group who followed a single party line. Their Lockeian themes pulled in one philosophical direction, while the philosophy of the *sensus communis* tugged in another. Modern researchers, reading these works from a golden age of philosophy of humour, will adopt useful elements for their own purposes, rather than accept the whole package. Most notably, the Lockeian theme that humans laugh at sudden incongruity has proved to have particular appeal. Researchers have refined this basic idea adding technical details. In so doing, they have removed the idea of incongruity from its original ideological context.

Alternatively, the disciplinary assumptions of Shaftesbury and Smith could be combined with Brown's anti-elitism, while removing both from their shared context of certainty. The result would be a move towards a more relativist sociological view of ridicule. The *sensus communis*, then, would not represent absolute good sense but that which is considered good sense by each social group. The advantage of this for a modern theorist is that it would help address the problem why humour is to be found in all societies. That is not a problem that bothered thinkers like Shaftesbury, Addison and others. They did not care to see humour as a common factor unifying humanity. They wanted to distinguish between types of humour, separating gentlemanly laughter from coarse laughter. They assumed that true and false wit would belong to different social circles. These theorists were pre-anthropological. If they imagined an immense gap between the laughter of the fair and that of the intellectual club in the same British city, then the gap between the wit of the English gentleman and the laughter of tribal peoples around the world was for them literally unimaginable.

The temptation to select useful bits and pieces shows how these works express themes that are familiar today. The philosophy of early modernity is not totally foreign to the inhabitants of late modernity. The ideal of the gentlemen's club, with its social and gendered elitism, no longer appeals. Nevertheless, it is easy for us to share the assumption of laughter's goodness and to sympathize with the desire to banish the gloomy heritage of Hobbes and other misogelasts. And we can note the insights that place laughter within its social context of conversation. Even critics, then, find themselves following the habits of their age by stressing the positives.

Reason and unreason

If the incongruity theorists were not a unified bunch, then this illustrates something about the way that the theory of humour reflects the practice of humour. Although humour is shared, not everyone shares the same taste. There will be social distinctions that are sometimes easy to claim. Thus the gentlemanly theorists were confident that their taste in wit differed from that of the peasantry in the country fair. Not all differences, however, follow the fissures of class or culture. John Brown could mock Shaftesbury's humour in a way that would irritate the Earl's later followers. When Brown was in one of his dark moods, little could raise him to laughter. Beattie's analysis of laughter is stodgy and earnest, lacking the lightness of Addison or Sydney Smith. One suspects a difference in temperament, at least with respect to the enjoyment of humour. It does not seem that Beattie kept his fellow philosophers laughing in the meetings of the Wise Club (Forbes, 1824).

Theories of humour can subtly express these differences in taste, which often prove to be more than just preferences of taste. Morality can be involved, as some things, but not others, are laughed at. A theory of humour does not merely comprise general ideas. Whatever the ideas of the theory, the theorist needs to write down the theory and choose examples. There is no neutral hiding place here beyond the reach of rhetoric. Even an avoidance of examples can express a morality of taste. This can be seen in the example of Schopenhauer.

Schopenhauer's great book *The World as Will and Idea*, which first appeared in 1819, is a landmark in European philosophy. In it Schopenhauer sought to go beyond the cognitive approach of the previous century, in order to introduce a psychology of emotions into philosophy. He argued that Locke, Kant and other rationalists were only dealing with part of human nature. In describing the origins of our ideas about the world, they only considered rational factors. Schopenhauer argued that rationality is constantly at odds with one of the greatest forces of human nature – the force of sensuous emotion. Thus, the will constantly battles against the idea. In all this, Schopenhauer was heralding a philosophical movement away from rationalism. Freud was to recognize that Schopenhauer's philosophy anticipated core psychoanalytic ideas. Freud declared that not only did Schopenhauer assert 'the dominance of the emotions and the supreme importance of sexuality but he was even aware of the mechanism of repression' (1925a: 244).

In *The World as Will and Idea* Schopenhauer included a brief section on humour. Surprisingly, he did not show himself to be a Freudian *avant la lettre*, basing his understanding of humour upon the forces of the emotion. In fact, his account is as bloodlessly cognitive as Locke's. Just like Locke, and indeed Kant, Schopenhauer explained humour in terms of the perception of incongruity. He proposed that 'the cause of laughter in every case is simply the sudden perception of the incongruity between a concept and the real objects which have been thought through it in some relation, and laughter itself is just the expression of this incongruity' (1987: 52).

The confidence of the assertion is apparent: in *every* instance, laughter was *simply* the perceived incongruity between our ideas of the world and the perception of its realities. No emotions were involved. In the first edition of *The World as Will and Idea*, he did not see the need for examples: 'I shall not pause here to relate anecdotes as examples to illustrate my theory; for it is so simple and comprehensible that it does not require them' (ibid.: 52). In the second edition, however, Schopenhauer had become persuaded of the necessity of examples. His concession was grudging: he would give examples 'in order to come to the assistance of the mental inertness of those readers who prefer always to remain in a passive condition' (ibid.: 55). It is seldom a good authorial tactic to insult one's readers so blatantly.

Some of Schopenhauer's examples were unfortunate, not because they failed to illustrate his theory but, by illustrating the theory only too well, they revealed the moral taste of the theorist. For his first example of a laughable incongruity, Schopenhauer cites a line touching the tangent of a circle at only one point. When the line touches the circle, it is actually parallel to it, yet it appears as if there is an angle between line and circle. There is an incongruity here: 'and if now such an angle lies visibly before us upon paper, this will easily excite a smile' (ibid.: 55). Schopenhauer seemed to believe that everyone would find the image of the circle and the line amusing. Only a high philosopher with little sense of humour and even less sense of conviviality could write something so odd. Perhaps Schopenhauer lacked a Wise Club, in which he could test reactions to philosophical drafts. The convivial types in the Wise Club would no doubt have demonstrated gently and tactfully that the incongruity of the circle does not always provoke mirth – at least in the way that Schopenhauer envisaged. It is easy to smirk at the image of the philosopher, looking at the diagram on his desk and laughing loudly on his own.

Schopenhauer distinguished between wit and folly. With wit, a person intentionally brings together two distinct objects under the same concept, but with folly, a person is led by a concept to treat two obviously distinct objects as if they were actually similar. Schopenhauer illustrates folly by the example of the pedant. This is someone 'who seeks to be guided by reason in everything; that is to say, he tries always to proceed from general concepts, rules and maxims' (ibid.: 53). The pedant's ideas are too abstract to serve as a guide for the complexities of the real world. In consequence 'the incongruity then between the concept and the reality soon shows itself here', and the pedant appears foolish (ibid.: 53). If only Schopenhauer had shifted his examples about. This is the place where the circle, its tangent and the theorist of humour would have made a good illustration.

But it gets worse and the smirking has to stop. Schopenhauer offered another example of an incongruity that he considered to be ludicrous 'to all'. He cited one of the freed 'negroes' in America, who took pains to imitate whites. The man's child had recently died and he chose the epitaph, 'Lovely, early broken lily' (ibid.: 57). Oh, how funny that a bereaved father should compare his lost child to a beautiful, broken flower! What a hilarious incongruity between the paleness of the lily and the dark skin of the dead child!

The incongruous mirth of Schopenhauer is shocking. How can anyone, let alone a philosopher, laugh at a grieving father on account of the colour of his skin? What moral blindness and sense of superiority make that possible? It is too easy to say that was the way of laughter in those days. Schopenhauer assumed that everyone would have found the example funny

– he implicitly excluded the grieving father in his imagined everybody. It is hard to think of Beattie, who was committed to political doctrines of equality, making the same assumption – and even harder to imagine Samuel Johnson doing so. Johnson was uncompromising in his opposition to slavery and in his advocacy of the civil rights of ex-slaves. Boswell records Johnson's mocking jokes against Scots, but there are none against Africans or slaves. Even had he made an incautious joke, his manservant Frank Barber, described by Boswell as more friend than servant, would have drawn him up short. And were Barber to suffer sudden, deep grief, it is unimaginable that Johnson would have made pitiless cracks about the colour of his skin.

Schopenhauer's remark indicates that a hardening of the heart accompanies particular types of laughter. There is no inevitability that all will harden their hearts simultaneously against the same target. There is more involved than the mere perception of incongruity. Those who fail to laugh have not necessarily failed to perceive the incongruity that Schopenhauer noticed, as if laughter will simply and inevitably result when the failure of perception is rectified.

Schopenhauer's philosophy may have less to tell us about the complexity of humour than did the British laughter-theorists with their debates about the morality of acceptable discourse. Yet, Schopenhauer by his choice of example does offer one important lesson. No-one should be misled by generations of intellectuals into believing that it is only the mass – the uneducated, non-philosophical *lumpen* mass – who laugh with bigoted cruelty.

5

Victorian Relief Theory

In 1902 a young French philosopher Ludovic Dugas commented that 'every theory of laughter bears the imprint of a philosophy' (1902: 138). It was a sensible observation, since all major theories of humour involve more than just making predictions about when laughter might erupt. If they hope to explain funniness, they have to make sense of seriousness. Certainly it has not been difficult to find philosophical imprints upon the theories of superiority or incongruity. These theories came into the world trailing the clouds of philosophical glory that are associated with figures such as Hobbes and Locke. Likewise, the relief theory of humour, to which Dugas was himself attracted, was much more than a simple prediction that laughter acts to relieve pressure. It too came with its philosophical imprint.

The origins of the relief theory lie within the materialist philosophy of the nineteenth century. To be precise, the theory can be traced to a debate between two British thinkers, Herbert Spencer and Alexander Bain. In seeking to depict the workings of the human mind in physiological terms, Spencer and Bain formulated respective versions of the relief theory. Bain discussed laughter in his book *The Emotions and the Will*, which was published in 1859. Spencer published a critical review of Bain's book in January 1860. Two months later Spencer's article on the physiology of laughter followed. Bain responded to Spencer's views on humour in later editions of *The Emotions and the Will*.

The time and place of the debate are significant. The same year, in which Bain's book was published, also saw the appearance of Darwin's *On the Origin of Species*, which threw educated Britain into the consternation of controversy and ensured that speculations about human nature would never again be the same. At first sight, the timing of Bain and Spencer's very minor debate about laughter seems to be a joke against Victorian Britain. One can easily imagine the side-whiskered Spencer and full-bearded Bain arguing earnestly about the causes of laughter, not noticing the revolution in thought taking place around them. But it was not like that. Spencer was a central figure in the Darwinian revolution. Bain, too, had his part to play. Just a few years later Darwin contributed to the debate about laughter, quoting both Spencer and Bain in his book *The Expression of the Emotions in Man and Animals* (1872).

The relief theory, therefore, was formulated at a crucial moment in intellectual history. Accordingly, it is appropriate to continue with the historical focus that has been adopted for understanding the other two major theoretical traditions. The relief theory bears the imprint of ideas that have subsequently become crucial to the development of physiological and evolutionary psychology. Some psychologists have suggested that the idea of

'neural networks', which is central in today's physiological psychology, originated with Bain (Wilkes and Wade, 1997; Wade, 2001). Spencer has been
praised for introducing evolutionary ideas into psychology (Young 1990); he
is also credited with being the intellectual founder of modern sociology
(Andreski, 1971). The debate between Spencer and Bain not only anticipated new ideas in psychology, but it also gave fresh form to the older clash
between the theories of superiority and incongruity.

Background to Bain and Spencer

The idea that each theory of laughter bears the imprint of a philosophy is
only half the story, because each philosophy is also imprinted with the
marks of its times. A philosophy will express, either implicitly or explicitly,
the hopes and fears of the age in which it was formulated. Its vocabulary and
style of expression will bear further imprints of its times. In a literal sense a
philosophy may directly bear its historical imprint. This is apparent to anyone who browses library shelves carrying original editions of philosophical
works, published in the last three hundred years. A quick glance conveys the
change between the times of the eighteenth-century incongruity theorists
and the nineteenth-century relief theorists. The eighteenth-century writers
on laughter, as literary figures of their day, tended to produce occasional,
slim, leather-bound treatises. With Bain and Spencer, we are looking at
numerous massive, cloth-backed volumes. Rows of such tomes bear these
same two authors' names. Second and third editions of their big works were
heavily revised, necessitating the purchase of further copies by good
libraries. The physical solidity of these books conveys earnest energy. These
are books that must be opened on a desk, not taken to the coffee-house to
be held in one hand while sipping a drink.

Bain, who was born in 1818, was two years older than Spencer. They
lived long productive lives, with both men dying in 1903. Both had written
autobiographies that were to be published during the year following their
deaths. Bain was for many years an eminent academic, holding a chair at
Aberdeen University and being appointed Lord Rector of that university
after his retirement. Initially he lectured on rhetoric and language, but his
specialist interests turned to philosophy and psychology. By contrast,
Spencer never held a university appointment. He attempted to support
himself through his writings, living frugally as a bachelor in rented accommodation. The circumstances of the two thinkers were adjusted to their
respective characters. Bain was the more convivial of the two, relishing in
the gossip and plots of the academic common-room. Spencer was a solitary
figure, frequently using the excuse of poor health to avoid company. If the
meal-time conversations in his lodging-house were distracting the train of
his thought, then he would insert ear-plugs. Constantly worried by his physical condition and by diminishing reserves of energy, Spencer claimed that he
needed his ear-plugs in order to avoid the dangers of undue nervous excitement. In practice he would resort to their use should others be talking about

matters that interested him little. For Spencer, big ideas and small talk did not mix.

Both men were recognized in their own day as original thinkers of substance. Bain was held in high regard by fellow philosophers such as John Stuart Mill, who appreciated the way he used new discoveries in physiology to re-examine traditional questions about the operations of human thinking. He founded the journal *Mind*, a specialist journal that attracted contributions from the major philosophers of the day. Spencer's reputation was of an altogether different magnitude. His name was as familiar as that of Darwin, with whom he was often linked. Hailed as the greatest philosopher of his generation, Spencer became known to admirers as 'the modern Aristotle' (Bowne, 1912: 217). Like his ancient forebear, this Victorian Aristotle was not content to be an expert in a particular discipline. The scope of his writings seemed limitless. The history of the solar system, social organization, the principles of biology, geology, morality, railway timetabling – nothing was exempt from Spencer's philosophizing. All were part of a grand project, to which Spencer dedicated over 40 years. His aim was to produce a single framework to accommodate all existing knowledge. Within this serious synthesis there would be, along with everything else, room enough for a theory of laughter.

Despite heavy competition, there is a good case for claiming Spencer to be one of the least qualified philosophers to write about laughter. Even his admirers noted that the modern Aristotle, for all his intellectual talents, lacked a sense of humour. It was said that Spencer's company was so exacting that a host and his family once escaped from their own house by the back door, leaving their distinguished guest sitting in the drawing-room oblivious (Sully, 1918: 292). Unintentionally this serious man spread fun, making others feel skittish by comparison. William James was never so delightfully malicious as when writing of Spencer. Reviewing Spencer's posthumously published autobiography, James dubbed Spencer 'a petty fault-finder and a stickler for trifles' (James, 1911: 111). He commented that Spencer gave a 'queer sense of having no emotional perspective, as if small things and large were on the same place of vision and equally commanded his attention' (ibid.: 112). There is something Pooterish about Spencer. Like the Grossmiths' great fictional character, Spencer showed the sort of dogged humorlessness that has others sniggering behind his back. His autobiography, however, certainly was not the diary of a nobody. Spencer was the great philosopher of the land of Pooter.

Neither Bain nor Spencer belonged to the traditional elites of British society as the Earl of Shaftesbury or Lord Kames had done. Spencer was brought up in Derby, the son of a schoolmaster, who taught him the virtues of self-reliance, hard work and religious scepticism. Spencer's father emphasized the importance of practical knowledge, rather than a high-cultured aesthetic sensibility. Having left school, Spencer worked as an engineer on the London–Birmingham railway. In his twenties, Spencer invented gadgets, such as a pin for securing together unbound sheets of paper and a device for calculating the time of a train's arrival from knowledge of its velocity. He also began contributing articles to magazines on diverse subjects and during his twenties he left his engineering post to work in journalism. He later gave this up, in order to devote himself to his philosophical writing. He found it difficult to support himself. His first books cost him money and he despaired of earning sufficient money to remain a full-time writer.

For his great system of philosophy, Spencer raised money in advance, promising subscribers that they would receive the parts in quarterly instalments. In common with other Victorian authors who attempted to live by publishing a set number of words at regular intervals, Spencer's economic interests were not served by writing concisely. When the great philosophical project was almost three-quarters done, Spencer could not forebear from reporting in *The Study of Sociology* – purely, as he assured readers, in the interests of sociological exactitude – that over 30 per cent of clergymen, mostly from the Established Church, had reneged on their quarterly payments (1897 edn: 439–40).

Spencer's early background was comfortable compared with that of Bain, who grew up in circumstances of extreme poverty in the highlands of Scotland. Having left school at 11, he went to work as a weaver like his father. He was able to rise above his origins by virtue of a recognizably sharp intelligence, dedication and the provision of schemes to educate the poor. As a young man, he attended night school. Like Spencer he was drawn to London and the world of the quarterly magazines. In this context he came into contact with Mill. For a number of years, Bain sought unsuccessfully to obtain an academic post. Well-placed supporters of the established church, as well as members of the Free Church in Scotland, opposed his various candidatures. Eventually in 1860 Bain obtained a chair in logic at the University of Aberdeen. He was to supplement his academic salary by writing magazine articles and textbooks for his various courses. His big books on psychology, *The Emotions and the Will* and *The Senses and the Intellect* became textbooks for his courses on philosophy, despite their being far too technical for undergraduate purposes.

Bain and Spencer might today appear to be typically Victorian figures, but by their backgrounds and their views they were outsiders. They were Victorian radicals, who prided themselves on their freedom from traditional conservatism. They were on the side of science against religion. Spencer in the course of his life became increasingly opposed to religion; Bain specifically asked that there should be no religious service at his funeral (Bain, 1904: 415). Neither had any time for the classical and theological curricula that dominated the higher institutions of learning. Both wrote strongly in favour of scientific education (Bain, 1879; Spencer, 1861). Bain disagreed with John Stuart Mill on the latter's attachment to the study of Latin and Greek (Bain, 1882). These were not men to share Shaftesbury's notion that moral sensibility depended on gentlemanly breeding and a taste for classical art. Achievement and discovery, not rank or religious orthodoxy, were to be respected.

The first paragraph of Spencer's essay on laughter shows his lack of concern for the old aesthetics. Spencer was questioning Hobbesian theory and commented that no-one's dignity is humiliated when 'we laugh at a good pun' (1864a: 105). The ghosts of Addison, Shaftesbury and Kames would have shuddered. Their gentlemanly sensibility did not permit the possibility of a good pun. Spencer and Bain represented the new world of the engineer and the scientist. In the Darwinian brouhaha, there was never any doubt about whose side they would take.

Today, it is easy to depict Spencer as an arch-conservative with a heartless social philosophy. His uncompromising social Darwinism has contributed to the current neglect of his writings. Spencer, rather than Darwin, popularized the phrase 'the survival of the fittest', which he advocated as a political philosophy. It is embarrassing to express any admiration for a figure who could have written against charity and the Poor Laws on the grounds that such measures enabled the weak and the biologically unfit to survive. Darwin was personally and politically more charitable.

Spencer set out his 'Darwinian' themes in *Social Statics* (1851) eight years before *On the Origin of Species*. He argued that human nature could be perfected, but only by following the strict laws that governed the development of species. The weaker members must be left to die out so that the stronger members could survive. Thus, the individual misery of the weak would serve the greater collective good:

> It seems hard that a labourer incapacitated by sickness from competing with his strong fellows, should have to bear the resulting privations. It seems hard that widows and orphans should be left to struggle for life or death. Nevertheless, when regarded not separately, but in connection with the interests of universal humanity, these harsh fatalities are seen to be full of the highest benificence – the same benificence which brings to early graves the children of diseased parents, and singles out the low-spirited, the intemperate, and debilitated as the victims of an epidemic (Spencer, 1851: 323).

Spencer argued that rational scientific thinking should replace unreasoning sentimentality. On many issues, such as religion and education, the so-called scientific principles were on the side of radicalism. *Social Statics* contains arguments in favour of the rights of women, against imperialism and against traditional deference especially to clerical authorities. Spencer argued that the popular appeal of monarchy demonstrated that humans had far to go in perfecting their nature. By the end of his life, Spencer claimed that his views on monarchy had somewhat mellowed. He still believed in its irrationality but he saw difficulties in abolishing it forthwith: 'While the average feelings of people continue to be those which are daily shown, it would be no more proper to deprive them of their king than it would be proper to deprive a child of its doll' (1904, vol. II: 465). There would be no offer of a knighthood that the English Aristotle could then refuse.

Spencer may have been a stickler, but he was no stickler for conventional propriety. One friendship that mattered greatly to Spencer was that of Marion Evans, the novelist George Eliot. They had met before either had become famous. Each had encouraged the other in their ambitions. It is probable that she had hoped for the sort of romantic attachment from which Spencer recoiled. When George Eliot set up house with the married literary critic George Henry Lewes, she was ostracized by polite society. Spencer remained a loyal, admiring friend. In his autobiography, Spencer commented pointedly that she and Lewes 'exceeded any married pair I have ever known in the constancy of their companionship' (1904, vol. II: 319).

Spencer may have disregarded conventional behaviour, but he did not seek to have fun mocking convention. In fact, he seldom sought to have fun outside of the occasional fishing trip. Whenever he took pleasure, he did so seriously. Even fishing had its serious side. He designed a new joint for fishing-rods, publishing a paper on the subject. In his autobiography, he noted the diversity of his interests 'from a classification of the sciences to an improved fishing-rod joint; from the general Law of Evolution to a better mode of dressing artificial flies'. There is, he commented 'something almost ludicrous in this contrast between the large and the small, the important and the trivial' (vol. II: 436). He had a theory to explain that ludicrousness.

Biology and function

It was not by chance that Spencer entitled his essay 'The physiology of laughter'. His theory of laughter, like that of Bain, was rooted in physiological ideas about the excitation and release of nervous energy. Neither Bain nor Spencer was actually a physiologist. They were using physiological knowledge in order to understand big issues about the nature of human thought and experience. Ostensibly, Bain and Spencer were dealing with the same problems that had concerned the British empirical philosophers of the previous century. Bain, in particular, was interested in the way that the mind combined sensations to produce knowledge. In this respect, he inhabits similar territory to Hobbes, Locke and the eighteenth-century associationists such as David Hume and Dugald Stewart. But his approach, and that of Spencer, were very different.

The biological approach can be seen clearly in Bain's *The Senses and the Intellect* and Spencer's *The Principles of Psychology*, both of whose first editions were published in 1855 (quotations will be taken from the third editions of each work). Both these books start with physiology. After nine preliminary pages of definitions, *The Senses and the Intellect* gets down to business with a detailed discussion of the nervous system, moving then in the following chapter to a discussion of muscular actions. Only after three hundred or so pages of physiology does Bain discuss directly what had been the starting-point of Locke, Hume, Stewart and company: namely, the association of sensations and ideas by the mind. Of course Bain was not the first thinker to suggest in general terms that body and mind might be closely related. David Hartley had suggested something similar in his *Observations of Man*, but he did so without a detailed knowledge of physiology. By placing anatomical detail right at the start of his investigation, Bain was asserting the importance of a biological understanding of the mind.

It was the same with Spencer's *The Principles of Psychology* which begins with a lengthy discussion of the nervous system. The opening sentence is so low key as to be shocking: 'The lowest animal and the highest animal present no contrast more striking than that between the small self-mobility of the one and the great self-mobility of the other' (1881, vol. I: 3). The great distinction of this new psychology was not between humans and other animals, based on the assertion that the former possess unique mental powers and perhaps a soul. The ability to move about provides the great distinction. Humans are immediately brought down with a biological bump. Within the context of Victorian England, the first statement of *The Principles of Psychology* was as provocative as any single sentence that Darwin would write.

Spencer's opening assertion was very different from the first sentence of Locke's *An Essay Concerning Human Understanding*. Locke declared that it was '*understanding* that sets man above the rest of sensible beings and gives him all the advantages and dominion which he has over them' ([1690] 1964:I, 1: i, emphasis in original). Even the great materialist Hobbes shared a similar assumption. Hobbes had begun *Human Nature* by distinguishing between the 'faculties of the mind' and the 'faculties of the body'. He described the three main powers of the body as 'power nutritive, power motive and power generative'. He asserted that these bodily powers have little to do with the analysis of the 'powers of the mind', and therefore, 'the minute and distinct anatomy of the powers of the body is nothing necessary to the present purpose' (1999: 22).

By contrast, Bain and Spencer were arguing that the powers of the body cannot be separated from mental powers. What Hobbes was terming 'power motive' was central to Bain's understanding of how cognition and emotion operate. He accorded great psychological significance to those muscular movements that earlier philosophers had dismissed as unimportant. Along with other muscular reflexes, the muscular reactions of laughter were about to come in from the philosophical cold.

The early chapters of both *The Senses and the Intellect* and *The Principles of Psychology* outline the anatomical nature of the nervous system. They describe nerve cells and the connections between nerve-centres, with Spencer's discussion ranging across the higher and lower animals and Bain's concentrating upon human physiology. Underlying the anatomical discussions of the nervous systems are questions about function. Like an engineer, Spencer wants to understand how the various parts of the nervous system operate together. How does the system function? Spencer suggested that questions about structures cannot be properly distinguished from those about functions: 'Structure and function are in our thoughts so intimately related, that it is scarcely possible to give a rational account of the one without some tacit reference to the other' (1881, vol. I: 46).

According to Spencer, the nervous system functions to receive and transmit energy (ibid.: 49). The nervous system receives disturbances and is thereby set in motion; then it operates actively as 'a liberator of motion' and 'as a distributor or apportioner of the motion liberated' (ibid.: 47). The act of perception, for instance, causes complex and multiple excitations within the nervous system. Bain agreed and proposed the Law of Diffusion to suggest how the excitation produced by sensation becomes diffused through the body: the greater the initial stimulation, the greater will be the diffusion (see Bain, 1865: 6–7). Accordingly, perception can involve secondary muscular activity such as clenching one's hands, turning one's head, moving one's eyes, etc. Even the visceral organs may be moved by these processes of energy being excited, diffused and expended in the course of perceptual stimulation.

This new psychological perspective was dethroning human experience. Conscious awareness was only half the story for much of human psychology was occurring beyond conscious awareness. Bain in *Emotions and the Will* emphasized the importance of habits and reflexes that are 'performed almost unconsciously' (Bain, 1865: 6). Spencer claimed that disturbances of the nervous system were going on all the time, emanating from pressure of touch, muscular strain, temperature, sounds etc, so that constantly 'there are multitudinous indistinct waves, secondary and tertiary, travelling in all directions working their indistinct effects' (1881, vol. I: 93).

We may be aware of immediate sensations and emotional feelings, but these are only the tips of the neurological iceberg. We will be unaware of the ceaseless voyaging of nervous energy, travelling to all parts of the body, activating gestures and reflexes, causing the visceral organs to react, and so on. William Carpenter, the British physiologist on whose work both Spencer and Bain were drawing, was to term such neurological processes as 'unconscious cerebration' (Carpenter, 1879). According to this image of human mentality, we can never properly know our own psychological states. A decisive move towards a psychology of the unconscious was being taken.

Spencer and evolution

In one crucial matter Spencer went further than Bain: his psychological theorizing formed part of a wider project to unite all scientific knowledge around the principles of evolution. In his autobiography, Spencer recounted the origins for his great scheme: 'The first days of 1858 saw the inception of the undertaking to which the rest of my life was to be devoted' (1904, vol. II: 18). The precise dating was important. Spencer became obsessed with showing that his project for an all-embracing evolutionary philosophy predated Darwin. In later works Spencer was to include detailed footnotes claiming that his evolutionary ideas could be found in *Social Statics*, the first edition of *The Principles of Psychology* or various magazine articles, all written before the fateful day when he came across *On the Origin of Species*.

Certainly, the general idea of evolution had been there in *Social Statics* (1851). In that book Spencer had suggested that societies and organisms follow the same principles of evolution or development. Originally societies were crude and undifferentiated, with all members partaking in the same activities. Over time, societies adapt by developing specialist roles for their members, just as biological organisms evolve by becoming more anatomically complex. Biological organisms might become differentiated but their parts become increasingly interlinked. Spencer commented that 'the same coalescence of like parts and separation of unlike ones – just this same increasing subdivision of functions – takes place in the development of society' (ibid.: 453).

This was to become his big idea. Biological organisms, societies and, indeed, the physical universe develop from undifferentiated, simple systems towards becoming more differentiated integrated structures. This was a theory of evolution, albeit lacking Darwin's notion of 'natural selection', with which many years later Spencer was to find fault (Spencer, 1893). Previous philosophers, according to Spencer, had assumed that humans possessed a fixed nature. However, human nature was in the process of development. Politics should aim to help that development. Spencer, however, was proposing more than a theory of biological evolution. He was suggesting that all systems – whether natural, biological or social – develop according to the same principles. In the twentieth century this notion would become known as 'systems theory'. Spencer's theory of laughter was intended to provide an illustration of these general principles of development.

Between the moment when Spencer devised his multi-volumed project for synthesizing knowledge and the publication of its first volume *First Principles of a New System of Philosophy* in 1862, came Darwin's *On the Origin of Species*. It was cruel timing. Spencer was to become fixed in the public mind as a follower of Darwin. In his *Autobiography* Spencer was at pains to record exactly when he first heard about the papers that Wallace and Darwin read to the Linnaean Society. He had sent Darwin a copy of his essays in 1858 and reports that Darwin replied praising his achievements. Spencer comments that the letter 'dispels, more effectually than anything else can, a current error respecting the relations between Mr Darwin's views and my own'. He is about to quote the letter. The reader turns the page. There is no letter published – only Spencer's comment that it would be 'out of taste' for him to repeat Darwin's praise (1904, vol. 2: 27–8; see Duncan, 1908: 87, for the text of the letter). Spencer claims to be observing the proprieties against boasting, while asserting that he has much to boast about. It is a moment of pure Pooter.

Spencer describes his reactions on first reading Darwin's *On the Origin of Species*. To be more precise – and precision is entirely appropriate – Spencer describes what might have been his reactions. He could not remember whether he felt vexed or annoyed: 'But I doubt not that any such feelings, if they arose, were overwhelmed in the gratification I felt at seeing the theory of organic evolution justified' (1904, vol. 2: 50). He adds, stressing the independence of his own thought, that if organic evolution had been justified by Darwin, then the theory of inorganic evolution, which was indubitably his own, was correspondingly strengthened. Hence, he presumed his gratitude.

It might seem odd that Spencer, who meticulously records so many trivial details, cannot recall what he felt when he read such a momentous work. He has sufficient self-awareness to realize that he may have felt jealousy. Perhaps, after the first shock he had put all feeling out of his mind, in a psychological equivalent of inserting ear-plugs. But still, his nervous energy had to be discharged; he had to get back to his writing table; there was always further work to be done. A letter had to be written to Mr Darwin, as one evolutionary theorist to another.

By the time Spencer's autobiography was published, Freud was putting the finishing touches to his book on jokes, having already published books on dream interpretation and lapses of memory. There is no reason for believing that Spencer, in the last years of his life, was aware of these new ideas about unconscious motivation. Certainly, when Spencer first read Darwin, there was no common vocabulary to describe how disturbing thoughts and jealous feelings might be repressed from conscious awareness. In a pre-Freudian world, Pooters could innocently convince themselves of their dignified intentions. And onlookers could smirk. The image of the high-minded philosopher being brought down by petty concerns continues to amuse – whether it is Socrates gazing at the skies, the flies buzzing about the bald head of Hobbes, or Spencer inserting his ear-plugs. There is something absurd about Spencer turning from the great theme of evolution to engage the following year with Bain on laughter – and, in so doing, to produce an original theory that could apparently explain why his own behaviour, whose incongruities he would never appreciate, was necessarily, indeed biologically, so funny.

Bain and relief

Bain's theory of laughter contained a number of elements, including Hobbesian assumptions, physiological speculation and a personal pleasure in the humour of naughtiness. Bain had made some preliminary comments about the physiological effects of laughter in *The Senses and the Intellect* where he outlined a general physiological account of pleasure and pain. He claimed that pleasure was associated with an increase of 'the vital functions', while pain was associated with a decrease (1868a edn: 283). He admitted that there were exceptions to this rule, but asserted that in general the principle was correct. Laughter fitted the principle because it represented an increase of vitality and a 'heightening of the powers of life' (ibid.: 291). The argument was somewhat weak, not least because of the vagueness of its key terms.

In *The Emotions and the Will* Bain treated the subject of laughter at greater length and switched his attentions from the effects of laughter to its causes. Here he rebelled against the eighteenth-century theorists of incongruity and went back to their old enemy, Hobbes's theory of superiority. He pointed out the implausibility of the incongruity theory. There were many incongruities that provoked anything but laughter: 'a decrepit man under a heavy burden, five loaves and two fishes among a multitude ... an instrument out of tune, a fly in ointment, snow in May', and so on (1865 edn: 247–8).

So if incongruity were not the cause of laughter, then what was? Hobbes had been wrong to suggest that a sense of superiority underlay the ludicrous, for one need not necessarily feel personally superior to the person that one laughs at. But Hobbes had been close. It was a feeling of degradation, rather than superiority. Pleasure is to be had by degrading a person or an idea: 'The occasion of the ludicrous is the Degradation of some person or interest possessing dignity, in circumstances that excite no other strong emotion' (1865: 248; Bain also included this definition in his *Mental and Moral Science* (1868b: 315). Bain expanded upon this basic idea in his textbook *English Composition and Rhetoric*, which was first published in 1866. He suggested that the main element of the ludicrous in writing 'is furnished by the degradation, direct or indirect, of some person or interest – something associated with power, dignity, or gravity' (1877 edn: 74). Bain included Hobbes's descriptions of laughter in an appendix, as an exercise for students to study the construction of sentences and paragraphs (ibid.: 274–7).

Bain in *The Emotions and the Will* took delight in demonstrating that an element of degradation lay in the examples of wit that the eighteenth-century theorists had produced to support their refutation of Hobbes. He suggested that the eighteenth century writers had missed the malevolent dimension. Even the most 'genial humour' has an element of degradation but 'the indignity is disguised, and, as it were, oiled by some kindly infusion' (Bain, 1865: 249). For instance, if one examines George Campbell's examples closely enough, they can be seen to bear traces of the very motivation that he was so keen to deny. They contained unacknowledged malice that delights in degrading an elevated figure. As an instance Bain quoted Alexander Pope on Queen Anne:

Here thou great Anna, whom three realms obey
Dost sometimes counsel take, and sometimes tea.
(quoted in Bain, 1865: 252n)

Bain's quotation indicates his own sense of rebellious fun. When he was writing, Britain had another dignified queen on the throne. James Sully would recall that Bain liked to tell 'amusing stories about Mill and other celebrities to the accompaniment of a mirthful falsetto laugh and shakings of the wee body' (Sully, 1918: 183).

Bain was suggesting that the pleasures of laughter might not entirely be estimable. In his later book, *Education as a Science*, Bain discussed humour under the general heading of 'anti-social and malign feeling'; and he described children's play and laughter as containing 'the zest of malevolence' (Bain, 1879: 76). In *English Composition*, he wrote that the exultation in degrading another is lessened by various rhetorical means. For instance, degradation might be combined with a compliment. He gave the example of de Quincey describing Kant as a great man but criticizing Kant for being so obtuse to the niceties of language that his sentences had to be measured by a carpenter and that 'some of them run two feet eight by six inches' (Bain, 1877: 76). Bain's general point was to emphasize the streak of malice even within seemingly gentle humour. 'We often hear of innocent raillery and harmless jokes', wrote Bain, but there is usually a core element of degradation (ibid.: 76). He did not discuss why the malevolent element should be disguised except to say that degradation 'cannot be acceptable to the honest sympathy of men generally' (ibid.: 76).

Many of Bain's examples in *The Emotions and the Will* did not deal directly with degradation, but were used to exemplify his other main theoretical point: laughter often accompanies a release from constraint. He suggested that if we are suddenly relieved from solemn posture, then 'the rebound of hilarity ensues, as in the case of children set free from school' (1865: 250). This fitted his general physiological law that a feeling of pleasure is normally associated with an increase of nervous energy. The release from constraint produces pleasure and an increase of nervous energy that can result in laughter. Bain connected the laughter that follows the release from constraint with the idea of degradation. Normally we have to maintain the posture of constraint in the face of 'the dignified, solemn and stately attributes of things' (ibid.: 250). If suddenly the dignified, solemn and stately are degraded, we delight in being momentarily released from our habitual constraint. A surge of freed energy passes through the body and we laugh like the schoolchildren rushing out of the school gates.

This implies that mockery provides momentary freedom. According to Bain, the serious and the mirthful are in 'perpetual contrast' (ibid.: 251). Ordinarily seriousness dominates the conditions of life. The sense of 'freedom, abandon and animal spirits', that schoolchildren display as they rush out of the school gates, is held in check by 'labour, difficulty, hardship and the necessities of our position' (ibid.: 251). This is a classic description of Victorian life and its ideals. Discipline and self-control are necessary; hard work should be the order of the day. The whole basis of society and morality depended on constraint. When Bain portrayed 'the serious' as comprising labour, difficulty and hardship, he added that such things 'give birth to the severe and constraining institutions of government, law, morality, education and etc' (ibid.: 251).

Yet, pleasure bursts out as we enjoy mocking 'hollow pretensions, affectation, assumption and self-importance, vanity, airs and coxcombry' (ibid.: 251). All these are targets that deserve to be ridiculed. In this, Bain was following the incongruity theorists of the previous century. Then Bain adds an extra remark that takes him into the psychology of modernity: 'We are occasionally disposed to waive even our serious feelings of respect and to hail the descent of a true dignity with sparkling countenance, but it is against our better nature to do so' (ibid.: 251). In short, we may take glee in mocking that which we should not mock. Laughter represents a rebellion against order – a temptation to a dangerous moment of anarchy against the severe demands of social constraint.

Scattered throughout these comments are the basic elements of a Freudian theory of laughter. There is the notion of a fundamental conflict between pleasure and the necessary demands of social life. Laughter has an aggressive element that erupts in rebellion against constraint, including those constraints that are vital for social life. Moreover, there is an element of disguise. The aggressive feelings appear as genial ones; unacceptable motives are disguised as acceptable ones. We are tempted to enjoy what we should not enjoy and to disguise the nature of this enjoyment. Bain did not pursue these matters. Like a naughty boy, he has glimpsed at rebellion. He laughs at the queen taking tea. His wee body shakes. Then it is back to serious, disciplined work. It was study, not laughter, that saved him from a harsh life of poverty.

Spencer and relief

Spencer had been commissioned by the magazine *Medico-Chirurgical Review* to review *The Emotions and the Will* soon after its publication in 1859. He agreed to the task because, as he was to say many years later, he felt that Bain had paid insufficient attention to the issue of evolution. Ever the stickler, Spencer depicted his relations with Bain as precisely as he could: 'Bain and I were on terms, if not exactly of friendship, yet of friendly acquaintanceship ... In after years we became more intimate and eventually established cordial relations' (Spencer, 1904, vol. 2: 46). The review was to be followed by the article on laughter, in which Spencer developed his own theory.

Spencer began his review by praising Bain for recognizing the importance of bodily organs in mental states. Spencer's main point was to criticize him for not going far enough. Bain's approach was 'essentially transitional', being an advance on the old ways of doing psychology but it was not yet fully scientific (1864b: 122: quotations are taken from Spencer's second series of *Essays*, which reproduced both the review of Bain and the essay on laughter). Bain had followed the old metaphysicians in classifying emotions by their outward characteristics. This, according to Spencer, was like the ancients classifying the whale as a fish. The procedures of the natural scientist should be adopted. The key was to examine the structures and functions of emotions in relation to the nervous system and then to 'study the evolution of the emotions up through the various grades of the animal kingdom' (ibid.: 129).

Regarding laughter, the procedures of natural science necessitated disputing Bain's theory of degradation. Hence, Spencer made the comment about the good pun in the opening paragraph of his essay. He was proposing a 'fatal objection' to Bain's theory, for not all degradation produces laughter and not all laughter, namely laughter at the good pun, is caused by degradation. This was an updating of the old argument that eighteenth-century thinkers had levelled against Hobbes. Spencer's aim was to reformulate incongruity theory as a theory about nervous energy, suggesting that 'unexpected contrasts of ideas' produce the reactions of smiling and laughing (1864a: 105).

Spencer started from the assumption that laughter is a display of 'muscular excitement' produced by emotional feeling. Like Bain, he agreed with 'the general law that feeling passing a certain pitch habitually vents itself in bodily action' (ibid.: 110–11). Some emotional states, he argued, produce bodily actions that are purposeful and some produce actions that are purposeless. Fear typically produces the purposeful reaction of flight. By contrast, laughter is 'purposeless' for the 'the movements of chest and limbs which we make when laughing have no object' (ibid.: 111). Because the act of laughing is not directed to any outwardly useful purpose its function must be to regulate nervous energy. Spencer's approach is physiological rather than social. He does not consider that laughter may fulfil social purposes in bringing people together or communicating enjoyment, etc. For Spencer, whose own body rarely shook with mirth, laughter was purposeless, except for serving the physiological function of expending an accumulation of nervous energy.

The question then is what might provoke the 'overflow of nerve-force' that is expended by the bodily movements of laughter (ibid.: 111). Recognizing Bain's point about flies in ointment and snow in May, Spencer conceded that it was inadequate to say that incongruities *per se* provoke the excess nervous energy. By the same token, he suggested, it is too simple to say that release from constraint is the cause of laughter. Spencer's solution is ingenious: 'Laughter naturally results only when consciousness is unawares transferred from great things to small – only when there is what we may call a *descending* incongruity' (ibid.: 116, emphasis in original).

The one example that Spencer used to demonstrate his thesis is somewhat odd. Spencer imagined a theatrical play where the audience is happily and sympathetically anticipating that the hero and heroine are about to be reconciled. Suddenly the performance is interrupted. A young goat wanders from the wings onto the stage. The animal sniffs around. The audience laughs. Because the audience is sympathetically disposed to the characters on the stage, the laughter cannot indicate any desire to humiliate them. It must have a different cause. The audience was concentrating on the play. Nervous energy would have accumulated in anticipation of the play's resolution. With the interruption, this energy needed an alternative release. This was a descending incongruity. The audience's attention was drawn from the big scene of the drama to the petty incongruity of the goat – hence an outbreak of laughter.

Other more convincing examples of descending incongruity might easily be given. The bathos of Pope's couplet about the queen sometimes taking counsel and sometimes tea fits the pattern. So does the image of the lofty philosopher swatting flies, or inserting ear-plugs at the dinner table. It is a descent from the sublime to the ridiculous, from the elevated to the petty – from the philosopher's great thoughts to the carpenter measuring his wooden sentences. Some modern psychologists have taken up this notion of descending incongruity to explain why some incongruities but not others are found funny (Apter, 1982; Wyer and Collins, 1992). Spencer's point was not to provide examples of ludicrous incongruities but to understand the function of laughter as a means of dissipating excess energy. Ascending incongruities produce no build-up of unreleased nervous energy for the energy is absorbed into the ascent. Sudden descending incongruities, by contrast, leave the observer with energy to spare. The individual is focused upon a big matter, for which nervous energy is required. Suddenly, the big matter is interrupted and the accumulated energy must find some other outlet.

Spencer's theory is itself a descending theory in that it goes from the larger unit to the smaller rather than vice versa. Laughter is to be explained in terms of the individual's nervous system rather than upwards in terms of the larger social unit. Thus, Spencer does not take up Bain's hints about the perpetual opposition between mirth and seriousness in social life. He could have argued, for instance, that laughter permits the 'social organism' to function, because it drains off tensions that accumulate as a result of necessary social constraint. The schoolboys rush out of the school gate, expending their excess energy. Because this energy is released so harmlessly, they will return with docility the following morning. Had Spencer sought to explain the social functions of laughter in this way, he might have discussed why laughter is typically shared. As it is, his theory of descending incongruity overlooks the social nature of laughter.

By the same token, Spencer might have linked his idea of descending incongruities with Bain's notion of degradation. By connecting the sublime with the ridiculous, one mocks the former. The dignity of the monarch is punctured by the descending incongruity of considering her taking counsel and tea. If one reverses the order of tea and counsel, the joke is spoilt. One might also interpret Spencer's example of the goat in this light. During a theatrical performance the members of the audience have to adopt a posture of restraint: they must not move, talk or cough. The breaking of the theatrical tension permits release from this restraint. In addition, the audience can gain pleasure at the expense of the actors who have demanded such restraint. Thus, the laughter at the goat is also an enjoyment at seeing the actors' discomfit and their performance spoiled.

Certainly Bain did not accept that Spencer had succeeded in refuting his idea of degradation. In the third edition of *The Emotions and the Will*, Bain took on Spencer's claim that puns could be made without degrading another person. Bain declared: 'I very much wish he [Spencer] had produced such a pun, as I have never yet met with one of the sort' (1899 edn: 263n). He challenged Spencer to produce a harmless, non-degrading pun. One gets the impression that Bain felt confident in offering the challenge.

Being on cordial terms of almost-friendship, Bain would have realised that his adversary was not a nimble joker.

Recent researchers, who have analyzed how speakers use puns in the course of ordinary conversations, have provided evidence that would have pleased Bain. Norrick (1993) claims that puns produce 'interactional aggression in disrupting topical turn-by-turn talk' and by setting recipients tests of understanding (ibid.: 25; see also Norrick, 2003). The degradation need not be aimed at a specific individual, although it can be, but at the conversational rules that constrain speakers. The pun signals a moment of relief from these rules, while disrupting the flow of other conversationalists who are following the rules. Hence punning can be an aggressive act that disrupts the talk of others.

In short, Bain's notions of degradation and relief from constraint could have been expanded into a social theory of rebellious humour that mocks serious convention. From there, it would have been a comparatively short step to extend the theory to cover the mockery that is used to discipline those who break social codes. Bain, whose interests in sociology were limited, did not take this step. By contrast, Spencer, whose philosophical remit included sociology along with everything else, did not wish to accord mockery such importance.

Spencer and the evolution of laughter

One reason why Spencer did not move theoretically upward to analyze the social functions of laughter was that he was using the topic of laughter to illustrate the laws of evolution. Descending incongruities were only part of his argument. The next step was to show why the build-up of nervous energy, that follows the perception of descending incongruities, should result in laughter. Spencer thought that laughter followed a general law of evolution that he called the Law of Least Resistance. This law suggested that systems will adapt by establishing patterns of movement that are easiest to make because they encounter least resistance. Spencer envisaged this evolutionary law to underwrite all regularly produced motions, whether those of organic or inorganic systems.

According to Spencer's law, nervous energy will tend to be expended in bodily movements that can be easily made without muscular resistance. Because the facial muscles are so frequently used, they provide little resistance to the pent-up energy. These muscles will be readily called into play when there is a need to discharge energy, such as the energy produced by descending incongruities. The resulting neuronal pathway will become well established, becoming transmitted from generation to generation as part of the biological make-up of the species. In this way, humans will inherit the physiological mechanisms of smiling and laughing as a response to the perception of descending incongruity. Spencer, in common with Darwin, believed that acquired characteristics could be inherited.

When Spencer subsequently referred to his analysis of laughter, he would be careful to note the origins of the 'Law of Least Resistance'. A footnote in later editions of *The Principles of Psychology* informs readers that the Law appeared in the first edition of that work and, indeed, in an even earlier article (1881, vol. 2: 539–60), as did a footnote in *First Principles* (1864c: 300). The origin of the Law was especially important for Spencer: it did not evolve from Darwin.

The discussion in *First Principles* shows how seriously Spencer was taking the topic of laughter, not because it was intrinsically important for him, but because it provided yet another illustration of the principles of evolution. The discussion of laughter comes in Chapter 10 of *First Principles* when Spencer deals with the laws of motion. All material bodies, whether organic or inorganic, follow laws of motion that guide their adaptation and evolution. Here Spencer discusses planetary movements before descending incongruously to laughter. Regarding the latter, there is 'an undirected discharge of feeling that affects first the muscles around the mouth, then those of the vocal and respiratory apparatus, then those of the limbs and then those of the spine' (1864c: 301). This demonstrates that 'when no special route is opened for it, a force evolved in the nervous centres produces motion along channels which offer the least resistance' (ibid.: 301). Then the reaction becomes a habitual motion that is transmitted by evolution. Laughter finds its place alongside a discussion of nebular condensation and the movement of the planets. That is, of course, why Spencer had discussed the topic in the first place. He would not have frivolously chanced upon the topic of frivolity.

Spencer's theory is one of the most integrated of all theories of laughter. Everything seems to fit together. He explains why some incongruities produce laughter while others do not. This is nothing to do with social custom, inner motive or immediate context. The reasons are physiological: energy is accumulated and must be released. If the descending incongruity is small, then the movement of the facial muscles into a smile will be suffice. Should the descending incongruity be large, then more muscles come into play: the vocal muscles may sound their ha-ha-has, sides may be slapped, the whole body may rock with mirth, until the energy is dissipated. The wider Law of Least Resistance, whose operations can be seen throughout the solar system, explains how the reaction of laughing should have evolved in this way. It is a reaction that is functional but essentially purposeless.

Spencer personally took the lessons of his own theories seriously. He did not wish to waste precious energy on something quite so purposeless as laughter. He is said to have permitted himself at most a 'quiet complacent smile' (Sully, 1918: 290). One historian of biological psychology has commented that today it is easier to mock Spencer than to recapture the power of his ideas (Young, 1990). Darwin paid tribute to Spencer's theory of laughter in *Expression of the Emotions in Man and Animals*. He believed that Spencer had provided a 'true theory' of many emotional expressions and that Spencer was 'the great expounder of the principle of Evolution'. He also praised Spencer's theory that when an emotion passes beyond a certain level, the nervous energy must spill over into bodily movement (1896: 8ff). By contrast, Darwin criticized Bain's theory of emotions for being imprecise (ibid.: 7).

It is fair to say that no philosopher before Spencer had produced a psychological theory of laughter that was quite so integrated yet at the same time so differentiated. His account puts the ideas of Hobbes, Locke and Schopenhauer into an earlier stage of psychological evolution. Like the engineer that he was, Spencer arranged his theoretical parts with care, oiling the conceptual mechanism to ensure its smooth running. From the hypothesis of descending incongruity through to the physiological theory of muscular energy, the concepts form a series of interlocking cogs and fly-wheels. Round they spin, whirring with precision, as the whole apparatus magnificently misses the point.

Towards pluralist orthodoxy

Bain and Spencer had formulated their respective versions of the relief theory just after the mid-point of the nineteenth century. Until the first years of the twentieth century, when Bergson and Freud wrote on humour, there were no further major psychological innovations into the nature of laughter. At this time psychology was becoming established as an academic discipline. Relief theory was not usurping the older two theoretical traditions but was finding its place beside them. As psychologists referred to humour, the conceptual elements of degradation, incongruity and relief were reshuffled and dealt out again in slightly different theoretical hands. Nor is this surprising. Bain and Spencer may have been proposing new theories of laughter based on the idea of physiological energy, but their combined effect was to give the older traditions a new boost by defining their central terms more precisely. Thus, Bain replaced the notion of superiority with the more satisfactory idea of degradation, while Spencer pointed to a particular class of incongruities as being involved in humour.

All the same, things went quiet in the psychology of laughter during the last part of the nineteenth century. Some of the new textbooks kept alive the old debates. The Norwegian psychologist Harald Höffding, whose *Outlines of Psychology* (1892) was translated into English and German, combined Spencer's Social Darwinism with Hobbesian ideas of superiority. He argued that life was 'above all a struggle for existence' and therefore 'strong and suddenly excited self-esteem easily breaks out in laughter' (ibid.: 292–3). His comments on the psychology of laughter lacked the physiological specificities that Bain and Spencer had aimed for.

On the other hand, William James ignored the subject in his great, two-volumed *The Principles of Psychology* (1890). The title suggests a rebuff to Spencer whose similarly named two volumes were still in print. Certainly James distanced himself from Spencer's evolutionary approach, using footnotes to complain of 'the scandalous vagueness' and 'inanity' of Spencer's ideas (1890, vol. 1: 149n). The high spot of James's *Principles* was his theory of emotions, which turned about the assumptions of Bain and Spencer. James asserted that emotional experience follows, rather than precedes, the relevant bodily state: 'We feel sorry because we cry, angry because we strike, afraid because we tremble, and not that we cry, strike, or tremble, because we are sorry, angry, or fearful' (1890, vol. 2: 450).

James's list of emotions is interesting for its omissions. Unsurprisingly, given the upright character of the writer, sexuality is left out. James did not say that we feel lust because our genitalia bestir themselves. James's list concentrates on what psychologists today would label 'negative' emotions. Happiness and laughter are absent. James could have plausibly claimed that we feel happy because we laugh. There are modern experiments to support the idea. Subjects who have been induced to bite tightly on a pencil, thereby employing the facial muscles involved in smiling, will report feeling happier than those who have been instructed to bite lightly (Strack et al., 1988). Apart from a passing reference to the physiology of laughter (vol. 2: 480), James ignored humour, thereby ignoring Bain and Spencer's contributions to the topic.

Spencer and Bain's theories of laughter faired better in France, thanks to the efforts of Théodule Ribot, the founder of French experimental psychology (Ferrand and Nicolas, 2000; Nicolas and Murray, 2000). Ribot greatly admired British psychology. His first book, *La psychologie anglaise* (1870), devoted separate chapters to the works of Bain and Spencer. Ribot summarized their debate on laughter, giving the edge to Spencer (ibid.: 270–4). Ribot was sympathetic to Spencer's evolutionary perspective and he translated Spencer's *The Principles of Psychology* into French. In *The Psychology of the Emotions* (1897) Ribot returned to the topic of laughter. Ribot's basic approach was integrative, combining all three major traditions within a broad evolutionary framework. Hobbesian laughter, he suggested, constituted a basic but lower form of humour, while the theory of incongruity dealt with a secondary but more developed type (ibid.: 352f). Ribot also provided Spencer with the opportunity for another Pooterish moment. He wrote to Spencer in June 1879 informing him that the French Minister of Public Instruction had decreed that Spencer's books would be awarded as prizes in French *lycées*. Spencer mentions the letter in his *Autobiography* but not without expressing some qualms. To quote from Ribot's letter would be 'in somewhat questionable taste and yet to say nothing about the endorsement it describes would be to leave out an occurrence of some significance' (1904, vol. 2: 326).

Dugas's book *Psychologie du rire* was very much influenced by his teacher Ribot to whom the work is dedicated. Dugas evaluates the main approaches rather than proposes a new theory. He was sympathetic to the relief theory, describing laughter as *'une détente'* (1902: 14). However, he felt Spencer's theory was somewhat narrow as it ignored the conscious, non-physiological aspects of humour. In general, Dugas's approach is integrative, seeking to combine the particular strengths of the various approaches. He followed

Ribot on Hobbes and evolution, distinguishing between the brutal giggling of 'savages' and the intellectual laugh of 'civilized' persons (Dugas, 1902: 99). Such a position not only suggests that ridicule is a lower form of humour, but that 'our' developed humour is not based on ridicule.

Sully's *Essay on Laughter* was published in the same year as Dugas's book. With Sully, we are moving towards the twentieth-century world of the professional academic psychologist. Sully was instrumental in founding the British Psychological Society. At the Society's first scientific conference in February 1902 he gave a paper on 'The evolution of laughter' (see Gurjeva, 2001, and Valentine, 1999, for discussions of Sully and the history of British psychology). Sully was the author of several textbooks, which summarized the current state of psychological knowledge rather than advanced a particular theory. His book on laughter aimed to organize and assess the relevant evidence. It did not argue partisanly for a particular approach. One new departure, which again gives Sully's book a modern touch, was the inclusion of evidence about the development of humour in children. This was not a topic that especially interested Spencer and Bain, neither of whom was a parent. Child development was, by contrast, of particular interest to Sully, as can be seen in *Studies in Childhood* (1895), probably the most creative of all his books.

Sully's *Essay on Laughter* resembles the modern 'literature review'. Every theory is given due accord. Sully concluded his discussion of the theories of incongruity and degradation, by claiming that 'whereas neither of the two chief types of theory covers the whole field of the laughable, each has its proper, limited domain' (ibid.: 135–6). Theoretical contradictions are seen as representing contradictory aspects of reality. Sully stresses that laughter is social in the sense that it unites people (ibid.: 255). On the following page Sully stresses that it would be wrong to say that laughter is just social, for we laugh at others. In this sense 'laughter would seem to be anti-social and dividing' (ibid.: 256). In this way, the book integrates by compiling, rather than resolving, the contradictory aspects of the topic.

Ideologically, too, Sully represents a step towards modernity. Like today's positive psychologists, Sully positions himself on the side of humour. In the opening pages, he declares an opposition to the 'rather sour-tempered laughter-haters' who are succeeding in reducing the 'friends of laughter' to the 'dimensions of a petty sect' (ibid.: 2). His style is cheerful and down-to-earth. Like Bain, he understands the fun of schoolchildren freed from constraint: one can see 'the laughter of joy' in 'the wild jubilant gladness of boys as they rush out of school'. Their explosive joy 'seems to be a way of throwing off the constraint and the dullness of the classroom, and getting a deep breath of the delicious sense of restored liberty' (ibid.: 72).

Sully writes as if he is being rebellious: he is battling on the side of laughter against its unnamed, implacable enemies. At the same time Sully displays the conservatism of a society in which apparent rebelliousness can function to preserve, rather than threaten, existing inequalities. He writes naturally of boys, not girls, rushing from school. The image also implies that the boys had been behaving dutifully during the hours of schooling. Spencer had criticized Bain for neglecting the evolution of emotions 'between the lower and the higher human races', as well as the evolution 'during the progress from infancy to maturity' (1864b: 129).

Sully does not neglect this evolutionary angle. He frequently makes a parallel between the development of laughter in children and its development within human evolution. He writes of the laughter of 'savages', which expresses 'particular mental conditions and attitudes similar to those which are expressed by the laughter of our children' (1902: 228). Some examples of 'savage laughter' indicate 'the coarse brutal forms of laughter which we associate with the rougher kinds of schoolboy' (ibid.: 251). Yet the laughter of 'savages' can also show 'a movement towards a more sympathetic laughter' and in this 'we detect the dim beginnings of that complex feeling or attitude which we call humour' (ibid.: 251). Sully speculates that the quality of humour 'improves as we pass from the lowest and most degraded to the higher savage tribes' (ibid.: 251). Again, 'our' laughter is presumed to be largely ridicule-free, although we can understand and sympathize with the inferior mirth of the less developed.

The stance is that of the European imperialist who is confident of his superiority and who imagines that power is being exercised with paternal benevolence. Just as parents need to exercise authority over their children, so the imperialist claims to watch over the 'child-like' peoples of Africa and elsewhere. Laughter, as a disciplinary force, has its place in this tale of imperialist justification. Sully suggests that humour can be a means of exercising parental/imperialist power. When dealing with Africans, laughter can be 'more effective than the harsher measures to which even a gentle Briton may think himself sometimes driven' (ibid.: 252). Sully cites a Miss Kingsley, who had much experience of Africa. She had written to Sully to say how she had been able to use humour with Africans in order to ensure that they complied with necessary demands: 'I could laugh them out of things other people would have to blow out of them with guns' (ibid.: 253).

Hat comedy

Sully's approach to the psychology of humour bears more than a passing resemblance to the ideological positivism of today. There is same general positioning of the analyst on the side of laughter. There is a similar emphasis on the good purposes of humour, while at the same time recognizing that humour can sometimes be 'anti-social' or, to use the modern terminology, 'negative'. Generally the view is benign. Bain's image of a conflict between harsh social necessity and momentary joys of freedom has been softened. So has Bain's equation of the pleasures of laughter with the spirit of malice. There are argumentative moves to attribute the negative, anti-social humour to others. In Sully's day, but not in today's liberal ethos, the others are seen to belong to supposedly earlier stages of evolution. There is class superiority, as well as racial superiority, as Sully suggests that the humour of 'the vulgar' may share 'the same unfeeling rejoicing of mishap in the laughter of the savage' (1902: 97).

Sully might have presented his work as summarizing the findings of science, but his exposition expresses an underlying ideology that is revealed both in what is said and what is left unsaid. The ideology employs sets of concepts to differentiate 'our' humour from 'theirs', just as eighteenth-century theorists distinguished between 'our' raillery and 'their' banter. Such differentiating rhetoric is particularly useful when talking of the way that 'we' might use humour in the cause of 'necessary' discipline. The term 'teasing' (as opposed to 'bullying' or 'ridiculing') can be used to convey 'our' good-nature. According to Sully, the adult teasing of children does not 'cross the boundary line of serious intention to annoy', for it is 'prompted by no serious desire to torment, by no motive more serious than the half-scientific curiosity to see how the subject of the experiment will take it' (ibid.: 77). A similar good-nature is optimistically assumed to accompany 'our' uses of disciplinary humour with social inferiors:

> One can only infer with some probability, from the relations of parents and adults, generally, to children, and of white masters to their coloured slaves, that power has always been tempered by some admixture of good-nature, which composition has produced a certain amount of playful jocosity, at once corrective and cementing. (ibid.: 263–4)

Yet, Sully was not blind to the possibility of wishful thinking and to the self-deceptions of humour. He followed Bain in claiming that 'malevolence or malice has its protean disguises' (ibid.: 143). But malevolence is easier to spot in others than in ourselves. Sully's terminological matrix was set to assign 'good-natured teasing' to authorities who are assumed to be acting in the interests of all. 'Cheerful rebelliousness' is ascribed to the young boys who will grow up to assume similar positions of authority, whereas 'unfeeling malevolence' is assumed to be a constitutional property of those who are separated from 'us' by chasms of evolutionary inferiority.

If ideology can provide the semantic tools that enable us to avoid self-critically examining 'our' own humour, then this is best examined by a specific example, rather than being asserted as a general principle. The chosen example – the comic potential of hats – also serves the purpose of illustrating the particularity of humour. What seems naturally and universally funny in one age can seem somewhat strange in another. The writers on humour in the nineteenth and early twentieth centuries frequently used hats to illustrate the unambiguously comic. Spencer's essay on laughter begins with the question: 'Why do we smile when a child puts on a man's hat?' (1864a: 105). Sully illustrated Hobbes's theory of superiority with a hat cameo: 'When I see my estimable fellow-pedestrian lose his hat at a street corner where the wind lies in ambush, my soul expands exultingly' (1902: 143). Bergson, in the opening chapter of *Laughter*, argued that laughable objects are always human. His first example was a hat: 'You may laugh at a hat, but what you are making fun of, in this case, is not the piece of felt or straw, but the shape that men have given it, – the human caprice whose mould it has assumed' (1911a: 3). No modern writer would assume that readers would laugh at hats.

On 12 September 1913, *The Times* reported that the psychologist William McDougall had delivered a talk to the British Association entitled 'A new theory of laughter'. In the talk McDougall criticized Spencer's theory of nervous energy. *The Times* reported the example that McDougall had used to confute Spencer. McDougall had asked his audience to consider 'the case of a man sitting down on his own tall hat'. Mr Spencer could offer no reason why that scene should liberate nervous energy. Later, McDougall was to incorporate his lecture into *An Outline of Psychology* (1923), where he discussed 'the types of the ludicrous' (ibid.: 167). The first 'basic examples of the ludicrous' – ahead of clowns and other comic characters – were the hats: 'the man sitting down on his own hat or pursuing it down the street before the breeze' (ibid.: 167).

The example of the child wearing the man's hat also featured in the work of the German psychologist Theodor Lipps, whose ideas were criticized by Sully. Lipps had assumed that observers first see the hat and then the child. The perception of the latter provokes the idea of incongruity. Spencer's theory of descending incongruity would also have predicted such an order of perception. Sully was sceptical: 'Do we, before the agreeable spasm seizes us, first mentally grasp the hat and then pass to the idea of its rightful wearer?' (1902: 11). Surely not, answered Sully. The spectacle 'would not impress you as being one whit more ludicrous' if you saw the hat first and then wearer, rather than 'if your eye lighted on the two together' (ibid.: 12). Sully suggested that we see the whole ensemble together, and, in arguing thus, he was being a *Gestaltist* before the birth of Gestalt psychology. The scene that he was imagining involved the child wearing a 'tall hat' (ibid.: 14). Sully added that 'the hat has become a symbol' and, as such, it represents 'the dignity' of the man who would rightfully wear it (ibid.: 16). The humour lay in the discrepancy between the child and the grown man's dignity. Again there is a reference to the delights of seeing dignity brought down to size.

The writers, in describing the child and the hat, assume the scene to be universally comic: anyone seeing the child in the adult hat would see the funny side. But even in their day not everyone would necessarily find such scenes funny. Imagine a new, expensive silken top hat and a child whose fingers were sticky with marmalade – would the first reaction of the hat's owner be to laugh? Perhaps onlookers might find the owner's consternation a matter for amusement, but the servant, whose task it was to place the hat out of children's reach, would not necessarily share the humour. The child wearing a guest's hat would be a sign that trouble was coming the servant's way.

The theorists may have used general terms but they had in mind something very specific. It is not any hat that is imagined. It was a man's hat. Sully and McDougall specified a 'tall hat'. A working man's flat cap was not part of this comic imagination. The scene is gendered. Presumably it is a boy, not a girl, who is trying on the high hat. McDougall did not invite his audience to imagine a woman sitting on feathered millinery. Nor did he evoke the somewhat unseemly image of a young woman sitting down upon a man's tall hat. The apparently universal statements about hat-comedy were not only located in a particular historical epoch, but they were to be understood in terms of class, gender and social norms of propriety.

None of this needed to be spelled out to the original readers of Sully, McDougall and Spencer. They would understand immediately. It is different for readers today. We cannot easily judge the social signals conveyed by different male hats: why one hat might be more dignified than another; or more appropriate to afternoon rather than evening wear; or how a slight adjustment in the angle of the hat on the head can convey rakishness or solemnity. There were also common-place social actions to be performed with the hat – to be raised, lowered or merely touched in greeting and deference. Today's baseball caps are as little made for doffing as are motor-cycle helmets. What do the young today know of doffing? A world and its iconography have passed.

The psychologists making their confident statements about the funniness of the child in the adult hat were omitting something. In Sully's account we can see the adults entering the children's nursery and registering amusement at the sight that greets their eyes. He writes of benign parents, whose teasing and laughter contain no malice. His account of the parent laughing at the child in the adult hat suddenly stops short. The perceptual account about the ordering of sensations tell us nothing about the reaction of the child – we can only imagine the audience of adults, pointing and guffawing as they confidently recognize something funny. What does the child see? What does the child do? Join in the laughter? Blush with embarrassment at being observed mid-game? Perhaps the child is upset to be the object of adult mirth. Not all those being teased recognize the benevolence of their superiors. There might be tears, or the tears might be hidden behind a brave, startled face that tries to smile.

We do not hear about these possibilities. The funniness of the child with the adult hat is presumed to exist as an objective fact of the world. This assumption may conceal the ambiguities and disguises of humour. The imagined scene contains an element of discipline, just like other incidents where adults laugh at childish mistakes. The adult laughter conveys the inappropriateness of the child's behaviour. If the child is seriously playing at being grown-up, then the adults are mocking the play. One might predict that the more seriously the child was playing, the greater the laughter. If the child has winsomely put on the hat in order to make the adults laugh, then the laughter will be diminished, even forced. It is the child's seriousness, not playfulness, that is being mocked. Perhaps the moment of laughter constitutes a release from adult, especially parental, constraint and responsibility. When children present themselves seriously but ludicrously as adults, so the adults can have a moment of childish release. And in that moment they do not care what effects their laughter might have on the child. Such is the avenging laughter of momentary freedom.

All these are possibilities, not certainties. But what is certain is that the psychological analysts, quoted above, do not discuss such possibilities, whose implications would disturb confidence in the goodness of 'our' laughter. The relief theory, which seems to be so naturally applied to children rushing from the school-gate, is not extended to cover adults childishly laughing at children. Instead, Sully and others apply a perceptual theory, seeking to find the cause of laughter through examining what exactly strikes the eye of the observer. The perceptual account omits so much and its omissions do not fall randomly. The laughers, as they laugh, do not see the hurt that their laughter may occasion. For them, it is just a good-natured, well-intentioned tease. But the laughter has occurred so suddenly, so unexpectedly that there could have been no prior intention. In the imagined hat-comedy, the perceptual account follows the scene from the perspective of the powerful. In the matter of laughter as in other matters, the perspective of power is protected by an element of blindness.

6

Bergson and the Function of Humour

The turn of the twentieth century was a grand time for theories of humour. The books by Sully and Dugas on the psychology of laughter appeared in 1902. Both writers found plenty of recent psychological research to review. The new century also saw the publication of the two most original books in the history of theories of humour – Henri Bergson's *Laughter* (1900) and Freud's *Jokes and their Relation to the Unconscious* (1905b). It is easy to suppose that this *éclat* of humour-theory reflected the gaiety of the times. In the popular imagination, this was a brief interregnum between the stuffiness of the nineteenth century and the murderous warfare of the new era. The last decade of the nineteenth century has become known as 'the naughty nineties', typified by images of the Moulin Rouge and can-can girls. In Britain the new century saw a new king, who was known to be a lover of cigars, card games and actresses. Neither Bergson nor Freud, however, belonged to the demi-monde of pleasure. Both led lives of extreme respectability. When they studied humour, they did so seriously.

Bergson's *Laughter* is probably his most read book, continuing to be republished in many translations. Its enduring popularity is perhaps surprising, for it is not an early version of ideological positivism. *Laughter* does not urge readers to smile through adversity nor does it sentimentally praise the life-enhancing goodness of a sense of humour. Instead Bergson, like Freud, placed laughter under suspicion. Bergson put the disciplinary functions of ridicule at the heart of humour and, as such, *Laughter* represents the first real social theory of laughter.

This aspect of Bergson's analysis has often been overlooked in favour of his curious, and ultimately unsatisfactory, idea that comedy is based upon bodily clumsiness. However, Bergson's ideas about humour are best appreciated within their philosophical context, rather than being decomposed into a series of separate hypotheses. The weaknesses of his theory, just as much as its strengths, are interesting because they reflect the depths of a distinctive vision.

Background to Bergson

The major figures in the philosophy of humour tend also to be major players in philosophy's serious business. Even Herbert Spencer, whose reputation evaporated like the face of the Cheshire cat in the twentieth century, was hailed as the greatest philosopher of his age. So too a generation later was Bergson. He was not a specialist in 'laughter studies', who happened to write an innovative book on his chosen speciality. He was a great philosopher, who happened to write on humour.

Bergson was born in 1859 in Paris. His father was of Polish Jewish origins, while his mother's family had come from Ireland. The family moved to London for a few years when Henri was a young child. He was to retain his proficiency in English after the family returned to Paris. In later years he worked closely with his translators to ensure that the English editions of his books captured the spirit and precision of the original French. From an early age Bergson showed a talent for mathematics and his first academic article, published when he was 19, was a solution to a mathematical problem. At university, his interests moved from the sciences to the humanities. After graduating, he taught in various *lycées* in France, and in this capacity worked for a few years at Clermont-Ferrand in the Auvergne. While at Clermont-Ferrand, he also gave lectures in philosophy at the local university. It was said that the seclusion of the Auvergne, with its fresh air and mountainous terrain, provided an ideal environment for Bergson to develop his philosophical speculations (Ruhe and Paul, 1914).

Late in life Bergson wrote an autobiographical essay, which described his philosophical development. Bergson recounted that as a young man he had been attracted by Herbert Spencer's philosophy. He had decided to become a philosopher with the mission to 'complete and consolidate' Spencer's *First Principles* (*The Creative Mind*, 1946: 12). He was soon to grow dissatisfied with Spencer's materialism that had placed the spiritual world beyond the reach of scientific knowledge. What Spencer had classified as 'unknowable' – namely, the spiritual, non-material world – was for Bergson most certainly knowable. Above all, Bergson came to believe that Spencer, along with most other philosophers, had failed to understand the nature of time. Spencer had assumed that the world simply evolved over time, without considering what is the basis for our understanding of time.

Bergson's first philosophical book *Time and Free Will* (*Essai sur les données immédiates de la conscience*) appeared in 1889, to be followed seven years later by *Matter and Memory* (*Matière et mémoire*). Both books were notable for the way that they re-examined the relations between body and mind in the light of recent research in psychology and physiology. They laid the basis for Bergson's philosophy of intuition that he was to develop over the course of his lifetime. Through intuition, the things that Spencer had dismissed as 'unknowable' could be grasped.

In 1900, the year in which *Laughter* was published, Bergson, was appointed professor at the Collège de France. His reputation as a philosopher was growing within France, but his books had yet to be translated into English or any other language. Much of the groundwork for *Laughter* had been prepared while Bergson was teaching in the Auvergne. However, Bergson was not to publish these ideas for sixteen years. First, three articles on the topic appeared in the *Revue de Paris* during 1900, and then later the same year Bergson combined these articles into the book *Le rire: essai sur la signification du comique*.

By the end of the decade, Bergson was being hailed internationally as the most original thinker of his time. It was *Creative Evolution* (*l'évolution créatrice*) that really established Bergson's reputation. For many years after its publication in 1907 this was considered to be Bergson's greatest work. In it Bergson attempted nothing less than the rewriting of Darwinian theory. He argued that evolution could not possibly be just a material process, and that the evolution of organic life depended upon spiritual factors just as much as on material ones.

After *Creative Evolution*, Bergson was regularly invited to lecture at the most prestigious universities in Europe and the United States. His lectures were major events that were reported in newspapers. Literary figures, such as George Bernard Shaw and T.S. Eliot, discussed his theories. It is said that Proust's *A la recherche du temps perdu* was heavily influenced by the Bergsonian philosophy of experience. William James wrote that the old generation of French professors was speaking of Bergson's talent 'almost with bated breath, while the youngsters flock to him as to a master' (1909: 227).

Rationalist philosophers felt the need to combat this new philosophy. Bertrand Russell described the argument between his own rationalism and Bergson's intuitionism as 'war to the knife' (quoted in Monk, 1997: 235). Although Russell and other rationalists attacked Bergson with full philosophical vigour, the arguments seldom became personal, as opponents respected Bergson for his personal modesty and his seriousness of purpose. Bergson's spiritual approach was the very antithesis of Karl Popper's attempt to establish the principles for a scientifically based philosophy. Whereas Popper did not hesitate to pour scorn on the mystical waffle of Hegelians, he praised Bergson for the 'lucidity and reasoned presentation of his thought', adding that this lucidity made it difficult to realize just how Hegelian Bergson really was (1984: 307).

In many ways, Bergson fitted the popular image of the philosopher. Unassuming and dedicated to the life of the mind, he strove to communicate metaphysical ideas as simply as possible. He did not seek to cut a dash at international symposia nor to stimulate controversy for the sake of publicity. He lived quietly with his wife and daughter in a suburb of Paris. Herbert Spencer's admirers may have compared him with Aristotle, but a generation later Bergson was being seen as the modern Socrates. Twelve years after the publication of *Laughter*, Edouard Le Roy began a book on Bergson by declaring that the Bergsonian revolution equalled in importance that of Socrates (Le Roy, 1913). Even opponents would not have dissented from Le Roy's claim that Bergson was the name on everyone's lips.

Honours were heaped on Bergson. Unlike Spencer he did not churlishly refuse them. Nor was he overwhelmed by their glitter, as he would later demonstrate. Bergson was elected to the Académie Française and made Officier de la Légion d'honneur. The League of Nations appointed Bergson to be president of its committee for intellectual cooperation. In 1927, he received the Nobel Prize for Literature. It was a fitting honour for a philosopher with the literary skills of a novelist. In his writings, Bergson offered concrete examples and wonderfully visual metaphors, in order to bring abstract principles down from the heavens to the earth, where, in his view, they belonged.

Intellectual fame of the proportions that Bergson attained depends either upon ruthless self-promotion – which was alien to Bergson – or upon creating ideas that encapsulate and re-direct wider currents of anxiety and hope. Thinkers in those times often seemed to suggest that a choice had to be made between religion and science. Russell's comment about 'war to the knife' was in this mode. Freud, who was Bergson's contemporary, made the choice unambiguously on the side of science. Bergson, however, offered the possibility of a third way. Both science and religion, he argued, were not just possible, but philosophically necessary. The world of the spirit was not rendered redundant by evolutionary science, as Spencer and others had supposed. *Creative Evolution* stressed that spiritual force, or the impulse to life, was a necessary part of the evolutionary process, providing the variation on which natural selection depended.

This mixing of the scientific with the spiritual, the material with the psychological, was a message that many wanted to hear. It seemed to save the scientific outlook from cold materialism, while enabling the religious perspective to escape from an irrational opposition to science. One Catholic admirer described his 'rapturous emotion' on reading *Creative Evolution* in the spring of 1907: 'I felt the presence of God in every page' (quoted in Chevalier, 1924: 65n). From the left, many syndicalists, who rejected the mechanistic doctrines of orthodox Marxism, took inspiration from Bergson's belief in the irreducibility of the human spirit.

Of course, not everyone was won over. Unwavering rationalists such as Russell were not the only ones to take exception. Many Marxists, whether or not orthodox party-liners, had little time for his work: members of the Frankfurt School dismissed him as a bourgeois idealist. Orthodox Catholics also found cause for complaint. The Catholic Church tried to stop believers from reading Bergson, putting several of his books on the Index in 1914. The Church's reaction might appear curious given that Bergson's philosophy was devoted to showing the limitations of materialism. However, Bergson did not directly invoke the notion of 'God', nor did he attempt to compress the processes of evolution into a period of six days. In France there were political considerations. Bergson was identified as a national enemy by Drumont whose *Action française* combined conservative Catholicism with anti-Semitism. Its policy of 'France for the French' excluded Bergson from citizenship on the grounds of his father's Jewish ancestry.

Bergson had not been raised religiously but in adult life he was drawn to Catholicism, without formally undergoing conversion. In 1937 Bergson wrote that he would have converted had it not been for the continuing growth of anti-Semitism. He wished to remain, he said, among the persecuted. It was a morally serious act: Bergson was prepared to jeopardize his place in the after-life, in order to oppose anti-Semitism in the present one. Bergson hoped, nevertheless, that a Catholic priest might feel able to recite prayers at his funeral (Levesque, 1973).

After the Nazi invasion of France, the Vichy government attempted to grant Bergson, France's most internationally famous philosopher, exclusion from the new racist laws. The government proposed to register him as an honorary Aryan. Bergson refused the offer. He did not wish to be the honoured citizen of a dishonourable society. So, he renounced all the honours that French government had previously bestowed upon him. He died shortly afterwards. The end in Occupied Paris must have seemed a long distance from those free days in the Auvergne and the intellectual delights of *Laughter*.

Experience and time

In his philosophical autobiography, Bergson describes the background to all his major books with one exception: he does not mention *Laughter*. Admirers have often treated the book similarly. Ruhe and Paul (1914) and Chevalier (1928) gave *Laughter* only passing mention, as Giles Deleuze (1988) would do in his warm account of Bergsonism. In the eyes of professional philosophers, the topic, not to mention the book's popularity, suggest a *divertissement* rather than serious metaphysics. *The Cambridge Dictionary of Philosophy* does not mention *Laughter* in its entry on Bergson (Audi, 1995). Bergson, too, was ambivalent about the topic. The original edition of *Laughter* contained a preface that was omitted in the English translation. Bergson offered a justification for not examining other theories of humour: that would have, he wrote, necessitated a much larger book 'out of proportion with the importance of the subject' (1900: v–vi).

Laughter stands apart from other works by Bergson, for its approach was not rooted in the sort of psychological analysis that characterized his first two books. Yet this did not of itself breach his philosophical principles. Bergson argued in *The Creative Mind* that philosophers should not apply the same method to each and every problem. No abstract principle will reveal 'the unity of our reality' (1946: 32). Therefore, philosophy demands a new approach for each new problem. We shall have to give up 'crowding universal science potentially into one principle' (ibid.: 32). That was a dig at Herbert Spencer and his intellectual descendants.

There were good philosophical reasons why Bergson, when examining humour, should have departed from the paths of Spencer and Bain. His first two books contained devastating arguments against the sort of psychology that both advocated. Psychological understanding stood at the heart of Bergson's philosophy. He argued that philosophy must start from the fact of human experience, especially the experience of time. Philosophers had failed to understand the particular nature of time. They erred in following common sense by treating time as if it were extended like space and as if it were essentially divisible into discrete moments. We may conventionally divide the day into hours and the hours into minutes and seconds – but in reality time contains no natural breaks. It flows through all our experiences, or, rather, our experiences flow through time.

Bergson argued that most psychologists also ignore the nature of time as unbroken duration, by imagining that human experience comprises discrete mental states, each following the other. Bergson argued that we are misled by language for 'our language is ill-suited to render the subtleties of psychological analysis' (*Time and Free Will*, 1913: 13). Language provides ready labels for mental states as if they are identifiable objects that have their own concrete existence – such as a state of 'happiness', 'love', 'hatred', etc. Academic psychologists might reject the labels of ordinary language and invent their technical terms for mental states, but they follow common sense in assuming that mental states exist as separate entities and can be accurately identified as such. For Bergson, the existence of discrete mental states is an illusion. He complained that conventional psychology 'arrests and solidifies into finished things' that which is fluid and unfinished (*Matter and Memory*, 1911c: 154).

By means of concrete examples, Bergson argued that our experience cannot comprise a sequence of distinct states of mind. Different themes from the past, as well as expectations for the future, are constantly weaving in and out of sensations of the present. In *Matter and Memory* Bergson argued that perception was not a simple process of receiving present stimuli in a defined moment. It necessarily involved memory of the past and readiness for future action. In this way, experience was constantly flowing through time, binding past, present and future indivisibly and giving experience its unique, changing patterns.

All this, Bergson argued, was ignored, or at best simplified, by most psychologists, especially by associationists such as Mill and Bain, who had assumed that it was the task of psychology to plot how one mental state, such as a perception, becomes associated with another, such as a memory. Bergson exempted William James from his criticisms, seeing similarities between his own ideas and James's notion of experience as 'a stream of consciousness' (Bergson, 1946). William James (1909) returned the compliment by saluting Bergson's stature as a great, original thinker.

Bergson's arguments against associationists are equally telling against the models of present-day psychologists (McNamara, 1996; Middleton and Brown, 2005). Cognitive psychologists often depict the mind as comprising interacting boxes of 'memories', 'attitudes', 'values', 'expectancies', 'emotional states', and so on. It is as if the mind were composed of various discrete components that operate in predictable directions. If one could halt the whole process at a given moment, one would be able to plot the position of each component. From a Bergsonian perspective, such a model confuses time with space, quality with quantity. It distorts the nature of lived experience, which cannot be understood by seeking to subdivide the mind into increasingly smaller units and ever shorter moments. Instead, psychology and philosophy need to start by recognizing the reality of duration, whose whole can only be grasped by an act of intuition.

What Bergson did not write

Bergson could well have used his critique of psychology as a starting-point for his analysis of humour. He could, for instance, have criticized the incongruity and superiority theories of laughter for assuming that laughter is produced by a sequence of separate mental states. Both theories assume a pattern of psychological change. The perceiver is in a serious frame of mind. Then there is a sudden perception, either of incongruity or of an inferior person, and this, in turn, is followed by the experience of joy which gives rise to the reaction of laughter.

A Bergsonian could point to a constant, but barely discussed, element in previous theories: the assumption of a sudden break in time. The notion of speed appears in Locke's definition of wit. According to Locke, wit does not merely consist of the assemblage of disparate ideas but of combining them 'with quickness' ([1690] 1964: 123). By 'quickness' Locke was not referring to an objectively measurable speed that could be checked against an agreed standard time for the assembly of ideas. The company does not stand by with its stop-watches at the ready in order to determine whether a remark is speedy enough to be deemed as witty. The quickness refers to listeners being caught by surprise and, thus, it refers to the expected tempo of interaction.

The notion of suddenness appears in other notable theories. Hobbes specified the feeling of superiority, which produces laughter, as an experience of 'sudden glory' (1999: 54). Campbell described wit as exciting 'in the mind an agreeable surprise' (*The Philosophy of Rhetoric*, 1856: 30). Schopenhauer ascribed laughter to 'the sudden perception of the incongruity' between a concept and the real objects that it describes (1987: 52). Thus, the theories do not assume that the perception of incongruity or a feeling of superiority is sufficient to provoke laughter on its own: the perception or feeling must be sudden. The theorists, however, did not specify what constitutes this suddenness.

Bain and Spencer implied a passage of time in their accounts of laughter. Pressure is built up and then it is released, not slowly but in a burst, as in Bain's image of schoolchildren rushing out of the school-gate. Spencer's idea of 'descending incongruities' implies an ordering that has to take place sequentially, as 'consciousness is unawares transferred from great things to small' (1864a: 206). In this context, 'unawares' indicates a temporal disjunction, as the mind has moved from one object to another without conscious intent. The same assumption is present in modern theories that claim humour is based upon a cognitive shift (e.g., Raskin, 1985; Giora, 1991).

Spencer's example of the goat wandering onto the theatrical stage depicts an unforeseen interruption as an expected sequence of action is suddenly, and without warning, disturbed. Groucho Marx in later life took to attending séances. During one, the medium claimed to have contacted a spirit from the other world. She asked if anyone in the room would like to ask it a question. Groucho called out 'What's the capital of North Dakota?' (Adamson, 1973).

A switch had been made from the ultra-serious to the comic. The medium had presumed that a certain type of question would be asked. Groucho had responded with a question that was knowingly inappropriate. The logic of Bergson's arguments in *Time and Free Will* and *Matter and Memory* would suggest that sequential theories of humour can only be approximations. There is no precise moment when the serious frame is broken and the comic one starts (Mulkay, 1988). Was Groucho funny the moment his hand shot up in the air? Or was it when he began to speak? Or when he began to say 'Dakota'? We imagine, even experience, a sudden disjunction in time. But each moment shades imperceptibly into the next. Because the start of Groucho's question seems to be in keeping with the expected movement of the social situation, the ending is unexpectedly funny. But that start is also reaching out towards the humorous ending. The precise moment of switching is unidentifiable. It is as if a conjuring trick has been performed, but the exact instant when the playing card was switched for the dove, or the innocent question switched for the disruptive one, is forever concealed. Therefore, Bergson's idea of duration could be used to criticize conventional psychological theories of humour. But Bergson did not attempt this explicitly in *Laughter*.

Bergson's critique of psychological theory contained another theme directly relevant to the study of humour. In *Time and Free Will* he discussed how easily we slip into the language of intensity when talking about feelings. But, he asks, is the difference between intense anger and not-so-intense anger really a difference in intensity? He suggests that ordinary people and psychological theorists confuse quality with quantity when they talk of emotions in this way.

There is no reason to go into the details of Bergson's subtle argument, except to note the implications for humour. We might imagine that loud, rollicking laughter is a sign of a more intensely felt experience than is a gentle smile. Bergson argued such an assumption would misunderstand the psychology of emotion. He followed Bain, Spencer and James in recognizing that muscular activity is centrally involved in the experience of emotion. For instance, the feeling of rage involves the clenching of teeth, the tightening of muscles, etc. However, Bergson argued that Spencer and Bain misunderstood the relation between experience and muscular activity. They had assumed that the emotion comprises nervous energy and that it is 'the emission of nervous force which consciousness perceives' (*Time and Free Will*, 1913: 21). The energy will seek muscular release, so a greater volume of energy will result in more muscular activity. Spencer and Bain assumed that because the energy is perceived as the emotion, a greater feeling of emotional intensity will accompany the increased muscular activity.

Bergson argued that Spencer and Bain had got things the wrong way round. The intensity of the emotion does not produce the muscular reaction, but the muscular reaction produces the feeling of intensity. We feel the muscular activity: the more muscles that are involved, the stronger will be the subjective experience of the emotion. This was in line with James's famous theory that we are sad because we weep and feel fear because we run. Accordingly, the feeling of intensity is related to the amount of the surface of the body that is involved in the muscular activity, rather than vice versa. Our trembling is not an outward sign of inner fear, as Spencer had supposed, but, as Bergson wrote in *Time and Free Will*, 'these movements form part of the terror itself: by their means the terror becomes an emotion capable of passing through different degrees of intensity' (1913: 30).

The implication for studying laughter is clear. Laughter is not the outward expression of an inner state, whose intensity determines the amount of nervous energy to be released in the muscular movements of laughing. Instead, the muscular reaction – whether the person uses a small number of muscles to register a weak smile or a much greater number to rock with loud laughter – is part of the sense of enjoyment. Because we laugh with muscular vigour, we will claim that we are feeling intense enjoyment.

Surprisingly little of this directly appears in *Laughter*. There are some passing criticisms of Bain and Spencer in relation to their respective theories of degradation and descending incongruities (1911a: 85ff., 124ff.). When Bergson discussed emotions in *Time and Free Will*, like James in his *The Principles of Psychology*, he omitted laughter. Yet, when Bergson specifically came to discuss laughter in his book on the subject, he largely omitted the psychological theorising.

Three observations

In *The Creative Mind* Bergson wrote that it was 'the duty of philosophy ... to lay down the general condition of the direct, immediate observation of oneself by oneself' (1946: 27). In accord with this principle, Bergson had begun *Matter and Memory* by observing his own perceptual experience. The opening sentence invited readers to assume that we know nothing about theories of matter and spirit. The second sentence then declared: 'Here I am in the presence of images, in the vaguest sense of the word, images perceived when my senses are opened to them, unperceived when they are closed' (*Matter and Memory*, 1911c: 1). He used a similar approach in a lecture about dreaming, delivered the year following the publication of *Laughter*. After a brief introduction he starts 'here, then am I dreaming', then proceeding to describe the complex nature of that experience (*Mind-Energy*, 1920: 84).

Bergson could have started *Laughter* in a similar way. 'Here I am laughing', he might have written, 'at something that has been perceived by my senses'. He might then have taken the topic from there, examining his own experience of a sudden change from seriousness to funniness. He could then have shown that there was no single point at which one mental state was suddenly replaced by an entirely different one. However, Bergson does not examine himself laughing. Instead, his stance is distanced and he puts the topic of laughter at a remove from himself.

In the opening section of *Laughter*, Bergson sets out three observations which 'we look upon as fundamental' because they indicate the field in which the comic is to be found (1911a: 3). He treats these observations not as hypotheses, but as facts. On their own, none of them is particularly original, or even controversial. When combined, they cease to be theoretically innocent, but dramatically point the study of laughter in a new theoretical direction. They jointly indicate the disciplinary functions of laughter.

The first observation, or fact, is that laughter is human. We laugh principally at humans, and only laugh at animals or things to the extent that they suggest human qualities. We do not typically find sunsets or mountain ranges hilarious, although we might laugh at a physical object produced by human hands – hence, we might laugh at a hat. Bergson notes that philosophers have often called humans 'the laughing animal', but they might have equally well defined humans as the animal 'which is laughed at' (ibid.: 4). By this reversal Bergson has immediately placed ridicule at the centre of his field. This is not to be an investigation, designed to leave readers with smiles on their faces and warmth in their hearts.

This impression is confirmed by Bergson's second observation that 'an absence of feeling' accompanies laughter. When we laugh 'we must, for the moment, put our affection out of court and impose silence upon our pity' (ibid.: 4). As always Bergson uses a striking phrase to express a striking idea: the comic 'demands something like a momentary anaesthesia of the heart' (ibid.: 5). In this regard, Bergson was depicting laughter as a temporary release from the usual demands of social feeling. George Herbert Mead was to express a similar idea. Normal social life involves us taking the attitude of the other, continually imagining how others feel and how they view ourselves. That attitude, which according to Mead, provides the basis for social life, involves 'a strenuous effort' (1962: 206). With laughter we free ourselves from the customary restrictions of social empathy, as the target of our mirth momentarily becomes an object, not a fellow human being.

Bergson's basic point about laughter's cruelty was not original, nor would he have claimed it so. James Beattie in *Essay on Laughter* had written of the opposition between laughter and sympathy (1779: 334). Sydney Smith argued that 'the sense of the humorous is as incompatible with tenderness and respect as with compassion' (1864: 134). Optimistically, Smith went on to suggest that it is 'a beautiful thing' that nature had affixed boundaries to the ridiculous, so that serious misfortune was never an object of laughter: 'Who is so *wicked* as to amuse himself with the infirmities of extreme old age? or to find subject for humour in the weakness of a perishing, dissolving body?' (ibid.: 134, emphasis in original). Perhaps Smith shielded himself from the crude laughter of the fair. Maybe the schoolboys of his time and class did not exchange the sort of 'sick jokes' that today take the infirmities of old age, not to mention corpses, as their subject matter (Dundes, 1987). Or perhaps, in asking his rhetorical questions, the Reverend Smith was trying to convince himself of the universal goodness of laughter.

In common with previous investigators of humour, Bergson did not discuss jokes. Had he done so, he would have found more than 'sick jokes' to confirm his second observation. Ordinarily, jokes depict scenes that bend the logic of everyday life. Listeners are expected to react to jokes differently than to non-joking stories (Mulkay, 1988; Norrick, 1993). After hearing the punch-line, it is inappropriate to ask what happened next: the joke and the world it depicts are finished. Crucially, listeners are not expected to express sympathy for the joke-figures. An example can be taken from the large collection of ethnic jokes discussed by Davies:

> An Aberdonian with a rotten molar went to a dentist who said he would charge £3 to pull it out.
> Aberdonian: 'Couldn't you loosen it for £1 so that I can pull it out myself?'
> (1990: 32)

To ask the joke-teller whether the Aberdonian had now recovered from his tooth-ache would demonstrate that the point of the joke had been missed, or that the recipient was displaying disapproval. Suffering often occurs in joke-stories. The following joke appears in a standard psychological test of reactions to humour:

> A blind man enters a department store, picks up his dog by the tail and begins to swing it over his head. A clerk hurries over and says, 'Can I help you, sir?' 'No thanks' the man replies. 'I'm just looking around.' (Mindess et al., 1985)

The point of the story is not to elicit concern for the pain suffered by the dog, nor for the owner's disability. Pain, cruelty and blindness pave the way to the punch-line and to the laughter.

Bergson's third observation was that laughter is socially shared: 'Laughter appears to stand in need of an echo' (1911a: 5). Significantly Bergson invites us to listen to the laughter of others, not to look inwardly at our own feelings when we laugh: 'Listen to it carefully: it is not an articulate, clear, well-defined sound' (ibid.: 5). He went on to suggest that laughter is something that reverberates from one person to another, 'something beginning with a crash, to continue in successive rumblings, like thunder in a mountain' (ibid.: 5–6). The imagery suggests the storms among the volcanic mountains of the Auvergne.

Bergson may not have invited his readers to imagine themselves laughing, but he asks them to imagine themselves not laughing. He writes that 'it may have perchance happened to you', when in a railway carriage or restaurant, to have witnessed a group laughing heartily at stories: 'Had you been one of their company, you would have laughed like them' (ibid.: 6). But you were not. You were on your own and had no desire to laugh.

The implication is that to understand laughter we must observe others, not draw inwards on ourselves. As Bergson argued, each subject demands its own approach. He notes that laughter is social: it is 'always the laughter of a group' (ibid.: 5). The theoretical movement is from psychology to sociology, from the intimacy of self-observation to the distance of observing others. It is as if we cannot be trusted to examine the anaesthesia of our own hearts.

Social functions

Bergson's third observation goes further than merely noting that people tend to laugh together. It sets up his theoretical reorientation. Having made the third observation, Bergson asserts: 'To understand laughter, we must put it back into its natural environment, which is society and above all must we determine the utility of its function which is a social one' (1911a: 7–8). Laughter, he claims, must 'answer to certain requirements of life in common' and thus must possess 'a *social* signification' (ibid.: 8, emphasis in original). Accordingly, the search for the social function of laughter 'will be the leading idea of all our investigations' (ibid.: 8).

Bergson's idea that one must seek the social function of laughter is not fortuitous. Echoes of Spencer can be heard, for Spencer had introduced the question of function into social analysis. In *The Study of Sociology*, Spencer had argued for a scientific approach to the study of society. That meant that the sociologist should adopt the methods of the biologist who studies organisms by examining their development, structure and function (1897: 59ff.). When considering any social practice or custom, the sociologist should seek to determine the structure of the practice and to discover how it functions, especially in relation to the ways it might enable the group to survive and to develop.

When Spencer examined laughter, he did not consider it to be a social practice. It was, for him, a physiological reflex, and, thus, its structure and function needed to be explored in physiological terms. Bergson transformed the question of humour by stressing that laughter belonged to the group. Its significance must, therefore, be social rather than physiological. Given the nature of Bergson's first two observations, the disturbing possibility is raised that ridicule and cruelty also have useful social functions.

Bergson's 'leading idea' turns the emphasis from the individual to the group and, crucially, from cause to effect. In this regard his approach to humour differed radically from that of most previous analysts, who had assumed that the key question was 'What causes the individual to laugh?' By contrast, Bergson was asking, 'What are the social effects of laughter?' Of earlier theorists, possibly only the Earl of Shaftesbury had looked at humour consistently in such a manner. He, too, saw ridicule as playing a central role in human affairs: it ensured that the truth of ideas could be tested in the right sort of social conditions. Unlike Bergson, Shaftesbury did not have the concept of 'function' in his conceptual vocabulary. For that, Bergson had Spencer to thank.

Modern sociologists take it as second nature to ask questions about the functions of social practices. They do so without pausing to ask where this habit of thinking originated. The sociologist Lewis Coser has claimed that it is 'a fact that very much sociological writing continues to use functional logic and reasoning but without doing so explicitly' (2003: 247). The usage is often implicit because structural-functionalism, which enjoyed great popularity as an explicit theory in the mid-twentieth century, has nowadays acquired a reputation for conservatism. The structural-functionalist assumes that each social practice possesses a useful function for maintaining the structure of society. If the sociologist concentrates on examining the structure of present social arrangements, then the resulting analysis can easily appear to carry conservative implications. In effect, the sociologist is saying that each social practice is usefully contributing to the functioning of the whole, and therefore change is either unnecessary or a threat to the structure of society.

By contrast, Spencer's sociology contained a historical theme, which ensures that the analysis does not necessarily defend present social structures. Spencer was asking whether social practices were functional to the extent that they aided the development and progress of society over time. Those practices that did not fulfil such developmental functions would tend to disappear if society is to progress. Spencer was not suggesting that every social practice necessarily possesses social utility for maintaining the social structure. In fact, he was greatly concerned that many social practices, such as the Poor Laws and the institution of the monarchy, were impeding social development. In the long term, according to Spencer, a society that preserves maladapted institutions, just like a biological organism that could not adapt to a changing environment, would be rendered extinct.

A few examples can be given to show how important the idea of functions has become to sociologists of humour. Over thirty years ago, Gary Fine (1983) wrote that, because the dominant theoretical paradigm in sociology was 'functionalism', sociologists should examine how humour functioned in social relations. He claimed that 'although dozens, if not hundreds, of specific functions of humour might be proposed, three seem of particular and general significance' (ibid.: 173). These were: promoting group cohesion, provoking intergroup conflict and providing social control. Apte (1983) has suggested that most anthropological approaches have been dominated by functional thinking. For instance, anthropologists see 'joking relationships' as serving the function of easing the strains of structurally problematic relations. Alberto Meluccci suggests that 'humour performs a vital function of releasing tension' (1996: 135).

In recent years, social analysts have attempted to examine the functions of humour within conversational interaction. Graham, Papa and Brooks (1992) claim to have identified twenty-four such functions. Hay (2000), examining conversation in friendship groups, claims that all humour functions to express solidarity with the audience. Beyond this 'general function', humour has, she argued, three 'specific functions', that fulfil 'solidarity-based, power-based or psychological based needs' (ibid.: 717ff.). Attardo in a semantic analysis of jokes claims that there are 'two general functions of humour in the broadest social and interpersonal perspective' (1993: 554): 'decommitment' and 'group identification'. By using the 'decommitment function' of humour, speakers can say things, such as criticisms or complaints, that would otherwise be socially threatening.

Janet Holmes (2000) has examined how 'humour functions in the workplace'. She shows that humour can be used to soften orders or to question authority – this is similar to what Attardo identifies as a 'decommitment' function. Du Pré (1998) uses functional terminology when examining how humour is used in health settings. She writes that 'some amount of "goofing off" may serve a useful function' (ibid.: 22) and that in potentially embarrassing situations humour 'performs a face-saving function' (ibid.: 24). Norrick (1993, 2003) emphasizes the 'metalingual function of joking' that enables groups to label some forms of talk as inappropriate within ongoing interaction.

Such analysts may not agree about the precise number or nature of the functions that humour serves, but they do agree that it does serve functions. The language of 'function' lends itself to a positive view of social action. Bergson sought to discover the functional utility, *la fonction utile*, of laughter (1900: 8): the phrase suggests that laughter, by serving a social function, will be useful. Today many analysts of laughter imply that humour is useful for maintaining social relations and averting a breakdown in communication. Norrick, having suggested the need to recognize 'a multiplicity of functions for laughter' (1993: 42), goes on to claim that 'we are developing an interactional perspective in which humour is seen as helping smooth the work in everyday conversation, as well as offering us a chance to present a self, test for common ground, and create rapport in an entertaining fashion' (ibid.: 43). The stress here is on the beneficial, useful things that humour can do. It is the same in Du Pré's analysis. Humour, she suggests, enables patients to maintain dignity, to facilitate empathy, to voice complaints in non-threatening ways and generally 'humour seems to facilitate quick and persuasive communication' (1998: 122). Again, these are assumed to be positive achievements. The writers of popular manuals do not hold back on humour's positive functions. According to Hageseth, 'humour's first function in life is to convey love and security' (1988: 39).

Of course, some analysts recognize that not all of humour's functions are so obviously positive. Gary Fine writes that humour can function to provoke conflict between groups, as well as to consolidate group cohesion. It has been found that people in high pressure jobs may tell jokes among themselves to alleviate pressure at the end of the day. Social workers, for example, may mock their clients and their problems (Sullivan, 2000). The morale of the social work team may be well served by such sessions of joking. However, the social workers may also be troubled by the problematic nature of their joking, but feel powerless to stop themselves from enjoying this fun.

Even when faced by both the positives and negatives of humour, researchers often show a tendency to stress the positive benefits over the negative consequences. As was noted earlier in Chapter 2, Berger (1997) asserts that the 'sociopositive' functions in general outweigh the 'socionegative' ones. Hay (2000) emphasizes the function of solidarity over division in her data. Norrick (1993) notes that mockery and sarcasm seem to be geared for 'animosity rather than rapport and this makes their interpersonal function as a whole problematic'. However, he suggests that 'a customary joking relationship may serve a rapport function between some conversationalists' and this helps to explain the apparently negative role of mocking and sarcasm in their talk exchanges (ibid.: 43–4). Thus, apparently negative functions are seen to be actually positive.

All this suggests the sort of bias towards the positive that characterizes the tone of ideological positivism. Bergson's *Laughter* might be seen to be taking a step towards this outlook, for he was proposing to search for humour's socially useful function. Yet, there is a crucial difference between Bergson's social analysis of humour and many later sociological approaches. Ideological positivists assume that humour is both intrinsically positive and also that it fulfils positive functions. The negatives are seen as unfortunate side-effects. By contrast, Bergson's observations suggest something more troubling. Humour, far from being intrinsically warm-hearted and positive, has a cold cruelty at its core. According to the assumptions of ideological positivism, Bergson was depicting humour to be essentially negative, while at the same time he was suggesting that it possesses useful functions. In so doing, he precludes the possibility that the positives can be brought into alignment.

Necessary and surplus functions

Herbert Spencer distinguished between different types of social function. There were some functions (and structures) that were universal, some that were general and some were specific. Biology provided his model. Biologists distinguish between those structures and functions that are common to all organisms, those that are common to species and those that are found in only particular sub-species (1897: 59). Given that human societies cannot be categorized as easily as biological organisms, one might collapse Spencer's tri-partite distinction into two: there are functions that are universal to all societies and there are functions that are specific to certain types of society. One might argue that universal functions are necessary for social life in general: the very continuity of social life would be threatened should these functions be unfulfilled. Then, there are practices that might be functional for certain types of social interaction, but these types of social interaction are not themselves necessary for the overall existence of social life. One might call the former types of function *necessary* and the latter *surplus*. This distinction echoes Herbert Marcuse's famous distinction in *Eros and Civilization* between necessary and surplus repression – a distinction that itself echoes Marx's even more famous distinction between necessary and surplus value.

Most of the modern sociological analyses of humour deal with surplus functions. Joking relationships are not presumed to be necessary for the continuation of social life in general, but they emerge in particular types of social arrangement, which marks some social relationships with structural tensions. Similarly, analysts might claim that joking enables commands or criticisms to be softened. They can point to types of social interaction where the humorous down-toning of criticisms enables the interaction to proceed without rupture. The analyst is not saying that every language must possess rhetorical devices for jokey down-toning, and that social life would be unsustainable without such devices. Although politeness might be universal – for every language must have codes for appropriate and inappropriate talk – particular codes of politeness need not be universal (Billig, 1999; Brown and Levinson, 1987).

Humour can be seen to provide useful rhetorical devices that help out in certain social situations. The doctor may use humour to ease a potentially embarrassing medical examination: the humour is a welcome extra, rather than integral to the examination itself. As described in the previous chapter, James Sully quoted a British colonialist who said she used humour to make Africans perform tasks, where other colonialists might have threatened them with a gun. Humour was here being seen as something surplus to the exercise of power. Similarly, modern business management books recommend that managers should show humour where appropriate (e.g. Barsoux, 1993). The books of good management practice are not suggesting that lack of humour would inevitably result in corporate bankruptcy, or that capitalism would implode were the managerial class incapable of delivering commands with jokey asides.

Most sociological work on humour points towards the surplus rather than necessary functions of humour. The trend in contemporary sociology is towards collecting details, as analysts observe the micro-aspects of interaction. The result is to proliferate functional analyses by seeing how particular ways of expressing laughter might function in various types of conversational context. The accumulation of such evidence about humour's various conversational and interactional functions is unlikely to produce an overall social theory of humour. The construction of social theory depends upon selection and exaggeration, rather than the accumulation of detail. The social theorist will accord one type of function particular importance, selecting it theoretically above other functions. Theory, in this respect, can involve a leap of imagination from the surplus to the necessary. The theorist will be saying that one type of social practice does more than help out social actors who happen to find themselves in a troubling social situation. The theorist will be asserting that one type of practice is necessary for social life.

This is what Bergson was aiming to do in *Laughter*. He sought the big picture – the big exaggeration. He was not attempting to categorize as many forms of humour as possible, in order to see how their micro-mechanisms operated in different forms of social interaction. By posing the question about humour's social function in the singular (*la fonction utile* rather than *les fonctions utiles*) and, then, by taking the risk of theoretical exaggeration, Bergson was able to produce the first social theory of humour.

The comic and its function

Laughter has become famous for Bergson's characterization of what is comic. He followed neither the theory of incongruity nor that of degradation, both of which he saw as covering only a small part of what is comic. In their place, he proposed a highly original account of the causes of laughter, drawing upon elements from both those earlier theories. Bergson argued that laughter was provoked by rigid or mechanical behaviour. He supported this idea with a series of examples. We laugh if a pedestrian fails to dodge an obstacle on the pavement; or we may laugh at an absent-minded professor, who dips his pen into a pot of glue that has been placed on his desk where his inkwell normally stands (1911a: 8–11).

Bergson argued that such misfortunes occur because of inelastic behaviour. The man tripping in the street should have altered his pace to avoid the obstacle in his path. Instead his behaviour demonstrated a lack of elasticity: 'That is the reason of the man's fall' and also of observers' laughter (ibid.: 9). Throughout the book Bergson discusses different forms of comedy, especially theatrical comedy. Each time he argues that the essence of the comedy resides in some form of rigidity. The examples are explained in terms of the general principle that 'the attitudes, gestures and movements of the human body are laughable in exact proportion as that body reminds us of a mere machine' (ibid.: 29). Thus, the comic is 'something mechanical encrusted on the living' (ibid.: 49) and 'we laugh every time a person gives us the impression of being a thing' (ibid.: 58). Bergson presents this idea, not as a hypothesis, but as a 'new law' (ibid.: 58; see also p. 29).

Since the person is not a thing, Bergson's 'law' suggests that we are laughing at the incongruity of the human appearing as a non-human object. Bergson's point is that we do not laugh at incongruity *per se* but at this very specific incongruity. Theories of incongruity fail to say why some incongruities, but not others, fail to raise laughter. It is the same with degradation. Rigid behaviour is liable to result in misfortune: the professor who dips his pen in the glue-pot looks stupid. Misfortune is not funny in itself, for many misfortunes are tragic rather than comic. It is this particular genus of misfortune that is found funny.

Having outlined what provokes laughter, Bergson then describes the function of laughter. He assumes that 'life and society require of each of us ... a constantly alert attention that discerns the outlines of the present situation, together with a certain elasticity of mind and body to enable us to adapt ourselves in consequence' (ibid.: 18). Bergson is suggesting that inelastic behaviour is non-adapted. His words again echo Spencer, who in *The Principles of Psychology* had distinguished between behaviour that is adapted to the environment and behaviour that is non-adapted. Bergson's argument proceeded along parallel lines, as he wrote that society needs a way to prevent 'the easy automatism of acquired habits' and to avoid 'inelasticity of character, of mind and even of body' (1911a: 19). Because such inelasticity is not functional, 'it is *rigidity* that society eyes with suspicion' (ibid.: 138, emphasis in original).

Bergson highlights the disciplinary function that laughter fulfils in helping to discourage inelasticity. Here he cashes out the theoretical reversal contained in his first observation, namely, that humans are the laughed-at animal. Laughter does not exist to ease the stresses and strains of social life, transmuting potentially negative situations into tolerably positive ones. It exists to discourage the sort of non-adapted behaviour that threatens all social development. In Bergson's phrase, 'rigidity is the comic, and laughter is its corrective' (ibid.: 21).

Members of society cannot shut themselves away from others; they must be attentive to their social surroundings and each person 'must model himself on his environment' (ibid.: 135). Laughter is a corrective because people dread being laughed at. Bergson's observation about laughter's cruelty is crucial. He comments that 'society holds suspended over each individual member, if not the threat of correction, at all events the prospect of a snubbing, which, although it is slight, is none the less dreaded' (ibid.: 135). Laughter, he continues, is 'always rather humiliating for the one against whom it is directed'; therein lies 'the function of laughter' (ibid.; 135).

The theory tightly links cause and effect. Laughter's cause – namely rigidity – produces the effect of ridicule that, in its turn, is designed to prevent further repetitions of the cause. Bergson was attributing a necessary function to laughter. He was proposing that all societies need to hold the threat of mockery over their members. Otherwise their members might be tempted into the sort of rigidity that would threaten the continuation of society. In consequence, laughter, by means of the disciplinary function of ridicule, 'pursues a utilitarian aim of general improvement' (ibid.: 20). Without laughter, social life would fall prey to rigidity; it would ossify. That is why the cruelty of ridicule is necessary.

Body and spirit of laughter

Bergson's theory is well equipped to account for the universality of humour. He assumes that by nature we are constituted to find rigidity comic, in order to assist our adaptation to a world that demands elasticity. Consequently, all human social life benefits from the disciplinary properties of laughter. In addition, Bergson's theory has no problem in accounting for the social aspects of laughter in the way that purely psychological theories do. The classic theories of superiority and incongruity have difficulty in explaining why communal laughter should be so much greater than individual laughter. Bergson turns around such theories by starting from the assumption that humour fulfils a social rather than a psychological function. His model differs from that of Bain who saw laughter as a release from social authority: the schoolboys rush out laughing from the disciplines of the schoolroom. The rebellious nature of laughter was also to feature strongly in Freud's theory. In Bergson's vision, by contrast, laughter is the mechanism of discipline, the punishment in the class-room of life.

In one sense, Bergson's theory finds common ground with Hogarth's analysis of the comic. Both Bergson and Hogarth give priority to the visual over the verbal. Hogarth in his *The Analysis of Beauty* (1753) suggested that comic figures should be drawn with sharp lines, for flowing, sinuous curves denoted grace. In a scene of dancers, included for illustrative purposes in *The Analysis of Beauty*, figures, whose limbs were angular, appear as comically ungainly, while the dancers whose figures comprise flowing lines are unfunnily graceful. Bergson goes further. The graceful movement can, in certain circumstances, be all the funnier. The more elegantly the absent-minded professor dips his pen into the glue-pot, the more comical is the result. It is not the action itself that is funny but the unadapted absent-mindedness that accompanies it. As Bergson commented, 'absent-mindedness is always comical' and 'the deeper the absent-mindedness the higher the comedy' (1911a: 146).

Bergson's identification of the comic with rigidity and absent-mindedness was connected to some of the most basic themes of his philosophy, although he did not specifically draw out these connections in *Laughter*. Bergson rigorously opposed abstract philosophical systems that seem to bear little or no relation to the complex reality of life as it is experienced. Philosophers, who step into puddles, because they are gazing at the clouds are, indeed, comical figures for Bergson – although he was too well mannered to dwell on the point. Not only are they comical figures, but also their philosophies are likely to be ludicrous. Again, Bergson was too polite to say this. But it is implied by his philosophical position.

Bergson had a number of philosophical reasons for identifying the comic with rigidity. First, Bergson placed great importance upon the operation of memory. In *Matter and Memory* he argued that we cannot experience the present in any meaningful way unless we have memory. However, the faculty of memory does not operate simply by associating the present sensation with a past one, as Bain and other associationists assumed. Memory is a form of preparedness for action. The selection of the past memory is the means of preparing for the future moment on which experience of the present depends. If absent-mindedness were a general condition, then the individual would not be able to function in the world. The smooth interweaving of past, present and future would be disrupted. Thus, absent-mindedness represents a practical failure. Fear of mockery will function to prevent the ordinary person from too much absent-mindedness.

There is another theme that directly connects Bergson's idea of comedy with his anti-materialist philosophy. Bergson constantly argued against materialists who viewed humans as just bodily machines. In Bergson's philosophy, life is not comprised purely of material elements: the world of the spirit, or the intangible force of life, has equal reality. Bergson's theory of comedy rules out the possibility that humans can merely be physical automata. We cannot just be machines, for the more machine-like we appear, the more risible we become in the eyes of our fellow humans. The theory of incongruity is correct inasmuch as it predicts that we will find comedy in the sight of a human behaving incongruously as a machine. This, of course, assumes that by nature humans are not machines. Our laughter, then, reflects that part of ourselves that is not machine-like.

Laughter contains hints of the evolutionary themes that Bergson was to develop in *Creative Evolution*. The echoes of Spencer contained in the terms 'adaptation' and 'function' were not accidental, but Bergson was to go way beyond Spencer. He wished to show that the non-material spirit worked within the processes of evolution. Indeed, it is only because of the force of the spirit, seeking to overcome the inertness of matter, that progressive evolution is possible. In *Laughter* Bergson alludes briefly to a conflict between matter and spirit. He claims that our imagination 'has a very clear-cut philosophy of its own' that is beyond the scope of reason (1911a: 28). When we look at our fellow humans, we see 'the effort of a soul which is shaping matter, a soul which is infinitely supple and perpetually in motion, subject to no law of gravitation' (ibid.: 28).

In *Creative Evolution* Bergson was to argue that living matter contains a vital impulse – a spiritual force – that is constantly seeking to overcome the limitations of matter. Because the vital impulse acts against the inertness of matter, living organisms do not simply reproduce themselves but change in the course of reproduction. Hence, the vital force provides the natural variation on which Darwinian theory is predicated. According to Bergson, there is a continual conflict between the spiritual impetus of life, or *élan vital*, and the material substances that enclose it. Such a conflict lies at the heart of evolution for 'the evolution of the organized world is the unrolling of this conflict' (1911b: 254).

The implication is clear. Without the spiritual force of life, there can be no evolution. At best, there would just be rigid reproduction of what already exists. Since circumstances change, this rigidity would preclude adaptation and, thus, life itself would be threatened. Traces of this argument can be found in *Laughter*, as Bergson suggests that the spirit through laughter prevents the human from being just a body. Bergson describes the soul as imparting 'a portion of its winged lightness to the body that it animates' (1911a: 28). Nevertheless, matter is 'obstinate and resists', forever obstructing and blunting the force of the soul: 'It would fain immobilize the intelligently varied movements of the body in stupidly contracted grooves' (ibid.: 28). When matter succeeds in dulling 'the outward life of the soul', it achieves 'an effect that is comic' (ibid.: 29). The body stumbles; scholars dip their pens in the glue – all because the clod-hopping body has momentarily eclipsed the lightness of the soul. Fear of mockery prevents this happening too frequently.

Bergson's account provides no equality between body and mind. It is not as if we sometimes laugh at the body and sometimes at the mind. The comic imagination represents a revenge of the spirit against the body, and not vice versa. By laughing at bodily stumbling and at absent-mindedness, society protects its creative spirit against the threatening dullness of the body. In this way, society can preserve its necessary elasticity. It is a paradox that the soul should trick the body by recruiting such a bodily response – the paroxysm of laughter – to achieve its mockery. But then, in Bergson's view, the body is a bit dim. It wouldn't get the joke.

Laughing at novelty and rigidity

Bergson's theory contains a tension between the idea that laughter serves a disciplinary function and the idea that laughter functions in the service of elasticity. The tension arises because the disciplinary functions of laughter often operate to achieve conservatism and conformity rather than elasticity and the free imagination of the spirit. This tension is a particular version of a more general problem facing any theory that claims to have discovered the objective nature of the comic. It has difficulty in explaining why humans do not uniformly laugh at the same 'objectively' funny things.

As far as Bergson's theory is concerned, the problem can be stated quite simply. He implies that rigid actions are inherently comic. However, not all people will laugh equally at the sight of rigidity. Some might sit stony-faced as the most skilled clowns go through their repertoire. Bergson's theory also can be taken as suggesting laughter is on the side of innovation against conservatism, although, to be fair, Bergson did not specifically assert this. But humour, just as much as any other rhetorical device, does not belong to one party. It can be recruited in the service of conservatism as well as radicalism.

Bergson's book *Le Rire* bore the same title as a popular Parisian magazine of the day. The magazine was on the side of the innovators as it mocked stuffy conservatism. It regularly reproduced illustrations by Toulouse-Lautrec and other free-spirited defiers of convention. In this regard it was so different from the British comic magazine *Punch* which by that time had become the voice of solid bourgeois sense, constantly comparing '"what an Englishman likes" with perceived threats to the standard' (Simpson, 1994: 135). *Punch* mocked the avant-garde, especially the aesthetic movement. The cartoons of George du Maurier poked fun at the 'Cimabue Browns', the fictional family who enthusiastically embraced all the artistic crazes of the period (Lambourne, 1983).

The tension between the conservative and radical tendencies of ridicule can be seen in Bergson's theory. He raises an idea that would have been shocking to the eighteenth-century theorists of humour, especially those who mentioned the disciplinary aspects of humour. Writers such as Lord Kames, Dugald Stewart and the Earl of Shaftesbury had presumed that mockery discouraged minor vice. By contrast, Bergson argued that immorality is not inherently comic in the way that inflexibility is, for 'a flexible vice may not be so easy to ridicule as a rigid virtue' (1911a: 138). Comic characters, he added, make us laugh 'by reason of their *unsociability* rather than their *immorality*' (ibid.: 139, emphasis in original).

By the term 'unsociability' (*insociabilité*) Bergson was describing the behaviour of someone who is removed from the company of others. But he also meant the person who constantly acts in ways that do not accord with demands of social life. In this wider sense of unsociability, the comic character may continually speak too loudly, dress too flamboyantly and show a general unawareness of the subtle codes of appropriate behaviour. Since the comic character fails to fit in with prevailing norms of conduct, then what is different can easily become the butt of humour. Therefore, according to Bergson, the comic is 'so frequently dependent on the manners or ideas, or to put it bluntly, on the prejudices of society' (ibid.: 138).

In an important respect, Bergson's contrast between flexibility and morality is too rigid. The apparently minor codes of politeness typically are codes of morality. As micro-sociologists have stressed, social actors often invest the little codes of everyday behaviour with a sense of morality (Brown and Levinson, 1987; Garfinkel, 1967; Goffman, 1981). The person who asks inappropriate questions or who wears the wrong clothing may be a comic figure in fictional television entertainment. In real life they are likely to be criticized for their 'rudeness' or lack of 'sensitivity', and so on. Being 'unsociable' itself often carries a tone of criticism – as in 'why are you always so unsociable?' Social ideals permeate the micro-processes of everyday talk and behaviour. Indeed, Bergson commented that 'there is no essential difference between the social ideal and the moral' (1911a: 138).

The 'unsociability' that the comic figure displays can represent a failure to comply, and, in such cases, laughter can be functioning to impose social conformity. Yet, it may be argued that social conformity demands flexibility and, therefore, Bergson was correct to identify the comic with inflexibility. In order to conform – to adapt oneself to the changing demands of a continuing social situation – one has to be aware of the actions of others. The rigidity of sticking to one's own purposes can appear socially inappropriate and, thus, comically ludicrous. However, the social awareness that is necessary for skilled adaptation can itself be a form of conservatism. The laughter, that, according to Bergson, was functioning to protect the elasticity of the spirit and to encourage social flexibility, may, in fact, be policing social actors to ensure that they follow the customs, routines and prejudices of society.

The power of Bergson's argument is that he gives theoretical priority to the disciplinary functions of laughter. Any rebellious function is secondary. The primary link is between conservatism and laughter. Society needs to impose its customs and rules; adults must teach the codes of talk and behaviour to the next generation; laughter has its primary function in discouraging infractions of such codes and customs. In this regard, and contrary to the tenor of some of Bergson's remarks, laughter functions conservatively to discourage the sort of social innovation that inevitably breaks rules.

Bergson implied that a certain type of human action – the rigid action – is by its nature the primary target of ridicule. However, the well-adapted social elasticity, that seems to be beyond ridicule, is itself a form of social obedience and, thus, a rigidity of the spirit. A Bergsonian could reply: that is precisely why socially conventional behaviour can be mocked. In so saying, the notion of 'rigidity' is in danger of becoming over-stretched or too elastic. It might be simpler to say that no form of social action is, by its nature, protected from the possibility of ridicule. Conventionality and unconventionality, social rigidity and social adaptability, all can be reduced to comic absurdity. As John Brown had argued in response to the Earl of Shaftesbury, even the great and good can be made to look ridiculous. Not even philosophical elasticity can provide shelter from mockery. The body can strike back humorously at the intellect. Philosophers present an easy target, even if they avoid puddles and glue-pots.

Imagine Bergson delivering a lecture on the vital spirit. He had an impressive presence and his lectures were great occasions. One observer described how 'silence would descend upon the hall and the audience feel a secret tremble within when they saw him quietly approach from the back of the amphitheatre, seat himself beneath the shaded lamp, his hands free of manuscript or notes' (Chevalier, 1928: 60). Imagine, too that the audience has sat still for over an hour, listening to his melodious voice. They have never heard anyone speak with such gentle authority and profundity. They are being taken to the heart of philosophy – to the nature of truth itself. At the end of the lecture, Bergson asks if anyone has a question they would like to ask. At the back, a man with a moustache, not unlike Bergson's own, stands up: 'Well then, professor, what's the capital of North Dakota?'

Pleasure and unconscious intent

Bergson's decision not to approach the topic of laughter through an analysis of experience fits well with his stress upon social function. The social significance of laughter is not to be found within the conscious experience of the person who is laughing. Someone observing a comic *faux pas* does not consciously think 'That person over there is behaving with untoward rigidity, so I had better chuckle to deter any repetition.' The laughter is spontaneously emitted without its function being represented in conscious awareness. This gap between function and experience is common within functional social analysis. Most functional explanations in sociology do not rest upon the assumption of conscious intent. The reasons that people give for their actions may not be the same as functional properties that the social analyst ascribes to those actions. As such, functions operate behind the back of the social actors. Bergson's analysis of the social functions of laughter, in part, bears the traces of such social functionalism. But in a crucial respect he goes further, to suggest that unconscious motives may also be operating.

The issue of pleasure must be central to an understanding of laughter. Why should there be pleasure in viewing what is to be disciplined? Bergson claimed that the 'pleasure caused by laughter ... is not an unadulterated pleasure' for 'it always implies a secret or unconscious intent' (1911a: 135–6). The unconscious intent refers to the disciplinary aspect: 'In laughter we always find an unavowed intention to humiliate, and consequently to correct our neighbour, if not in his will, at least in his deed' (ibid.: 136). The notion of 'a secret or unconscious intent' is interesting. Actually, the phrase does not appear in the original French text, where Bergson says that laughter is always mixed with *'une arrière pensée'* (an ultimate aim) that society has for us and that we may not have ourselves (1900: 139).

One might ask how *une arrière pensée* came to be rendered in the English translation as 'a secret or unconscious intent'. Given the care with which Bergson supervised the English translations of his works, a simple error is highly improbable. The translators of *Laughter* specifically declared that their translation 'has been revised in detail by the author himself' ('Translators' preface', 1911a: v). Between the original publication in 1900 and 1911, when the translation appeared, the intellectual landscape had changed. Not only had Bergson's name become well known but so also had Freud's. By 1911 the phrase 'a secret and unconscious intent' would carry a Freudian resonance lacking in *une arrière pensée*. It would convey that a motive had been repressed, or censored, from conscious awareness.

Bergson, an early reader of Freud's work, would have been well aware of the resonance. Elsewhere he indicated that his approach could be combined with that of Freud (i.e., 1920: 107). The Freudian idea of secret intentions implies much more than that social actors may not be aware of the effects of their actions on society. It implies a hidden secret. In the case of laughter, Bergson implies what this secret might be. There is an unavowed intention to humiliate our neighbour. The phrase *'l'intention inavouée d'humilier'* appears in the original edition (1900: 139). There the intention is simply 'unavowed', but the addition of psychoanalytic echoes takes the argument a step further. The intention is disavowed, or subjected to the processes of denial.

Bergson did not elaborate a theory of the unconscious. His two earlier psychological works emphasized that the perception of the present did not merely consist of passively receiving incoming sensations, but was affected by the motives of the perceiver. In *Laughter*, Bergson alludes to these ideas. He says that 'I look and I think I see' and that 'I listen and I think I hear'. However, we deceive ourselves if we believe that we perceive the world directly and dispassionately: 'What I see and hear of the outer world is purely and simply a selection made by my senses to serve as a light to my conduct.' In consequence, 'my senses and my consciousness ... give me no more than a practical simplification of reality' (1911a: 151). Indeed, our senses simplify the nature of our inner sensations. All is distorted, or at least simplified, in order that we may function practically in everyday life.

It is a short step from this to say that, in order to function comfortably in the social world, we hide aspects of our own conduct from our own understanding. The components of Bergson's argument suggest such a possibility. The pleasure of laughter depends on a lack of sympathy or a temporary anaesthesia of the heart. The cruelty of our laughter does not reflect well on us. The desire to humiliate the person at whom we laugh is unadmitted, unavowed – to be disavowed should we ever be challenged. This is a secret intent – secret, not just from others, but also from ourselves.

This suggests that the analysis of laughter's pleasures requires a psychology of unconscious motivation. Bergson did not explicitly provide this, but his own writing exemplifies the resistance that such an undertaking might elicit. Right at the end of *Laughter*, Bergson returns to the issue of laughter's cruelty. He comments that 'there is nothing very benevolent in laughter' for 'it seems rather inclined to return evil for evil' (ibid.: 194). Bergson mentions that laughter cannot be 'kind-hearted' for its 'function is to intimidate by humiliating' (p. 198). In order to function as a corrective, 'it must make a painful impression on the person against whom it is directed' for 'by laughter society avenges itself for the liberties taken with it'. It would, comments Bergson, 'fail in its object if it bore the stamp of sympathy or kindness' (ibid.: 197).

Worse than bringing pain to its victims, the practitioners of laughter take pleasure in doing so. Laughter, writes Bergson, could not fulfil its functions had nature not 'implanted in the best of men, a spark of spitefulness' (ibid.: 198). Hobbes seems to return, as Bergson writes that the person who laughs at another becomes 'more self-assertive and conceited than ever' (ibid.: 199). This is pointing towards a psychology of laughter's sadistic pleasures. Bergson, having opened up this possibility, suddenly closes it down: 'Perhaps we had better not investigate this point too closely, for we should not find anything very flattering to ourselves' (ibid.: 198–9).

Two paragraphs later the book ends, shut tight. Bergson has illustrated, but not explained, something about the cruelty of laughter. He suggests that we do not want to look too severely upon this aspect of ourselves. Bergson expresses sympathy with this avoidance. It is a curious position for a philosopher, who devoted himself to investigating the nature of human experience.

Ridicule may depend on more than anaesthesia of the heart; it may also require anaesthesia of self-knowledge. Ridicule and cruelty may supply two sharp angles, with self-deception making the third point of humour's triangle. When the triangle of laughter is displayed as a decoration of social life, the whole shape glitters with the allure of a diamond catching the sun. We admire and enjoy the comic spirit. Dazzled by the light and trusting in our sense of beauty, we forget the cutting power of the diamond's edges.

Without words

Bergson's view of humour is characterized by a further, highly individual feature – the priority given to the visual over the verbal. Bergson's prototypes of the comic tend to be wordless, such as the slapstick of the professor's pen or the pedestrian tripping in the street. This is so different from the great incongruity theorists of the eighteenth century. Bodily humour was definitely of a lower order, associated with the crudities of the carnival. In those days, even rhetoricians of gesture tended to look down on the humour of bodily pantomime (e.g., Gilbert Austin's *Chironomia: Or a Treatise on Rhetorical Delivery*, 1806). To be sure, Addison and other incongruity theorists did not like word play for its own sake. The pun was in bad taste. Nevertheless, they presumed that true wit combined dissonant ideas. To accomplish such witty combinations, words were required. The summit of wit did not involve glue-pots. It was *le bon mot*.

In the twentieth century, some theorists, most notably Mikhail Bakhtin, have looked favourably on the vulgar laughter of the carnival, seeing it as an act of riotous subversion. Bergson's appreciation of wordless, bodily humour did not have this aesthetic. He was not championing the vulgar over the elite. He was careful to praise the construction of character in 'high-class comedy' (1911a: 142). High-class theatrical comedy does not aspire to heights of tragic drama. Whereas tragedy transcends ordinary life, comedy 'is situated on the border-line between art and life' (ibid.: 150). The comic writer must dull the audience's sympathy for the character and allow gesture to appear more important than action.

By means of close-up shots, film and television can convey a subtlety of gesture that the old stage actor could not. It would be presumptuous to speculate which modern television comedies Bergson would have liked or disliked. Nevertheless, some comedies seem to fit his descriptions well. Comedies of embarrassment such as Larry David's *Curb Your Enthusiasm* or Ricky Gervais's *The Office* situate themselves on that border between real-ity and fiction. The gestures and expressions of the characters count for more than the scripted wit. The Larry David character is a professional comedy-writer and Gervais plays a would-be comedian. The audience is not invited to laugh at their comic gags but at their gestures when their wit fails.

Bergson's theoretical downgrading of verbal humour reflects intuition-ism's search for the reality of constant change behind the appearance of fixity. Language can hinder this search, for it contains fixed categories that seem to take objects for granted. Moreover, language contains psychological terms that distort the reality of inner psychological states. We would not be able to talk of our feelings of 'love' or 'hate' if we did not have these terms in our vocabulary. However, the language of emotions comes at a cost. To have such general concepts, we have to reduce our inner states 'to a more and more impersonal form and to impose names on them – in short, to make them enter the current of social life' (*Matter and Memory*, 1911c: 242). Yet, each of us, writes Bergson, has our own style of loving and hating and this 'love or hatred reflects his whole personality' (*Time and Free Will*, 1913: 164).

Our shared vocabulary cannot represent this individuality. It reduces the individual elements, indeed the very nature of the experience, to 'the imper-sonal aspect' (ibid.: 164). If the impersonal nature of language, which permits social communication, distorts the unique nature of experience, then philosophers should seek to look behind language, in order to intuit those realities that transcend the verbal world. The paradox is that Bergson, like any philosopher, had to use words to produce his philosophy.

The distrust of language appears as a theme in *Laughter*. Bergson suggested that we do not see things themselves but in most cases 'we confine ourselves to reading the labels affixed to them'. This occurs because the 'word, which only takes note of the most ordinary function and commonplace aspect of the thing, intervenes between it and ourselves, and would conceal its form from our eyes' (ibid.: 153). This is as true of the perception of inner states as it is of outer physical objects. Our inner states, writes Bergson, are screened from us, because we interpret them with the categories of impersonal language. Instead, we should be paying attention to the feeling itself 'with those innumerable fleeting shades of meaning and deep resounding echoes that make it something altogether our own' (ibid.: 153). Only novelists, poets and artists can really capture this inner reality. The fixed terms of everyday language or conventional psychology come nowhere near to doing so.

Bergson affirms the need to place laughter in its social context, but social contexts, in general, are saturated with language and communication. The social context of humour is no exception. Bergson may be correct in supposing that much of what we laugh at is bodily gesture or social inelasticity – although verbal jokes, puns and ironic remarks, etc. also play large roles in social life. However, the analysis of laughter is not confined to identifying the objects of humour. As Bergson stressed, the action of laughing is itself a social act. Here Bergson does not develop his analysis.

Bergson's commitment to a social analysis of laughter would seem to be pointing towards the need to analyze the micro-functions of laughter within social interaction. Having asserted that laughter in general plays a necessary, disciplinary function, Bergson then becomes impatient with social analysis. He wants to get beyond language, beyond the petty details of ordinary interaction, in order to reach towards the truths of experience that we ignore in our everyday understandings. Only if laughter is an expression of the winged spirit of the soul in its battle against the inertness of matter does it continue to interest Bergson philosophically.

Sometimes a theoretical weakness – or a commitment, despite everything else, to a particular way of viewing the world – can reflect well on the theorist. Bergson was committed to the idea that philosophy should not start with abstract systems. It should start with the experience of the philosopher. Yet, Bergson, by upbringing, class and personal taste, was not someone who would consider it proper to divulge private information in public. None of his books remotely resembles Rousseau's *Confessions* or even Descartes' personal account of how he came to doubt all but his own existence. Bergson's analyses of his own experiences are cut off from the particularities of his own life. He gives away no secrets. Certainly, he does not parade suffering as a warrant for his credentials to speak about experience. He is, thus, remote from today's culture that values public self-revelation as a morally existential act.

Bergson lived a quiet life with his wife and daughter Jeanne in their secluded house in Anteuil. The quietness would have been significant. Jeanne, who was born seven years before the publication of *Laughter*, could neither hear nor speak. Bergson's philosophy, that downgraded the importance of language, must have matched the quality of his home life. He could utter no *bons mots* or funny jokes to Jeanne, nor receive them in return. Her spirit of creativity – her life force – would be deadened had it purely depended upon the utterance of words. No doubt, those proud devoted parents played with their daughter. Perhaps papa, the philosopher, pretended to dip his pen in the glue-pot. And perhaps Jeanne's whole face sparkled with silent delight. The imperfections of the body and the words that she would never speak must have seemed trivial in those shared moments. The spirit of life would have been present, really present, profoundly present, in her laughing eyes.

7

Freud and the Hidden Secrets of Jokes

The second great twentieth-century book of humour-theory was Freud's *Jokes and their Relation to the Unconscious* ([1905b] 1991). As theoretically daring as Bergson's *Laughter*, Freud's book was part of his project to transform our understanding of human nature. Freud was suggesting that the human condition is marked by self-deception. We wish to conceal from ourselves knowledge about the dangerous psychological forces that guide our daily conduct. Even the innocent gaiety of mirth was compromised. The joke is seldom 'just' a joke, but it hides secrets even more discreditable than Hobbes ever imagined.

The Freudian perspective would seem to be ideal for providing the missing ingredient in Bergson's analysis. When analyzing laughter, Bergson had looked into the human heart and seen an absence of feeling just where we would like to believe there is warmth and good nature. However, Bergson drew back from the uncomfortable implications of his theory. By contrast, it is easy to imagine Freud striding on, chin jutting out in defiance, to uncover the momentous secrets that everyone else had overlooked.

Such an image of Freud is familiar. The cartoonist Ralph Steadman plays with this image in his wonderful book *Sigmund Freud* (1979), which slips in and out of seriousness as it explains and illustrates, admires and gently mocks Freud's theory of humour. Steadman's drawings develop the traditional joke against philosophers – the contradiction between the philosopher who can tame the world in theory but not in practice. There is Freud, the intellectual, working out his new theory of humour, and then we smile at his awkwardness in the world. Steadman's Freud holds his head in his hands as his patients talk unstoppably at him. He looks exasperated as his daughter utters a *double entendre*. The big city dwarfs this giant of ideas, a little man with beady eyes, unruly beard and phallic nose.

It is appropriate to stress the tensions between the world of ideas and daily life in the case of Freud, and particularly so in relation to his theory of humour. It is too simple to say that Freud found the missing psychological component that all previous investigators had neglected. To be sure, Bergson's argument about the disciplinary nature of laughter can well be combined with Freud's idea that laughter has its own secrets. And such a combination points the way toward a critique of ideological positivism. Yet, Freud's theory of humour also had its own surprising omissions. The man himself – his preferences, his fears and his jokes – are present in his book on humour. So, it is not just a matter of sorting out the strengths and the weaknesses of the theory as if the theorist is irrelevant to the balance-sheet. As will be seen, the gaps in Freud's analysis of humour tell us about the author and about the hidden nature of humour.

The apparent weaknesses of the analysis can act as testimony to the enduring inner strength of the theory and the humanity of its originator.

Background to psychoanalytic theory

Freud was a contemporary of Bergson. He was born in 1856, three years before Bergson, and was to die in 1939, two years earlier than Bergson. The Freud family was comparatively poor and moved to Vienna from Moravia when Sigmund was a young child. Actually, the child was not then 'Sigmund'. He had been named 'Sigismund Schlomo Freud', but when he became an independent young man, he dropped the middle syllable from his first name as well as his entire middle name. The change signified the journey that the Freud family, and particularly Sigmund, was taking. They were moving from the ghetto that cramped the lives of Eastern European Jews into the mainstream world of modern Europe. Sigmund's father, as a young boy, had worn the traditional dress of pious Jews and, like Sigmund's mother, grew up speaking Yiddish. They would always speak German with a markedly Jewish accent. Their children, however, would wear modern clothes, learn the manners of bourgeois Austrians and speak perfect German. 'Sigmund Freud' was a much more fitting name for a young man who wanted to enter the great German culture. Ernest Jones, many years later, would write that 'a Gentile would have said that Freud had few overt Jewish characteristics, a fondness for relating Jewish jokes and anecdotes being perhaps the most prominent one' (1964: 49).

Freud's *Jokes* appeared in 1905 during the most creative period of his life. He may no longer have been a young man, but he was formulating the key ideas of psychoanalysis. Freud had originally trained as a doctor and then conducted neurological research. Henri Bergson must be one of the few philosophers to quote from Freud's early physiological research papers (*Matter and Memory*, 1911c: 157). Increasingly, the young Freud was drawn to psychiatry, travelling to Paris to study under the great Charcot, who was using hypnosis to treat neurotic disorders. On his return to Vienna, Freud worked with Josef Breuer, an older psychiatrist, and together they came to believe that hypnosis had its weaknesses as a form of treatment. It was better to talk with patients, encouraging them to reminisce about their past. Freud and Breuer became convinced that wilfully forgotten memories lay at the root of neurotic disorders. Something had happened in the past that the patient had been motivated to forget. The task of treatment was to bring this neglected memory back to conscious awareness, so that a cure could be effected through self-knowledge. Such was the basis of the theory of repression that Freud and Breuer outlined in their book *Studies on Hysteria* (1895).

Freud was to break with Breuer shortly after the publication of their book. There are different accounts of their separation. As is so often the case in the history of psychoanalysis, personal and intellectual factors were intermixed. What seems clear is that Freud was being drawn to the idea that the repressed memories at the root of neurosis were sexual desires of which the patient was ashamed. Breuer had grave misgivings, both about the hypothesis and about its possible effects upon the good reputation of his medical practice. Nevertheless, in his work with Breuer, Freud had taken the first, decisive step towards psychoanalytic theory by formulating the concept of repression. Years later, Freud was to claim, 'the theory of repression is the corner-stone on which the whole structure of psychoanalysis rests' ([1914] 1993: 73).

After the split from Breuer, Freud engaged in a period of introspection that has become known as his 'self-analysis'. For over a year, he sought to explore his own mind, searching his own memories for hidden elements. The self-analysis took him back to his childhood recollections and from these he attempted to reconstruct that which he had forgotten. In a number of respects this self-analysis was to provide the model for later psychoanalytic practice. There was the assumption that the key to the present lay in the forgotten memories of childhood. Also, Freud claimed that the forgotten memories were expressions of childish desire, especially sexual desire for the mother. Because these memories were sexual, they had been wilfully forgotten or repressed. Freud was dealing with shocking ideas, including his own shameful, childish desires. No wonder he used circumspect language when writing about such matters to his friend and mentor, Wilhelm Fliess, a psychiatrist several years older than himself.

There was another outcome of the self-analysis that was to become important. Freud believed that the sorts of repression he was uncovering in himself were universal. The work with Breuer had suggested that repression was the cause of neurosis. The implication was that 'normal', non-neurotic people would not need to repress, for they can confront their daemons consciously. The self-analysis contradicted this. If Freud, an ambitious doctor who could function 'normally' within the world, had repressed memories and childhood sexual desires, then so would anybody. Thus, Freud was moving from the specialist psychiatry of neurosis towards proposing a general psychology that was describing a very strange normality.

Freud's interest in general psychology was to be expressed in a trio of major books – *The Interpretation of Dreams*, *The Psychopathology of Everyday Life* and, finally, *Jokes*. In each book, Freud examined a waste product of the mind: dreams, slips of the tongue and then jokes. Every normal person has dreams, suffers occasional lapses of memories and laughs at jokes. Most ordinary people, not to mention psychologists, considered these activities to be of little significance. But Freud believed that they held the key to mental functioning for in their very triviality the workings of the unconscious were detectable.

Background to Jokes

During the period of his self-analysis, Freud wrote to Fliess that he was starting to collect 'profound Jewish stories' (letter of 22 June 1897, Freud, 1985: 254). Jews like Freud and Fliess grew up hearing Jewish anecdotes and jokes and they would cite them in conversation. Certainly Freud's letters to Fliess are full of references to well known Jewish stories. Freud's pupil, the psychoanalyst Theodor Reik, recounted that Freud often told Jewish jokes. He never did so, according to Reik, just to raise a laugh, but it was always to make a serious point: 'It was as if he brought the joke forward as an example of how wisdom is expressed in wit' (Reik, 1956: 36). The Jewish stories that Freud was collecting would provide a substantial amount of the material for *Jokes*.

Some background is necessary to appreciate just how radical a step this was. One might suppose that Freud, in collecting his Jewish jokes, was enjoying a contented period in his life. This was at a time when the theatres of Paris, London and Vienna were filled with light comedies and, as we have seen, the thoughts of serious psychologists were turning towards laughter. Happy days, it might be supposed. And one can envision the youngish Viennese doctor, full of energy and with several serious books to his name, taking time out to write a fun book.

The image would be wrong both psychologically and historically. The first years of the twentieth century were for Freud a bleak period. He was struggling to support his young family. His days would be spent seeing patients and he would write late into the night. He was isolated from the medical establishment of Vienna. He sought to obtain a professorship at the University of Vienna, but his application was being regularly rejected. He strongly suspected anti-Semitic discrimination was at work. Freud had hoped that his intellectual isolation would be ended by the publication of *The Interpretation of Dreams*. Surely a daring book on that topic would capture the public imagination and draw praise from the specialists. Nothing changed when the great book appeared. In the first six years of publication, *Dreams* sold only 351 copies (Gay, 1995: 3). *The Psychopathology of Everyday Life* did not fare much better.

The political situation in Vienna was not good for Jews. When Freud entered university in the late 1870s he could expect that the ancient prejudices against Jews were about to be finally rendered obsolete by the movement of rational Enlightenment. Things did not work out that way. By the turn of the twentieth century, anti-Semitism was increasing throughout the Austro-Hungarian Empire. Jews were once again being accused of the old mediaeval crime of ritually sacrificing Christian children. In the outer provinces there was mob violence against Jews. The capital offered little protection. Karl Lueger was elected mayor of Vienna on an anti-Semitic platform, promising to remove Jews from public life. Freud had good grounds for suspecting that increasing anti-Semitism was responsible for blocking his chances of a university chair.

At no other time in his life was Freud to feel so isolated. 'I have been virtually cut off from the outside world', he wrote to Fliess in March 1900 (Freud, 1985: 402). Freud did have a few friends, who were interested in the same medical and psychological issues as he was. From 1902 they met regularly at his house on Wednesday evenings. From these informal Wednesday meetings, the Vienna Psychoanalytic Society was to grow. All the early members were Jewish, as were practically all Freud's patients at that time. Freud's only other forum was the local B'nai Brith Society, to whom he gave lectures about the ideas that he was developing. In these meetings, Freud could feel welcomed as a friend. The sole surviving text of one of these lectures shows that he used Jewish jokes to illustrate his themes (Freud, 1993). He omitted such jokes from the version to be later published in the journal *Imago*. Among the wider medical establishment – and more generally in the world of successful gentiles – Freud was a stranger, a nobody.

Later Freud would claim that his early experiences as a Jew in a gentile world were crucial to his intellectual development. He had learnt to be suspicious of the prejudices of 'the compact majority' (Freud, [1925a] 1993: 191). His feeling of estrangement prepared him to follow new paths of thought. It was no coincidence, he would assert, that psychoanalysis had been discovered by a Jew for 'belief in this new theory called for a certain degree of readiness to accept a situation of solitary opposition – a situation with which no one is more familiar than a Jew' (Freud, [1925b] 1993: 273).

It was possible, however, for a Jew with an interest in sex and psychology to write a best-seller in Vienna. In 1903 a young philosopher showed how it could be done. Otto Weininger published *Sex and Character* ([1903] 1906), creating the sort of stir that Freud could only dream about. Weininger's ideas, rather than Freud's, struck the mood of the times. Weininger was arguing that Jews were a degenerate, effeminate race, whose character was a threat to the manly, strong race of Germans. This was what the educated gentiles of Vienna wanted to read. Weininger, who was not only Jewish but also homosexual, was to commit suicide shortly afterwards.

Freud was appalled by Weininger's work whose success deepened his own sense of gloom. In fact, Weininger's success was also to bring personal problems for Freud. Fliess accused Weininger of plagiarising his own ideas about the normality of bisexuality. More than this, Fliess accused Freud of being the instrument of this plagiarism, suggesting that Freud had communicated these ideas casually to a patient who was a good friend of Weininger's. Fliess demanded an explanation from Freud, who, in turn tried to placate his friend. But the more Freud tried to smooth things over, the worse they became. Freud omitted to mention that Weininger had visited him with a copy of the manuscript of *Sex and Character*. When Fliess challenged him on this, Freud conceded that the visit had indeed taken place.

In all this correspondence about Weininger, the chief concern was whether Weininger had stolen Fliess's ideas about sexuality and whether Freud, wittingly or unwittingly, had aided the theft. The two men did not discuss the anti-Jewish nature of Weininger's work. The strain of the growing estrangement between the friends was telling on Freud. In his final letter to Fliess on this matter and, indeed, on any other, Freud concluded that he felt unable to work, not even to complete his book on jokes (see Freud, 1985: 463–8). Their friendship never recovered. In jealousy of Weininger and fear of what his success represented, they had turned on each other.

And how does Freud, despairing of ever being taken seriously by the wider world, react to the gravity of his professional situation? Does he follow Weininger down the path of intellectual self-hatred, in the knowledge that this would increase the likelihood of achieving fame? Or does he try the other tactic of removing all traces of personal ethnicity from his writings, so as not to appear as a Jewish author in the eyes of the gentile world? Not a bit of it. He rebels against his situation. Freud, the sex doctor who was unashamedly Jewish, tells jokes. Not only this, he tells Jewish jokes. He does this in a book that was to argue that telling jokes was seldom a purely innocent action.

The rebellious unconscious

Although Freud intended *Jokes* to be understood as a self-contained book, it belonged to his wider theoretical project. Not only was Freud's theory designed to show the importance of unconscious factors in mental life, but it was also based on a general vision about the relations between the individual and society. This social vision is particularly important for understanding Freud's view of humour. More than the first two works of the trilogy, *Jokes* was exploring a phenomenon that was inherently social. According to Freud, a joke is 'the most social of all the mental functions that aim at a yield of pleasure' (*Jokes*, [1905b] 1991: 238).

Herbert Marcuse made the point in *Eros and Civilization* that Freud's theory 'is in its very substance "sociological"', for it was a theory about the way society demands the repression of instincts (1972: 24). Freud was to develop these themes in later works such as *Group Psychology and the Analysis of the Ego* and *Civilization and its Discontents*. These more social psychological writings, however, did not represent a new theoretical development. They elaborate basic themes that were present in Freud's earlier writings such as *Jokes* and that, according to Marcuse, lay at the heart of the inner logic of Freudian theory.

Like Hobbes almost three centuries earlier, Freud depicted a conflict between individual desire and social order. As humans, we inherit the instincts of sexuality and aggression that promise to afford us the most intense of pleasures. However, these instincts are dangerous, for they are fundamentally anti-social. Because individual pleasure conflicts with social demands, sexuality and aggression have to be curbed from an early age. If people continually let themselves be ruled by their instincts, then the cooperation, discipline and moral sense that are essential for social life would be impossible. Not only must the instinctual desires be thwarted, but they must also be pushed from conscious awareness, so that we are not continually conscious of desire and temptation. Repression, thus, is necessary for collective life.

This means that repression is a disciplinary force, exerting control over undisciplined instinctual forces and turning the unsocialized infant into a civilized being. However, the instinctual urges do not simply disappear once they are repressed. The problem of repression is never completely solved. Society may attempt to divert, or sublimate, instinctual energy into socially useful ends, but this process is always unfinished. There still remains instinctual energy left over. And this residual energy seeks to tempt the individual into pursuing the paths of pleasure.

Freud saw the normal psyche as being split by conflict. The forces of unconscious instinct try to force their way into consciousness, but the ego – or, to be more precise, particular aspects of the ego – seeks to repel these dangerous, disruptive instincts. The battle is never-ending. The instinctual forces, that Freud was to call the id, are constantly trying to take advantage of the ego. This was why the detritus of the mind was so significant. When we go to sleep, consciousness drops its guard, and the instincts make play in our dreams. It is the same when we forget a word. The unconscious is up to its tricks again, pushing the proper word out of our minds and trying to get us to say a dangerously suggestive one. Similar processes are at work with jokes. In all these cases, the instincts are breaking through the necessary disciplines of social order, leaving traces of their purposes as they do so.

According to Freud, unconscious desires must disguise themselves if they are to evade the mental censor. Psychoanalysis sought to reveal these disguises. In *The Interpretation of Dreams* Freud claimed to provide codes for understanding dreams. Freud introduced the important concept of 'dream-work'. This is the process by which the hidden, or latent, meaning of a dream is represented in its outward or manifest content. The dream-work ensures that the underlying desire is 'translated', often through complex processes of condensation and substitution, into what seems to be the incoherent, nonsense of dreams. It was Freud's claim that he had cracked the code by which dreams disguise their real meaning.

Two implications can be noted. First, Freud's theory asserts that dreams express desires: they are 'wish-fulfilments'. This includes dreams whose manifest content seems *prima facie* to indicate anxiety. Even nightmares are expressing hidden, denied wishes. The second point is the sweeping nature of Freud's theorizing. He did not suggest that some dreams are wish-fulfilments but that they all are: 'Every dream is the fulfilment of a wish, that is to say there cannot be any dreams but wishful dreams' (*The Interpretation of Dreams*, [1900] 1990: 214). In consequence there are 'no "innocent" dreams' and all seemingly innocent dreams turn out on analysis to be 'wolves in sheep's clothing' (ibid.: 270).

It was the same with slips of the tongue. In *Psychopathology* ([1901] 1975) Freud argued that apparently random acts of forgetfulness do not in reality operate by chance. Hidden desires were at work just as they are in dreams. In both cases condensations and substitutions operate so that 'unconscious thoughts find expression as modification of other thoughts' (ibid.: 342). Again, there were, according to Freud, no innocent lapses. Mental life was strictly determined.

So the general theory of mind was in place for the final work of the trio. The first two books had argued that what seems to be trivial is by its very triviality psychologically significant. The step from dreams and slips of the tongue to jokes is small. If unconscious desires are at work in the former two phenomena, then it is expected that they can be found in the absurdity of jokes. But, as will be seen, jokes differed from the other two waste products of the mind. Freud loved neither dreams nor moments of forgetfulness in the way that he loved the jokes of his ancestors.

A theory of repression

Freud's theory depicts repression as the means by which unruly human nature is socially disciplined. The unconscious rebels against this discipline in dreams, slips of the tongue and jokes. So far so good, one might say. But there is a question. How does society enforce repression? In particular, how does it coerce the young to give up their instinctual freedom? To answer these questions, one requires a theory that outlines the processes by which the social order is reproduced. Such a theory, for example, might describe how adults impose discipline on the young. Following Bergson's analysis, one might presume that the disciplinary side of laughter would feature in such an account. Ridicule might be used to drive away, or rather drive underground, the wayward desire.

Although Freud's theory has a crucial sociological dimension, it becomes somewhat unsociological when it comes to describing how repression occurs. Broadly, Freud did not inquire how society might impose repression, especially through the agency of parents. Instead, Freud tended to presume that the psychological imperatives come from within the individual child. This was implied by his theory of the Oedipus Complex, which basically acquits adults of the desire to discipline children and which loads everything on the developing child.

At the time when Freud was writing *Jokes*, he was not yet using the term 'Oedipus Complex', although he had already formulated its basic ideas. His self-analysis had laid the groundwork. In 1897, he wrote to Fliess saying that the feelings of 'being in love with my mother and jealous of my father' were not peculiar to his own childish self but represented 'a universal event in early childhood'; this accounted for the 'gripping power of *Oedipus Rex*' (Freud, 1985: 272). Freud was to develop these ideas in his *Three Essays on the Theory of Sexuality* ([1905a] 1977). According to Ernest Jones, Freud wrote *Three Essays* in parallel to *Jokes*. Apparently, he kept the manuscripts on adjoining tables and 'wrote now on one and now on the other as the mood took him' (Jones, 1964: 315).

The two works are united by many similar preoccupations, including sharing the same theoretical logic that downplays the social processes of discipline and repression. Having derived the idea of the Oedipal situation from his own self-analysis, Freud based his developmental theory of repression on the young boy, despite the fact that most of his patients were women. He believed that young girls went through analogous processes of development. There is no need to go into the details of this famous theory

– the broad outlines will suffice. Freud made the daring assertion that the young infant has sexual feelings, which are initially expressed in a sensual love for the mother. At around the age of three, the young boy experiences a conflict of emotions. He wishes to possess the mother sexually, but feels the father to be a rival. The child starts to feel a murderous jealousy against the father. If only daddy were dead, then mummy would be mine, the child is thinking. The child fears that the father can read his mind and wishes to punish him by castration. The child still loves his father and feels guilt. These conflicting feelings of desire, hate and guilt form the basis of the Oedipal situation.

The young boy resolves the uncomfortable conflict by imagining himself as the father. If I were daddy, so the young boy thinks, then I would be able to sleep in mummy's bed. So the child identifies with his father. The problem is that the father is the image of discipline, the person who is telling the child how to behave. The result is that the child takes the father's disciplining voice as his own. From then on, he has an internal voice telling him what to do and what not to do. This is the origin of the moral conscience, according to Freud. The moral conscience, of course, disapproves of all those murderous and sexual desires. They have to be denied, or repressed from awareness. Thus, the child emerges from the Oedipal situation as a self-repressing moral individual, ready to accept the restrictions of the social order by internalizing the disciplinary voice of authority. The curious feature of this theory is that the child does everything. The parents are passive figures, the objects of their children's desires and hatreds.

Freud was aware that he had developed the Oedipal theory by attempting to reconstruct the past from fragments of adult memories. To sustain the theory, he needed direct evidence about the behaviour of children. His wife Martha forbade him from conducting psychoanalytic studies on their own children. So, Freud asked whether any of his small group of followers would observe their own young children. The year following the publication of *Jokes*, Max Graf, one of the Wednesday regulars, started taking notes about his own boy. These notes formed the basis of the famous case study of Little Hans.

The focus on the child and the corresponding neglect of the parents are notable features of Freud's report on Little Hans and of his Oedipal theory in general. Again there is no need to go into the details here (see Billig, 1999, for details). In the case of Hans, the parents were engaging in precisely the sort of behaviour that Freud was attributing to Hans. Freud diagnosed Hans as feeling aggression towards his younger sister, but it is his mother who regularly beat the girl. The father, who allegedly was the object of Hans's jealous feelings, was obviously jealous of Hans, objecting that his wife was cuddling the boy too much. Both parents seemed obsessed lest the young boy touch his own penis. They even made him sleep in a bag to prevent this from happening. Freud claims that Hans had a fear of castration, which he attributed to the boy's guilt about supposedly wishing to kill his father. Yet, the mother had threatened to cut off the boy's 'widdler' if he continued to touch it.

Young Hans developed a fear of horses, which Freud interpreted as an unconscious fear of his father. Hans's father blamed his wife for the child's neurosis because she had shown the child too much affection. Freud thought these criticisms were unjust. Had she been less affectionate, the results would have been just the same. Several times in the report, Freud asserts that Hans's mother had nothing to reproach herself for. There was nothing she could have done to stop the boy acting as he did: 'She had a predestined part to play, and her position was a hard one' (Freud, [1909] 1990: 190). In other words, the actions of the parents were largely irrelevant. Similarly Freud believed that his own childish desires for his mother and his jealous feelings towards his father were not caused by anything his parents had actually done. The parents were not to blame for the universal and inevitable complex of feelings experienced by the young child.

The real drama of love and hate, thus, occurs within the imagination of the child. In taking this line, Freud's account of Little Hans overlooked the ways that 'Oedipal parents' might be producing an 'Oedipal child'. Freud was not interested in how they exert discipline, ensuring that patterns of repression are reproduced across the generations. Certainly, he overlooked how laughter might play a part in the disciplinary process. Freud was much more interested in the child's fantasies, dreams and failures of memory, for these, he believed, held the clue to the hidden processes of repression.

At one point, Little Hans is 'remembering' holiday events that could not possibly have taken place. Freud reproduces the father's notes, taken when the conversation occurred. Hans is claiming that his young sister, Hanna, had been on family holidays to Gmunden twice. The father points out that this was highly implausible, and Hans responds:

> Hans: 'Yes. Just you write it down. I can remember quite well. – Why are you laughing?'
> I: 'Because you're a fraud; because you know quite well that Hanna's only been at Gmunden once.'
> Hans: 'No, that isn't true. The first time she rode on the horse ... and the second time...' (he showed signs of evident uncertainty) (Freud, [1909] 1990: 236).

Freud and Hans's father seek to discover the psychological meaning of Hans's fantasy. They do not discuss the father's reaction. 'Why are you laughing?' asks the little boy. The father does not answer by referring to his own feelings. His reply suggests that there is something out there that is objectively risible. He laughed, he explained, because Hans is a fraud.

The father thereby provides Hans with an example and explanation of the rhetoric of mockery. Adults can use laughter to indicate displeasure rather than pleasure – to discipline rather than to enjoy rebellion. You mock what has been said, indicating that you are not taking seriously words that have been seriously uttered. It is a powerful rhetorical tool. It has upset the flow of Hans's story. This laughter, contrary to Bergson's notion, does not stand in need of an echo. Or rather there may be a deferred echo in the child. Hans, clever young boy that he is, will have learnt something about the laughter of mockery. His turn to use this laughter will come. When it does, it will not constitute the return of the repressed but the return of the repressive.

This is only a small detail that Freud ignored in his long and richly described case-study. A further example of Freud ignoring disciplinary laughter in the case of Little Hans will be discussed in detail in Chapter 9. Such examples would scarcely be worth mentioning at this stage but for a point of theoretical importance: Freud also neglected this sort of disciplinary laughter in his book on *Jokes*. As will be seen, when Freud discussed parents laughing at children, he did so benignly. It was as if his general theory of psychological suspicion had limits when it came to examining the nature of parental authority and the parental laughter of ridicule.

Jokes and wit

Theodor Reik, writing nearly 50 years ago, declared that the 'psychological profoundness' of *Jokes* had not yet been appreciated (1956: 36). Ernest Jones similarly described *Jokes* as 'the least read of Freud's books' (1964: 315). Today, Freud's most dedicated critics, such as Erwin (1996), Crews (1995, 1998) and Webster (1996), tend to ignore the work. Given their tenacious delight in exposing as many of Freud's weaknesses as possible, their neglect of *Jokes* might be taken as an implicit commendation. As will be seen, *Jokes*, as well as being creatively imaginative, contains few of those psychoanalytic overstatements that Freud's critics love to pounce upon.

The first thing to note about *Jokes* is that it is about jokes. To modern English-speaking readers this may hardly be worth noting. The English title should lead us to expect this. However, the translator, James Strachey, faced a dilemma. As he wrote in his Introduction to the translation for the Standard Edition, the original German title was *Der Witz und seine Beziehung zum Unbewussten*. *Der Witz* could easily have been rendered in English as 'wit'. Both the English 'wit' and the German *Witz* refer principally to verbal humour and the two words have a shared etymological history. Theodor Reik always called the book in English 'Wit and its Relation to the Unconscious'. This was also the title used by A.A. Brill in the first English translation that was published in 1911. Nevertheless, there are differences between the ways that wit and *Witz* are used in their respective languages. 'Wit' is more specific than *Witz*, for it carries an implication that the humour is of good quality. Strachey noted that English words 'wit' and 'witty' are 'applied only to the most refined and intellectual kind of joke' (1991: 35). Although the German term *Witz* can be used in this way, it is often used in a wider sense that does not imply a judgement of praise. In this respect, *Witz* parallels the English 'joke', which linguistically permits bad jokes as well as good ones. In German *ein alter Witz* is a stale joke. In English the phrase would not normally be rendered as 'stale wit', for that would be, if not a contradiction of terms, at least an oxymoron.

Strachey noted that Freud tended to use *der Witz* in the wider rather than restricted sense for he intended to discuss verbal humour in general, rather than just concentrating upon humour of good quality. For this reason, Strachey justified rendering *Witz* as 'jokes'. There was another reason, which makes 'jokes' a felicitous translation but which Strachey did not mention. Some of the examples that Freud used to illustrate his humour would not have been considered particularly 'witty' by many past authorities, especially those eighteenth-century theorists who were concerned with establishing aesthetic standards. Specifically, Freud included jokes *qua* jokes, along with *bons mots* and witty sayings.

As was mentioned in Chapter 4, eighteenth-century writers had tended not to discuss jokes. Nor had Bain and Spencer presented jokes to illustrate their respective theories. When discussing verbal humour, Bergson used examples of *bons mots*. The wit of the *bon mot* typically consists in being a reaction to a particular context, whereas a joke 'is not tied to a particular context but is self-contained, thus enabling a joke to be performed successfully on a number of occasions' (Davies, 1990: 3; see also Norrick, 1993). Bergson cites the comic character who wore a row of medals, although he has received but a single decoration. The character, who was an official of Monte Carlo, comments at one point in the play 'I staked my medal on a number at roulette ... and as my number turned up, I was entitled to thirty-six times my stake' (Bergson, 1911a: 118). Without knowing the Monte Carlo connection, the remark would not make sense and its witticism would be lost. The remark is a *bon mot*. It may be a joking *bon mot* but technically it is not a joke.

Of the four books on the theory of humour published in the first five years of the twentieth century, only *Jokes* deals with jokes. In this regard, Freud's book is more democratic than the corresponding books of Sully, Dugas and Bergson. In Freud's book, the humble joke, passed from common mouth to common mouth, finds its place alongside the witty sayings of the great and the good. In a modern analysis of humour, the absence of jokes – or to be more precise the absence of the topic of jokes – would be unthinkable.

Yet, it is too simple just to say that Freud was merely using *der Witz* in the wider, non-evaluative sense. Freud invites his readers to share in the jokes that he presents. In the introductory chapter, Freud writes that it is natural that he should illustrate his topic with 'examples of jokes by which we ourselves have been most struck in the course of our lives and which have made us laugh the most' ([1905b] 1991: 46). Some writers have sought to read Freud's inner motivations from his favourite jokes (e.g., Oring, 1984), just as critics and admirers alike have done from the very partial analyses that Freud provided of his own dreams and lapses of memory (e.g., Billig, 2000; Grinstein, 1990; Swales, 1982, 2003). It is a reasonable tactic because psychoanalytic theory in general, and Freud's work in particular, inevitably mix the personal with the intellectual (Forrester, 1991).

There is a central tension in *Jokes*. Psychoanalytic theory is a theory of suspicion. In *Jokes* Freud invites us to be suspicious of laughter by showing how unconscious motives might be at play. In this regard, Freud was continuing Hobbes's task of uncovering base motives behind laughter. But Freud's rhetorical practice simultaneously seeks to promote laughter, as he shares with his readers the jokes that have made him laugh. In his writings Hobbes was never so benevolent about laughter.

Joke-work

Towards the end of the introductory chapter in *Jokes*, Freud asserts that 'there is an intimate connection between all mental happenings', so that a discovery in one field, even in a remote field, 'will be of an unpredictable value in other fields' ([1905b] 1991: 46). The principle is an important one in psychoanalytic theory and it guided the way that Freud approached the topic of humour. He wanted to show that there was an intimate connection between the various waste products of the human mind. In *Dreams*, Freud had drawn attention to the similarity between dreams and jokes: 'If my dreams seem amusing, that is not on my account, but on account of the peculiar psychological conditions under which dreams are constructed; and the fact is intimately connected with the theory of jokes and the comic' ([1900] 1991: 405n). Now, for similar reasons, he wanted to show that jokes resembled dreams.

In the first analytic section of *Jokes*, Freud examined the structure of verbal humour, looking at the 'joke-work', or the internal structure of jokes and witty remarks. The terminology was designed to evoke a parallel with his earlier analysis of 'dream-work'. The analysis of joke-work in this first section is not really psychological. It resembles what today's analysts would call 'semantics' or 'discourse analysis' in that it focuses on the language of humour.

The first joke, or *bon mot*, whose technique Freud analyzes, comes from Heine's play *Reisebilder*. A poor lottery agent boasts that the great Baron Rothschild treats him as an equal – in fact, quite 'famillionairely' (*Jokes*, [1905b] 1991: 43). Freud explains how this joke, and others like it, operates. Two meanings are contained in the seemingly non-sensical word 'famillionairely'. First, the great Baron honours the poorer man by treating him familiarly as if he were an equal. Second, the familiar manner of a millionaire is not the same as the familiar manner of an ordinary person. As Freud put it, the rich man's condescension 'always involves something not quite pleasant for whoever experiences it' (ibid.: 48). The word 'famillionairely' condenses these two meanings. The joke also misdirects listeners, who expect to hear 'familiarly'. At the last moment a substitution occurs to transform the expected compliment into sly criticism. Thus, the joke-work operates by 'condensation' and 'substitution'.

Freud showed how other jokes use these same techniques. He quoted de Quincey's remark that old people are likely to fall into their 'anecdotage' (ibid.: 53). Again, a made-up word condenses two meanings and substitutes them for an ordinary word. Given that the two meanings are separate, even incongruous, the joke creates what recent theorists have termed a 'synergy' out of disparate components (Apter, 1982a, 1982b; Giora, 1991). After discussing the processes of condensation and substitution in relation to the 'famillionairely' and 'anecdotage' jokes, Freud then asks a seemingly innocent question: 'Are processes similar to those which we have described here as the techniques of jokes known already in any other field of mental events?' (ibid.: 61). He answers his own question. Yes, they are just like the processes of dream-work.

Besides 'condensation' and 'substitution', Freud used a number of other psychoanalytically evocative terms to describe joke-work. For instance, there are 'displacement' jokes, in which one idea suddenly displaces another. Freud used this term, when he moved from witty *bons mots* to jokes *qua* jokes. The first of Freud's jokes were Jewish bath jokes, which depict Galician Jews and their supposed 'aversion to baths' (ibid.: 84). Freud justifies telling such low jokes: 'We do not insist upon a patent of nobility from our examples. We make no inquiries about their origin but only about their efficiency – whether they are capable of making us laugh and whether they deserve our theoretical interest' (ibid.: 84–5). Freud suggests that his two requirements of 'efficiency' and theoretical interest are 'best fulfilled precisely by Jewish jokes' (ibid.: 85).

No modern writer on humour would feel required to write in this way. The analysis of jokes now needs no justification. In fact, the situation is reversed, such that a writer of a book on humour, that did not discuss jokes, would be expected to justify that omission. Nor does the study of Jewish jokes constitute a risk. Jewish jokes are so familiar that within the field of 'humour-studies', they have become a specialist sub-topic in their own right (Ziv, 1998). Peter Berger, who is a practising Christian, devotes a whole chapter of *Redeeming Laughter* to Jewish jokes on the grounds that the 'best jokes are Jewish jokes' (1997: 87). Freud may have been of the same opinion. He could have said as much in his letters to Fliess or to the local B'nai Brith. But he would not have uttered the thought to a general audience. That would have been courting disaster.

Freud's first Jewish bath joke is a displacement joke.

> One Jew says to another 'Have you taken a bath?'
> The other replies: 'No, is one missing?'

Freud explains that this joke operates on the 'double meaning' of the word 'take'. The joke disappears if the first speaker is quoted as saying 'Have you had a bath?' The joke, however, does not just depend on the double meaning of a single word. In the imagined dialogue, the second speaker replaces the first speaker's train of thought by another. The result is that the idea of washing is displaced by that of theft – the proper thought by the improper one.

In discussing joke-work, Freud was preparing the way for his psychological argument. He had chosen his theoretical terms with care. Without them the parallel between jokes and dreams might have disappeared, just as the humour of the bath-joke disappears without the verb 'take'. His strategy should not to be dismissed as mere rhetorical sleight-of-hand, although Freud pulls off the necessary rhetorical tricks with aplomb. This is 'theory-work' of the highest order, condensing the complexity of reality and displacing prior ideas with unexpected insights.

Innocent and tendentious jokes

Having discussed joke-work, Freud then made a number of subtle distinctions, the most important of which was between 'innocent' and 'tendentious' jokes. He claimed that there were two types of joke: 'In the one case, the joke is an end in itself and serves no particular aim.' This was the innocent joke. By contrast, when a joke 'does serve an aim – it becomes *tendentious*' ([1905b] 1991: 132, emphasis in original). In making this distinction, Freud was departing from *Dreams* and *Psychopathology*, where he had argued that there were no such things as innocent dreams or innocent lapses of memory. The critics have delighted in showing the implausibility of such sweeping claims. With jokes Freud was more cautious. The same critics have remained significantly silent.

Freud began by discussing innocent jokes because they permit us to observe the joke 'in its purest form' (ibid.: 137). According to Freud, innocent jokes use joking techniques for their own sake. Freud presented an example of a supposedly innocent piece of humour. He was dining with friends and a chocolate roulard was served for dessert. One of the guests asked whether the roulard had been made in the home. The host replied that it was indeed home made – it was a 'home-*roulard*'. The answer was a multilingual pun on 'Home Rule', a term then associated with the Irish political situation. Everyone at the table laughed.

Freud presented the remark to illustrate innocent humour. The speaker was not wishing to make a political point, despite using a political term. Nor, most importantly, was the remark expressing any hidden psychological desire. The sole purpose of the pun was to bring about pleasure. Therefore, concluded Freud, 'there is nothing left open to us but to bring that feeling of pleasure into connection with the technique of the joke' (ibid.: 137–8). In other words, the diners were simply enjoying the host's play with words. As we shall see, things may not have been that simple.

Freud then made a further distinction between the joke technique and the underlying thought that the joke expressed. In the case of the 'home-roulard', there was only the joke-technique of word-play. Sometimes, however, innocent jokes will have a 'kernel of thought' that will be enclosed within a 'joking envelope' (ibid.: 135). Freud cited the sayings of Lichtenberg, a humorist whom he greatly admired. There was Lichtenberg's description of a disbeliever: 'Not only did he disbelieve in ghosts; he was not even frightened of them' (ibid.: 134). This remark suggested that someone who rationally did not believe in ghosts nevertheless might still be afraid of them.

Then there was Lichtenberg's aphorism that 'experience consists in experiencing what one does not wish to experience' (ibid.: 135), which Freud had earlier presented as demonstrating the technique of 'multiple uses of the same material' (ibid.: 105). The aphorism plays on the different senses of 'experience', just as the bath-joke depends on two senses of 'take'. At first hearing the aphorism sounds profound. Yet, suggests Freud, if we discard the joke-work, we can see that it is only expressing the old platitude 'adversity is the best teacher'. The pleasure, in this case, comes entirely from the joke technique, because the underlying thought is so banal.

Both tendentious and innocent jokes use similar techniques, the difference between the two lying in the kernel of thought that is expressed. The kernel of thought for tendentious jokes is not banal, as in the Lichtenberg aphorism about experience. It is typically something that cannot be directly uttered because there are social restrictions against such expression. Since childhood we have learnt not to express hostile or sexual feelings directly. That is why tendentious jokes tend to be either hostile, obscene or both. The joking envelope enables us to express what otherwise would have to be repressed from polite conversation.

Freud asserts that a tendentious joke 'will evade restrictions and open sources of pleasure that have become inaccessible' (ibid.: 147). Because the thought is expressed as a joke, and is seemingly non-serious, it avoids social censorship. Thus, the joke-form makes possible 'the satisfaction of an instinct (whether lustful or hostile) in the face of an obstacle that stands in its way' (ibid.: 144). In this way, a tendentious joke functions to circumvent a taboo and, in so doing, it brings pleasure to the joke-teller and the recipients of the joke. The tendentious joke can be rhetorically useful, for it 'bribes the hearer with its yield of pleasure into taking sides with us without any very close investigation' (ibid.: 147). Freud used this tactic in his own writings and he recommended it to younger followers. Once when Reik was preparing to write an angry review against a German psychiatrist, Freud cautioned: 'Humour – as much as you wish...but no insults! More cheerful and superior' (1956: 631). We might not be able to strike our enemy directly, but, as Freud wrote in *Jokes*, by mocking our enemy, 'we achieve in a roundabout way the enjoyment of overcoming him' ([1905b] 1991: 147).

By connecting humour with taboos, Freud can explain why the subject matter of jokes is not randomly distributed across the fields of human activity. In theory, one can joke about any conceivable topic: one might have jokes about flower-arranging, stock-market trading and theoretical physics. However, jokes will abound where there are social prohibitions. According to Alan Dundes, 'it is precisely those topics culturally defined as sacred, taboo or disgusting that tend to provide the principal grist for humour mills' (1987: 43). As such, jokes provide a mirror image of a culture's sense of morality (Zijderveld, 1982). Today the quickest of visits to those web sites that collect jokes will reveal a super-abundance of sexual, lavatorial and racial jokes. It has been suggested that the growth of sadistic, 'killing' jokes in the United States is related to trends in right-wing politics (Lewis, 1997).

According to the logic of Freud's argument, there will be wider, more universal factors at work. Peter Berger argues that aggressive jokes circumvent 'the taboo against aggressive actions, a taboo that in one way or another exists in every society' (1997: 54). Similarly, there are good reasons for supposing that sex is accompanied by taboos and restrictions in all known societies, as are excretory functions. In consequence, one should find sexual, aggressive and excretory jokes universally, although the particularities of the jokes will vary depending on the particularities of the social restrictions.

In his anthropological book, *Totem and Taboo*, Freud suggested that in strict traditional cultures some festivals act as a release from restraint. During the festive time, prohibitions that are strictly enforced for the rest of the year are lifted. Authorities are mocked, rules flouted and social conventions are broken – and all this is done in obedience with the social imperatives of the festival. In this way the festival can provide a 'licence for every kind of gratification' (*Totem and Taboo*, [1913] 1990: 201; see also *Group Psychology*, [1921] 1985: 163f). A tendentious joke acts like a mini-festival, lifting customary restrictions for a very brief moment during the course of social interaction. Generally, when joking, people can say things that would be taboo in normal 'serious' talk. The obligation of empathy is relaxed as soon as someone begins a standard joke format: 'A blind man walks into a shop …'. The standard joke format signals the temporary, conversational festival.

It is not only formal jokes that can operate in this way. The joking envelope permits speakers to criticize, give orders and flirt with listeners in ways that can otherwise be found offensive. The joke can also become coercive in this respect. Recipients may have difficulty in complaining at the criticism, command or flirtation, for they risk the accusation that they lack a sense of humour. It was 'only a joke', the joker can say, implying a criticism of the complainant, who has apparently failed to 'get' the joke. There is nothing new in this coercive power of humour. Jonathan Swift complained that all too often raillery consisted in nothing but running 'a man down in discourse', but the butt of the mockery 'is obliged not to be angry, to avoid the imputation of not being able to take a jest' (1909b: 231).

Critics commonly maintain that Freud stretched his theories far too widely, in order to find traces of unconscious motivation in every piece of human conduct. They have found it easy to criticize Freud on the grounds that some dreams and memory-lapses do not express repressed wishes (e.g., Webster, 1996; Macmillan, 1997; Timpanero, 1985). However, in the case of jokes, Freud was over-cautious. Far from finding tendentiousness in every piece of humour, he seems to have been over-ready to accept the innocence of laughter.

Regarding the episode of the chocolate roulard, it is not difficult to think of tendentious aspects. The question that prompted the witty remark was potentially awkward: 'Made in the house?' the guest had inquired ([1905b] 1991: 137). It would not be difficult to claim that the question represented an act of social aggression. As Freud noted, a roulard demands much culinary skill. The question implies that the hostess and her cook might lack such skill. One might imagine an alternative turn to the scenario. Following the question, host and hostess exchange glances and the host replies, 'No, the roulard was delivered earlier.' There is a moment's silence, as the hostess, her face slightly reddening, looks down before cutting the first slice.

The host's joke dispelled the possibility of such awkwardness: it makes light of the question and the questioner's intent. The social occasion sails onwards. The dangerous reef of social embarrassment is left well behind. No-one round the table comments on the potential rudeness of the guest, who had asked the question. Nor did Freud when he came to write about the episode. It is forgotten.

Freud's failure to comment on the possible social functions of the home-roulard remark reflects his general approach to studying jokes and their meanings. Freud tended to assume that the meaning of a joke was contained within the content of the joke itself, and could be examined apart from the context in which the joke is told. Thus, he examines the bath jokes as self-contained entities that will possess the same meaning regardless of who utters the joke and in what context. Similarly, he considered that the phrase 'Home-roulard' carried no tendentious echoes in itself and, therefore, it must be an innocent remark. But the remark need not have been socially innocent in the context in which it was uttered.

Freud's approach, nevertheless, has the virtue of being theoretically focused. He has an important point to make: some jokes – the tendentious ones – avoid social prohibitions. They permit speakers to say things that would otherwise be forbidden. In this regard, humour is a means of evading the inevitable restrictions of social life, permitting brief moments of shared freedom. As Freud was to write in a later essay, humour is not 'resigned' but 'it is rebellious' ([1927] 1990: 429). The idea was to become incorporated within the psychoanalytic tradition. Alberto Melucci has remarked that psychoanalytic theorists have followed Freud in viewing laughter as the means by which 'the ego launches a momentary mutiny against the super-ego, its grey and severe mentor' (1996: 136). In this way, Freud situated humour on the side of rebellion not discipline. This was a tendentious move, reflected in a series of observations and omissions at the core of Freud's analysis of humour.

Freud's three observations

Freud follows his distinction between innocent and tendentious jokes with three observations of great theoretical importance. Freud's three observations, unlike the three observations made by Bergson at the start of *Laughter*, are not explicitly presented as such. They have to be distilled from the complex, inter-twined argument that Freud was presenting. When combined, these three observations provide the basis of an ingenious and innovative theory of tendentious humour.

The first observation is that tendentious jokes produce much greater laughter than do innocent ones. As a rule, an innocent joke provokes only 'a slight smile', and it 'scarcely ever achieves the sudden burst of laugher which makes tendentious ones so irresistible' (Freud, [1905b] 1991: 139). In terms of evoking laughter, Lichtenberg's witty aphorisms cannot compete with jokes about lavatories and bath-houses. One might note that the home-roulard remark, had it been purely innocent, should not have produced much laughter. That it did suggests, according to Freud's own theory, that the fun might not have been entirely innocent.

Taken on its own, Freud's first observation was not particularly original. Eighteenth-century theorists often remarked how feeble were the effects of clever wit as compared with those of humour. In those days humour denoted the mockery of an individual's character. Sydney Smith asserted that 'laughter is not so long and so loud in wit as it is in humour' (1864 edn: 139). Dugald Stewart, commenting on the justness of Lord Chesterfield's remark that genuine wit never made anyone laugh, claimed wit 'wholly divested of every mixture of humour' is unlikely to produce more than a smile (1814 edn: 306). Neither Smith nor Stewart could offer a satisfactory reason for the differential effects of wit and humour.

Freud's second observation goes far to providing a persuasive explanation. Freud had argued that both tendentious and innocent jokes employ similar sorts of techniques, such as condensation, displacement, double meanings, etc. If both types use the same techniques and if tendentious jokes evoke greater laughter than do innocent ones, then the greater laughter of tendentious jokes cannot arise from the technical qualities of the joke-work. Freud stated that 'a suspicion may be aroused in us that tendentious jokes, by virtue of their purpose, must have sources of pleasure at their disposal to which innocent jokes have no access' ([1905b] 1991: 140).

This second observation is based on the distinction between the form of a joke and its content. What counts in producing the big amounts of laughter is the underlying content and not the joke-form. Any theory, such as the incongruity theory, which concentrates on the technical aspects of jokes, cannot explain the popularity of dirty or aggressive jokes (Herzog and Karafa, 1998). In fact, Freud's theory could be taken further. Aggressive feelings need not be expressed within the formal content of a joke, but may depend on the act of telling the joke. A speaker may be acting aggressively by making a joke or humorous remark, which in Freud's terms has an innocent content. A pun, such as the 'home-roulard' phrase, may appear to be an innocent play on words, expressing no ulterior message. However, a speaker may be suspected of possessing ulterior, even hidden purposes, in uttering an innocent pun at a particular point of the conversation. The punning speaker may be engaging in a conversationally aggressive manner, disrupting the seriousness of others or displaying competitive cleverness – and this is why, so it is claimed, males engage in more conversational punning than do females (Norrick, 1993).

The roulard remark seems to have functioned tendentiously in context. As well as rescuing the conversation from a potentially awkward moment, the remark may also have accomplished an unacknowledged put-down of the speaker who was threatening to disrupt the politeness of the occasion. 'More humour, less anger' urged Freud. He and his fellow guests signalled their appreciation of a not particularly clever pun. Change the context slightly – remove the element of potential rudeness – and the same pun might not have produced similar effects. Would the guests have laughed so much had the hostess declared, when the dessert was brought to the table, 'And now we have a home-roulard'? Some polite smiles perhaps, but little more.

Freud's second observation is supported by later psychological studies of humour that have shown that a joke's choice of target will affect the reaction of recipients. In general, it has also been found that people will enjoy jokes more about taboo topics than about non-taboo ones (Kuhlman, 1985), although there will be individual differences in the types of jokes preferred (Herzog and Bush, 1994). Importantly, the enjoyment of the joke will often depend on the nature of the target. In an experimental study Zillman (1983) presented participants with jokes in which either a social superior mocked a subordinate or *vice versa*. In both cases, the content of the joke was the same. Respondents, who occupied socially subordinate positions, preferred jokes that mocked superiors, whereas those who occupied socially superior positions enjoyed jokes at the expense of subordinates. Around the world, the same basic ethnic jokes are told, but each group will have its preferred stock choice of victims (Davies, 1990). Danes tell jokes about Norwegians and Swedes, while the latter two nationalities tell the same jokes about each other but not about Danes (Gundelach, 2000). In Israel, Jews will find the same joke funnier if its butt is an Arab rather than a Jew while the position is reversed for Israeli Arabs (Nevo, 1998). There is evidence that women prefer jokes that mock men, whereas men prefer jokes that have women as their targets (Gruner, 1997: 114f; Herzog, 1999). However, as Lampert and Ervin-Tripp (1998) emphasize in their careful review of studies on gender and humour, the meaning of a joke can depend on the context in which it is told. Males and females might, in fact, enjoy similar types of joke but only among like-minded people who are unlikely to misinterpret the humour as being hostile to their own gender. According to Lampert and Ervin-Tripp, both sexes will prefer to tell sexually tendentious jokes to members of their own sex. All this supports Freud's contention that recipients' reactions to aggressive jokes are not merely, or even principally, determined by the joke-work itself, but by tendentious factors.

The basic phenomenon can be observed in the writing of theorists about humour. Simon Critchley writes in *On Humour* about the way that 'a true joke' challenges the existing order by making the familiar seem unfamiliar. He comments that 'jokes are a play on form, where what is played with are the accepted powers of a given society' (2002: 10). As an example of such true humour, he cites a radical feminist joke: '"How many men does it take to tile a bath-room?", "I don't know", "It depends how thinly you slice them"' (ibid.: 11). Critchley does not mention that there are racist versions of the same joke. The joke can be found, for instance, on the 'joke websites' of the Ku Klux Klan, where it is asked how many blacks or Jews (usually denoted by insulting epithets) does it take to tile a room (Billig, 2001, 2005). These jokes use the same 'play on form' as the version that Critchley praises. Like the bath-house jokes, the tiling joke uses a sudden switch in the meaning of 'take'. The joke-work, or semantic structure, is identical in the racist and feminist versions. However, Critchley would not dream of classifying the racist versions as 'true' jokes. This has nothing to do with the form or technical wit of the jokes, and everything to do with their tendentious politics.

This illustrates Freud's basic point that recipients of tendentious humour have reasons for laughing that lie beyond the joke-work. In this regard, Freud's theory points to the close link between laughter and moral judgement in tendentious humour. Extreme reactions are to be expected: the joke-form that is liable to be greeted by intense laughter is also liable, under other circumstances, to evoke strong disapproval. Sexual humour or sick jokes can produce such disparate extremes, as would the different versions of the tiling joke. Laughter at an aggressive joke does not merely express an appreciation of the joke-work but validates the mocking of a particular target. If the target is deemed morally inappropriate, then the result is likely to be explicit disapproval, or what in the next chapter will be called 'unlaughter'. In introducing the notion of tendentious jokes, Freud makes a profoundly important comment: 'Only jokes that have a purpose run the risk of meeting with people who do not want to listen to them' ([1905b] 1991: 132).

Such considerations lead directly to the third of Freud's observations and possibly the most brilliant of the three. According to Freud, we tend to delude ourselves about the nature of our tendentious laughter. Freud states that when reacting to obscene or hostile jokes, 'we are subject to glaring errors of judgment about the "goodness" of jokes' (ibid.: 146). Freud suggested that, when we hear a joke, we do not separate the content from the joke-work (ibid.: 136). We think we are laughing at the cleverness of a joke's technique, whereas in fact we laugh at the tendentious thought behind the joke. Recipients might think the tile joke to be extremely clever, at least when their preferred target has been selected; and they might attribute their amusement to the cleverness rather than to the aggressive intent of the joke. As Freud pointed out, the techniques of jokes are 'often quite wretched, but they have immense success in provoking laughter' (ibid.: 146). By attributing our own laughter to the joke-work, we avoid recognizing the extent our laughter reflects the tendentious impulse. Freud's conclusion is striking: 'Strictly speaking, we do not know what we are laughing at' (ibid.: 146).

According to psychoanalytic theory, the ignorance, shown by those who laugh at tendentious jokes, fits a pattern by which we hide our 'true', socially questionable motives from ourselves. In the joking moment, the repressed desire is released but it is hidden as a joke. In Zillman's experimental study the subjects were unaware that their responses had been affected by the joke's choice of target. When asked to describe why they found a particular joke funny, they cited the joke-work, not the target of the joke. Zillman specifically claimed that his results supported Freud's idea that 'people are poor judges of what, exactly, makes them laugh' (1983: 101). In short, we like to believe in the innocence of our laughter – that our jokes are 'just' jokes, or 'just' a clever play of form, and not the expression of problematic motives.

Freud's third observation is extremely important within the history of humour-theory. It completes the dethroning of consciousness that had been begun by Bain and Spencer and continued by Bergson. Freud was claiming that the conscious experience of the person who laughs does not contain the key to understanding the nature of laughter. It is not good enough to refute Hobbes or any other motivational theorist of humour by saying that 'when I laugh, I don't experience a sense of superiority or a desire to disparage others'. The fact that such a feeling is not consciously experienced at the point of laugher is not the deciding factor. If it were, we would not be able to explain why the selection of a joke's target is so important in determining whether laughter or disapproval is the result: those who laugh will claim that the joke-work, rather than the choice of the target, is the source of their laughter.

Freud was not highlighting a chance failure of judgement, as if people occasionally are mistaken about the nature of their laughter. He was suggesting something much more systematic: we are driven to avoid self-knowledge about our laughter, and to repress awareness of our feelings. In wanting to believe the best of ourselves, we claim that we laugh because something is objectively funny, not because we take delight in cruelty or obscenity. That is why jokes are experienced as if they possess, to quote Peter Berger, a 'putative objectivity' – as if there is '*something out there*, something outside one's own mind, that is comical' (1997: 208, emphasis in original). If the comic is an escape from reality, as Berger suggests, then, according to Freud's theory, this includes an escape from the reality of our selves and our motives.

It is not merely that we should distrust our experience at the point of laughter as a guide for explaining why we laugh: we should also distrust the accounts that are given subsequently. The person who laughs has no superior knowledge about the nature of their laughter. If challenged for joking inappropriately, especially if the joke is aggressive, the joker may claim that 'it is just a joke – no harm is meant, etc.'. There may be no conscious intent to deceive, but Freudian theory recommends that we should treat such claims with suspicion.

There is evidence to support this. When teasing occurs in close relationships, the teasers tend to over-estimate the extent to which their partners enjoy being teased (Keltner et al., 1998; Shapiro et al., 1991). The teasers will want to believe that their pleasure is not one-sided. They will convince themselves that they are acting in good spirits and they seem unaware that the recipients of the teasing might view things differently. As Boxer and Cortés-Conde (1997) point out, teasing can become a very useful tool for social control. Not only do the teasers seek to control the behaviour of the recipients but by insisting that their actions be described as 'teasing' or 'joking', not 'bullying' or 'mocking', the 'teasers' also protect themselves from criticism, including self-criticism. In this regard, the discourse of 'teasing' is part of the activity of control (Hepburn, 1997, 2000). This is the rhetoric of the tease-spray, dispelling humour's bad odours. The tease-spray, in common with other rhetorical devices, may be designed to persuade others. In practice it may convince its users more than its recipients. As Swift noted, the recipients may feel powerless to object to 'just a tease' for it will expose them to further mockery that they are unable to take a joke. The 'teasers', more than their victims, will need to believe in the goodness, cleverness and essential innocence of their sense of humour.

An important but simple point follows from Freud's view that the tendentious joke can never be just a joke. The reasons for objecting to particular sorts of humour – for finding fault with sexist, racist or bullying humour – need not be felt to reside in the quality of the humour itself. There is no reason for believing that 'our' jokes are 'true jokes' in the sense of being truly or objectively funny and that the jokes of our opponents indicate no 'real' sense of humour. Anti-racists should not object to racist jokes on the grounds of technical quality. That would imply that such humour would be acceptable if only it were a bit funnier. The reason why racist humour is not funnier has little to do with the joke-work. It is offensive because it is racist. By the same token racists do not become any less racist on account of telling jokes or by turning racism into a joke. Thus, Freud's distinction between the joke-work and the tendentious purpose of a joke provides the basis for a critical approach to humour: it avoids the dangerous supposition that humour is necessarily to be applauded for being wittily clever.

No sex, please

Jokes is a curious work not least because Freud seemed reluctant to use the sort of examples that would best support his theory. It is as if he had two basic aims that are in tension with each other. On the one hand, Freud was formulating a general theory of humour, in order to expose the hidden, repressed basis of tendentious humour. He was warning his readers to beware of tendentious jokes, for dangerous instincts may be contained within the joking envelope. On the other hand, Freud wanted to celebrate humour. As he wrote in the introduction, he wanted to illustrate his theory with jokes that made him laugh. He was on the side of rebellious naughtiness. The impersonal requirements of a theory, that exposes discreditable desires, exist uneasily with Freud's personal enjoyment of the humour that he analyzed. In consequence, *Jokes* contains some surprising omissions.

The most glaring omission is the virtual absence of sexual jokes. A detailed analysis of sexual jokes would have helped Freud sustain his theory of tendentiousness. It would have been easy to argue that the prevalence of sexual jokes indicates that humour must be reflecting some murkier depths of the human psyche, especially the male psyche. Despite the fact that Freud was bravely developing a controversial theory of child sexuality, his book on *Jokes* is rather cautious about sex. Something curious seems to have happened in those long nights when Freud worked on his two manuscripts. In writing his *Three Essays*, he did not flinch from citing evidence that children had sexual desires. When he turned to the other desk where his manuscript on humour lay, he was overtaken by reticence.

In the section on tendentious jokes, Freud does discuss 'smut'. He suggests that men use dirty talk as a form of voyeurism, speaking smuttily in front of women as an act of degradation: 'A person who laughs at smut is laughing as though he were the spectator of an act of sexual aggression' ([1905b] 1991: 141). Such smutty talk is a male revenge against women who have denied them satisfaction. Freud's argument is theoretically interesting for the way that he links male sexual joking with both sexual frustration and aggressive degradation. It is also rhetorically interesting: the section contains not a single example. Freud did not want smutty talk in his book.

Freud included very few sexual jokes. One such was the umbrella joke: 'A wife is like an umbrella. Sooner or later one takes a cab' (ibid.: 119, 156f). Freud explains that the joke condenses two thoughts, one of which can be spoken outright while the other must be disguised. The first thought is that an umbrella does not provide full protection against the rain. Sooner or later one has to take a cab to avoid a heavy downpour. The second thought is that one marries 'in order to protect oneself against the temptations of sensuality' (ibid.: 156). Just as the umbrella fails to provide protection against heavy rain, so does the wife fail to protect against her husband's frustration. Consequently, a man must hire a woman, as he might hire a public cab.

Disguised in the form of a joke, the tellers and hearers (who, of course, are assumed to be respectable, married men of a certain age) can share a thought that they would not otherwise admit to each other. After the dessert has been finished and the wives have adjourned to the drawing-room, the men might be left to smoke, drink and joke. The bourgeois host would surely embarrass his guests were he suddenly to say: 'My dear little wife might be excellent with the chocolate-roulard, as you have seen, but in bed, it's a different story; so I need to visit prostitutes.' The guests might stare into their brandy glasses; or take out their fob-watches, claiming an early start for the morrow. On the other hand, the unutterable thought can be expressed obliquely in terms of umbrellas and cabs. The gentlemen can then laugh together, ostensibly at their wit, not at their wives, while covering up all insecurities with the loud sounds of their shared guffaws.

Significantly, Freud says how he came to hear of the umbrella joke: he found it in a joke-book produced for an artists' carnival in Vienna (ibid.: 118). Most of the other jokes that he reproduces in *Jokes* come without a provenance, unless they are the *bons mots* of a celebrity or quotations from writers. By citing a respectable provenance, Freud reassures his readers that the joke has not come straight from unseemly company. Freud belonged to respectable circles, where men did not engage in post-roulard smutty talk. Reik in his memoir said that Freud was 'old-fashioned in his gallantry toward women'. He would jest about wives, money and shopping, saying things such as 'a wife is expensive but you have her a long time' (Reik, 1956: 56). He was not the sort of man to drool over the idea of opening up a woman like an umbrella.

Freud's *Jokes* is very different from Legman's *Rationale of the Dirty Joke* (1969) which is the classic psychoanalytically influenced work on male sexual humour. Legman presents his life-time collection of filthy jokes. The collection is carefully arranged by theme, going from the merely dirty to the absolutely disgusting. Everything is there: jokes about private parts, sexual positions, bizarre practices, excretions, animals, and so on. Legman holds nothing back. Taken together, the collection conveys the Freudian impression that there is something seriously odd about the things that men have found funny – something that cries out for a psychoanalytic understanding.

Legman's book creates another impression. There is also something seriously odd about a man who devotes so much time and energy to collecting dirty jokes. Legman's own motives inevitably come under question, especially if one accepts the logic of Freud's psychoanalytic arguments. Legman claims to be a dispassionate inquirer, professing distaste for much of his collection. Much of his material comes from library sources, but significant amounts also derive from what he calls 'field work'. He must have spent many hours hanging around locker-rooms, bars and masculine clubs (see Legman, 1969: 45). No-one made him do this. To elicit new jokes from his sources, he would need to have told old ones, displaying suitable enjoyment in the process. The more the collector of the dirty joke disclaims unworthy motives, the higher must rise the psychoanalytic eye-brows of doubt.

Freud, by contrast, is beyond this sort of suspicion. His book is almost prim. Any male reader hoping to find a dirty joke to swap with his locker-room buddies will be disappointed. Freud was not that sort of writer. It doesn't get worse than the umbrella joke. And that is hardly likely to induce suspiciously loud belly laughs.

Omissions of race

There is another type of joke that is conspicuous by its near absence in Freud's book – the racist joke. The nasty oddity of racist humour would have strengthened Freud's theory by providing further evidence that aggressive motives can be wrapped within the pleasures of humour. But again Freud forbore to use the obvious evidence. One might speculate on Freud's motives. In fact, psychoanalytic theory invites us to do so. If all lapses of memory are psychoanalytically significant, then so must be those that take place within the construction of intellectual theory.

To see what Freud omits, it is necessary to appreciate what he includes. As has been mentioned, *Jokes* is notable for its Jewish jokes. The bath-house jokes come first. Following them come other genres of Jewish joke, such as the *Schnorrer* (beggar) jokes, the matchmaker (*Schädchen*) jokes and the Little Itzig anecdotes, etc. By and large, these Jewish jokes fit easily into Freud's view of humour as rebellion. The *Schnorrer* reverses social order by treating his patron with superiority; Little Itzig overturns the militarist logic of the army; the *Schädchen* presents the bride's defects as advantageous qualities. In each case, the little man (and invariably it is a Jewish male) takes on the world with no other weapon than an ability to subvert the logic of convention.

Theodor Reik stressed the way that Jewish jokes mock military ideals and aristocratic authority: 'Jewish wit considers the hero ideal as funny – in both meanings of the word – and does not appreciate the fame of knighthood' (1962: 63). Reik offers an example of such a joke:

'Take a seat, Baron,' says the Jewish businessman to the Duc of Gramont, who replies huffily, 'I'm a duke'. 'Take another chair,' says the businessman.

As Reik noted, the joke has to be delivered with an intonation that certainly is not that of the aristocrat. The outsider mocks aristocratic authority as if oblivious to the petty distinctions of noble rank. Freud called the best of this humour 'cynical' or 'sceptical' ([1905b] 1991: 161). He also speculated that cynical jokes might be tendentious because they possess the ulterior purpose of belittling the demands and social conventions of the world.

If the classic Jewish joke can be heard as the voice of rebellion, celebrating the unbroken spirit of the powerless, then there is another type of Jewish joke. This is the joke that is a Jewish joke, not because it belongs to the Jewish tradition of joking, but because of its target. Its tendentious object is to mock and degrade Jews. Its voice is that of the superior, mocking inferiors for their supposed inferiority. Freud does not specifically discuss this latter type of humour in *Jokes*. Twice he mentions that the Jewish jokes told by Jews differ from those told by non-Jews. He claims that the anecdotes told about the Jews 'from other sources scarcely ever rise above the level of comic stories or of brutal derision' (ibid.: 194). Earlier he had commented that the jokes told by 'foreigners' are in the main part 'brutal comic stories in which a joke is made unnecessary by the fact that Jews are regarded by foreigners as comic figures'. In contrast the jokes told by Jews about themselves acknowledge 'their real faults as well as the connection between them and their good qualities' (ibid.: 157).

Freud's distinction between the Jewish jokes told by Jews and by non-Jews is revealing. Like his distinction between tendentious and innocent jokes, it rests on the content of the jokes, abstracted from any context in which the joking might occur. Freud assumes that the differences in content will be clear. If the joke embodies positive as well as negative stereotypes, it will be an insider joke – if not, it will be an outsider one. In fact, Freud suggests that the outsider jokes may not be proper jokes because they scarcely ever employ the techniques of the joke. They are just brutal derision or anecdotes of mockery. It may be comforting to believe that one's enemies do not tell proper jokes, but it means overlooking that some jokes, such as the bathroom-tiling joke, can have their racist and non-racist variants.

Freud's distinction assumes it is easy to decide whether or not a joke is racist. However, there is often controversy whether a particular joke or joking remark should be branded as 'racist'. In such controversies, defenders will typically claim that the joke is 'just a joke' whereas accusers will contend that a racist joke can never be 'just a joke' (e.g. Jaret 1999). Academics debate the matter too. Christie Davies (1990) defends ethnic jokes on the grounds that such jokes are generally harmless because the jokers do not believe in the stereotypes that the jokes employ. He claims that genuine anti-Semites use devices other than jokes to express their animosity (ibid.: 125) and he urges 'let us not also forget that jokes are first and foremost jokes' (ibid.: 119). His defence resembles the claim for the harmlessness of the so-called friendly 'tease': the teasing is only teasing, nothing serious. In answer, critics will claim that ethnic jokes recycle stereotypes and that anyone laughing at such jokes is validating prejudiced images, regardless of the claims to be 'just joking' (Boskin, 1987; Husband, 1988). In arguing thus, the critics are pointing to the effects of the joking rather than making claims about the purity or otherwise of the jokers' motives.

Davies specifically argues that most Jewish jokes are not genuinely anti-semitic because Jews will often tell the same Jewish jokes as non-Jews (1990: 121–2). Like Freud, Davies analyzes jokes in terms of their content abstracted from any context in which they might be told. However, the context in which a joke is told can influence how the joke is understood. The same joke may be enjoyed in different ways. One can imagine aristocrats in Freud's day laughing at the ignorant Jew who did not know the difference between a Duke and a Baron. Others, laughing at the same joke, might enjoy the rudeness of the Jew who did not care about the niceties of aristocratic status. A Jewish audience listening to a Jew telling a Jewish joke would know that certain limits of meaning were in place, which would not be so were the joke being told in a gathering of anti-Semites. Any stereotypes, which are to be momentarily enjoyed by insiders, are assumed to be 'just stereotypes'. The outsider is in a different position – their very being does not distance themselves from the stereotypes. In consequence, insiders may distrust the laughter of outsiders, even though they might laugh at the same joke. Lampert and Ervin-Tripp (1998) make a similar point with respect to jokes about sensitive topics in gender relations. They cite 'Mary Jane rape jokes' in which a female character answers back a potential rapist. Women are likely to tell such jokes to other women, but may feel uncomfortable when men tell these same jokes. By the same token, men do not seem to enjoy listening to women telling castration jokes.

The context in which Freud was presenting his Jewish jokes must be understood. The jokes appear in a book, published in Vienna at a time of widespread anti-Semitism. Freud was addressing a general audience, not a specifically Jewish one. He was not using Jewish jokes in the way he did when writing to Fliess or lecturing to the B'nai Brith. The jokes are the object of theoretical analysis, which itself proceeds unjokingly. The analysis, then, gives pointers as to how the writer conceives that the ambiguous jokes are to be interpreted.

Freud explained *Schnorrer* jokes from the rich patron's point of view. In such jokes the beggar acts as if he is doing the rich man a favour. The *Schnorrer* tells the Baron that his doctor has recommended sea-bathing for his health; so he asks for money to stay at the expensive resort of Ostend. The Baron queries the expense – couldn't he stay somewhere cheaper? The *Schnorrer* replies: 'I consider nothing too good for my health.' Freud claimed that these jokes are directed against the Jewish religious law that commands rich Jews to give charity to the poor. This law is 'highly oppressive even to pious people' ([1905b] 1991: 158) and stands in 'open rebellion' to conventional views of charity (ibid.: 159). But tendentious jokes need not have a single interpretation. The Schnorrer joke can be enjoyed from the other perspective. We can claim to laugh at the rich Jew, taking enjoyment in seeing him bettered by the poor Jew who treats him 'famillionairely'. The rich Jew might be rich but he is still just a Jew. His wealth gives him no advantage in the battle of wits. Thus, the poor Jew, by subverting the logic of the world, turns the tables on his rich patron and triumphantly rebels against his inferior status.

Freud's relation to his Jewish jokes was not straightforward. Given his opposition to religious belief, it is not surprising that he would interpret his enjoyment of the *Schnorrer* jokes in terms of a rebellion against religious orthodoxy. There is also an ethnic rather than theological dimension that Freud does not discuss in *Jokes*. Although Freud was alluding to himself as an insider, he hardly resembled the figures in most of his jokes. The bathhouse jokes depict *Ostjuden*, the unassimilated ghetto Jews of Eastern Europe. Freud's parents may have grown up as *Ostjuden* but they were raising their children to be Austrian Jews. Only in his earliest years, before the family moved to Vienna, did Freud visit a bath-house. He spoke perfect German without a Yiddish accent. Jews of his circle did not use matchmakers. Certainly no matchmaker brought the young Sigmund and Martha together. The bath-house jokes may have depicted unclean Jews of the ghetto. Freud, a Jew of the Viennese suburbs, was fastidious about his appearance.

Yet, it would be wrong then to conclude that, when Freud was laughing at the Jews of the bath-house, he was reproducing a wider prejudice against the *Ostjuden*. His jokes do not necessarily indicate an element of self-hatred, albeit in a more genial form than Weininger's, as if his laughter were denying that he had inherited the characteristics of his ancestors. As Ernest Jones wrote, Freud had none of the identifiable characteristics of a Jew, except his habit of telling Jewish jokes. In many circles, he would have been able to 'pass' as a gentile. Certainly as the author of a book on humour he could have 'passed' in the eyes of his readers, just as Bergson did not reveal his Jewish background in *Laughter*. But Freud does not seek to 'pass' in this way. He may not have been a bath-house Jew, but he did not aspire to be a member of the compact majority. By telling Jewish jokes in his book, he presents himself to his readers as a Jew. Moreover he celebrates the Jewish traditions of humour. He may not write his theory in a Yiddish accent, but he tells his jokes with one. By including his Jewish jokes, Freud stands against the prejudices that sought to make educated, German-speaking Jews ashamed of their Jewishness.

Freud writes as if the insider jokes recognize the good qualities of Jews as well as the not so good. His bath-house jokes, however, appear to trade on the 'dirty Jew' stereotype. Where are the counter-balancing admirable qualities? Surely, their absence cannot have escaped Freud's notice. It would not be difficult to interpret Freud's enjoyment of such jokes as expressing an aggression that he would not have wished to discuss publicly. The bath-house Jews mock the necessity of regular bathing. The jokes can be heard as a rebellion against the clean order of the gentile world. Was Freud, in his retelling of such jokes, rebelling against the respectable world to which he simultaneously belonged and from which he was being excluded? One can have suspicions.

There is another form of ethnic joke that is less ambiguous and that does not make its appearance in Freud's book. Not all ethnic jokes make use of stereotypes, whether of desirable or undesirable qualities. These non-stereotyping jokes have tended to be ignored by academics studying ethnic humour. For instance, Christie Davies in his survey of ethnic jokes specifically excludes those that do not ascribe a quality to an ethnic group on the grounds that such jokes are comparatively unimportant (1990: 6). The tiling joke imputes no stereotyped characteristics, whatever its target. The audience is expected to know why the teller should wish aggression upon the particular target and to share that aggressive wish. Such jokes can be called 'pure aggression' jokes since they play with the idea of violence not with stereotypes.

In an analysis of Ku Klux Klan joke websites, it was found that over 10 per cent of racist jokes were pure violent jokes in this sense. For example: 'What do you call three blacks at the bottom of a river? – A good start' (for details see Billig, 2001,2005). These are outsiders' jokes and, contrary to Freud's assumption, they do use conventional joke-forms. 'Pure aggression jokes', such as the tiling joke, can be found with different targets. On some websites the target of the 'bottom of the river' joke is three Jews. A common version depicts the target as three lawyers.

The lawyer version differs from racist versions, in that it plays with the idea of violence as a knowingly disproportionate reaction to the irritation that lawyers are generally believed to occasion. No-one outside the world of the joke is seriously advocating violence against lawyers. In the unreal context of the joke, the idea can be entertained, and the entertaining of it provides the entertainment. The racist versions are different in that they are treating actual violence, not the idea of inappropriate violence, as a matter for laughter. Racist violence, which the teller and recipients know to occur, becomes a matter of fun, not outrage. The victims of such actual violence are highly unlikely to find this humorous – especially when members of a racist organization with a long history of violent atrocities are telling the jokes.

Freud would have been aware of violent racist jokes. As the political situation of the Austro-Hungarian Empire was deteriorating and riots against Jews became common, so violent jokes against Jews attained a certain respectability. In 1901, when Freud was still collecting his Jewish jokes, Ernst Schneider, a close associate of Vienna's anti-Semitic mayor Karl Lueger, had publicly recommended an improved technique for converting Jews: they should be immersed in the baptismal water for a period of five minutes (Wistrich, 1989: 222). Freud would probably have heard about this particular crack in *Neue Freie Presse*, the newspaper that he read daily.

Freud kept this type of humour out of his joke book. Perhaps he did not trust some of his gentile readers not to laugh. Maybe the idea of such humour was too painful even for Freud to contemplate. It was easier to assume that such humour was not 'real' humour. His brief comments in *Jokes* suggest that he could not bring himself to dignify these as jokes. Whatever the reasons for Freud's omission, the rhetorical and theoretical effects are clear. His book preserves its air of celebrating humour. It contains no lengthy sections in which jokes are presented in ways that aim to evoke the reader's disapproval, or even disgust. The omission enabled Freud to maintain his theme that humour was rebellious.

Forgetting disciplinary laughter

In Freud's vision, humour is seen to be on the side of the powerless. It teases the world delightfully; it challenges authority and evades restriction; it is the child laughing at the parent. Although Freud calls humour 'rebellious', this joking rebellion is a form of accommodation. It is not the rebellion that challenges power seriously. The sort of cynical humour, that Freud enjoyed and that he found in much traditional Jewish humour, distances the joker from the exigencies of the world, but it does little to distance those exigencies from the world.

There is a further omission in Freud's approach. Rebellious humour may resemble the child laughing at the parent rather than the parent laughing at the child, and Freud, by concentrating upon the rebelliousness of laughter, ignores its disciplinary tendencies. At several points in *Jokes*, Freud refers to Bergson. He cites Bergson's ideas that machine-like behaviour is comic. Freud calls *Laughter* 'a charming and lively' book ([1905b] 1991: 286). He does not, however, mention Bergson's central argument that laughter functioned principally to discipline. Again an omission of significance can be suspected.

The main part of Freud's analysis deals with verbal humour, but Freud was too ambitious a theorist to confine himself to just one type of humour.

In the last part of *Jokes* he develops a theory that applies to non-verbal humour. In doing this, Freud made a distinction between the comic and the joke: 'A joke is made, the comic is found' (ibid.: 238). Much of what Bergson was discussing fell under Freud's heading of the comic, such as exaggerated gestures, absent-mindedness, accidental slips, etc. These are actions or incidents that just happen to occur and that onlookers find amusing. Freud's distinction between what is made and what is found does not fully stand up. Professional clowns and writers of fictional comedy can deliberately create comic actions. At this point, however, it is not so much the cogency of Freud's theory that matters, but what the theory overlooks.

When Freud discussed the comic, he made a theoretical switch. He proposed another theory of humour that does not directly follow from his wider psychoanalytic perspective. He went back to the relief theory of Bain and Spencer, and especially to their assumption that laughter provides a means of expending nervous energy. In this way, he hoped to explain why we laugh at comic actions. Freud cited Spencer's physiological theory of laughter, commenting that Spencer's notion of descending incongruities 'fits in excellently with our own line of thought' (ibid.: 198). One might have expected that Freud would have added something to Spencer's theory. It would have been easy to argue along with Bain that Spencer's theory really describes the humour of degradation, making the 'high' descend to the level of the 'lower'. Had he argued in this way, Freud would have been back with the familiar psychology of tendentious, aggressive motives.

But Freud does not take this line. He uses the relief theory in a purely physiological way that avoids assuming the existence of tendentious motives. Freud's explanation of comic laughter claims that observers build up energy by imagining themselves engaging in the actions that they are observing. They make a comparison between their own way of acting and what they see. Since comic actions are exaggerated and require more nervous energy, the observer has nervous energy to spare. This is then expended in the action of laughter (ibid.: 249f). Had Freud's whole book been based upon this theory, it would hardly have deserved attention. This aspect is neither original nor convincing. Moreover, it lacks the coherence of Spencer's original formulation. It did, however, fit Freud's long-held belief that one day psychoanalytic theory might be translatable into a physiological theory of nervous energy.

Under the heading of the comic, Freud considers why onlookers often laugh at naïveté. Someone may unintentionally say something funny – perhaps a remark will have a double meaning. The onlookers will know that the speaker did not intend the secondary meaning and this adds to the pleasure. Had the double-meaning been intended the onlookers might well have been indignant rather than amused. Significantly Freud uses this essentially motiveless theory of humour when he comes to discussing parents laughing at children, particularly at the naïveté of children. He says that 'it will not surprise us to find that the naive occurs far the most often in children and is then carried over to uneducated adults' (ibid.: 241). The phrasing is indicative. Children and the uneducated are being portrayed as displaying comic behaviour. It is not the onlookers who are psychologically motivated to laugh at such behaviour. The educated adults merely have to 'find' this behaviour, in order to find it funny.

Freud presents a number of examples of childish naïve humour. For example, a brother and sister are presenting a home-made drama to uncles and aunts. They are playing at being husband and wife. In their little play, the husband goes overseas and has various adventures. On returning home he tells of his deeds. His 'wife' then says proudly, 'I too have not been idle', as she displays 12 dolls sleeping in their cots. The adult audience laughs at the naïveté of the remark (ibid.: 242).

Freud uses his relief theory to explain this type of laughter. If the theory attributes any motive to the adult audience, it is one of empathy. Freud writes that 'we take the producing person's psychical state into consideration, put ourselves into it and try to understand it by comparing it with our own'. These processes of 'comparison and empathy' produce an expenditure of energy that 'we discharge by laughing' (ibid.: 245). Far from being driven by tendentious motives and the temporary suspension of empathy, this laughter, according to Freud, relies upon the friendliness of empathy. Freud's argument here is, in effect, a continuation of his Oedipal approach to child sexuality. The adults are psychologically blameless. Their desires, like those of Little Hans's parents, are ignored. In Chapter 9 an episode from the Little Hans case will be discussed. This concerns the way that adults laughed at the little boy and that Freud did not question whether the laughter expressed any tendentious motives. In short, Freud tended to assume that those adults, who laugh at childish naïveté, do so with the innocence of children.

In arguing thus, Freud puts aside his observation that generally we do not know why we laugh. So too he abandons his suspicions. Freud does not wonder whether the adult laughter might be revenge against the demands of children. The uncles and aunts have had to sit still, while the niece and nephew perform their childish drama. The children are exerting a control over the adults who have no power except to remain quiet, and to stifle criticism, boredom and irritation. Then comes the moment of release – the moment they can laugh at those children, who cannot understand what is going on. In this regard, Freud's description resembles Sully's account of the 'hat-comedy': the adult laughter is presumed innocent – 'just laughter' – and the reactions of the laughed-at children are ignored.

Nor does Freud dwell too much on the moment of empathy, in which the adults supposedly compare their mental states with those of the naïve child. Adults do not have the freedom to speak as innocently as does the child, for they regularly have to curtail their thoughts and actions. As the adults laugh at the naïveté of the child, they collectively celebrate the evasion of the restrictions that curtail their own behaviour. However, their laughter signals that the rebellion is momentary and doomed to failure, for the adult laughter serves to strengthen social restrictions, disciplining the very naïve freedom that it celebrates, making childish naïveté less, not more, likely. Thus, the enjoyment is hedged by limitation, as the adult laughter reinforces power and discipline. But, of course, the adults will not claim to be doing this: they will believe that their laughter is purely innocent. Such is the weighted mixture of rebellion, discipline and lack of self-awareness when the powerful laugh at the innocent.

On this matter, Freud's theory sides with the adult over the child. He does not do this by justifying the disciplinary powers of laughter, as Bergson had done, but by assuming the innocence of such laughter. Freud's theoretical switch aids this. Out goes the suspiciousness of psychoanalytic theory. Back comes the innocence of pre-Freudian relief theory. To put it bluntly, there is too much Spencer and not enough Freud. In other circumstances this might be quite funny.

However, the criticisms should not detract from recognizing that Freud produced the greatest suspicious theory of humour. Earlier accounts, such as those by Hobbes and Bain, seem fragmentary and superficial by comparison. Freud not only viewed laughter as a sign of hidden desires, but his theory suggested what these desires might be and why they have to be hidden. His theory may have used the concept of the 'innocent' joke, but if one takes Freud seriously, it is hard to rest easily with the assumption of laughter's innocence. Ideological positivism has to forget the lessons of Freud – to push his scepticism from conceptual awareness – in order to maintain its sentimental vision of humour. That is one reason why Freudian insight is so valuable for critical analysis.

Freud's analysis concentrates on the unconscious motives of individuals, but his insights can be combined with Bergson's analysis of the social significance of laughter. This would mean taking seriously the sorts of disciplinary laughter that Freud overlooked. In a further respect, Freud's analysis of humour points to something important that was often neglected by previous theorists of humour – the developmental aspect. Psychoanalytic theory stresses the childhood origins of adult psychology. Above all, for Freud this meant tracing the infantile roots of those aggressive and sexual desires that in adulthood become indirectly expressed in dreams and jokes. However, if we take seriously Bergson's ideas about the disciplinary purposes of humour, then there is another aspect of childhood to consider. Adults may teach children through mockery. Through this teaching, children may learn not just how to follow desired social codes, but how to laugh. To pursue these matters further the analyst will have to venture into one sensitive area, into which Freud did not even care to tiptoe: the tendentious laughter of the parents.

A coda

Freud left it late to leave Vienna after the Nazis had invaded Austria. He was tired and old. Only when his daughter Anna had been taken for questioning by the Gestapo did he fully confront the seriousness of the situation. Freud's last moments in Vienna indicate both the conservative and rebellious nature of humour. When the Nazis took over Vienna, it was by no means the end of laughter. A majority of the gentile population celebrated. Jews were forced to scrub the streets with toothbrushes. The crowds gathered to laugh at respectable citizens so demeaned. It was fun, just as it would be a year later when German troops pulled the beards of old Polish Jews. Photographs show the soldiers laughing as their victims stand scared and humbled. This was not humour as rebellion but the humour of power, or, to be more precise, the humour of recently acquired power.

At almost the last moment, Freud managed to obtain the paperwork to leave Vienna for England. As a final step, he had to sign a form saying that he had not been mistreated by the Nazis. He told his son that he had added the words 'I can thoroughly recommend the Gestapo'. It seemed one last act of rebellion from someone who had been rebelling throughout his life. The document has surfaced recently, and it appears that Freud never wrote those words (Ferris, 1997). Even the Gestapo would have understood that Freud was being ironical. The joke might literally have been the death of his wife and children. As it was, four of his sisters failed to escape.

The joke could not be spoken, nor written. But it could be thought. Thinking a joke is not enough, for joking needs to be a social act. As Freud had written in *Jokes* many years earlier, the person to whom the joke is told is 'indispensable for the completion of the pleasure-seeking process' ([1905b] 1991: 239). So Freud told his Gestapo joke to his son, pretending that he had already made it in writing. In this respect, the joke contained an element of deceit. Such is the strangeness of humour that this element of deceit does not diminish the essential morality of the joke. Nor does it detract from the greatness of its creator.

II

Theoretical Aspects

8

Laughter and Unlaughter

A critical approach to humour needs to recover some of the elements that have been omitted in previous theories, especially the so-called negatives that tend to get lost in the loose assumptions of ideological positivism. This will mean paying particular attention to the nature of ridicule. The historical discussion has shown that ridicule was not always treated as the enemy in the way that it is by today's ideological positivists. For Plato, ridicule was, under certain circumstances, one of the few permitted forms of humour. According to the Earl of Shaftesbury in the eighteenth century, gentlemanly ridicule was vital for the maintenance of reasonable discourse. And, of course, ridicule lies at the centre of Bergson's analysis of humour. As Bergson argued, without the laughter of mockery, social life would become rigid and ultimately unsustainable. All these ideas suggest that the critic should not go along with the prevailing mood, taking for granted that ridicule constitutes the unnecessary, subtractable negative of laughter's positive value.

However, the historical discussion has also suggested that there is no complete theory of ridicule that can be pulled off the shelf, dusted down and then applied to the relevant phenomena. Shaftesbury's ideas, and those of his followers, were tied to a confident view that what was ridiculous could be objectively identified. And it just so happened that the objectively ridiculous coincided with the prejudices of eighteenth-century gentlemen. Superiority theories such as those of Hobbes or Bain failed to place the act of ridicule in its social context: it was as if ridicule depended on a psychological state, which, in any case, ridiculers have denied experiencing. Bergson proposed an explicitly social theory of ridicule, but then he stopped short of appreciating what this implied for the psychology of laughter. The scepticism of Freudian theory is needed to take Bergson further than he intended – and, indeed, further than Freud intended. For even Freud was at times too willing to take the side of laughter.

The historical discussion suggests that no single theory can hope to explain the complexity of humour. The proponents of the three main theories – superiority, incongruity and relief theories – focus upon one factor, which they claim to be the cause of laughter. But, as their theoretical rivals point out, the chosen factor always omits something important. Incongruity theorists cannot explain why some incongruities fail to provoke laughter while others provoke it in abundance. It is the same with the feeling of superiority or the relief of nervous energy. And so long as these theories are expressed in psychological terms, none can explain why laughter is primarily a social act.

The present approach does not seek to reduce laughter to a single cause. Indeed, humour is not to be considered as a unitary entity. The paradoxical nature of humour is to be stressed. Three paradoxes can be identified – the first two will be discussed explicitly in this chapter, while the third will be a guiding principle of this and the subsequent chapter. The first paradox is that humour is both universal and particular. It is to be found in all societies, but not all humans find the same things funny. The second paradox is that humour is social and anti-social: it can bring people together in a bond of enjoyment, and, by mockery, it can exclude people. Previous theorists have noted these paradoxes. For instance, as mentioned in Chapter 5, Sully in his *Essay on Laughter*, drew attention to such contrary aspects of humour. The third paradoxical feature is that humour appears mysterious and resistant to analysis, but it is also understandable and analyzable. Freud helped show why humour might appear so intractable: we have good reason to recoil from understanding the tendentiously unpleasant aspects of our laughter. Yet, Freud's own way of analyzing jokes showed that much insight is to be gained from seeking to understand this resistance to understanding.

As a first step, the relations between laughter and humour need to be examined. All too often theorists, whether they were superiority, incongruity or relief theorists, have assumed that laughter in itself was unproblematic. What needed to be discovered was the cause of this strange reaction. In an age that values 'a sense of humour' as something self-evidently desirable, the links between laughter and humour cannot be taken for granted. Eighteenth-century theorists of language often made a distinction between natural and artificial signs. Natural signs were the expressions of the face, including smiling and laughing. Because of the limitations of natural signs as a method of communicating thoughts, humans invented languages or artificial signs. According to James Beattie's 'The theory of language', language and artificial signs 'have been employed universally for the purpose of communicating thought; and are found so convenient, as to have superseded in a great measure, at least in many nations, the use of the Natural' (1783: 294).

In such ideas there is a sense that laughter as a natural reaction stands apart from language rather than being a part of it. With the development of Darwinian thinking, such ideas have been interpreted biologically, with laughter being seen as the biologically given reaction to the inner emotions elicited by humour. Such an assumption was to be found in the Victorian relief theorists, who supposed that inner emotional states are accompanied by observable physiological reactions. Darwin described laughter as 'the natural and universal expression' of joy (1896 edn: 218). Today, many writers, not just positive psychologists, also suggest that laughter is a 'natural' response. The philosopher John Morreall, who has written extensively on humour, describes laughter 'as the natural expression of pleasure' (1983: 58). The word 'natural' implies that the relation between the sounds of laughter and the inner state, whether joy or pleasure, is biologically determined. There is a double 'naturalness' in ideological positivism: the inner experience of joy is assumed to be naturally positive as is the outer reaction of laughter/smiling.

These assumptions will be critically examined in the present chapter. The rhetorical nature of laughter will be stressed. This is a prerequisite for the argument, to be developed in the following chapter, that ridicule is both a means of disciplinary teaching and the lesson of that teaching. Like language and other aspects of rhetorical communication, laughter has to be learnt and taught. The rhetorical nature of laughter helps us to understand why humour might be paradoxical. Language is paradoxical to the extent that it enables us to perform contrary discursive acts: we can assert, because we can deny; we can question because we can answer; we can criticize because we can justify, and so on. Because laughter is rhetorical, it cannot be a single, simple thing that can be considered apart from the rhetoric of communication. So the rhetorical opposite of laughter, which here will be termed 'unlaughter', will need examining. Laughter and unlaughter are very much part of the processes of learning and imposing the disciplines of social life. In this respect, the social links between humour and laughter take us to the heart of serious living.

An unamusing anecdote

Many of today's psychological works on humour start with a humorous anecdote. Not only does the humorous anecdote serve to present the humorous credentials of the author, but it also sets up the investigation to be on the side of humour, thereby exemplifying the positives of humour. The critic should be aware of the traps set by the humorous anecdote. Yet, on the other hand, anecdotes are good for theory, for they prevent abstract concepts becoming too far removed from the ambiguous details of social life. So, it is appropriate to start discussing the relations between laughter and humour with an anecdote – an unamusing one.

On 2 July 2003, the Italian Prime Minister, Silvio Berlusconi, addressed the European Parliament. It was a formal speech to inaugurate the start of his presidency of the European Union. Such occasions have already developed into rituals. The incoming president utters platitudes about the future of Europe and the European parliamentary members (MEPs) politely receive the speech. Berlusconi was, to use the conventional euphemism, 'a controversial figure'. Among his controversial acts, the billionaire right-winger had changed Italy's criminal law in order to avoid prosecution for corruption; he had brought fascists into his coalition government; he had supported the American invasion of Iraq. In his own country he was accustomed to his words being received with respect, for he owned the major channels of mass communication.

Berlusconi's speech to the European Parliament was not going well. Across the chamber could be heard the sounds of dissent. Some members were booing; others were banging on their desks. Berlusconi turned to one of the protesters, a German MEP: 'Mr Schultz, I know there is a producer in Italy who is making a film on Nazi concentration camps. I will suggest you for the role of commandant. You'd be perfect.' He beamed at his own wit.

There was a pause, as his Italian words were translated into the various languages of the MEPs, followed by audible gasps and increased booing. He was being 'ironic', he added over the noise. He continued to display his smile, as if it proved his point.

The controversial figure had stirred up yet another controversy. The episode was reported prominently in the newspapers and television studios of Europe, except those owned by the controversialist himself. The German Prime Minister demanded an apology for the insult to his country. Mr Berlusconi, under pressure, issued a statement of regret two days later. He regretted that anyone could have interpreted 'an ironic joke' as an insult to the German nation. He made it clear that this expression of regret did not constitute an apology. Why should he apologize? He was the one who had been insulted. The parliamentarians had treated him with discourtesy. Besides, as he repeated once more, his words were ironical.

The episode illustrates a number of features about the topic of humour. It shows that humour is not the preserve of the 'positive' or the good-hearted. Mr Berlusconi's self-proclaimed irony was not the sort of 'positive' humour that is celebrated by positive psychologists. It is an example of the mockery that such psychology has trouble in accepting as humour. The episode also shows that humour can be a matter of controversy, for there are differences in the appreciation of humour. What may have amused Mr Berlusconi and his supporters certainly offended others.

Because there are differences in reaction, it is difficult to define humour in terms of the laughter that it evokes. There may be attempts to be humorous that result in just a small number of people laughing and with many more people registering outrage. Should we define Berlusconi's remark as not being humorous because it failed to produce laughter in the majority of its recipients? But should humour need to pass some sort of statistical test of success in order to qualify as humour, as if sheer weight of numbers should always be used to define what is humorous? There may be some attempts at humour that fail entirely in producing laughter.

The key issue is not to define humour in terms of its effects but to examine how it may succeed or fail in its effects. Similarly, analysts should try to avoid becoming prescriptive in their definitions of humour, by claiming what they find funny to be 'genuine humour' and what they find unfunny to be not properly humorous. The theoretical danger is that analysts would deny that they find certain forms of ridicule to be funny. Then, ridicule and mockery can easily slip through the definitional net. The end-result becomes cosy and comforting. Humour is something good and those with a sense of humour are good people. Mr Berlusconi and his offensive remarks would be removed from the agenda of humour. However, this would represent an uncritical approach, for the critic needs to take seriously the negative, rather than eliminate it theoretically.

The Berlusconi episode shows that jokes and humorous remarks are not merely uttered, but they have to be received. Moreover, the reception cannot be guaranteed. There can be a mismatch between the attempt at humour and the effect of laughter. Accordingly, humour cannot be defined purely as that which elicits the response of laughter. Humour might involve the *attempt* to produce laughter in its recipients but it must be recognizable as humour even if it fails in its end. Besides, humour can have other ends than seeking to make the addressed recipient laugh. Mr Berlusconi was not seeking to amuse Mr Schultz. He was intending to insult him, to silence him, to trap him within the mocking laughter of others.

There is a 'meta-discourse' of humour. As will be suggested, humorous remarks, having been made, are also commented upon. This is particularly evident when wit goes wrong or provokes divided reactions. Mr Berlusconi was quick to comment on his humour – or use a meta-discourse of humour – by claiming that he was just being ironic. In fact, the issue was not whether his offending remarks were ironic or not. His critics did not doubt the irony. No-one actually believed that the media proprietor was in fact recommending his opponent for an acting career. There was a gap between the literal and intended meaning of his remarks that is characteristic of irony (Attardo, 1993). The issue was whether it was appropriate to use irony in this way. Berlusconi's opponents, including the German Prime Minister, were affronted that a joke on the topic of concentration camps should be made, especially when publicly addressed to a German national. The German Prime Minister had called it an insult to his nation. He did not add that it was singularly inappropriate for a man, who had introduced the political heirs of Mussolini into the Italian government, to imply that those who objected to his politics must be Nazis.

The episode illustrates that laughter and humour do not stand alone, outside the normal or serious, processes of communication. If laughter is rhetorical, then so is the refusal of audiences to respond with laughter. This means that theories of humour should not be reduced to the biology of laughter. Mr Berlusconi's inherited capacities to stretch his facial muscles into a narrowed-eyed smile do not explain the incident. There are political, moral and aesthetic dimensions to humour, as well as psychological ones. Mr Berlusconi may have been claiming just to be ironic, but he also aimed to humiliate his opponents. Imagine the width of his smile had the joke succeeded and the rest of the chamber had joined with him in laughing at Mr Schultz. Imagine, too, how Berlusconi's own newspapers and television stations would have carried the picture of that triumphant smile.

Such a smile would have represented more than just a movement of facial musculature – it would have been more than just a smile. It would have represented a potent, self-serving rhetoric expressing both what could and could not be said openly in words. Mr Berlusconi could not have declared that he wished to humiliate the Germans who were spoiling his great day as President of the European Union. Nor would he have been able to admit to deriving pleasure from disrupting the serious routines of the occasion. He, the media magnate who had broken rules and had pushed his way through the niceties of democratic politics, was showing a thing or two to the MEPs who make their little speeches, pass their sanctimonious resolutions and never exercise real power.

This, too, points towards another dimension: the power of humour to disrupt order. Even bad humour – whether its badness is moral, political or aesthetic – possesses this potential. It can also possess the power, or at least the ambition, to impose order. Berlusconi depicted himself as the injured party, reacting to disruption. Around the chamber, MEPs were interrupting his speech with their booing and their banging. If only irony could have restored order, good behaviour and silent admiration.

In this way, humour needs to be understood in relation to the social order. This means more than decoding jokes in terms of their social impact or in terms of their potentiality for disrupting solemn occasions. A simplified sorting of the world into its psychological positives and negatives will not suffice. It means having a wider psychological view about the complex relations between the individual and the social. The dynamics of humour are situated within, as well as reacting against, these complex relations.

Laughter and biology

Many philosophers and psychologists have begun discussing the topic of humour by declaring words to the effect that humans are 'the laughing animal'. Aristotle set the pattern, writing that 'no animal laughs save Man' (*On the Parts of Animals*, 1968, x: 29). His lead has often been followed down the ages. Voltaire, in his *Philosophical Dictionary*, called man 'a risible animal', stressing that 'man is the only animal which laughs and weeps' (n.d.: 136). James Beattie likewise claimed that 'risibility' was 'one of the characters that distinguish man from the inferior animals' (1779: 299). In the era of modern psychology, the same assertion is made, with William McDougall declaring that 'man is the only animal that laughs' (1923: 165).

It seems reasonable to start with a striking phrase whose literal truth seems easy to justify. Other animals do not laugh spontaneously in the way that humans do. Hyenas may make laughter-like noises, but that is an acoustic accident. Their screechings no more correspond to the functions of human laughter than do the barking of dogs or the roaring of lions. Certainly, hyenas have not been observed to swap jokes or tell funny stories. But humans laugh; and throughout humanity laughter is used to indicate enjoyment. Thus, the epithet the 'laughing animal' seems to suggest something about our biological nature. We are the species that has been formed to enjoy humour.

Perhaps a qualification should be made in the case of humans' nearest relatives. Darwin, whose *The Expression of the Emotions in Man and Animals* remains as insightful as anything published subsequently on the topic, notes that anthropoid apes, when tickled under the armpits, will make 'a reiterated sound, corresponding to our laughter' (1896 edn: 201). There are detectable acoustic differences between human laughter and that of primates (Provine, 2000). Nevertheless, Darwin's observation highlights the complex relations between laughter and humour. Being able to display pleasure when tickled does not indicate what is meant by a sense of humour.

In Chapter 2, the value of humour was noted in the small ads of those seeking partners for marriage and/or romance. Anyone wishing to meet a special other with a 'good sense of humour' is not primarily searching for a partner who wishes to have their armpits tickled.

There is evidence that some primates can show the rudiments of what humans would recognize as humour. Chimpanzees, who have been taught to communicate using basic elements of human sign language, will occasionally make wrong signs or throw things at their keepers, and then use the 'funny' sign (McGhee, 1983). These very crude forms of humour are not necessarily accompanied by laughter. They are made by chimps after being taught by members of the 'laughing animal' species. In natural conditions chimpanzees neither spontaneously develop elaborate systems of sign language, nor signify their own actions as 'funny'. Perhaps the lesson of such studies is not that apes or chimps are almost-laughing animals. It is that the laughing animal, which is also the language-using animal, can with considerable effort instruct its nearest evolutionary relatives in some very basic language and humour.

That humans may have inherited the capacity to make the noises of laughter does not mean that humour is biologically inherited, even though it is universal. Humans may have inherited the capacity to eat: without that capacity the species would die out. It also may be the case that every society has customs, taboos and rituals associated with eating. However, this does not mean that food customs are biologically inherited or that there is a gene to ensure that eating and drinking carry complex social meanings. At some point, culture takes over from biology. The demands of social living, rather than the imperatives of biology, might ensure that food has cultural meaning.

So it is with humour. It is hard to doubt that the capacity to smile and laugh, just like the capacity to cry, is biologically inherited. Darwin's observations on the development of smiling and laughing in infants have hardly been bettered. The ability to scream is present from the moment of birth. Smiling and laughing develop later. These reactions are not learnt as such. Moreover, they form the basis for later adult reactions. Darwin comments that 'in joy the face expands, in grief it lengthens' and that these patterns are to be found in 'all races of man' (1896: 213). Some modern psychologists have gone on to propose that there are some basic facial expressions of emotion and that these have a biological basis (i.e., Ekman, 1984, 1992; but see Parkinson, 1995, and Wierzbicka, 1995, for reservations and qualifications).

There are good biological reasons why infants should be able to produce laughing, smiling and crying within the first few months of life. Compared with other species, human infants have a long period in which they are utterly dependent on others for food, comfort and warmth. This period of dependency occurs before the young human has acquired the means to communicate in the distinctively human way, namely, by means of language. If during this period the infant could not communicate basic discontent and contentment, then it would be at a disadvantage in making its needs known to its carers. Those infants with an ability to communicate in such ways would be at an evolutionary advantage. Similarly, there are good reasons why the sign for happiness should have evolved to be as distinct as possible from that of discontent – hence the face expanding in the case of the former and lengthening in the latter. Whatever the details, it makes sense to say that infant crying, smiling and laughter possess survival value for the survival of the species with the longest childhood.

If we take the evolutionary argument seriously, then we are led to a paradoxical conclusion. The period in which humans show the most biologically controlled laughter is the period when they have not acquired a sense of humour. Infants do not understand jokes, make puns or play practical jokes. The infant's laughter resembles the ape's reaction to tickling. It is directly controlled by stimuli, whether internal or external. To acquire a sense of humour – or an appreciation of funniness and an ability to create funniness for others – infants, and all primates, must do more than merely laugh.

Development of humour

John Morreall, in his book *Taking Laughter Seriously* (1983), has suggested that infants lack a sense of humour because they cannot make the sort of 'cognitive shift' that is essential to humour. Morreall had in mind the sort of shift in meaning that word-play depends upon. However, there is also a more basic shift in humour. At the minimum this shift involves, as Michael Mulkay (1988) has emphasized, being able to recognize and communicate a shift from the world of seriousness. In this respect humour resembles playfulness. The newly born infant is serious. It reacts directly to its own bodily states and to the outside world. It cannot indicate playfulness. To do so, some sort of linguistic or representational ability is required, in order to transcend the world of here-and-now. James Sully, in his *Studies of Childhood*, reported the case of two sisters who one day said to each other 'Let us play being sisters' (1895: 48). The statement might appear curious to adult observers but it is not meaningless. Kurt Koffka, the great Gestalt psychologist, was to cite this anecdote in his *The Growth of the Mind* in order to illustrate how real the world of play was for children (1928: 381). Playing at being sisters, Koffka suggested, was more vivid than merely being sisters.

The preface 'let us play' was indicating a shift. The world of play was being entered with its own rules, fantasies and outcomes, distinguishing it from the mundane world. In the game of 'playing sisters', the sisters can imagine themselves with different parents. The preface conveys that what is to come is 'play'. Thus, the ability to play in this way depends upon possessing the ability to distinguish play from non-play. So it is with humour. As the child acquires the ability to engage in humour – to make puns, act in funny ways, etc. – so the child learns to communicate that such actions are to be taken humorously.

A study by Kathy Johnson and Carolyn Marvis (1997) illustrates this well. They examined the emergence of verbal humour in a single infant, named Ari, who was actually the child of one of the authors. When Ari was learning to speak, he inevitably made some mistakes, inadvertently calling things by their wrong name. Some instances provoked adult laughter, which, according to Johnson and Marvis, provided 'a social cue that such mislabels are considered funny' (ibid.: 194). In time, Ari began to mislabel deliberately in order to evoke laughter. To do this, he needed to accompany his mislabelling with signs that what was being said was 'funny'. The simplest way was to smile or laugh as he spoke. He would point to a picture of a cow and call it a duck while laughing loudly (ibid.: 190).

When adults told Ari that his mislabelling was funny, they were teaching him what should be counted as 'funny'. There is evidence that parents can do this quite directly. Judith Dunn (1988), in a fascinating study, analyzed in detail the interaction between mothers and children. She provides several instances of mothers telling children what is funny. In one example, a mother and child are watching a puppet show. The mother tells child to watch the dog talking to the puppet. The child says that dogs don't talk. The mother tells the child to keep watching. The child does so, and then declares 'Funny dog.' The mother replies, 'He is' (Dunn, 1988: 163). The child is learning how to use 'funny' – funny dogs can talk and funny dogs can be laughed at. In another example the child is wearing inappropriate trousers. The child says that her father dressed her. The mother says, 'Silly old Daddy' and the child laughs (ibid.: 158). Again, the child is learning the appropriateness of laughter – and blaming others – in such a situation.

In these examples laughter does not just occur but the funniness is signalled by talk. There is, in this respect, a 'meta-discourse' of humour that is used to comment on what is to be considered funny (Norrick, 1993, 2003). The meta-discourse has serious, unfunny meaning. Adults told Ari jokes, deliberately playing with words. These might be preceded by a remark such as 'Now, grandpa will tell you a joke' (Johnson and Marvis, 1997: 191). Ari would know that grandpa's verbal 'mistakes' then were not to be taken seriously – but the preface is to be taken seriously. When Ari started making his own jokes, he would preface them with something like 'Ari tell mommy a joke' (ibid.: 191). When the joke had been told, his mother might say 'that's funny' (ibid.: 191). In this way, the adult indicates what funniness is, as well as giving approval to the child's 'funny' remark. As the child develops humour, so the child is acquiring the ability to engage in the meta-discourse of humour.

Laughter, as a way of demonstrating 'that's funny', can also be part of the meta-discourse of humour. Such meta-discourse is vital for the adult world of humour. Through language it is possible to indicate that some things are funny, and thereby to demarcate a distinction between the world of seriousness and that of humour. Joke-tellers will often preface their joke by a remark that indicates that there is a shift: 'I've got a joke for you', they might say (Norrick, 1993: 125f). In so doing, they would be indicating, to use

Berger's phrase, a 'temporary emigration from the reality of everyday life' (1997: 11). Of course, it is possible to use bodily gestures, such as smiling, for this purpose too. Mr Berlusconi used his grinning face to indicate non-seriousness as he delivered his 'ironic' remark.

Failure to indicate the transition from seriousness to playfulness can fatally injure the attempt to be humorous. It is said that the British philosopher C.B. Broad was a ponderous lecturer. According to his students, he would read each sentence twice, except for jokes which he would read three times. The extra repetition was the only means of knowing that he was telling a joke (Edmonds and Eidinow, 2001: 54). The boundary-markers between humour and seriousness are not absolute and they, too, can be used for the purposes of humour. One can blur the boundary, as in the case of straight-faced irony, when something that is not to be taken literally, is uttered, even momentarily, without markers of humour (Attardo, 2000; Mulkay, 1988). In this case, fooling others, by not indicating the passage to humour, is part of the humour. It is a verbal, practical joke.

Perhaps other species of primate might be able to produce a facial grin to resemble Mr Berlusconi's. But not even the most talented sign-using chimp is able to deliver an insult and then to claim that their insult should be understood as irony, all the while holding a gesture of grinning. Something peculiarly human is involved in such actions. However, the necessary skills have to be learnt, for the world of humour is barred to the infant whose laughter is held in thrall to biological imperatives. The child, who is learning the enjoyment to be gained by calling a cow 'a duck', is preparing for bigger things to come. It may be charming to watch these first steps along the path to full-grown humour. Sully wrote at the start of his *Studies of Childhood* that the child 'makes a large and many-voiced appeal ... to our sense of the laughter of things' (1895: 3). However, we should not sentimentalize the 'positives', diluting red warning signs into a rosy glow. With the example of Berlusconi's irony in mind, we should be prepared for the possibility that not all need be positively charming in the world of humour.

Universality and particularity

There are infinite ways of being humorous. That is part of the problem. The child, who has learnt that approving laughter can be elicited by misnaming objects, is only just beginning. There is so much more to learn – whether it be puns, irony, standardized jokes, gestures of mimicry, anecdotes about minor mishaps, *bons mots*, imitation farting, actual farting, insult disguised as irony, irony disguised as insult, etc. The child has to learn that humour is not one thing, but its range matches the range of the human imagination. Cleverness and stupidity, rebelliousness and conservatism, tolerance and bigotry – all can find their expression in humour. The world of humour is democratic, for it is not restricted only to those who possess a particular talent, background or status. Everyone can participate. And there are different ways of participating.

Consequently, humour should not be understood as a simple phenomenon. It has its contradictory elements. As was mentioned, humour is both universal and particular. And it is both social and anti-social. A simplified psychology, that seeks to explain humour in terms of a single factor – whether it be a single impulse, motive or intellectual operation – will not be able to give due weight to the paradoxes of humour. These are not paradoxes to be resolved, for they express the complex, indeed contrary, demands that social life makes upon individual.

The first paradox – that of humour's universality and particularity – relates directly to laughter's rhetorical rather than biological nature. Humour is universal: this statement, at the minimum, implies that humour can be found in all societies. During the period of colonial expansion, European travellers would sometimes claim to have come across a people who did not seem to have a sense of humour and who, by this failure, showed that they belonged to a lower level of civilization. James Sully in *An Essay on Laughter* (1902) dismissed such reports. He pointed out that the 'natives' sometimes did not care to laugh in front of their powerful conquerors (ibid.: 225f). They might prefer to laugh behind their backs for the good reason that they were laughing at them. Subsequent anthropological investigations have given no reason to doubt Sully's conclusion. As one anthropologist has claimed, humour is pan-human, for no humour-free culture has been discovered (Apte, 1983).

It is most certainly not the case that only societies living in happy circumstances experience humour. Joking can appear in the direst of social environments; in fact, it can provide a way of demonstrating that one has not succumbed to exigency. Some observers have commented that political humour may be more vigorous in tyrannies than in democracies (Benton, 1988; Speier, 1998). Some prisoners in the concentration camps told jokes (Cohen, 1953). When the anthropologist Colin Turnbull stayed with the Ik, a mountain people in Uganda, their social fabric was disintegrating under conditions of starvation. Nevertheless, the Ik would often break into laughter, especially when they witnessed misfortunes happening to others. Particularly amusing was the sight of an enfeebled old woman slipping and plunging to her death (Turnbull, 1972). This laughter was not just signifying an inner state of pleasure, as they witnessed such misfortunes. There is an 'out-thereness' about the laughter of humour. The Ik were indicating that the misfortunes, happening before their eyes, were funny. In doing this, the Ik might not have been displaying humanity, but they were showing themselves to be essentially human.

To say that humour is universal, or that it is pan-human, is not the same as saying that all humans share the same sense of humour. In fact, quite the opposite can be asserted. Humour might be universal, but humans do not find the same things funny. There are cultural and historical differences. To quote Peter Berger's paraphrase of Pascal, 'what is funny on one side of the

Pyrenees is not funny on the other side' (1997: 14). Thankfully, not all societies have shared the grim humour of the starving Ik. There does not exist a particular joke, scene or anecdote that will universally amuse all members of the laughing animal species. Any attempt to find the objectively laughable – the holy grail of comedy that will guarantee to unleash the biological mechanism of laughter – will be doomed to failure.

Even individuals within a culture do not share the same humour, as the Berlusconi episode illustrates. Indeed, the same person may not find the same things funny at all times. Presumably little Ari, and certainly his family, grew bored with the joke of calling a duck a cow and vice versa. Perhaps there were serious moments when Ari's parents might have been irritated by his deliberate mislabelling. What was charmingly funny would then become unfunny – in fact, it has to if the child is to learn more sophisticated ways of being humorous, and that there are times and places for laughter.

Almost a hundred years ago, mass audiences in the new cinemas laughed regularly and loudly at the films of Charlie Chaplin. It seemed as if the little clown with the bowler hat and cane had found the secret to universal laughter. Rich and poor, educated and uneducated, English, French, Americans and Germans, laughed long and loud. Here, it could be imagined, was an objectively and universally funny figure. Now, three generations later, the laughter appears somewhat mystifying. An audience today might raise the occasional smile, if they could be persuaded to watch old films of Chaplin. But modern audiences would be unable to reproduce anything like the shared hilarity of their great-grandparents. Towards the end of his life Chaplin commented in an interview with a journalist that the Tramp could not work in modern times: 'There's not the same humility now ... so it has become something of an antique...it belongs to another era' (Merryman, 2003). What once seemed universally funny no longer appears funny at all.

The premise of universality on its own cannot explain how this can happen. It is not just that humour changes as one crosses borders of culture and time. Even in Chaplin's heyday, not everyone was impressed. Some preferred other silent movie stars and others, including Freud, preferred to read rather than watch films. Today, researchers have studied differences in humour in relation to such variables as gender, ethnicity, mood, personality, etc. (e.g., Gruner, 1997; Herzog, 1999; Jaret, 1999; Kelly and Osborne, 1999; Lampert and Ervin-Tripp, 1998; Nevo, 1998; Ruch, 1998). Having a sense of humour does not mean laughing indiscriminately at every type of joke. It involves preferences and judgement. Chapter 2 mentioned a British public opinion survey that found people valued humour rather than seriousness in their partner. The survey contained another interesting finding. Overwhelmingly respondents wanted their partners to be 'intelligent' rather than 'frivolous' (Observer, 16 October 2003). What counts as 'humour' and what counts as 'frivolous' can be contested. Two people may claim to value a sense of humour equally highly, but this does not mean that they are made for each other. One partner's humour can easily become the other's irksome frivolity.

William Hogarth beautifully captured the variety of reactions to a comedy in his print 'The Laughing Audience', published in 1733 (reproduced in Uglow, 1997: 18). We cannot see the scene that is amusing the audience in the theatre – we only see the faces of the audience. Those in the pit are staring at the stage and laughing. It is Hogarth's genius that he portrays individual character, as the faces laugh in their different ways. Only a bare majority of faces in the picture are laughing. At the bottom of the picture, three musicians are concentrating seriously on their job. At the top of the picture in the gallery, no-one is looking at the events on the stage. Three orange-sellers are trying to attract the attentions of two young beaux, who in their turn are more interested in the sellers' charms than in their wares. Hogarth's laughing audience is not a universal audience. Some have to earn their living while others can find better amusement to hand.

One figure in the audience is staring intently at the stage. He is looking down his thin nose with disapproval. Although he is depicted as sitting at the end of the back row, the engraving is so subtly constructed that this disapproving figure is almost at the centre of the picture. As Derek Jarrett has commented on the print, 'once noticed the face cannot easily be ignored' (1976: 165). Nor does the disapproving figure appear to wish to be ignored. He could have slipped out of the theatre unnoticed. Instead he remains there, displaying his disapproval of the entertainment. No-one else in the audience notices this display for they are all too preoccupied. But Hogarth notices. And so, throughout the years, has Hogarth's audience. Thus, the print's title, 'The Laughing Audience', contains its own joke.

Hogarth's print illustrates that any universal statement about what the laughing animal finds funny will founder. To be sure, writers have not hesitated to write in the most universal terms about what 'we' find funny. William Hazlitt, in his 'Lectures on English comic writers', listed a number of things that make 'us' laugh. He wrote: 'we laugh at deformity ... we laugh at the dress of foreigners...we laugh at people on the top of a stagecoach', and so on (1987: 69). For all the confidence of Hazlitt's statements, he is not describing a universal community of laughers. Not all humans laugh at deformity or the dress of foreigners. Most of us today have had no opportunity to laugh at the passengers on a stagecoach. Hazlitt's apparently universal 'we' is circumscribed by time, place and background: he is talking about Englishmen like himself.

There is something deeper at work than the mere fact of difference when it comes to different preferences in humour. Such differences are frequently invested with moral meaning, for humour has its politics, morality and aesthetics. Hogarth's sternly depicted face in the pit was expressing a moral disapproval, the force of which Hogarth well knew. Strict religious moralists not only objected to the obscene frivolities of the theatre, but they found fault with the very idea of caricature in general and with Hogarth's art in particular (Uglow, 1997; Donald, 1996). Thus, 'The Laughing Audience' seeks its own laughing revenge on unamused critics.

By the same token, it was not merely personal preference that stopped most MEPs from sharing Mr Berlusconi's demonstration of irony. They were not commenting on the technical deficiencies of his irony. Theirs was a moral rejection of the utterance: no such joke about concentration camps should have been made. Today, people object to the idea of laughing at deformity, foreigners or those too poor to travel inside a coach. Were Hazlitt to write his piece today in a newspaper, he would be met with a barrage of angry criticism. 'Quite frankly', outraged letter writers would declare, 'I don't find these things in the least funny and Mr Hazlitt represents the sort of smug, prejudiced Englishman, whom we had hoped was no longer around ...' In fact, such is the social expectancy nowadays that people should enjoy funniness that contemporary letter writers are likely to begin by presenting credentials for their own sense of humour (Lockyer and Pickering, 2001): 'I have always enjoyed a joke and a laugh, but I wish to protest at ...' No-one complaining about particular instances of humour would wish to appear as generally lacking a sense of humour.

Our moral sensitivities may have changed from Hazlitt's day. But this cannot occur without detailed instruction about the ethics of laughter. One might predict that young Ari's mother would react with strong, immediate disapproval should her child have displayed inappropriate laugher – whether at foreigners, poor people, physical deformity or whatever. 'That's not funny', she might say, as firmly and as confidently as if she were identifying a table, chair or any other physical object in the world.

If there are no universal ethics, politics and aesthetics, which are shared by all cultures, then likewise there can be no universal humour. However, the fact that there might be no universal humour does not explain why humour is to be found universally. It is a truism to assert that all cultures have codes, which encourage some sorts of behaviour and which forbid others. There could be no social order, and thereby no culture, if there were no such codes. In this regard, ethics, politics and aesthetic preference are to be found universally. However, different social groups have different codes – they do not share the same ethics, politics and aesthetics. We might assume that it is part of the biological nature of humans to live in social groups with cultural norms. This does not mean that any particular cultural norms are genetically inherited. A code that permits horse flesh to be eaten is no more or less a reflection of human biology than a cultural code that forbids its consumption. What we can say is that all known cultures have codes about the eatable and the non-eatable, but that no code, nor personal preference, is more 'natural' than any other.

The paradox of humour's simultaneous particularity and universality can be understood in the same light. Since the cultural codes differ from society to society and across time, then so will the content of the humour. However, this still leaves a problem. The necessity for a culture to have cultural codes seems self-evident. But why should all cultures have codes of humour? What is the social function, or necessity, of these codes? Why is a completely serious society unknown? The possibility can be raised that the universality of humour derives from the necessity of having social codes, rather than directly from the biological characteristics of humans. To put the question individually, rather than phrase it in terms of abstract theory: why does Ari's family, along with families across time and space, find it so natural to tell the young child not only the names of things but also what is funny and what is not funny?

Laughter as rhetoric

Smiling and laughing might appear to be natural, spontaneous reactions, but there is much that has to be learnt in order to accomplish culturally appropriate ways of producing the smile or the laugh. Jonathan Swift, in his essay 'A Complete Collection of Genteel and Ingenious Conversation', observed that persons of good taste display the sort of laughter that can only be acquired by 'much observation, long practice and sound judgment' (1909a edn: 238). Young ladies, who seek to be proficient in the graces of conversation, must learn 'the contortions of every muscular motion of the face', 'the proper juncture of smiling and frowning' and 'when to jibe and when to flout'. Then there was 'the whole military management of the fan' that must be proficiently mastered (ibid.: 247–8).

In recent years, analysts equipped with the advantages of recording devices have been able to demonstrate Swift's point that conversational laughing is no simple, 'natural' matter. Gail Jefferson has investigated the complex rhetoric of laughter in conversations, examining what meaning the particles of laughter might have (Jefferson, 1984, 1985). In doing this, she has paid great attention to where speakers place particles of laughter in their utterances. Her evidence demonstrates that laughter does not just occur at the end of jokes. It can be subtly placed in serious remarks. And when it occurs at the end of jokes, it does not occur in a simple, 'natural' way. Jefferson's general argument is that laughter does much more than signify a sense of inner joy. In fact, often it does not even do this.

Laughter has a rhetorical character, for it is typically used to communicate meaning to others, rather than being a reflex reaction following a particular inner state. In this regard, laughter is not like a hiccup or facial tic. Moerman (1988), building on Jefferson's work and using data from both American and Thai conversations, shows that there are many different ways of laughing. According to Moerman, laughter can vary along four dimensions: (1) delayed/prompt; (2) few particles/many particles; (3) soft/loud; and (4) slow/rapid. By varying their laughter along these dimensions, speakers convey meaning. For instance, a speaker might deliver a verbal insult with accompanying loud, many particled laughter to indicate that the insult is not to be taken literally but as a joke. If the recipient responds with significantly lower grade laughter – for instance, if the laugh is noticeably delayed and contains many fewer particles – then the recipient can be indicating that offence is being taken at the insulting words. Offence can be taken despite the original speaker's mitigating laughter and despite the recipient's acknowledgement that humour had been originally intended.

The 'military management' occurs with successful joke-telling. Harvey Sacks (1992) analyzed in detail the way adolescents told a dirty joke (see Mulkay, 1988, for an alternative analysis of the same episode). As Sacks shows, there is nothing automatic or artless about laughing at a joke. Recipients should be able to produce 'laughter in an appropriately timed way', coming not too soon or too late after the joke (Sacks, 1992: 486). This laughter needs to be delicately coordinated between speakers, so that the recipients upgrade the laughter made by the joke-teller in delivering the joke. Sacks comments: 'The thing about laughing is that to do laughing right, it *should* be done together' (ibid.: 571, emphasis in original). At the same time, the laughter should appear natural and unfeigned, if the recipients are to indicate their pleasure at the joke. As Swift realized, much practice and sound judgement are required to deliver laughs in just the right, natural-seeming way.

Laughter does not stand on its own as a reaction to humour. It can be mixed with words to produce the rhetoric of appreciation. Deborah Tannen (1989) shows how the recipients of a joke can indicate their appreciation by repeating the punch-line amidst particles of laughter. Kotthoff (1999) gives an example of a man telling a humorous story about a flat-mate. In the course of the story, the teller scattered particles of laughter, thereby indicating that a funny ending was on the way and that appreciative laughter was being sought from the recipients. When the anecdote was completed, the recipients responded with suitably amplified laughter. When the main burst of laughter has subsided, one of the recipients declared without laughter particles, 'that is really marvellous' (ibid.: 73). His comment was a rhetorical judgement, but so was the recipients' laughter which also was saying 'that is really marvellous'.

The placement of laughter particles can perform subtle conversational functions. For instance, a laugh may precede the introduction of a conversationally problematic phrase, such as an obscene word. The laugh signals to the listener that the speaker is aware that the word might give offence (Jefferson, 1984). Coupland and Coupland (2001) provide examples of young persons talking about age with old people. The young person, on being told an old person's age, may use laughter particles to indicate surprise: 'eighty-seven, ha-ha, you don't look a day over sixty-five, ha-ha'. In such a case, the laughter-particles specifically accompany the numbers. They are not generally scattered in the utterance as if the young person were merely laughing at what the old person has said. The precision enables the communication of a specific polite meaning, namely, conveying surprise at the age of the older person, who, so it is suggested, had appeared to be substantially younger.

A laugh or a smile can also mitigate an utterance, such as a complaint or direct request, that otherwise recipients may find too strong or too direct (Holmes, 2000; Jefferson, 1985). Again, the laughter particles have to be precisely placed within utterances, in order to indicate exactly what is to be softened, mitigated, marked as problematic, etc. In these cases, the laugh becomes part of the rhetoric of politeness, smoothing over conversational difficulties that otherwise would arise (Brown and Levinson, 1987; Jefferson, 1984; Mulkay, 1988: 112ff).

Laughter particles can also be used to convey argumentative meaning, sometimes ambiguously and without the need to spell out all assumptions. One study has looked at the way that native-born Greeks talk about Moslem minorities (Figgou, 2002). Greek speakers often told stories about how some Moslem minorities, such as the Pontians, show prejudiced attitudes against others, such as Albanians. Signs of laughter often accompany such tales. For example, one woman talked of a Pontian woman who complained 'because an Albanian has moved into a flat next to hers [laughs] can you believe it? She has been living here for a few years and she has already started to treat others as unwelcome, as inferior' (Figgou, 2002: 252). The laughter does more than signify irony at one minority group complaining about another. The speaker downgrades the importance of such complaints: they are to be treated with amusement, not moral outrage. In this way, the speaker justifies her own complaints against Moslem minorities, by implying that she is treating Moslems just as they treat others. More than this, she conveys that the whole business, because it is amusing, is not so important and, thus, she should not be criticized for her views about minorities. In this way, the woman presented her own character or *ethos* through the laughter particles that also serve the rhetorical purpose of seeking to dispel the suspicion of prejudice as the speaker complains against ethnic minorities.

Perhaps 'problems talk' provides the most striking example of the gap between laughter and humour. Jefferson (1984) has looked at the way that speakers, who wish to discuss their problems with professional care-workers or with friends, often introduce their problems. They often use interpolated particles of laughter. By doing this, speakers with serious illnesses can demonstrate that they are 'coping' with their difficulties, showing what Jefferson calls 'brave laughter' (see also Chapman, 2001). Those with less serious complaints can use laughter in problems talk to forestall criticism that they might be complaining unnecessarily (Du Pré, 1998). By placing laughter at the end of a description of a problem the speaker can ease the way for the recipient to respond. Jefferson (1984) gives the example of a speaker who says of her problem 'I've stopped crying' and follows this with a laugh. Her laughter indicates that the problem is not too painful to talk about rather than that the problem is funny. The recipient then asks without laughter 'Why were you crying?' In this way, the laughter thereby facilitates the serious talk about the past crying.

In such troubles-talk, the recipient is not supposed to repeat the laughter of the speaker who is introducing the troubles. For the speaker's careful introduction to her problems to be met with a burst of laugher would be a solecism indeed. It would belittle the problems, as well as demonstrate that the recipient had not learnt the socially appropriate management of the laughter-particle. In troubles-talk, the laughter is 'humourless' (Du Pré, 1998: 104). A laugh can be so much more than just a laugh. In conventional terms, it is not even a laugh: it is a serious part of conversational language.

Rhetoric of unlaughter

To say that laughter can be rhetorical implies more than saying that laughter communicates meaning. Rhetorical meaning is always potentially contestable. In speech every rhetorical move can in theory be countered by an opposing move, for whatever can be asserted rhetorically can also be negated rhetorically (Billig, 1996). Just as words can indicate praise for a funny story – 'that is really marvellous' – so the opposite judgement is possible 'that is really not funny'. One person can claim their jokes as proof of good humour, while recipients might see them as evidence of irritating frivolity. It is the same with the rhetorical uses of laughter. If laughter can be used to communicate appreciation and amusement, then there are ways of conveying disapproval and unamusement. The rhetorical nature of laughter is possible because there is a corresponding rhetoric of unlaughter.

The idea of 'unlaughter' indicates the rhetorical nature of laughter. If someone is showing 'unlaughter', this implies more than that they happen not to be laughing. Much of the time people are not laughing as they go about their daily business. Someone engaged in actions that do not involve laughter, such as walking down the street on their own, is simply not laughing, rather than showing unlaughter. A parallel can be made with the English words 'smiling' and 'unsmiling'. A person is typically described as 'unsmiling' when they are conveying seriousness in moments when they might be expected to smile. The word communicates more than the absence of a smile – it is a significant absence. Politicians might be described as 'unsmiling' as they emerge from an unsuccessful meeting. Their unsmiling faces will convey serious deadlock, rather than the triumph of brokering a deal. Expressions of disappointment, grimness and general seriousness will be needed to convey this unsmilingness.

'Unlaughter' can be used to describe a display of not laughing when laughter might otherwise be expected, hoped for or demanded. Mr Berlusconi's critics reacted with unlaughter. They demonstrated their unlaughing outrage in the European Parliament to the television cameras that were recording the events. In this sense, their actions and expressions were conveying the significant absence of humorous reactions. Similarly, the unlaughing member of Hogarth's laughing audience is doing more than merely happening not to laugh. His face is constructed to indicate disapproval, if not to others in the audience, then at least to Hogarth's own audience. His laughter is a significant absence.

A complete absence of laughter or smiling can be disconcerting to the joke-teller. Every professional comedian has tales of 'dying a death', when an audience greets the jokes with silence, refusing to occupy the slots which the comic has left for the audience reaction. Xenophon describes a banquet at the house of Callias, with Socrates among the guests. Philip, a professional buffoon, invites himself, promising to amuse the company in return for a free meal. He said 'a thousand ridiculous things', but each remark was greeted with silence. He failed even to provoke a smile. Finally, he threw himself on a couch, covering his head with his cloak, groaning and refusing his food. Only then did he succeed in his original aim. Critobulus, one of the diners, 'almost burst his sides' (*The Banquet*, 1910: 165; for a discussion of the role of the professional buffoon in Ancient Greece, see Bremner, 1997).

Xenophon provides no description of how exactly the diners failed to laugh at Philip's jests and what precisely was his reaction to their silence. In this context silence can indicate much more than an absence. It is itself a rhetorical presence, speaking volumes of criticism. Moerman (1988) offers a Thai example to indicate how a recipient of a joke can demonstrate displeasure. After a particular joke had been told, one recipient did not laugh and immediately cut in to change the subject of the conversation. This person was doing more than personally not appreciating the joke. He was outwardly displaying his disapproval, his unlaughter. It was unclear whether he disapproved of the particular joke or to the fact that a joke was being told at this particular moment. He was not reacting like someone who had failed to understand a joke. Instead, he was cutting in to halt the enjoyment of others.

If a speaker makes a teasing remark, then the recipient can indicate disapproval by withholding laughter and reacting with a 'po-face' (Drew, 1987). The po-face can simultaneously indicate understanding and disapproval of what is being understood – although it can also be used as a joke against the joker. If speakers can demonstrate their appreciation of a jest by loud, immediate and prolonged laughter, then they can also indicate lack of appreciation by delayed and meanly particled laughter. The groan or the deliberately slow 'oh-hah-hah' can indicate a minor lack of amusement rather than the full-scale disapproval of unlaughter (Norrick, 1993: 123–5).

Just as there are varieties of ways of conveying appreciation of humour, so there are many ways of displaying unlaughter. The put-down, following a joke, can be accomplished verbally. Queen Victoria, on hearing a slightly risqué joke told by a groom-in-waiting, declared decisively that 'we are not amused'. Verbal unlaughter requires appropriate facial expression. The effect of Queen Victoria's statement would have been undermined had she displayed a broad smile, or even added a mitigating 'laughter-particle' of politeness. Lytton Strachey described how Queen Victoria would customarily show displeasure at impropriety: at such moments 'the royal lips sank down at their corners, the royal eyes stared in astonished protusion' (1928: 251). One suspects that Victoria's famous declaration of first person plural unamusement was accompanied by face of singular *hauteur*.

Silence and an appropriately forbidding expression can be sufficient on their own to deliver magnified and magnificent unlaughter. The novelist P.G. Wodehouse recounted how as a young man he had attended a luncheon at which the comic poet W.S. Gilbert was the honoured guest. At one point, Gilbert started to tell the assembled company a lengthy anecdote that was obviously going to work its way towards a humorous conclusion. Wodehouse misjudged the end of the story and let out a premature burst of laughter across the table. In the ensuing silence, he received a stare from the great man: 'His eyes were like fire, and his whiskers quivered. It was a horrid experience' (Sutherland, 1987: 271). Few can attain such heightened skills of unlaughter. Mobilizing its heavy, silent weaponry takes considerable practice, status and dyspepsia.

Just as joke-tellers cannot guarantee themselves a reaction of laughter, so unlaughter, however fearsome its weaponry of display, cannot guarantee to silence the laughter of others. In fact, the laughter may be deferred. Unlaughter is a favourite target for the laughter of ridicule. As Wodehouse told the story of that luncheon, so he was presenting Gilbert as a comic figure to be mocked. We are to imagine the whiskers and the mute outrage, and we are to smile. Similarly, Victoria becomes an object of amusement with her superior non-amusement. Again, Hogarth captures this to perfection. We cannot see what amuses the laughing figures in his print. In consequence, we cannot directly participate in their laugher. But we can spy the incongruously unlaughing figure in their midst. Then we can smile. In this way, Hogarth invites us to laugh at unlaughter and thereby recruits us into his laughing audience.

Learning to ridicule

Another paradox of humour was mentioned earlier, namely that humour is both social and anti-social. With rhetoric, speakers can do opposing things, criticizing or praising, asserting or negating, and so on. Similarly, speakers can be serious or humorous. Laughter does not possess a single rhetorical force even within the context of humour. It can be the laughter of hostile ridicule or the laughter of friendly appreciation: one can laugh *with* others and *at* others. As such, laughter can join people together and it can divide; and it can do both simultaneously when a group laughs together at others. The laughter itself does not accomplish this uniting and dividing, for the laughter takes its meaning from the wider rhetorical context of humour. Consequently, one might say that humour, rather than laughter itself, can be both social and anti-social. This duality of humour directly relates to ideological positivism. As was discussed in Chapter 2, psychologists have sought to distinguish positive humour, which supposedly brings people together in shared amusement, from the negative humour of ridicule, which hurtfully divides people. Positive psychologists aim to encourage positive humour, while eliminating the negative varieties. This good intention, however, is not so simple in practice.

Certainly, it is easy to sustain the idea that humour can be a positive social force that brings people together. As one sociologist has written, 'we rarely laugh alone and never tell ourselves jokes out loud or play jokes on ourselves' (Fine, 1983: 176). As was seen in Chapter 6, Henri Bergson gave particular attention to this aspect of laughter, declaring that laughter stands in need of an echo. More properly, he should have said that humour stands in need of an echo, for some types of laughter, such as the laughter of 'problems-talk', most certainly are not to be echoed. Sociologists such as Fine emphasize that humour can help sustain the morale and cohesion of groups. That is why positive psychologists recommend the use of humour in therapy, work groups, family life, and so on. As Bergson appreciated, this social aspect of laughter also has its cruel side.

It may seem obvious that humour is social, but the theoretical implications are important. In the first place, any psychological explanation of humour must inevitably be limited if it takes as its model the individual perceiving a particular comic stimulus. This was a weakness in the classic versions of all three major theoretical approaches. The superiority, incongruity and relief theories were essentially individualist rather than social theories, for they sought to discover what stimuli or feelings induce individuals to laugh. Such stimulus-response models cannot explain why laughter should be so much greater in company.

By contrast, there is no such problem, if laughter is seen to be rhetorical, for rhetoric is part of social communication. The primary purpose of laughter or unlaughter will be to communicate with others. It is possible to talk with oneself and, thus, to laugh with oneself, but this must be a secondary use of rhetoric (Billig, 1996). One might note that little Ari learns the rhetoric of laughter within the context of his family. In this regard, humour is not, and cannot be, a solitary discovery. Ari becomes the centre of amused attention when he makes his little errors of labelling. Mommy, grandpa and Ari love to swap jokes, their laughter creating shared moments of enjoyment. The positivist psychologists do not lie when they stress the force of humour in bringing people happily together.

But that is not the whole story. The shadow of ridicule remains. The rhetoric can be reversed with the positives turned to negatives. Laughter can hurt and divide. It can have its victims. Hazlitt talks of laughing at deformity and at foreigners. He also mentions how hard it is to stop children laughing at 'a negro' (1987: 69). Hazlitt was, of course, imagining his own audience to be full-bodied, English and white. He would know that the targets of the laughter could hardly be expected to share the mirth. They are the objects of the laughter, excluded from the party of the mirth-makers. In the early nineteenth century, Sydney Smith declared that 'laughter is, to many men, worse than death'. He went on to declare that 'there are very few who would not rather be hated than be laughed at' (1864 edn: 139). Smith's exaggeration is pardonable. There may be some people who welcome a gentle teasing on a topic of their choosing; they may bask in the attention. Nevertheless, the exceptions do not undermine the rule. Smith's general estimate was correct: ridicule can be more hurtful than hatred. After all, hatred can often be more easily returned than ridicule. Hating those who ridicule us does not necessarily ease the pain.

Positive psychologists and other contemporary theorists have shown a tendency to downplay the importance of derogatory humour. Peter Berger has suggested benign humour 'is the most common expression of the comic in everyday life' (1997: 100). He offers no evidence for this assertion. Other writers have claimed ridicule to be a primitive form of humour that individuals and societies will outgrow. This was the position of Sully, Ribot and Dugas over a hundred years ago, as they compared the humour of 'primitive peoples' with that of children (see Chapter 5 above). The assumption can still be found. John Morreall writes of children's 'natural propensity to derisive laughter'; he suggests that modern society has not entirely outgrown such childish pleasures, although they are much diminished nowadays (1983: 10).

Such comments depict ridicule as a detachable aspect of humour. It is something that will disappear as the world and its inhabitants mature. Only benign humour then will be left. This optimistic hope fits in well with the assumptions of ideological positivism, just as it did with the imperialism of Sully's day. There is, however, another possibility that was taken seriously by Bergson. Ridicule, far from being a detachable negative, lies at the heart of humour. The origins of little Ari's humour are suggestive. His parents were laughing at linguistic mistakes that he made unwittingly and unwittily. In such moments, it will be suggested in the following chapter, one can glimpse ridicule's social functions that help to explain why humour might be universal.

For the present one can note a developmental implication. Children will have to learn the rhetoric of laughter, in order to laugh appropriately and to understand the laughter of others. It is reasonable to assume that, in common with other aspects of language, children will learn through interacting with and imitating older speakers, particularly adult care-takers. Two further observations, that have often been made and that have already been mentioned, can be added. The first is that children engage in the laughter of ridicule. And the second is that parents gain delight in laughing at their children.

In relation to the latter assumption, James Sully, who was one of the first psychologists to discuss at length the development of humour in children, has already been quoted. With regard to the first observation, he also wrote that children's humour at first tends to have an element of mockery: 'Regarding now the child as teaser, we see that he very early begins to exercise at once his own powers and others' endurance' (1902: 201). Sully specified that he was not just referring to boys but 'a vigorous child, even when a girl, grows aggressive and attempts various forms of playful attack' (ibid.: 201). In the eighteenth century, the Scottish philosopher David Hartley made similar observations. Children do not laugh spontaneously at birth but 'they learn to laugh as they learn to talk and walk' ([1749] 1834: 274). He also commented that 'the most natural occasions of mirth and laughter in adults seem to be the little mistakes and follies of children' (ibid.: 276).

In such observations, there is an implicit thought that tends not to be brought into the open. If children learn humour from adults and if they delight in the humour of ridicule, then possibly they do so by copying adults who are laughing at them. However, it seems easier to recognize the cruelty and crudity of the child's laughter than that of the adult. The rhetorical tease-spray comes in handy when considering adult mockery of children. The word 'teasing' is used to imply something playful and good-natured (Yedes, 1996). In the hat example, discussed in Chapter 6, Sully down-played the motives of the adult laughing at the child – the 'teasing' was devoid of malice. It was, he suggests, as benign as the rule of the British over the child-like natives. Freud made no such parallel between the laughter of parents and that of imperialists. But he too assumed that the laughter of parents was devoid of aggressive motive and beyond suspicion.

The tease-spray downgrades the possible 'negative' effects: the adult is only teasing, not being seriously aggressive through humour. 'Our' laughter, especially 'our' parental laugher is asserted to be good-hearted. The assumption is boosted by an imbalance of research interest, which has not happened by chance. Developmental psychologists have often studied children's humorous aggression, but they have tended to avoid looking at parents' use of aggressive humour against children, except as a problem that characterizes malfunctioning parents (for a fine analysis of the way that such adults may use aggression, including sarcasm, against their children, see Scheff, 1997: 81f). Freud was good at describing the origins of aggression, including aggressive humour, in children. He discussed the unconscious aggression that children may feel for their parents, but, strikingly, he ignored the unconscious aggression that parents may feel against their children. A particularly telling example of Freud's neglect in this matter will be discussed in the next chapter.

In modern developmental psychology children are often described as going through stages of cognitive development: only when they reach a sufficient stage of cognitive complexity can 'real' humour begin (i.e. Bergen, 1998; McGhee, 1983). The more that psychologists stress the stages of development, the more the actions of the parents slip from sight. Even when the social aspects of development are taken into account, there is a tendency to stress the positives. For example, Barbara Rogoff, in a notable account of child development, depicts development as an 'apprenticeship' in which children are guided by adults in 'skilled, valued sociocultural activity' (1990: 39).

There is another possibility. Mockery may be one of the ways in which the 'apprenticeship' can occur. According to Buss, 'one of the prime means of socialisation is through teasing, laughter, and ridicule' (1980: 232). Since Buss wrote those words some twenty or so years ago, psychologists have not systematically studied the ways in which 'normal' parents might use the humour of mockery to discipline their children – although there has been much research in the ways that children and adolescents tease or bully each other (e.g., Crozier and Dimmock, 1999; Eder, 1990; Smith, 1999; Smith and Sharp, 1994; but see Hepburn, 1997, 2000). With respect to mockery, the psychological emphasis tends to be on what children, rather than parents, do. It is as if the aggression of ridicule has to be projected upon children and 'bad' parents.

Nevertheless, there is anthropological evidence to suggest that in a variety of cultures, mothers may use teasing to control their children. Bambi Schieffelin (1986, 1990) has studied the way that Kulali children acquire language. The Kulali live in Papua New Guinea and teasing is, according to Schieffelin, 'pervasive in everyday social interactions', for teasing enables people to make and resist demands in this egalitarian society (1986: 166). Because mothers frequently tease their children, the children in their turn learn how to tease others. Anthropologists have noted similar maternal teasing amongst the Kwara'ae of the Solomon Islands (Watson-Gegeo and Gegeo, 1986), Mexicanos in California (Eisenberg, 1986), Japanese families (Clancy, 1986) and working-class Americans (Miller, 1986). In these cases, mothers use teasing to control their children, mocking inappropriate behaviour, including inappropriate use of speech. Kulali mothers rarely if ever use physical chastisement. They often tease their children to discourage them from asking for food that the mother does not wish to give. There is also pleasure to be gained from teasing. One working-class mother in Baltimore told the anthropologist that she enjoyed seeing her child 'get mad' (Miller, 1986). She then added that teasing helped make her child more independent – as if realizing that it is not acceptable to enjoy making a young child tearfully angry. A more selfless, pragmatic justification is provided for what is typically unplanned, spontaneous behaviour.

The anthropological evidence about mothers teasing their children is intriguing. Indeed, the very word 'teasing' might be downplaying the significance and the force of the activity that is being described. There is a temptation to assume that anthropologists study exotic peoples who differ greatly from ourselves. In the case of parental teasing, it would be comforting to imagine that parents in Papua New Guinea or in the deprived areas of American cities tease their children to a much greater extent and with far more aggressiveness than do 'our' kindly, educated, liberal Western selves. However, as will be discussed in the next chapter, there are reasons for supposing that caregivers in most cultures, if not all, might tease or mock children. Ridicule is a cost-effective means of social discipline, especially for those like the Kulali and Western liberals who look askance at the physical punishment of young children.

The lack of research into how 'we' might discipline 'our' children through mockery is itself a significant absence. Nevertheless, glimpses of parental mockery near at home can be found. Judith Dunn (1988), in her study of the interactions between mothers and children, depicts something more fraught and full of conflict than is implied by Rogoff's notion of 'apprenticeship'. At around the age of two, the child begins to thwart parents regularly. Humour plays its part, as the child sees humour in what the mother is saying seriously. The mothers can also use humour against the child, deriving pleasure in mockery. Dunn notes that mothers' sense of humour is rarely if ever studied by psychologists (ibid.:166).

In one episode, the little boy has been noisier than the mother would like. The mother calls him a lion and starts treating him as if he were a lion. She laughs at him. He protests in distress, 'I not a lion, I John' (ibid.: 164). He is crying. It is the mother, who is mislabelling and getting pleasure from it. The more that the child wants to return to serious labelling, the more she can assert her authority by laughing at him, showing that she is not taking him seriously. She is no longer calling him her little boy. He is now the object that is being labelled unwillingly as 'funny'. A serious lesson about behaviour is being taught through laughter. John is being shown how to use the laughter of ridicule. He is not enjoying his lesson.

Little Ari represents one image that can be universalized: the child who is happily learning the pleasures of laughter and funniness, serving, as it were, an apprenticeship in the rhetoric of humour. Little John represents another image: the parent using the laughter of ridicule to exert control and to impose the codes of social living. That image, too, can be universalized. Across time and place, children are learning the pleasures of ridicule and its pains from the disciplinary moves of adults. How else would ridicule acquire its fearsome aspects? And how else would the young learn of its cruel pleasures?

These questions are theoretically important. They derive from considering laughter to be rhetorical rather than a 'natural' reaction. If laughter is rhetorical, then, like all the devices of rhetorical communication, it has to be learnt and can be mobilized in various ways. The possibility is raised that the rhetorical aspects of laughter are not merely social practices that have to be learnt; they are also part of the techniques of learning social practices and discouraging infractions. This would help explain why humour is both universal and particular. Maybe ridicule provides a key force in maintaining social order – maintaining not this or that particular social order, but social order more generally. If this is so, then ideological positivism's promise of constant, warm-hearted happy laughter is positively self-deluding.

9

Embarrassment, Humour and the Social Order

Humour is universal. That much has already been asserted. But assertion is not sufficient for theoretical analysis. Reasons have to be given to account for this universality. If laughter is rhetorical, as was argued in the previous chapter, then the universality of humour is not to be satisfactorily explained in biological terms. It does not take us far to say that humour is culturally universal because humans are biologically equipped to laugh. The social practices of laughter and its relations to the cultural specificities of humour will still need explication. The question, then, will be why all societies have social codes of laughter and humour.

An alternative way of accounting for the universality of humour would be to follow Bergson by asking whether humour possesses a vital social function. In Chapter 6 when discussing Bergson's theory of laughter, a distinction was made between necessary and surplus functions. A function is necessary if social life in general – rather than a particular form of social life – depends upon the fulfilment of that function. Bergson suggested humour fulfilled such a function. Not only this, the aspect of humour that fulfilled this function was ridicule. Without the possibility of ridicule, social behaviour would be in danger of becoming impossibly rigid. Accordingly, the social practice of ridicule is necessary for the maintenance of social life. In this way, Bergson attempted to provide a social rather than biological answer to the question of humour's universality. It will be argued in this chapter that Bergson was basically correct but for the wrong reasons.

Before going into the argument why ridicule might be necessary for the maintenance of social order, a few words need to be said about the implications of such an argument. The idea of ridicule fulfilling a necessary function will find itself at odds with the prevailing assumptions and theories of ideological positivism. Far from viewing ridicule as a basic part of humour, ideological positivists see it as an unfortunate negative side effect. Moreover, they view this negative as something that needs be subtracted from social life, rather than being a vital component on which much else depends.

But it is not only ideological positivists who hold such assumptions. Even social critics often do. Freud, as was seen, took humour to be primarily rebellious. But if ridicule is necessary for maintaining social order, then humour will not be intrinsically or essentially rebellious, as Freud supposed. It may even help maintain the order that it appears to mock. Critical theorists also have a preference for rebellion over discipline. Views that applaud laughter as an instrument of rebellion are likely to receive a favourable hearing. In recent years the work of Mikhail Bakhtin has justifiably been much praised by critical thinkers in the social sciences (e.g., Bell and Gardner, 1998). Bakhtin has provided great insight into the dialogical nature of language. His views on humour, however, parallel aspects of ideological positivism. Bakhtin, who lived most of his adult life under tyranny in the Soviet Union, sympathized with the anarchic counter-world of the carnival (1981: 84f). He claimed that anger and indignation divide people, while 'laughter only unites' (1986: 135). But, of course, laughter can divide as well as unite. So, Bakhtin followed the long tradition of distinguishing between the good and the bad laugh. There was 'the joyful, open festive laugh' and 'the closed, purely negative, satirical laugh' (ibid.: 135). Ridicule was festive if it mocked authority, but was negative if it served the interests of maintaining social order.

So the present argument cuts against a number of contemporary grains. As the historical survey suggested, there is nothing 'natural' about present assumptions. Past figures, as intellectually and ideologically diverse as the Earl of Shaftesbury and Henri Bergson, have commended ridicule for its essential place in social life. Significantly both those figures are out of fashion today. The theories and self-help books of ideological positivism rarely mention either of them. Similarly, radical social theorists today are unlikely to take to their hearts an eighteenth-century English aristocrat with unambiguously snobbish views, or a spiritual philosopher drawn to Catholicism.

However, the purpose is not to resurrect their particular claims why ridicule might be so necessary to social life: neither the winged lightness of the Bergsonian spirit, nor the civility of the gentleman's club will make their appearance here. In fact, much of the argument will focus upon something to which neither Bergson nor Shaftesbury gave much theoretical significance: the place of ridicule in the social development of children. Freud, of course, gave developmental issues greater priority than any previous theorist of humour. But the present position examines development from a different perspective than Freud. It seeks to notice the ridicule of parents that Freud overlooked.

By looking at the ridicule of parents, one can see how humour, social customs and the practices of mockery are reproduced over time. But to sustain the argument, a further element needs to identified in order to be connect the practices of ridicule with the conduct of social life. This extra linking element is, it will be suggested, another social universal: the practice of embarrassment.

Outline of the argument

The present argument about ridicule might rub against the prevailing common sense, but it is not a difficult argument to make. It does not require a new toolbox of technical terminology. Nor does the argument need to be put in an allusive, difficult style, as if the ideas must be distanced semantically and syntactically from the linguistic conventions of common sense. The argument can be simply put. Everyday codes of behaviour are protected by the practice of embarrassment. If one infringes expected codes of interaction, particularly if one does so unwittingly, one might expect to be embarrassed.

What is embarrassing is typically comic to onlookers. Social actors fear this laughter. Accordingly, the prospect of ridicule and embarrassment protects the codes of daily behaviour, ensuring much routine conformity with social order. This is likely to occur within all cultures. Therefore, ridicule has a universal role in the maintenance of order.

The argument, however, will not be presented as if it were a stand-alone theory, for it is part of a critique of ideological positivism. What is remarkable about the argument is not its originality, nor its complexity, but that it needs to be made at all. The logic of some notable sociological and psychological theories seems to be leading towards the general argument, only to stop curiously short. So it will be necessary to demonstrate, not the originality of the argument, but how it seems to have been avoided.

Therefore, this chapter will have a dual strategy. It will suggest that the argument for the importance of ridicule in social life is supported by the inner logic of Erving Goffman's sociology, as well as by some findings of social psychologists. Yet, it will also be suggested that there is a curious gap between the inner logic and the outer theorizing of Goffman and social psychologists. All the elements for the argument exist, yet analysts seem to avoid making connections. It is as if they have carefully threaded the positive and negative wires into an electric plug. They stand before the socket with plug in hand, but for some reason they do not bend down to insert the plug. They look but do not notice the socket. Their unnoticing eyes save them from using the negative wires to bring light.

The present aim is both to develop the argument and to show how its obviousness seems to have been overlooked. When such sophisticated observers as Goffman, and even at one point Freud, fail to notice something that is before their eyes, then one can suspect that the act of overlooking is at least as significant as that which is being overlooked.

Disciplinary humour

To begin with, a distinction can be made between two sorts of humour: disciplinary and rebellious humour. Both types can be seen as forms of ridicule. Disciplinary humour mocks those who break social rules, and thus can be seen to aid the maintenance of those rules. Rebellious humour mocks the social rules, and, in its turn, can be seen to challenge, or rebel against, the rules. Disciplinary humour contains an intrinsic conservatism, while rebellious humour seems to be on the side of radicalism. This distinction is not original. Janet Holmes (2000), in her analysis of the way that humour is used in places of work, distinguishes between repressive and contestive humour. The former is used by superiors to maintain their power in the work-place, while contestive humour is used by subordinates to challenge that authority. The distinction does not rest upon the intrinsic nature of the humour itself, or what Freud called 'the joke-work', but upon the social position of the person using the humour and the uses to which the humour is put.

The distinction between disciplinary and rebellious humour – or between repressive and contestive humour – may be helpful theoretically. Nevertheless, in practice it might be difficult to classify unambiguously a particular piece of humour as belonging to one or other type. The classification can be contentious, because wider ethical, personal and ideological considerations are involved in how we classify our jokes and those of others. In the eighteenth century Shaftesbury thought that the ludicrous could be clearly and unambiguously identified: some things, he believed, were objectively ludicrous. His critic John Brown had fun pointing out that what appears ludicrous to an aristocrat may not appear so funny to a commoner.

As Freud suggested, people are motivated to think well of their own laughter and, in consequence, they may make self-interested and self-deceiving claims about what they find funny. If there is a cultural or ideological value for either rebellious or disciplinary humour, then we are likely to find a claim and counter-claim. In the Platonic republic, a guardian who giggled, may claim that they were not being unnecessarily frivolous and certainly not mocking the order of state; they were laughing with the good disciplinary purpose of discouraging others from error. Today, by contrast, laughers are more likely to justify themselves by claiming that no offence was meant or that they were merely mocking those in authority who deserve mockery. In Bakhtinian terms, we are more likely to claim to be laughing in the subversively festive way than the negative sarcastic manner. If there is a debate whether a particular remark is positive or negative, disciplinary or rebellious, there can be no objective proof to settle the matter to the satisfaction of all parties. Self-deceit can always be suspected in the application of the desirable label to one's own humour.

Regarding the Berlusconi episode, that was discussed in the previous chapter, it would have been possible for Berlusconi to claim that his 'ironic' remark was contestive, because he was rebelling against the demands of the formal situation, and outraging conventionalists in the process. His critics, by contrast, could claim his remark to have been a coercive and repressive misuse of power. Those who make racist or sexist jokes often claim to be rebelling against the demands of 'political correctness', placing themselves on the naughty, contestive, powerless side. Even academics can sometimes take this line. Gruner (1997), in his psychological analysis of humour, mentions that at conferences he shows cartoons of men eyeing up women. This brings complaints from 'politically correct' women. Gruner comments: 'these complaining ladies not only dislike the cartoon humour, they don't even *understand* it (ibid.: 90, emphasis in original). Gruner, in defending himself, points to the so-called social power of 'political correctness', as do others who justify controversial, right-wing remarks on the grounds of rebelling against 'political correctness' (for analyses of the way 'political correctness' has become part of right-wing rhetoric, see, for instance, Fairclough, 2003; Johnson et al., 2003). Gruner's critics will see him as more powerfully coercive than he sees himself. In such arguments, one's own power is curiously invisible, for power is always claimed to reside on the other side. Thus even the powerful can justify their humour on the grounds that it is challenging, not exercising, power.

That is why one needs to be cautious about describing disciplinary humour as being unambiguously conservative, and rebellious humour as being objectively radical. It is not quite so straightforward. Denial, self-deceit and self-righteousness can all be at work. This is particularly so in an ideological climate that favours the rebellious over the disciplinary. Nevertheless, some broad distinctions between rebellious and disciplinary humour can be made.

In order to illustrate these differences, we can go back to the childish roots of humour, at least as studied by psychologists in North America and Britain. As mentioned in the previous chapter, Johnson and Marvis (1997) have looked at the origins of humour in one child, Ari. The earliest incidents of verbal humour occurred unwittingly. Little Ari made linguistic mistakes, calling things by their wrong name, and his parents laughed. Their laughter was informing Ari of his errors. In this sense, the laughter had a corrective function. It was also mocking the mistake. However, the mockery was enacted with displays of delight to ensure that the child, who was being mocked, was not being excluded from joining in the laughter, however perplexed he might be about its nature. Corrective mockery need not performed in this inclusive manner. In the case of little John, the mother's mockery was more direct and the child reacted with tears not laughter (Dunn, 1988).

The disciplinary teaching of children is typically double-edged. There is the overt message of the adult, laying down the rules. Then there is the covert teaching that indicates how the adult world of rules can be disrupted. This can be seen in the teaching of appropriate speaking. Language-learning does not consist in merely learning the rules by which objects are named or by which grammatically acceptable sentences are formed. To speak appropriately also involves following codes of interaction. The child must learn to speak in ways that are considered socially acceptable or polite (Brown and Levinson, 1987). Speakers must learn the appropriate, or culturally polite, ways to intervene, to cede the floor and to end their turns of speaking, and so on. As conversation analysts have revealed, each utterance, that proficient speakers make, bears the marks of the complex codes of appropriateness (Nofsinger, 1993; Psathas, 1995).

Anthropologists have noted that there are wide cultural differences in the ways children and adults converse; in some cultures adults will adopt childish forms of language when speaking to children; in others they will speak as they do to other adults, correcting childish mistakes (Schieffelin and Ochs, 1986). Whatever the practices of such talk, in all cultures children eventually have to learn to talk in the appropriate way and adults are required to ensure that they do. In the process, young children, in learning the complex codes of politeness, will make errors. This will occur in all cultures, regardless of what is considered to be an error and at what ages children are still permitted to speak childishly.

Children are likely to butt in when they should not, use inappropriate forms of address, speak too loudly, too softly, too directly, mumble too much, and so on. Their care-givers will inform them that certain ways of talking are unacceptably 'rude'. This is dangerously double-edged. Each time care-givers tell the child, 'don't say that, it's rude', they will be showing the child how to be rude. They will be establishing a domain of forbidden talk. Sometimes, especially in the case of taboo words, what is forbidden becomes an object of temptation and desire. The child will take delight in breaking the rules and uttering forbidden words (for more details, see Billig, 1999). In consequence, the child, in learning how to talk, will not only learn how to be polite but also how to be rude, for there cannot be politeness without rudeness.

Something similar occurs with disciplinary laughter. The laughter that greets the 'wrong' utterance points out the childish error. It is an easier form of discipline than physical punishment or withdrawal of love, especially for minor infringements. It is discipline with a loving smile – and all the more ambiguous for that. When disciplinary laughter occurs, the child may learn that a certain way of speaking is incorrect. Just as the teaching of politeness involves the teaching of rudeness, so disciplinary laughter teaches the rules that should be followed and, in so doing, it teaches how the rules can be broken. Little Ari learns the rules of labelling. He also learns that breaking these rules – calling a duck 'a cow' – can produce smiles and laughter. He would repeat the trick intentionally to the delight of his family. In addition, there is the covert message. Little Ari, by observing his parents' laughter, will be learning how to mock. If anyone else makes an error, he knows that laughter can be an appropriate response. He will be able to take social pleasure in the mistakes of others.

Children can turn around the lessons that they learn in order to take their revenge against parents. They can mock the parents' attempts to impose rules. They can even wait years to enjoy the opportunity. Norrick (1993), in his analysis of conversational humour, gives the example of a mother who uses the wrong phrase, when talking to her grown-up daughters. She notes that there is a pencil on the couch and asks 'Who belongs to it?' Her daughters laugh at the mother's failure to use language properly. One of them remarks that the kitten is playing with the pen, so the kitten belongs to it. The other daughter laughs and adds her own joking remark, mocking the original mistake. The two daughters, but not the mother, are laughing. Finally, one of the daughters asks the mother 'Don't you want to say, "Who does the red pen belong to?"' The mother interrupts her to say that she had deliberately said '"Who belongs to it." I meant it as a *joke*' (Norrick, 1993: 89–90).

The daughters can suspect that the claim was made *post hoc* to save face. It would be an instance of what Attardo (1993) calls the 'decommitment' function of humour: one separates oneself from the serious or literal meaning of one's utterance, in order to claim that it had only been a joke. The mother had not previously displayed the conventional signs that she was making a humorous remark. She had not scattered laughter particles on the way, nor joined in her daughters' laughter. The analyst, with the benefit of a recorded version of the interchange, can point to the implausibility of the mother's claim. But implausibility cannot be turned into incontrovertible fact. There is no way of looking into the mother's head to identify a precise mental state that would settle the matter once and for all. Claim and counter-claim are still possible. As Norrick writes, much conversational joking revolves around ambiguity and 'conversationalists can take advantage of this ambiguity as a face-saving device' (1993: 136).

Power can be directly enforced by disciplinary laughter as groups maintain their unity by mocking transgression of their customs. Michael Wolf, in an interesting discussion of humour, claims that laughter can protect the norms of correctness by discouraging deviance; in this way humour 'implicitly invokes a certain sense of social commonality' and can achieve an 'enhancement of solidarity' (2002: 334). In work groups new members, who wear inappropriate clothing, may find themselves the butt of humour (Fine, 1983). This laughter is a form of instruction, just as it is when older hands play practical jokes on apprentices. Derrick Allsop's *Kicking in the Wind* (1997) describes life in an English Third Division professional football team. A young apprentice is playing his first match in the first team. On the coach to the game, the senior players tell him to fetch the sandwiches. He goes to do so, without realizing that the sandwiches are for the return journey after the game. The manager is initially angry, before realising that a joke is being played. The young professional 'slinks back to his place among the elders' and, comments Allsop, it's 'all part of the initiation process' (ibid.: 148). The apprentice learns the rituals, while the senior professionals exercise their power, sharing pleasure as they do so.

The way that humour can be used to bolster convention has long been remarked upon. In the mid-eighteenth century Francis Hutcheson in his *Thoughts on Laughter* wrote that 'in the more polite nations there are certain modes of dress, behaviour, ceremony, generally received by all the better sort, as they are commonly called'. If in any assembly 'a contrary dress, behaviour, or ceremony appear ... a laugh does ordinarily arise, or a disposition to it, in those who have the thorough good-breeding, or reflection, to restrain themselves' (1758: 32–3). According to Hazlitt, 'anyone dressed in the height of fashion, or quite out of, is equally an object of ridicule' (1987: 69). In these instances, what is 'normal' or socially conventional is assumed to be unfunny.

Christie Davies (1990), in his extensive survey of ethnic jokes, suggests that majority members of a culture will often tell ethnic jokes about marginal groups who speak with a noticeable and low-status accent. The English, for instance, will make ethnic jokes, putting on mock Irish/West Indian/Pakistani accents. Such jokes mark out these accents as being 'funny', not quite 'proper' English. In the nineteenth century the magazine *Punch* contained many cartoons that mocked the speech of servants (Pearsall, 1975). The magazine was reflecting its readers' assumptions that the speech of the lower orders was a sub-standard form of English. These sorts of jokes take 'our' accent, dress, customs as the implicit 'correct', unfunny standard against which the differences of others are to be found simultaneously wanting and humorous.

It is the same with childish mistakes of the so-called rules of language. When Ari's mother tells him that one type of animal is called a 'duck' and another is called a 'cow', she does not expect to be laughed at. This is normal, unludicrous language, whose rules are to be learned and followed. But when Ari gets the rules wrong, earnestly calling the duck a 'cow', then the grown-ups smile. Similarly when the grown-up children finally told their mother that she had spoken incorrectly, they were not laughing: they were giving a serious explanation for their laughter. In this way, disciplinary humour, in ridiculing those who fail to comply with the codes of appropriateness, stands guard over rules, which are not assumed to be funny.

Rebellious humour

By contrast, rebellious humour outwardly mocks the rules and the rulers. If the social world is full of codes that restrict what can be said and done, then delight can be taken in breaking the rules that constrain social actors. The child may derive pleasure from uttering words that the parents have expressly forbidden. Dunn (1988) recounts an episode when a young girl has been told not to utter the words 'Mr Piggyface', when a certain visitor comes to the house. The young girl then repeats the words with obvious pleasure out of earshot. It is the same with scabrous terms. The delight in talking about farts, poo-poos and wee-wees is not innate. It derives from the prohibitions attached to such terms and from the pleasure to be gained from breaking such prohibitions (Billig, 1999). Thus, the pleasure of the dirty joke comes not from its 'dirtiness' as such, but from the fact that the dirtiness has been forbidden and marked out as 'dirty'. It is the same with 'sick' jokes: whatever is taboo becomes the topic of the joke because it is taboo (Dundes, 1987). The worse the tragedy – whether natural disaster, epidemic or mass terrorism – the more the sick jokes are told, especially by adolescent boys (see Lampert and Ervin-Tripp, 1998, for a discussion of such gender differences).

Significantly, humour can be found in breaking the codes of language. Calling a duck a 'cow' is just the beginning. Much adult humour involves breaking the shared rules of conversation. Analysts have stressed that conversation depends upon speakers sharing common codes. Participants in a conversation will accept certain 'maxims' that they will assume are being followed by other speakers. For instance conversationalists will assume that the remarks of others are relevant, orderly, understandable, etc. This assumption enables them to derive meaning from remarks that otherwise might be difficult to interpret. Similarly, when conversationalists talk, they will attempt to make their utterances, relevant, orderly understandable, etc., otherwise conversations are liable to break down (Grice, 1975; Sperber and Wilson, 1986).

Humour can flout such maxims of conversation. Puns may disrupt the flow of conversation, as a speaker intentionally takes the words of a previous speaker in their 'wrong', unintended sense (Norrick, 1993, 2003). Irony, especially when speakers say the opposite of what they mean in a dead-pan manner, breaches the maxims of cooperation and relevance (Attardo, 2000). If speakers phrase demands, orders or refusals with recognizable signs of humour, they can break conventional codes of politeness without offence (Holmes, 2000; Kotthoff, 2003). It has been claimed that every maxim of conversation can be broken to comic effect, but they cannot all be broken at once without conversational interaction descending into unfunny meaninglessness (Attardo, 1993; Morreall, 1983). Joke-telling will have its codes, that indicate the switch from seriousness to joking (Mulkay, 1988; Norrick, 1993; Sacks, 1992). Even the person telling a 'sick' joke, that makes light of tabooed topics, must follow the codes of joke-telling, in order that the recipients are able to recognize that a joke is being told (Dundes, 1987).

The notion of rebellious humour conveys an image of momentary freedom from the restraints of social convention. It constitutes a brief escape, or, to use the terminology of Peter Berger (1997), a moment of transcendence. It fits Bain's image of the children rushing out in release from the constraints of the school-room. As James Sully wrote in his *Essay on Laughter*, 'the laughter at what is lawless, and still more at the indecent and the profane, certainly derives a part of its gusto from a sense of relief from restraint, which is a main ingredient in the enjoyment of all license' (1902: 118). Freud developed this idea with his claim that tendentious humour provides a means of temporarily escaping from a prohibition.

Just as disciplinary humour has to be understood in relation to the operation of order and power, so conversely does rebellious humour. Authority is challenged and the guardians of rules are mocked. Whereas disciplinary humour mocks the powerless, rebellious humour can delight in taking the powerful as its target. As Bakhtin well knew, the subversive culture of joking often flourishes in dictatorships (Benton, 1988). Those who are denied direct political expression may mock their leaders' pretensions. Under the communist regimes, where the official media presented the leaders with all respect, jokes about the leaders' stupidity and bodily functions were circulated popularly. Hans Speier (1998) identified these as the 'whispered jokes' that are told unofficially in all totalitarian regimes.

The impulse to mockery is by no means confined to totalitarian regimes. Political caricature has developed at the same time as the beginnings of democracy in Britain. Gombrich and Kris, combining their respective expertises in art history and psychoanalysis, argued that William Hogarth was the decisive figure in developing the anti-authoritarian tradition of British caricature. Hogarth extended the targets of middle-class visual mockery from the powerless to the powerful. For Hogarth, 'not only the outcast, the low and the servile were funny, but every fool whatever his position' (Gombrich and Kris, 1940: 17). Folly, hypocrisy and pretension in the highest positions were especially ludicrous, especially if the perpetrators could be depicted as being outrageously fat or thin.

By the end of the eighteenth century, cartoonists such as Gillray and Rowlandson, had pushed the bounds of mockery even further than Hogarth had done. The powerful were portrayed in all their bodily inadequacy. No dignity was safe from the sharpness of Gillray's burin. Certainly royalty was not spared. The crowds would press against the print shop windows to view the latest cartoons. The politicians, fearing the effects of such mockery, would pay popular cartoonists to lampoon their rivals (Donald, 1996). Occasionally self-righteous observers would condemn the general lack of moral respect. In the German magazine *London und Paris*, one correspondent denounced the English cartoonists for encouraging 'an eccentric and distorted judgement of everything that should be precious and important to Englishmen' (included in Banerji and Donald, 1999: 204).

Those are the tones of unlaughing rectitude that rebellious humour has provoked down the ages and that in its turn can become an object for further mockery. In the present age, we are drawn to the side of Gillray and Rowlandson, not to the *London und Paris* critic, whose words appear ripe for mockery. It is easy, then, to imagine a clear distinction between the laughter of rebellion and the seriousness of authority. Bakhtin, whose remarks on humour were quoted at the start of this chapter, implied such a distinction. In notes made towards the end of his life, Bakhtin commented that 'only dogmatic and authoritarian cultures are one-sidedly serious' for 'violence does not know laughter' (1986: 134). It is an attractive message that seems to place laughter – or rather, genuine festive laughter – on the side of the rebels and in their whisperings against intolerant authority.

However, there are difficulties with an equation between rebelliousness and humour. A feeling of rebellion and an enjoyment of humour that transgresses social demands do not necessarily equate with a politics of rebellion. The conditions of late capitalism illustrate this. The position of the joking rebel is a valued one. It is much celebrated in the entertainment products of the media. These products do not encourage their audiences to become rebels in an absolute sense, for their rebelliousness conforms to the standards of the times. At the flick of a switch (and after the proper payment by credit card), we can enjoy regular programmes of fun and mockery. Dutiful consumption encourages us to mock apparent authority, enabling us to enjoy the feeling of constant rebelliousness in economic conditions that demand continual dissatisfaction with yesterday's products.

There are other difficulties with any attempt to equate humour with rebelliousness and authority with seriousness. Radicalism has no monopoly on rebellious humour. If laughter is rhetorical, then it can no more be the property of radicals than any other type of rhetorical device. In the Platonic society, the high-minded guardians would be expected to mock romantic poetry. Plato himself was rebelling against the Athenian order that had condemned Socrates to death. More generally, it should not be thought that laughter, even laughter that is claimed to be rebellious, belongs to the enemies of bigotry. Not only can bigots laugh, but they can also position their laughter as rebellious, mocking the seriousness of tolerance and reason.

Ethnic humour has become a matter of contention in recent years. Those who defend ethnic jokes will typically claim that such humour is harmless fun. For example, some academics will claim that ethnic jokes are far removed from 'real' prejudice. Christie Davies suggests that 'real' racists have better things to do than tell jokes (1990: 125f; see also Gruner, 1997). The general value of humour is evident in such claims. It is as if the 'really' prejudiced would not show the humanity of laughter. There is, however, little reason for supposing that the bigoted, or even the socially powerful, are devoid of humour.

Sartre (1948), in his essay on anti-Semitism, suggested that bigotry and humour were integrally connected. Bigotry resembled a joke, because bigots do not, indeed cannot, really believe in the literal truth of their outrageously expressed opinions and grossly exaggerated stereotypes. In expressing their views, bigots knowingly mock the standards of liberalism and tolerance; and they enjoy freeing themselves from the constraining standards of rationality, decency and evidence. Hence, the discourse of bigotry can have the character of a joke. Certainly, Ku Klux Klan members tell racist jokes and publish them on websites (Billig, 2001). These jokes mockingly transgress the liberal moral order that forbids racist humour. Even extreme racists will claim the position of 'naughty-boy' racists. And, contrary to Bakhtin's assumption that violence does not know laughter, such racists will make jokes about torturing, lynching and burning their victims. Part of the pleasure resides in being offensive, leaving the liberal in the position of unlaughing seriousness. In this respect, the mocking jokes of the extreme racists do have a serious message.

Present ideology is not comfortable with the image of the tyrant with a sense of humour, enjoying the delights of rebellious humour. It prefers the wishful thinking of Bakhtin that tyrants do not laugh properly. Ron Rosenbaum (1998), in his survey of differing interpretations of Hitler, comes to the disturbing conclusion that Hitler's evil resided in his sense of mockery. The image of the laughing Hitler is, Rosenbaum argues, the most disturbing image of all – more disturbing than Hitler the lunatic or the monster. The image contradicts ideological assumptions about the goodness and positive benefits of laughter.

Grown men often like to tell tales of their schooldays, depicting themselves as having been cheekily mischievous. They like to laugh at the idea of mocking the pompous, irrational authority of the old-style schoolmaster. In such tales, the sympathy is with the boy not the master. Here is an example of a successful adult man talking about his schooldays. One teacher had a huge blue handkerchief, which he would often use in class. Once he dropped it without realizing. The mischievous boy, to the delight of his laughing school chums, returned the handkerchief to the master, keeping it arm's length as if it were a truly disgusting object. Another teacher had a speech impediment that the boys found funny. He could not pronounce the letter 'h'. One day, as he read the register, the mischievous boy did not answer to his name. The teacher repeated the name several times. Silence each time. Finally, the mischievous boy said to the delight of his chums: 'My name's not Itler, sir. My name is Hitler' (*Hitler's Table Talk*, 1988: 189, 192). It is a disturbing tale, not least because it upsets moral sensibilities that are ready to applaud small rebellious victories over authority.

Disciplinary functions of rebellious humour

At first sight disciplinary and rebellious humour appear to be quite distinct. The former is driven by a conforming spirit and functions conservatively to protect the rules of social life, while the latter is motivated by the spirit of rebellion and threatens those rules. However, in practice the distinction is not quite so clear. Motive, content and effect do not fall into distinct rebellious or conservative piles. The 'positives' and 'negatives' are not in necessary alignment.

It might, therefore, be helpful to introduce a rough distinction between the psychological nature of humour and its sociological consequences. Some acts of humour might appear rebellious to the participants. Those who laugh might imagine that they are daringly challenging the status quo or are transgressing stuffy codes of behaviour. In their meta-discourse of laughter they might claim to occupy the position of rebelliousness. However, the consequences of such humour might be conformist rather than radical, disciplinary not rebellious. In the matter of humour, there might well be a disjunction between experience and consequence, so that what is experienced as rebellious humour possesses disciplinary functions.

The practical joke may well appear to participants as 'just a joke', that subverts the normal order of seriousness. When the professionals tell the apprentice to fetch the sandwiches, they seemingly flaunt the authority of the manager. But there is no actual rebellion in these jokes. The old professionals may take pleasure in the momentary infraction of the codes, as if they are momentarily escaping like schoolboys from the demands of serious living. But they are not abandoning such codes. Moreover, the manager recognizes what is happening and smiles knowingly. By teaching the apprentice a lesson that will not be forgotten easily, the professionals are strengthening the codes that maintain the structure of differential power. Thus, the momentary release takes meaning from the enduring power of constraint. The joke simultaneously teaches the conventions and takes innocuous revenge against them. There is rebellion against the codes in the disciplining of the apprentice.

The ambivalence of such humour can be seen in another example of a male sporting practical joke. This was one that was played on the British cyclist Tommy Simpson in the early days of his career as a professional in France before he had learned to speak French proficiently (Fife, 1999: 190; see also Fotheringham, 2003). Simpson had asked the French professionals how to ask for the lavatory in a smart hotel. They had told him to say in colloquial impolite French 'Have you a shit-house?' They witnessed the effects with glee. This practical joke, like all such practical jokes, humiliates victims and teaches them an unforgettable lesson. Simultaneously the joke humiliates the moral order, as the rules of politeness and expected routine are broken. The onlookers – professional cyclists from working-class origins who would never be able to stay in such a hotel had they not subjected their bodies to the punishing disciplines of their sport – could enjoy hearing the obscenity being uttered. In this way, the disciplining of the speaker is accompanied by an enjoyment of social disruption.

However, the disruption is only momentary. The hotelier might be offended; a sandwich might even be inappropriately eaten. The victim has learnt a lesson. And the vicarious enjoyment of the jokers is ended. They have needed to recruit an innocent in order to act against convention and power. They themselves have not acted seriously or rebelliously. They have not questioned the authority of the team-manager; nor have they undermined the order of a hotel designed for the rich. They have turned rebellion into a joke and the consequences are hardly rebellious. In any case, the little act of rebellion is serving disciplinary functions.

Thus, there can be a gap between the nature of humour as an act of rebelliousness and the social effects of the humour. Rebellious humour need not have uniformly rebellious effects. Gillray did not subvert the moral order. His admirers and victims continued to occupy their positions in good society, from which the artist was excluded. He was not invited to those smart gatherings where his cartoons would be displayed. By enjoying such cartoons, well-bred admirers could congratulate themselves on their fashionable daring, freedom of thought and, above all, their Englishness. When Gillray died, driven half-mad by poverty and the effects of inhaling the fumes of etching acid, not a single obituary was published (Donald, 1996; Hill, 1966). The well-born admirers did not condescend to attend his funeral.

This suggests that rebellious humour need not have rebellious consequences. The argument, however, can be taken further. At times, rebellious humour – or humour that is claimed and experienced as rebellious – can have conservative and disciplinary functions. Far from subverting the serious world of power, the humour can strengthen it. In the world of late capitalism, the enjoyment of mass-marketed rebellious humour directly aids the economic structures that have produced such enjoyment. The more we laugh and the more we imagine ourselves to be daringly free in the moments of our laughter, the more we are complying with the demands of the so-called free market. And the more we reveal ourselves captive to the demand that we possess a naughty sense of humour.

The point is not confined to the conditions of late capitalism. The disciplinary functions of rebellious humour are much more general. Anton Zijderveld (1982) has examined the role of folly in traditional pre-modern Europe. Travelling performers would amuse their audiences by mocking all authorities, whether secular or religious. The goliards, who themselves were often impoverished unemployed clergy, would depict bishops and even popes as venal idiots; they would parody religious services and beliefs; they would enact obscenities. In Zijderveld's words, they held up a looking-glass to the world of normality. Though they mocked authority, the goliards were not rebels. They did not seek to stir up movements of protest. They were not trying to destroy the figures, on whose continued existence as targets of mockery they depended for a meagre living.

Zijderveld's argument went further than denying that goliards and fools were in actual practice rebels. Zijderveld suggested that their humour actually strengthened the power of those figures that they mocked. According to him, the goliards stripped the pretence of morality from the authorities. Thus, the fool 'is prone to lift the veil of authority from the positions of power by silly remarks, irreverent antics' (p. 28). Having lifted the veil of dignity, the fool reveals not the powerless nakedness of the authority – but the fact of authority's naked power. The audience, having laughed at authority, becomes all the more aware of authority's power. Thus the fool demonstrates, and thereby reaffirms, the power of the authority.

Where there is a social demand to imagine oneself as rebellious, then the enjoyment of rebellious humour offers the possibility of self-persuasion. Speier (1998) has argued that the whispered jokes that are circulated in totalitarian regimes are not actually rebellious. Instead, they provide alibis for those who do not dare to rebel. Mockery does not equate with rebellion. In all armies soldiers tell jokes at the expense of their commanding officers, but the joking does not stop them from obeying orders. Similarly, the jokes against dictatorial authority do not produce political change. As Speier points out, the jokes enable those who do not risk rebellion to live with their conscience. They can convince themselves, even as they live cowed under the dictatorship, that they were really rebelling. They must be rebels after all, for hadn't they whispered jokes? In this regard, the jokes can fulfil conservative functions while being seemingly rebellious in content. This does not occur because the joking relieves pressures in any literal sense as Bain, Spencer and, to a lesser extent, Freud believed. It is not as if accumulated energy is expended so that the act of joking becomes a safety valve that regulates pressure within the system. The mechanism is that of self-persuasion. Rebellious joking permits a clear conscience that does not recognize that rebellion has thus become a joke.

The ambiguity of humour, especially its moral ambiguity, leaves ample room for self-persuasion and self-deceit. The mother in Norrick's example can persuade herself, but not her daughters, that she was in control of the joke. Nothing would convince her otherwise. The possibilities for self-persuasion may be all the greater when issues of morality are at stake. The whispering joke-tellers can convince themselves that they rebelled in their hearts. They joked about the dictator's mental shortcomings, so they could not possibly be true believers. Practical jokers can feel themselves to be like naughty little boys, who harmlessly show that they have not yet become boring adults. Today, with humour being considered to be self-evidently desirable, there is a bias towards the supposed naughtiness of rebellious humour. There is more virtue in being the child who mocks the parents, than in being an adult who mocks children. That is why the image of the dictator as a naughty rebellious boy is so unsettling.

Self-persuasion depends upon formulating claims and explanations that reflect well upon the self. The moment of humour itself is not what counts– whether or not one actually laughs at the joke about the dictator or powerful authority, or what one is existentially experiencing in that moment of such laughter. What counts is what one believes to be the moral point of one's laughter. This is where the idea of function comes in. The belief can reinforce the sense of rebelliousness but that reinforced sense of the self as a rebel can function to protect the social order from rebelliousness. This is only possible because rebellious humour can serve disciplinary functions. Again positives and negatives do not fall neatly and separately into place.

The power of social order

To show how important the disciplinary aspects of humour are for social life, it is necessary to turn from the topic of humour. Instead of asking how particular forms of humour operate, there is a wider question to pose. Why does social life continue from day to day, from moment to moment? The broad answer would be that humans are social animals that need to live in groups. Customs and social codes are necessary for group life. Moreover, such customs and social codes would soon disintegrate, if social actors did not act as if they were solid, objective realities. It is the same with languages. No language can continue to exist as a living entity if individual speakers arbitrarily decide to ignore all its codes and conventions. If there were no agreements about which words should be used for 'duck', 'cow' or anything else, then language would soon fall apart. If everyone suddenly stopped using a particular language with its particular codes of grammar, vocabulary and practices for appropriate speech, then that language would be added to the long list of dead languages. To live the language has to fill the minds of its speakers, framing their thoughts and reactions, with its codes being followed routinely and unthinkingly. And if all shared language codes collapsed, then not just would language die, but so would the basis of all social life.

Therefore, one can ask the question slightly differently: what impels social actors to continue to accept the social realities of everyday life? As Berger and Luckmann (1967) in their classic *The Social Construction of Reality* argued, the world in which we live might be socially constructed, but we act as if it is solidly real. 'Our' world is experienced as more than just 'our' world. It is experienced as 'the' world with an objective 'out-there-ness', which, 30 years later, Berger (1997) was arguing also characterized humour. Just as customs and institutions confront us as realities, so we believe that some things are objectively and 'really' funny. It is as if the comic is also an order of reality 'out-there' beyond our personal preferences.

The two phenomena – the seriousness of the social world and its comedy – may be integrally connected. The social basis of the connection cannot be demonstrated merely by examining in increasing detail how humour operates in particular social situations. Instead, it is necessary to take broad view of the so-called serious world and its power over social actors. A social theory of humour, in this regard, requires a social theory of seriousness.

This is where the idea of embarrassment as a social force comes in. To say that codes must be followed for the continuation of social life, does not stipulate why social actors actually follow codes routinely, even when such obedience might make demands upon them. There must be an internalized force to protect codes and ensure routine social compliance. Some social scientists have claimed that what impels social actors is an incipient sense of shame and a fear of embarrassment. The idea of a social world driven by such disciplinary fears is plausible. But, as will be seen, there are gaps in the theory. Theorists, who attempt to explain the power of the social world in terms of embarrassment, still have to explain how the fear of embarrassment comes to exert its social power. To do this, a link to laughter can be made, thereby providing something that is missing both in theories of humour and theories of embarrassment.

At the root of social life is a dilemma that perplexed Freud. Social customs, codes and institutions may permit us to live socially, realizing our nature as social animals. However, social life constrains us. It takes away our freedom. This was something that Bain recognized with his description of life demanding restraint, work and seriousness. Freud was to make a similar point in *Civilization and its Discontents* ([1930] 1987). According to Freud, social life curtails our possibilities for happiness by making demands on our freedom. We cannot behave just as we might like. The infant may bawl, scream and gurgle at will. Mature adults cannot, at least if they wish to remain part of social life. Somewhere along the line between infancy and maturity, freedom has to be renounced in the cause of becoming socialized.

Practically every moment of our social life provides evidence of this renunciation, or at least, evidence of the demands of social life. Micro-sociologists and discursive psychologists have in recent years documented the extent to which the practices and talk of everyday life are hedged by shared codes (see, for instance, Edwards, 1997; Edwards and Potter, 1993; Potter, 1996). Nothing illustrates this better than the practice of conversation. Our utterances in conversation cannot dispense with the demands of appropriateness. Politeness makes demands on social actors, who have to display their consideration of others (Brown and Levinson, 1987). Sometimes polite remarks must be phrased indirectly rather than directly, requiring more linguistic effort.

In Anglo-American society, one does not usually make direct demands, in the way that Socrates could order the slave boy in the *Meno*. Diners at the table, for instance, are not expected to demand: 'Salt'. Instead they have been taught to use extra words, delivered at an appropriate speed with an appropriate intonation: 'Please could you pass the salt?'. Conversation analysts have analyzed the ways that requests are accepted or refused (Bilmes, 1987; Heritage, 1984; Nofsinger, 1993; Pomerantz, 1984). Typically, an invitation or a request can be accepted quite briefly. However, rejections require something extra, such as an apology, justification, and excuse: 'I'm so sorry, I would love to, but I've already promised to do so something else, sorry'. To refuse a request or an invitation with a direct, unadorned 'no' can threaten the continuation of the interaction, although this is not the case in all cultures (Katriel, 1986; see also Holtgraves, 2001).

The power of social demands can be seen in the codes of turn-taking, which, as has been mentioned, all languages need for conversation to proceed. As Goffman noted, in all spoken interaction 'conventions and procedural rules come into play which function as a means of guiding and organizing the flow of messages' (1967: 33). Above all there must be codes for speakers to indicate that their turn has come to an end and that it is others' turn to take the floor. The force of social pressure in dialogue can be seen in what conversation analysts have called 'adjacency pairs'. A question represents the first part of an 'adjacency pair'. When a question has been asked, the recipient is placed in a position where an answer of some sort is expected. The answer might be that 'no answer' can be satisfactorily provided. Even a shake of the head might suffice. But an absolute silence, that totally ignores the question, is rare, especially when the question is addressed directly on a one-to-one basis. Such an absence of response would indicate a refusal to continue the dialogue. In 2002, there was a distressing case of child murder in Britain. It was reported that the suspect had refused to answer any questions during police interrogation. After the murderer had been convicted, video-tapes of the police interview were released. The tapes showed that after each question, the suspect answered 'No comment'. This went on for hours. Of course, 'no comment' is a comment. One might ask why the suspect bothered to say again and again 'no comment'. Why did he not sit in total silence? The very response illustrated the power of a question. It seems to drag forth a response, even if the recipient wishes not to reply and the response that is elicited signifies no response.

Conversation analysts have shown the extent to which social pressures constrain us in social interaction, as we practise the codes of dialogue habitually. Speakers may not be consciously aware of the details of the codes that they follow. They normally will be unable to articulate the rules as formal principles. Nevertheless they are likely to be aware when another speaker is breaking such codes, by being, for instance, too abrupt or too expansive, too quiet or too loud, too high-pitched or too low-pitched, etc. Before speaking, we do not in general consciously adjust our words to fit the codes. Habitually, questions are answered, requests acknowledged, adjacency pairs completed, speaking turns awaited and then taken up at precisely the expected moment. Our words spill out, in dutiful and routine fulfilment of the micro-codes that ensure there is no absolute freedom of speech if dialogue is to continue.

From Freud's perspective, the whole intricate display of social life is threatened by the selfishness of individual desire. Freud may have recognized this tension underlying social life, but he could not say why individual actors, on a day-to-day basis, feel at home in these conditions of curtailment. His theory, which was discussed in Chapter 7, suggested that the individual, at a decisive moment in childhood, begins to repress the desires that threaten social order. But Freud provided no real account of how such repression is renewed in detail throughout adult social interaction. Social order must have some disciplinary power over us to ensure habitual compliance. What exactly this power is and how it is habitually exercised in social interaction Freud could not say. He imagined that there was some sort of hydraulic mechanism within the psyche, damning up instinctual energy that nevertheless continued to leak out in jokes and dreams. In fact, Freud was looking in the wrong place. He was searching within the individual for hidden psychological forces, rather than looking at the processes of daily interaction. When he looked at humour, it certainly was not to look for its disciplinary force in maintaining the constraints of serious life.

Goffman and embarrassment

Probably the greatest sociologist to examine the routines and codes of everyday life was Erving Goffman. In a series of books and essays, Goffman explored how ordinary life was socially organized. He was particularly interested in social interaction occurring within institutional or semi-formal situations, such as work-places, restaurants, mental institutions, etc. He was less interested in the informal interactions of families; and he certainly was uninterested in developmental matters. His genius was to notice, often with wry humour, the little details of life that we daily take for granted. According to Goffman, much interaction is structured around the need for social actors to present themselves acceptably to others and, thereby, to 'maintain face'. Threats to face can be threats to social order, so codes of interaction function to enable social actors to engage in the patterns of everyday life without the loss of face. Goffman was addressing the big question 'How does social life continue?' The broad answer was that social actors fear losing face so they comply with the social demands of the situations in which they find themselves.

A key essay in Goffman's book *Interaction Ritual* (1967) deals with the issue of embarrassment. Goffman begins the essay with a description of the signs of embarrassment. He says that individuals can easily recognize these signs in themselves and in others. The signs include blushing, fumbling, sweating, breaking of the voice, etc. Being embarrassed is a feeling of discomfiture that 'seems always to be unpleasant' (ibid.: 101). It is something that one would wish to avoid. Goffman suggests that in general terms embarrassment is connected with 'unfulfilled expectations' (ibid.: 105). All social life depends on expectations. We cannot have face-to-face encounters in shops, restaurants or work-places unless we have some expectation how others will behave. Embarrassment is likely to occur when someone produces behaviour that breaches the codes of expected behaviour. In this sense, as Goffman comments, the expectations relating to embarrassment are moral ones. Someone is producing behaviour that is improper for the situation and will be judged for doing so. Embarrassment is not generally concerned with the big issues of morality, but with the everyday morality of someone 'who carries on social encounters' (ibid.: 105). Goffman is dealing more with the morality of etiquette rather than sin.

Goffman wished to examine how embarrassment contributes to the maintenance of daily life. In this respect his analysis is social rather than psychological. He assumed that being embarrassed is unpleasant, but he did not wish to explore the nature of the feeling, just as Bergson had preferred to discuss the function rather than experience of laughter. Rather he wanted to demonstrate its social function. He assumes that there are social codes of embarrassment – when and how it should be displayed. To this purpose, his essay offers two arguments that he did not clearly distinguish. In the first place, he offers a general argument that positions embarrassment as the disciplinary agent of the social world. On the other hand, he also makes a more restricted argument about the sort of situations in which displays of embarrassment are necessary for overcoming structural tensions. In the first argument, Goffman ignores the role of humour and laughter. In the second argument, Goffman does discuss the role of humour, but it is part of an argument that seems to concentrate optimistically on the nicer side of things.

The first argument is the general one. Embarrassment is, according to Goffman, something that is social. We are unlikely to feel embarrassment when alone. It occurs when we strike a false note in front of an audience. Later researchers have amplified this point (i.e. Marcus and Miller, 1999; Parrott and Harré, 1996; Tangney, 1992; Tangney et al., 1996). For instance, it has been argued that blushing is likely to occur when something, that people wish to hide, is revealed to others (Crozier, 2001). This is not surprising if embarrassment is connected with social evaluation and the loss of social face. There can be no loss of face if we drop a plate or leave our clothes unbuttoned when alone at home. But these are just the sorts of things to cause embarrassment if they occur before others. Interestingly, there is some evidence that people are more likely to feel embarrassment in front of strangers and acquaintances than in front of close friends and family (Miller, 1996: 42f). The mother, who got her statement the wrong grammatical way round when speaking to her adult daughters, did not appear to display signs of embarrassment. Had she been corrected when speaking thus to a shop assistant, her manager at work or a television interviewer, one might predict that she would be more likely to have displayed the signs of embarrassed discomfiture.

Goffman, in connecting embarrassment with the everyday morality of interaction, is implicitly distinguishing the feeling of embarrassment from that of shame. One can be ashamed, or feel guilt, on one's own in ways that do not happen with embarrassment (Tangney et al., 1996). It has been suggested that shame involves a general and enduring sense that the self is unworthy, whereas embarrassment is much more temporary and tied to particular situations (Tangney et al., 1996, 1998). However, the distinction between shame and embarrassment may be as much quantitative as qualitative. According to Thomas Scheff who was written widely on shame, embarrassment is 'a less intense, brief, and overtly experienced form of shame' (1990: 18).

Goffman's general argument is that any social encounter, especially that which has to be enacted in a public or semi-formal setting, holds the potential for embarrassment. There are codes and expectations for appropriate behaviour. A *faux pas* or gaffe is always possible and this will bring about the embarrassing moment. Thus, according to Goffman, 'in our Anglo-American society at least, there seems to be no social encounter which cannot become embarrassing to one or more of its participants' (1967: 99). Goffman may have been unnecessarily cautious here. Embarrassment is not confined to Anglo-American society. As Darwin suggested in *Emotions and their Expression*, in all peoples the reactions of embarrassment can be detected. One might speculate that the potentiality for embarrassment is universal, although social infractions that might be merely embarrassing in one culture may be experienced as shameful in another (Imahori and Cupach, 1994).

Embarrassment, then, can be seen to possess a universal role in supporting the moral order of everyday life, whatever the nature of that moral order. What this suggests is that the social patterning of embarrassment may provide the answer to the big question about the continuation of social life. The short answer is that fear of embarrassment keeps us on track. As one researcher into embarrassment has put it, 'for many of us, a quiet but compelling drive to avoid embarrassment pervades our daily life' and this observation points to 'an important conclusion about social life' (Miller, 1996: 164; see also Modigliani, 1968). This 'conclusion' accords well with Goffman's work. In his brilliant essay 'On face-work', Goffman argued that people tend to avoid social situations in which they might lose face. Social actors tend to stay away from socially difficult situations and they cooperate to save their face 'finding that there is much to be gained from venturing nothing' (1967: 42).

Thomas Scheff, in a series of important books, has developed Goffman's basic insight to suggest that fear of shame protects the 'social bond' (Scheff, 1990, 1994 and 1997). Shame, according to Scheff, is the 'master emotion of social life' that stalks all social relations, whether personal and private. As has been noted, Scheff specifically identifies embarrassment as a lesser form of shame. One might say that the sorts of social interaction that concerned Goffman, are policed by embarrassment rather than shame. Lesser though embarrassment might be, it can be experienced intensely. One might point to a disjunction. The intensity of feeling associated with embarrassment often seems out of all proportion to the provoking cause. Calling an acquaintance by the wrong name, forgetting to zip up one's clothing, spilling a cup of coffee – these are all trivial misdemeanours in the big scheme of things. Yet, the embarrassment at the time, and the haunting after-effects of memory, can be far more intensely uncomfortable than feelings of guilt following an unobserved act of immorality.

The logic of Goffman's 'Embarrassment and social organization' points towards a conclusion of great importance. It explains why social actors do not regularly throw off the codes of behaviour. There is no need to formulate elaborate psychoanalytic theories in order to explain our routine acceptance of constraint. Built into the fabric of social life is the mechanism for social embarrassment, threatening social actors with a form of social death each time they forget the codes of appropriateness. However, as will be seen, something crucial is being left out.

Goffman's essay, instead of advancing triumphantly to a big conclusion, seems to drift towards a lesser end. The signs were there from the start. When discussing what he called the 'vocabulary of embarrassment', Goffman suggests that the gaffe or the *faux pas* does not comprise the typical case of embarrassment. He does not really offer convincing arguments for the assertion. Later researchers have asked respondents what sorts of situation they find to be embarrassing. A study by Sabini et al. (2000) has suggested that there are three main types of embarrassing situation: *faux pas*, sticky situations and being the centre of attention. They suggest that being the centre of attention is different from the other two types. A *faux pas* refers to occasions when the social actor fails to negotiate routine social interaction. A false step is taken – the wrong clothing is worn, or the right clothing is worn wrongly, etc. Sticky situations refer to occasions when things are turning out wrongly. An ex-partner, parent or minister of the faith turns up at a most inopportune moment. The social actor, then, must do something that 'will discredit the performance of someone else in the interaction' (2000: 216, see also Parrott and Smith, 1991).

Goffman, in the second part of his essay, concentrates on the tricky situation rather than on the *faux pas*. He is interested in a particular type of sociologically determined tricky situation. He discusses the embarrassment that is felt when participants find themselves in situations where there is a conflict of expectations. In the work situation, there will be codes for interactions between managers and workers. The codes, which govern the interaction, will permit differences in status to be displayed. On the other hand, there are situations in which egalitarian behaviour is expected – for instance, when employees meet at the drinking fountain or in the elevator. When a manager meets a worker in one of these egalitarian situations, then, according to Goffman, displays of fumbling and embarrassment might occur, indeed they might be expected. These displays, far from indicating a breakdown of social order, contribute to the maintenance of social order for they show that the individual actors have other selves apart from the one that they are displaying at the particular moment. Goffman ends the essay with a typical sparkling epigram on the nature of embarrassment: 'Social structure gains elasticity; the individual merely loses composure' (1967: 112).

In the article Goffman does not link humour with embarrassment, save for a footnote towards the end of the article. This footnote refers to the sort of embarrassment that arises between a superior and junior in a situation of expected equality. Goffman suggests that joking can help to relieve the tension of the moment. Participants may 'josh' each other, delivering mock insults and making mock claims. Joking and joshing, comments Goffman, undermine the seriousness of the conflicting situation in which the participants find themselves. A display of demonstrating that one is flustered or embarrassed can function similarly. Thus, according to Goffman, 'it is natural, then, to find embarrassment and joking going together, for both help in denying the same reality' (ibid.: 112n).

Goffman's footnote contains both a significant presence and a significant absence. The significant presence is the linking of humour with a particular type of embarrassment. He is suggesting how humour might enable participants to come through a tricky moment. In the language of ideological positivism, one might say that Goffman sees a positive role for this sort of shared humour. Subsequent research could easily be cited in support of this idea (e.g., Beck, 1997; Du Pré, 1998). The significant absence is that Goffman does not link humour with the embarrassment of the *faux pas* or social gaffe. In particular, he does not discuss the possibility that onlookers might find embarrassing gaffes funny and that this type of humour, which the ideological positivists would term as negative, may also have a 'positive' function. Goffman's significant presence and his significant absence fit a wider pattern. So does the fact that one of the most influential articles on embarrassment in the modern social sciences confines the link with humour to a mere footnote.

Laughing at embarrassment

As it stands, Goffman does not explain, nor seek to explain, why social actors should dread being embarrassed, especially when making observed social gaffes. He avoided psychological explanations and he was generally uninterested in developmental questions. Accordingly, he did not explore the origins of embarrassment. It is as if embarrassment is a physiological syndrome that 'naturally' occurs. Put people in an awkward situation then blushing, stammering, etc. will result, as if it is a physiological response to social circumstances. There is a parallel with theories of humour that link humour with laughter, but treat the latter reaction as a 'natural' given, rather than examining how children learn to laugh at what is socially considered to be funny.

The parallel between humour and embarrassment can be taken further. Just as infants cannot be said to possess a sense of humour, so very young children cannot be said to show embarrassment. In fact, infants do not even show the physiological characteristics of embarrassment, such as blushing (Buss, 1980). The infant is regularly placed in situations that would be embarrassing to an older child. Its body is open to the regular inspection and touch of its care-givers. If embarrassment is a social reaction, then it has to be learnt. Unsocialized infants cannot display appropriate signs of being flustered when behaving in a socially inappropriate manner, because they do not know how to behave in socially appropriate ways. If displays of embarrassment are expected in awkward social situations – and such displays function to reduce disapproving reactions from onlookers (Manstead and Semin, 1981) – then the child has to learn how to deliver these displays appropriately. There is then, to adapt Jonathan Swift, the military management of the blush and the downward glance to be mastered.

Virtually everything that an infant does would be considered as socially inappropriate if performed by an older child. Somewhere along the line the child has to acquire the knowledge of social appropriateness, including knowledge about embarrassment. From having its toilet needs being cared for, the child must learn to feel embarrassment, if not shame, if such functions become publicly exposed. The psychological evidence about the development of embarrassment is scant. What little evidence there is suggests that children below the age of nine rarely show the reactions of embarrassment. A sense of embarrassment comes with the development of a sense of social self (Buss, 1980). Significantly it appears that signs of embarrassment are first shown in response to ridicule (Bennett, 1989; Bennett and Gillingham, 1991). The child behaves inappropriately and others laugh. Such laughter is, of course, disciplinary. It is teaching the child about inappropriate behaviour: it says 'if you behave in this way, others will laugh at you'. Interestingly, these studies refer to the laughter of older children, not to the laughter of parents. Whether parents – and mothers in particular – laugh at young children as part of toilet-training has not been studied by psychologists. But the child not only has to learn to wipe its own bottom, but to be ashamed of failing to do so. How exactly care-givers accomplish this necessary, but delicate, task is unclear.

The first reactions of the child to the ridicule of older children do not constitute full-blown embarrassment as such. The child below about the age of nine might display proto-embarrassment – the outward signs of flustering are produced without the full knowledge of the social proprieties involved (Bennett, 1989; Bennett and Gillingham, 1991). However, the lessons of such early ridicule contain an important element that will stand the child in good stead for learning the nature of embarrassment. The child is on the way to learning that if one behaves in an embarrassing way, onlookers may well laugh. And here lies the central connection between laughter and embarrassment that Goffman overlooked.

The matter can be put simply. Embarrassment may be painful for the one who is embarrassed, but it is frequently funny to onlookers. Tricky situations provide the subject matter for comedies: bosses are inadvertently addressed as if they are underlings; prospective parents-in-law as if they are prying strangers; former lovers arrive on the scene when least wanted; parents unwittingly expose the ill-founded social pretensions of their offspring and vice versa etc. The possibilities are endless. The audience enjoys the discomfort of the characters. It is the same with gaffes. As William Hazlitt remarked, 'we laugh at those misfortunes in which we are spectators, not sharers' (1987: 70).

The link between humour and embarrassment can be detected in the research findings of those who study embarrassment, although the link is seldom explicit in their theories. Interestingly, such researchers rarely draw specific attention to this aspect of their findings. Miller and Tangney (1994) asked students to recall situations that caused them embarrassment and situations that caused them shame. They were interested in what distinguished the two types of situation. One of the prime differences was that respondents described the embarrassing situations, but not the shameful ones, as being humorous. Parrott and Smith (1991) report similar findings. In their study more than 40 per cent of respondents, who described embarrassing situations, mentioned that others were laughing at them.

Researchers often use examples of embarrassing situations to illustrate their theories or to include in their questionnaires. Such examples frequently include the ridicule of others, although, as will be seen, the researchers' theories tend to downgrade the importance of mockery. One of Sabini et al.'s (2000) *faux pas* vignettes depicts a lecture hall on the first day of a new semester. A student, who knows no-one else, is sitting in the hall, preoccupied and biting the end of her pen. Suddenly, some of the other students started staring 'and a few began to laugh' (ibid.: 238). She looked down and realized her hands were blue; she fled to the bathroom and her mouth was blue with ink from her pen.

Another example can be given. Parrott and Harré (1996) discussed the 'family resemblances' between different episodes that are classified as embarrassing. They stressed three overlapping themes: (1) failure to perform a social role; (2) loss of self-esteem; and (3) social anxiety. They presented an example that contained all three elements. During a chemistry class, a particular student broke a beaker, which set in motion a chain of catastrophes, involving splashing water, breaking a thermometer, upsetting chemicals and causing the room to be filled with a cloud of smoke. Parrott and Harré recount that 'her classmates laughed at her, and, not surprisingly, she felt embarrassed ... she began sweating and trembling and burst into tears'. (ibid.: 44).

One might note how, in telling the story, Parrott and Harré link the laughter of others with the feeling of embarrassment. They do not feel the need to explain why the classmates might have laughed. The phrase 'not surprisingly' indicates how 'natural' they assume to be the link between embarrassment and laughter. Similarly, Sabini et al. (2000) do not explain why onlookers should find it funny to see a young woman sitting alone with inappropriately blue hands and mouth. The absence of explanations indicates that the authors expect their readers to understand why the embarrassing scenario should be found funny.

Miller (1992, 1996) provides a taxonomy of embarrassing situations. The most common type of embarrassing situation is one where the actor displays what Miller calls 'normative public deficiencies'. Sometimes the deficiency is bodily, when the social actors lose control, laughing, coughing or farting far too loudly for the occasion. No embarrassment ensues if the bodily eruptions occur in private without the possibility of witnesses. Miller uses the term 'temporary stupidity' to indicate those situations, in which an otherwise competent social actor makes a cognitive error, such as forgetting the name of a friend, wearing inappropriate clothes or noticeably saying the wrong word. For instance, George Bush senior, when Vice-President of the United States, said that he'd worked for seven and a half years with President Reagan and 'we've had triumphs. Made some mistakes. We've had some sex...Uh...setbacks' (quoted in Miller, 1996: 54).

It is said that a hundred years ago the Irish politician Sir Boyle Roche was much laughed at for his inappropriate comments that indicated the extent to which he regularly missed the point. On one occasion in the Irish Parliament, he claimed with due seriousness that we should not put ourselves out for posterity; he asked rhetorically 'what has posterity done for us?'. In the face of mounting laughter, he tried to explain his remark: he meant immediate posterity, not distant posterity, etc. Each serious explanation increased the laughter. As one observer commented, on hearing his explanations 'it was impossible to do any serious business for half an hour' (quoted in Davies, 1990: 142).

Gaffes, like those of Sir Boyle or George Bush, resemble loud bodily eruptions in a hushed formal occasion. They are likely to provoke onlookers to laughter. As the example of Sir Boyle shows, the more that perpetrators react with seriousness and the more they show that they have failed to get the joke, the greater the fun can often be. The general point is that, as James Sully wrote, there is 'ample evidence to show that what is embarrassing, what is contrary to rule' move onlookers to laughter, at least 'under certain limiting conditions' (1902: 114). One limiting condition is that the resulting gaffe does not transgress deep moral codes – in other words, that it should be embarrassing not shameful.

Perhaps the strongest evidence about the link between embarrassment and humour comes from a study of humour. Researchers studying embarrassment have often asked respondents to describe embarrassing episodes that have happened to them. By contrast researchers studying humour rarely ask their respondents to recount funny events in their lives. In one of the few such studies, Van Giffen and Maher (1995) asked people to describe events that made them laugh. They specifically requested respondents to confine their answers to actual events, and to exclude jokes or scenes from television or films. Although Van Giffen and Maher present their results briefly, nevertheless one fact is clear. The situations described by their respondents as being funny are very similar to those situations that respondents in the embarrassment studies describe as being embarrassing.

Van Giffen and Maher present some of the funny episodes in an appendix. Some of the episodes clearly fit the category of 'normative public deficiencies' that Miller used to describe embarrassing incidents. There is a story about friends at the dinner table laughing at another diner, whose dessert slipped from his plate into his lap. There is a story about a group teasing a woman about the size of her jaw. The butt of the joke then looks into the mirror to check her jaw and, it is said, that 'this made everyone (excluding the butt-of-the-joke) laugh even louder' (Van Giffen and Maher, 1995: 49).

Some of incidents, reported by Van Giffen and Maher, fit the type of 'temporary stupidity' that Miller (1996) identified in embarrassment tales. For instance, there is a story of someone forgetting to pay for groceries at the supermarket. There is also a tale about watching the next-door neighbours ease their car out of their garage, wave and then drive straight into the wall. The teller of that story remembers: 'I had to hurry my sister in the car because she was laughing uncontrollably. I gave a slight smile and look of sympathy as I tried to hold in my laughter and get into the car' (Van Giffen and Maher, 1995: 50).

This story suggests a conflict between empathy and laughter, which Bergson highlighted and which was discussed in Chapter 6. The story-teller recounts having attempted to display a look of sympathy while seeking at the same time to contain laughter. The implication is that a display of sympathy was expected but this was in danger of being swept aside by uncontrolled laughter. The sister, who could not produce the display, was being hurried out of sight. Hearers of the tale cannot simultaneously laugh and enquire whether the neighbour was badly hurt. The query might follow the laughter, but it cannot accompany it. Similarly, the members of the Irish parliament, as they slapped their thighs and hooted at Sir Boyle's solecisms, did not pause to consider whether they might be causing him hurt. Who cares whether George Bush woke in the middle of the night, sweating with embarrassment at the thought of his misplaced word? In fact, the idea of the vice-president in his pyjamas seriously worrying over saying the word 'sex' adds to the joke. Those who enjoy such moments of mirth, and who delight in the gaffes and social stupidity of others, find themselves temporarily freed from the constraints of empathy. For a moment, the objects of their laughter do indeed become objects.

Embarrassing incidents and empathetic reactions

There is nothing particularly remarkable in the argument that embarrassment can be funny to onlookers. One might think it curious that such an acute observer of human foibles as Goffman could overlook this aspect. Goffman is rightly celebrated for his insights into human conduct. He steps back from the routines of everyday life, as if he were an ethologist observing the ritual displays of a strange species. Yet, his detachment has its limits. In his essay on embarrassment he seems to be giving a positive bill-of-health to humour. Does ideological positivism, with its optimistic views of human nature, reach into the work of this great observer of modern social life?

The issue stretches beyond Goffman. The question is whether social scientists more generally have been reluctant to consider the connections between disciplinary laughter and embarrassment. The researchers into the psychology and sociology of embarrassment often display a discrepancy between their illustrations theory and their explanations. In the examples, the role of ridicule is apparent, as onlookers are seen to enjoy the embarrassment of others. However, the theories tend to portray onlookers as 'nice guys', empathizing with the victims of embarrassment, not mocking them.

There are two elements in this 'nice guy' view of embarrassment. First, the onlookers are said to feel for victims of embarrassment, sharing with them secondary feelings of embarrassment. In this respect, empathy is held to be a spontaneous reaction. Second, the theories suggest that onlookers do what they can to smooth over the interaction and to rescue perpetrators of social gaffes from the awful social holes in which they find themselves. According to this view, people are sympathetic repairers of social breakdowns.

Both elements of the 'nice guy' view can be found in Goffman's writings. He suggested that sympathy was a customary reaction when observing the embarrassment of others. He claimed that actors often collaborate to save the face of someone who is embarrassed. He wrote that 'when an individual finds himself in a situation which ought to make him blush, others present usually will blush with and for him' (1967: 99–100). Sir Boyle should have blushed at his own verbal solecisms. But his audience was laughing at him, not blushing for him. The sister, who had to be hurried out of sight, was not blushing for the motoring ineptitude of her neighbour.

Goffman's observations about behaviour in embarrassing situations were part of a more general view of social conduct. An optimistic view on human helpfulness and fellow-feeling can be detected. In his essay 'On face-work', Goffman wrote about 'the rule of self-respect and the rule of considerateness'. This rule leads actors to do what they can to save their own face and that of 'the other participants' (1967: 11). If there has been a gaffe, the rule of considerateness will lead onlookers to try to remedy the situation, showing 'a protective orientation toward saving the others' face' (ibid.: 14).

Subsequent researchers have tended to follow Goffman in stressing both the contagious nature of embarrassment and the tendency for onlookers to engage in remedial work. Modigliani (1968) wrote that embarrassment is a 'highly infectious form of discomfort' (ibid.: 314). Miller (1987) conducted an experiment on empathetic embarrassment. Pairs of subjects were assigned different roles. One had to perform an embarrassing task, such as singing the 'Star-Spangled Banner', while the other subject observed the performance. Miller found that observers reported empathy for the embarrassed other, claiming to share the feeling of embarrassment. Metts and Cupach (1989) have examined the sorts of remedial strategies used both by embarrassed actors and by onlookers in embarrassing situations. Remedial strategies include apologies, excuses, justifications and humour. Both the embarrassed actor and onlookers may make jokes in order to lighten the situation and downgrade its seriousness, as Goffman implied in the concluding footnote of his embarrassment essay. Du Pré (1998) refers to the way that humour can perform face-saving work in embarrassing situations. Reviewing past work on humour and embarrassment, she concludes that 'overall, this research suggests that people commonly use humour to manage face-threatening situations' (ibid.: 24).

The 'nice guy' theory finds its place in social psychology textbooks. John Sabini, who is an embarrassment researcher, has a section in his textbook discussing embarrassment (Sabini, 1992). He includes a short sub-section on empathetic, or secondary, embarrassment, in which he quotes Miller's (1987) empathetic experiment. Franzoi (2000), in his textbook *Social Psychology*, outlines research indicating how unpleasant the feeling of embarrassment is. After giving the bad news about the unpleasantness of experiencing embarrassment, Franzoi states, as if offering a general law, that 'the good news is that embarrassing situations are also unpleasant for onlookers, and thus, they often help us recover our self-presentations' (ibid.: 78).

It is not difficult to feel that the 'nice guy' view is missing something. Miller's experiment may have produced some evidence for empathetic embarrassment, as onlookers reported feeling embarrassed for the subjects singing the 'Star-Spangled Banner'. It is not clear whether such reports reflected an inner discomfort or the social demand to appear sympathetic. Nevertheless, Miller's results also indicated that the onlookers, in contrast to the embarrassed actors, enjoyed participating in the experiment. Could the witnessing of others' embarrassment have contributed to that enjoyment? But this enjoyment is not something that can be openly admitted. There is certainly other laboratory evidence to suggest that onlookers tend to underestimate the extent of embarrassment felt by others (Marcus and Miller, 1999).

The two social psychology textbooks, when they discuss Miller's finding as evidence for sympathy, do not mention the findings about observers enjoying the experiment more. Sabini's section on empathetic embarrassment shows how the 'not-so-nice-guy' aspects can be glossed over. Sabini mentions a friend who cannot watch re-runs of *I Love Lucy*, because the comedy show invariably depicted Lucy in some scheme that was about to disintegrate to her immense embarrassment: 'The reason my friend can't watch them is that he becomes so embarrassed watching that it is painful!' (1992: 253). The anecdote is designed to illustrate the reality of empathetic embarrassment, but it is revealing in another way. Sabini does not have another section entitled 'The Enjoyment of Watching Embarrassment'. Nor does he mention the millions who have watched *I Love Lucy*, in order to laugh at the character in her embarrassing situations. Indeed, there may be occasions when people enjoy deliberately embarrassing others. This element is vital to certain sorts of practical joke, such as those played upon apprentices. Perhaps enjoyment, not empathetic embarrassment, may be a major reaction to watching the embarrassment of others. As Sharkey (1992) has remarked, this has not been an object of much research. Social psychologists have been reluctant to explore, even to mention, this less-than-nice-side of human behaviour.

Of course, it would be wrong to dispute that such empathy does not exist and that people will sometimes work to smooth over the embarrassing situation. The problem is not the occurrence of such reactions but their elevation as the norm – as if empathy were the dominant motive underlying social life. Instead of sympathy for the Vice President, who implausibly talks of sex with the President, there can be malicious pleasure in seeing a politician publicly making a fool of himself. Concentrating on the nice kindly things that social actors do leaves too much unexplained, especially in relation to the social force of embarrassment. If embarrassment plays such a vital role in the continuation of social life, then at its core is not necessarily a harmony of social motives. In the typical situation of embarrassment, there may be dissonance. Instead of the social imperatives of empathy, onlookers might be enjoying a momentary release from such imperatives, as they partake in the cruel pleasures of disciplinary humour. The embarrassed individual is dying a social death, while the onlookers are filled with the joys of life.

The embarrassment of Little Hans

If there is such an underlying dissonance, then one can expect denial and self-deceit. There is too much at stake for people to admit the cruelty of their own pleasures in an age when we are expected to be both sympathetic nice guys and lovers of good humour. Even hard-headed social scientists can be swept along. As they direct their gaze to the positives, so they turn from the negatives. Their conclusions will then reflect what they see and what they avoid seeing. Even Goffman was affected by this. At this stage what is required is a detailed example, not more theoretical statements.

The example is taken from Freud's famous case of Little Hans, the young boy whose parents were early followers of Freud and whose father, Max Graf, took notes of his son's behaviour, which he passed on to Freud. The case has been discussed above in Chapter 7. An episode, relating to the learning of embarrassment, occurred when Hans was four and a half years old (Freud, [1909] 1990: 181–2). The Graf family was on holiday and regularly went to a particular restaurant for lunch. A young girl of about eight also went there with her family. Hans clearly wished to be friends with her. Hans's father described a particular episode, which he said 'has given us a great deal of entertainment, for Hans has really behaved like a grown-up person in love' (ibid.: 181):

> For the last few days a pretty little girl of about eight has been coming to the restaurant where we have lunch. Of course, Hans fell in love with her on the spot. He keeps constantly turning around in his chair to take furtive looks at her; when he has finished eating, he stations himself in her vicinity so as to flirt with her, but if he finds he is being observed, he blushes scarlet. If his glances are returned by the little girl, he at once looks shamefacedly away. (ibid.: 181)

Graf concludes the description with the comment that Hans's behaviour 'is naturally a great joy to everyone lunching at the restaurant' (ibid.: 181).

The tale is one of embarrassment and laughter. According to the father – and to Freud who reproduces the tale – the boy is embarrassed because his desires have been exposed. He shows the signs of being flustered if he sees that he is being watched. He blushes; he looks away shamefacedly. The adults watching the childish behaviour find it amusing. Neither Graf nor Freud felt any need to explain why the adults were so amused. It is presumed that readers will understand: 'naturally' Hans's behaviour is a great joy to everyone. What gives the joy, according to Graf and Freud, is the display of adult love in one so young.

So outwardly this is a tale of embarrassment, love and laughter. It is charming, loving and joyous. Naturally readers can share the feelings down the ages. But there are other aspects. In the story, as told by Freud and Graf, the adults are passive observers. They are watching what is intrinsically funny, namely the behaviour of the little boy, who is supposedly in love but ashamed of his desires. This depiction of the passive adults and the desiring child fits Freud's Oedipal story (see Chapter 7). The restaurant incident is transformed if the analytic gaze is transferred from the child to the adult diners. The locus of pleasure, as well as the practice of denial, is shifted from the child to the adults.

We can see the adults looking at the young boy, laughing and enjoying his discomfort. Presumably the adults, at their separate tables, catch each other's eye to share the fun. At the start of the meal, as Hans is staring and hoping for the girl to appear, so the adults are staring and hoping for Hans to begin his comic behaviour. Each time he blushes, he becomes funnier. It is further proof of his inappropriately adult love. So the more he is embarrassed, the more the adults laugh. Graf's report depicts the funniness as 'natural'. Freud, the initial reader of the report, is invited by proxy to enjoy the scene. When Freud repeats the story in the published case report, so his readers are invited across time and place to join in the fun. To do this, they must smile at a little boy in love, not at an embarrassed little boy being laughed at by adults.

To join in the fun at second hand, we must ignore some implausible aspects of the story. Not only must we believe that Hans is in love, but that he is embarrassed by his desires. However, when alone with his father, he seems to show no signs of embarrassment. 'Do you think the little girl might be there today?' he asks papa directly and unashamedly. Another day, he tells his father that he has discovered where the little girl has been staying: he had seen her entering a particular house (ibid.: 191). But in the restaurant, it is all head-down blushing. Graf and Freud attribute the difference to the possibility that the girl – the object of his desires – might enter the restaurant at any time. They do not explain the difference in terms of the presence of the adults and their laughter.

The laughter of the adults contained a disciplinary aspect that was hidden from them in the moments of their enjoyment. Hans was being 'naturally' funny because he was behaving inappropriately in the restaurant.

Young men in bourgeois *fin-de-siècle* Austria should not stare at respectable young ladies in restaurants. Very young infants need not be so restricted. Hans in breaking the codes of polite behaviour is not being understood as behaving childishly. His behaviour is interpreted as being beyond his years, as if he were a young man in love. The incongruity between the childish body and the supposed adult feelings is seen to be comic. The adult laughter is telling Hans that if he acts in this way – turning round in his chair to stare – he will be behaving inappropriately. He may become the focus of unwanted attention. The laughter is teaching him how to behave in a public place.

There are further aspects to this teaching. Just as the teaching of politeness generally involves indicating what rudeness is, so disciplinary laughter has implicit consequences. It not only indicates that inappropriate behaviour is 'naturally' funny, but, in so doing, it provides a model of discipline. Hans is to learn that what is socially inappropriate can be socially funny. He is not just being given a lesson in how to behave in a restaurant, but he also is receiving tuition in how to ridicule. Becoming a socialized member of society means more than learning how to behave in public. It involves learning how to laugh at those who behave inappropriately, for polite adults must be able to discipline the socially deviant with momentary heartless mockery.

Yet, the discipline seems to occur beyond the awareness of those who are exacting the discipline. A rhetorical spray is at hand. The adults can claim to be 'just' laughing. But they are not 'just' laughing, especially if they believe that they are 'just' laughing. To believe that one is 'just' laughing is to do more than 'just' laugh: it is to believe and to laugh. In the case of disciplinary laughter, the belief reassures, as it hides the cruelty of the laughter from the laugher. The adults in the restaurant need not believe that they are in any way causing the discomfort of the young boy; nor even that they are teaching him a lesson. They are just laughing innocently, or so they might care to believe.

Hans is a bright boy. In time he will learn how to mock. He will also learn how to claim to be 'just laughing' or 'just joking'. If such claims hide aspects of his own laughter from himself, then he will be learning the sort of self-deception that constitutes repression. Freud never properly explained how the skills of repression are learnt. He assumed that they were deeply hidden, inner processes that cannot be taught and that arise spontaneously within the Oedipal child. Of course, adults cannot directly teach how to repress. They cannot directly tell the child that 'if you think this way and do that, you will succeed in accomplishing adult repression'. But unwittingly they can provide displays of repression. That summer holiday, the adults in the restaurant with their laughter and their interpretations were providing models of repression.

There is a further turn to the story. The adults' disciplinary laughter was enabling them to engage in the very behaviour for which Hans was being made to feel embarrassed. We can imagine the scene. They were turning in their seats and staring – staring at Hans. They were catching the eyes of strangers as they laughed. The respectable men could smile at the women at the next table, as they joined in the mockery of Hans, who only wants to catch the eyes of the young girl. In short, the adults are enjoying the licence to do the very things that are forbidden.

Here lies one of the central ambiguities of disciplinary laughter. It permits the laughers to enjoy what is being outwardly sanctioned. This can be seen in the practical joke that simultaneously disrupts and reinforces the social order. The social order is reinforced when the new group member unwittingly disrupts its accepted practices. The observers stand back and laugh at the resulting confusion and embarrassment. They are not outraged, but amused. They can enjoy the disruption vicariously. In this enjoyment can be detected, not just the mockery that ensures the reproduction of the social order, but a rebellious delight in seeing the order disrupted. Onlookers are freed from the constraints that they impose on themselves and on others. So the adults delight in the freedom of Hans, even as they are constraining it through their disciplinary ridicule.

Laughing about it later

If children have to learn that embarrassing situations are ludicrous, then this knowledge must cover their own embarrassments. The nice guy theory of embarrassment is not totally without foundation. The embarrassed social actor can smile during the moments of their embarrassment, but this is not necessarily an indication of joining in the joke and sharing the humour of the onlookers. Those who are embarrassed might show wry smiles that recognize the ludicrousness of their own position in the sight of others. Such smiles are different from the smiles of the mockers. Wry smilers avert their gaze before smiling, as if avoiding eye contact. This basically is a smile of appeasement, going along with the laughter of others, so as to prevent further outbursts (Keltner, 1995; Keltner et al., 1998; see Retzinger, 1991, for a discussion of shame and smiling). It is a display of smiling, or laughing, *with* those whom one suspects are laughing *at* oneself.

The embarrassing moment, painful though it may be at the time, can later become a humorous story for the embarrassed person. Freud in 1922 added a postscript to his case-history of Little Hans. He had recently met Hans who was by now an adult. Hans had told Freud that when he read the case-history he had no recollection of the events. Perhaps, he too smiled at the behaviour of the child who blushed scarlet in the restaurant. As an adult, who understood the proprieties of behaviour in public places, he could now appreciate the funniness of his former self. In this, he would be engaging in something quite common – the turning of one's own embarrassment into an amusing story to be told later.

Embarrassment researchers tend not to comment upon the significance of 'laughing about it later', although their examples suggest it occurs regularly. Miller (1996), in the first chapter of his book *Embarrassment*, presents an example of an embarrassing incident. A 41-year-old graduate student was late for work and, in her haste to dress, had put on an old maternity slip that was too big for her. On her way to work she had to cross a busy road. The traffic stopped for her. As she began to cross, she could feel her slip slide down. The drivers were watching and her slip fell to the ground. She stepped out of the undergarment and carried on walking, burning with embarrassment and burying her head in her umbrella. Miller describes the story as 'a typical example of embarrassment' (ibid.: 3). He mentions two aspects without drawing particular attention to them: 'this event may have been delightful for the drivers who witnessed it, and the hapless victim was able to laugh about it later on' (ibid.: 3; see also Miller, 1996: 201n, for another 'laugh about it later' example). 'Laughing about it later', of course, implies that it was no laughing matter at the time. The very comprehensibility of the phrase suggests something general.

One might ask how, and in what contexts, people later laugh about embarrassing episodes. The linguist Helga Kotthoff (1999) has provided a detailed analysis of conversations, in which speakers tell humorous stories against themselves. Mostly these relate to embarrassing situations. In the later retellings, the episodes have become humorous tales. Among her examples is a restaurant story. Several speakers are talking about the time when they were eating in a Japanese restaurant. At the next table was a famous actress. Suddenly one of them knocked the soy sauce off their table. As the story is told, there are increasingly more interpolated laughs (which, in the transcript, are indicated by H, HE or HO, with the capitalization signifying increased volume). The main speaker continues: 'OFFHE THE TABLE HEHEHEHEHE and with that HEHEHE the meal was tempoHOrariHIly interruHUpted HE' (ibid.: 71). Another speaker, who was not present at the original episode, then asks 'Why?' Her lack of laughter indicates that she is not getting the joke. One of the speakers, who had been present, replies: 'By accident. It slipped. HEHE'. The questioner, who had not got the joke, then takes up and increases the laughter 'HAHAHA oh God', thereby indicating that she now understands the humour (in Kotthoff's transcription HAHA indicates greater laughter than HEHE). And another speaker, who also had been present, adds without laughter 'we simply made a bad impression'.

One can ask what is going on in such a story: why should making a bad impression be a matter for laughter? This story is not explicitly *about* embarrassment. The story does not end with a statement about the participants' feelings, with the teller, for instance, concluding 'and we were so embarrassed'. The speakers have signalled early in the telling what is required from the hearers – namely, laughter. The story is being told literally for laughs. In this way, speakers can indicate that they find the past event humorous rather than embarrassing (Norrick, 1993: 39). The reaction of the hearer who asks 'Why?' indicates that the basis of the humour may not be obvious despite the signals of laughter. As Kotthoff comments, 'for an outsider, the episode is not funny; this is an instance of "you had to be there"' (1999: 71). This would have been an example of what Freud called 'the comic' which is found and, unlike wit, is not created. When the speaker replies 'we simply made a bad impression', the hearer does not then need to ask again why that was funny. She can join in the laughter. Story-tellers and hearers assume that making a bad impression in front of a famous actress is a sufficient matter for humour.

The 'you had to be there' nature of the story is not straightforward. The tellers are not conveying that 'if you had been there, you would have laughed'. Laughter is the mode of telling the story, not part of its content. The speaker does not conclude the tale by saying words to the effect 'and then we all started laughing'. The 'laugh about it later' story is generally a story about an event that was not funny to the tellers at the time, but becomes funny in its re-telling. It can be so re-presented without the addition of wit, simply because it tells of a type of event – namely, an embarrassing event – which is socially recognized to be funny, at least to onlookers. In the retelling, the recipients of the story, and also the story-teller, have become observers of the past.

If laughter is absent in the content of the stories, then this is a double absence. In these examples, the tellers do not say that the onlookers were laughing and that they themselves had become objects of ridicule. The famous actress is just a passive onlooker: she is not depicted as having mocked the clumsy diners at the next table. We do not know how the pedestrian with the loose slip recounted her tale. It is possible to imagine two different formulations. The first might include passive onlookers. It could become a story about 'how surprised they must have been to see me step out of my slip and carry on walking!' A different tone of story would be indicated if the teller says that 'I could tell they were all laughing at me; I had to carry on walking, but I could feel their laughter.' The story about laughter would be less likely to be a story told for laughs. It is much more likely to be told for sympathy.

In the 'laugh about it later' story, the laughter must now belong to the teller and to their hearers, not to the witnesses of the original episode. In this respect, the story can become one about how 'I/we disrupted the social interaction'. We interrupted the dinner; I surprised the motorists; and you, the hearers, are invited to laugh at the temporary disruption of social life. The teller, far from being a humiliated victim of embarrassment, becomes the unconventional hero/heroine, who can laugh at the surprise of others.

The humour involved in the 'laugh about it later' story reveals something important about the nature of social life. On one level these stories might be understood as the means of coping with the painful memories of embarrassing episodes. The stories transform the pain of the past into the pleasure of the present, recruiting an audience to give laughing validity to that transformation. More importantly, the shared laughter indicates pleasure at the idea of disrupting the social order whose power was painfully felt at the time. The humour in the stories about the undergarment falling down or the soy sauce crashing to the floor derives from the disruption of social routine. In the retold stories, surprised, even outraged, onlookers are necessary. A soy sauce bottle being knocked off a table, when no-one is looking, is not a funny story. The hearers laugh with delight at the idea of making a bad impression, subverting the normal behaviour expected in a restaurant, especially when celebrities are present. Thus, the later laughter indicates the pleasures of subversion and revenge against the ridicule of embarrassment.

Paradoxes of discipline and rebellion

The ridicule of onlookers may be necessary to ensure that the mechanism of embarrassment acquires and retains its power to enforce the demands of social order. However, the laughter at those, who commit *faux pas* and inadvertently break the codes of social life, may not be straightforward. Certainly, the spontaneity of laughter, including the laughter of disciplinary mockery, typically precludes the conscious aim of disciplining. The pleasure of the onlookers may be experienced as pain by the disrupter. This can be detected in the case of Little Hans in the restaurant. Yet, there is a paradox: the same mechanism that ensures social compliance also expresses pleasure at subversion.

In order to understand this paradox, it might be helpful to return to the basic vision of Freud. In *Civilization and its Discontents* Freud expressly argued that civilized life requires the renunciation of pleasure. There was a conflict between the individual's pleasure and the demands of social order. The positives could not be brought into alignment. The more that people acted in responsible, ethical ways, the more temptations there were to repress. As has been suggested, the conversational codes of politeness make continual demands on speakers, who habitually and unthinkingly follow such codes in their daily conversations. Because it is impossible to have habitual politeness without the possibility of rudeness, the demands of politeness create rudeness as a hidden pleasurable temptation that needs to be routinely repressed, or driven from conscious awareness. The child must acquire the skills of routine repression in order to develop into a mature, conventionally appropriate speaker. Goffman (1967) hinted as much in his essay 'Where the action is', when he suggested that social life presents opportunities for mischief and physical destruction. Infants, he wrote, cannot be trusted to 'forgo these easy opportunities', and development was 'the process by which the individual learns to forgo these opportunities voluntarily' (ibid.: 169–70). Characteristically, Goffman does not say how the child is induced to give up such easy opportunities. Nor does he trace the psychological residues that such renunciation may leave in the conduct of day-to-day life.

It is a tenet of Freudian theory that repression can never be complete. As Freud suggested, repressed desires return in the form of dreams, neuroses and, above all, jokes. It can be no coincidence that so much humour involves the disruption of social codes: comedians voice the unsayable, often rudely insulting others as they do so. As Zijderveld suggested, the traditional fool turns the world of seriousness upside-down. In contemporary society millions regularly choose to watch situation comedies that present images of social disruption for pure enjoyment, although there may be occasional viewers who find the scenes of *I Love Lucy* too embarrassing to watch.

As Freud recognized, tendentious humour often contains an element of aggression as it rebels against the demands of order. The pleasure of the soy sauce story is to be found in the disruption of the famous actress's meal. Both the embarrassment at the time and the humour of the later story are enhanced because the onlooker is someone famous, possessing greater status than the social disrupter. The teller can exult in the heroics of making a bad impression, thereby subverting the deference normally paid to the famous. Yet, as Hans Speier (1998) so acutely observed, rebellious political jokes often support the social order that they seem to mock. There can be a conservative function in the pleasures of rebellious humour. The famous actress needs to be famous for the story to work fully. The story-tellers delight in recalling the moment when their humbly non-famous lives briefly, and so absurdly, impinged on hers. In this way, the story depends upon the continuing social division between the famous and ordinary that it seems to subvert.

The link between embarrassment and humour is ambivalent. It can function to protect the social order, keeping social actors in line, but simultaneously it can express pleasure at subverting that same order. All this helps understand why humour is universal to the extent that it is found in all cultures. One might suppose that ridicule is universally useful both as a means of socialization and as a means of preserving everyday social order through the disciplines of embarrassment. Similarly, one can predict that all cultures make demands on their members. In consequence, the need to repress disruptive temptations will be universal, although the precise nature of the temptations will vary from culture to culture. From this it follows that the possibility of pleasure at seeing order disrupted and at seeing authorities discomfited should also be universal. The very conditions of social life may produce the necessity for empathy and compliance, but at the same time they enable the pleasures of ridicule and disruption. If one wants to say that this ambivalence reflects human nature, then this is because human nature is, and must be, a social nature.

10

Final Remarks

The arguments for a critical approach to humour have been outlined, and their historical antecedents have been discussed. Humour may be paradoxical in that it is social and anti-social, as well as being universal and highly particular. The preceding arguments also have their own paradoxical, even contradictory, features. Two such features merit brief attention. First, the arguments seem to be suggesting that humour is both more important and also less important than is often believed. Second, the arguments have been posed in very general terms, while, at the same time, it has been suggested that theories of humour should be understood in terms of the particular circumstances of their formulation.

To begin with, there is the paradox of humour's importance and unimportance. The argument has been that humour in the form of ridicule lies at the heart of social life. Among major theorists of humour, only Henri Bergson and to a lesser extent the Earl of Shaftesbury in the eighteenth century, have taken this line, at least in a systematic fashion. Often, theorists seem to be moving towards recognizing the social importance of ridicule, only to shy away at the last moment. Even Bergson seemed unwilling to consider too directly the implications for an understanding of human nature. Freud's work bears the marks of avoidance, as he emphasized the rebellious aspects of humour while overlooking its disciplinary functions.

Goffman's analysis of embarrassment is another example of simultaneous insight and avoidance. He suggested that fear of embarrassment makes us comply with the social order. It is the glue of social life – the substance that keeps the social world together. Goffman did not deal with the developmental issue. Babies are never embarrassed and young children can rush about without the self-consciousness of adults. Somewhere along the line, we have to learn how to be embarrassed. This is where humour, or at least ridicule, comes in. It is through ridicule that embarrassment is learnt. The fear of embarrassment continues to be related to the fear that others will laugh at us. If embarrassment lies at the heart of social life, as Goffman suggested, then so must humour in the guise of ridicule. In consequence, humour, because it plays such a key role in the maintenance of social life, is much more important than social theorists have often assumed.

On the other hand, the argument has been saying that humour is less important than it is often thought to be. There is nowadays a widespread belief in the self-evident desirability of humour. This is part of a general outlook that here has been called ideological positivism. The assumptions of ideological positivism are manifest in common-sense beliefs, in professional and self-help therapies, as well as in theories of academic psychology. The message of ideological positivism is both prescriptive and descriptive in relation to humour. Popular and academic writers describe the apparent positive benefits of humour. Laughter is said to be good for physical and psychological health – although there are grounds for treating with caution sweeping statements to this effect. Then there are the prescriptive recommendations. One should learn to smile through adversity, laugh to relieve tension, joke with subordinates at work, and so on. With a sense of humour people will enjoy better bodily and psychological health, relationships will run more smoothly and businesses will be more productive. In this image, humour offers many important possibilities for making the world a positively better place.

The critical approach questions such assumptions, especially when expressed in the context of popular and academic psychology. Accordingly, the critical approach, that is being developed here, warns that humour is neither as important, nor as good-natured, as its supporters often advocate. This is not because humour plays a marginal role in social life. On the contrary, it is precisely because humour has a vital, disciplinary role in the maintenance of social life that it is less important in the sense that ideological positivism accords it. The problem for ideological positivism is that ridicule – the great negative side of humour – fulfils the vital social role. As a result, ideological positivism overlooks the social core of humour. If ideological positivism overestimates the importance of the secondary aspects, while downgrading the primary one, then the critical argument seeks to turn things topsy-turvy. What is unimportant and sometimes completely overlooked by ideological positivism becomes the central element of this critical approach.

The critical argument suggests that the optimism of ideological positivism should be treated with caution. Some versions of ideological positivism imply that the world can be transformed by realizing the positives of human nature. Strategies for improving humour can play a part in this transformation. It is as if inner psychological change takes precedence over fundamental social change. The idea of necessary repression, derived from Herbert Marcuse, throws doubt on the optimism of this positivism. Marcuse ended *Eros and Civilization* with the caution that no future utopia could avoid the shadow of death, or Thanatos. The inevitability of future death is not the only shadow cast upon the possibility of freedom. There are shadows from childhood. Repression cannot be evaded if the disciplines of language and social practices are to be learned by the child. And laughter, far from indicating an escape from such disciplines, is complicit within them.

The second paradox relates to the generality of the critical theory that has been outlined here. This theory does not connect humour with a particular sort of social arrangement. Instead, it is a universal theory, claiming that all social life requires the disciplinary force of ridicule. This is why humour is to be found in all cultures. The argument connects humour with discipline and, hence, with power. Even the micro-dynamics of power are involved when parents joke with children. All too often, theorists have overlooked the power dynamics of humour, especially those that occur when adults find amusement in the behaviour of children. Even Freud, the great exposer of human self-deception, overlooked this. He let himself be taken in. Or rather he rushed to assume the innocence of parental laughter.

One implication of the present argument is that power is necessarily involved in social order. There could be no language unless adults seek to instil the established codes of meaning in the younger generation. There is no developmental equality between the babbling of children and the conventions of the adult language. The latter has to replace the former. The child has to accept the disciplines of language, in order to enter the world of dialogue as an appropriate speaker. It was in this sense that Roland Barthes, with characteristic exaggeration, claimed that language was 'quite simply fascist' (1982: 461). If meaning has to be socially policed, then mockery and laughter are the friendly neighbourhood officers, who cheerily maintain order. And sometimes they wield their truncheons with punishing effect.

This may have been proposed as a universal theory, yet, at the same time, a historical argument has been developed. Theories of humour are not to be abstracted from their particular intellectual and social context. Each theory of humour is also a theory of serious meaning. Most of the main theories are general, universal theories. For instance, the theory of superiority did not confine itself to those feelings of superiority that might arise during a particular historical epoch or within a particular culture. Hobbes's theory reached out to all laughter, regardless who is laughing or where the laughter is occurring. In all cases, he argued that laughter is symptomatic of a sudden feeling of superiority. Similarly the theory of incongruity is typically phrased in terms of a universal psychology. It asserts that whenever a certain pattern of incongruity is perceived, the response of laughter is likely to follow. This is proposed as a universal law of human behaviour and this universality characterizes modern versions of the incongruity theory as well as the classical formulations.

Yet, these general theories have tended to arise in particular circumstances and they take much of their meaning from the wider philosophical and political contexts of their formulation. In this regard, the analysis of these general theories has itself been particular and historical. Hobbes's fear of laughter was part of his general fear of untrammelled emotion being given political rein. The theories of incongruity were part of an ideology of gentlemanly taste and class superiority. And today, theories of humour are touched by the wider climate of ideological positivism and its positive psychology.

The same critical focus can be turned self-reflexively on the present enterprise. So, one might ask, what are the general relations between the present theory and the particular conditions under which it is being proposed? The theory is not being proposed merely to make technical points about theories of humour, although it is hoped that, along the way, there have been some suggestions for improving particular theoretical perspectives. Bergson's vision, like so many old French farm-houses, requires renovation and the installation of modern utilities. Goffman's theory of embarrassment could do with a new extension. But the basic impetus is not to renovate the old sites of theory, hoping to make a profit in today's market of ideas with a period-style Shaftesbury villa or fully modernized Spencerian town-house. The impetus for the theory comes from the argument with ideological positivism. This argument is not merely whether the brochure for the estate of happy humour has omitted the suspicion of dry rot and structural weakness. The argument is not even confined to the particular topic of humour, for ideological positivism's assumptions about humour are part of a much wider viewpoint.

The current theoretical perspective has been proposed in general, universalized terms. It has not focused upon exploring differences in humour – whether these are differences of culture, gender, ethnicity or whatever. Two interrelated problems with such a universalized approach can be mentioned. First, such universalism is somewhat out of fashion today with social theorists, who often stress the importance of difference. Sometimes universal theorizing conveys the impression that human nature has a fixed character. A stress on difference shows the variety of human natures and suggests that we are not bound to reproduce a particular, fixed pattern of behaviour. Instead we can create and re-create our natures. However, in a divided world of differences, where small distinctions can be the occasion for mass destruction, it is sometimes beneficial to stress the unity of humanity. This unity does not arise because we possess a fixed human nature in a simple biological sense. With regard to humour, we are not biologically obliged to laugh at the same things. Whatever differences there might be between cultures, the very fact that humans live within culture and within language creates commonality. If all cultures possess humour because they are cultures, then we are united by the possibility of humour, whatever the cultural, political and personal differences. In this, we share a common humanity.

The second drawback of a universalized approach is that it fails to get down to the business of examining the conditions of contemporary society. The present analysis has not examined the particular social conditions that have produced ideological positivism and its theory of humour. By contrast, the historical conditions that might have produced the superiority, incongruity and relief theories have been discussed. Clearly, much could be said about the relations between the structures of late capitalism and contemporary common-sense views on humour. This big and important topic is beyond the scope of the present work. What has been attempted here has been much more limited. The aim has been to highlight some of the confusions and evasions that have characterized some theoretical discussions of humour. The hope has been to move *toward* a critical theory of humour, rather than to claim to have arrived at one. A full critical approach would, of course, analyse the particularities of today's varieties of humour.

Instead, some very brief remarks can be offered in order to suggest how such an analysis might relate to some of the ideas that have discussed earlier. It has been argued that the apparent rebelliousness of humour need not, in fact, indicate an actual rebelliousness, for rebellious humour can have disciplinary functions. The mocking of authority can help to sustain, rather than undermine, existing relations of power. In today's culture, there is no set time that is marked off for carnival. Instead, huge quasi-monopolies carry the carnival nightly into the homes of rich and poor, who expect more varied fare than mere bread and circuses. The popular media is characterized by a continual tone of irreverence. Within the daily carnival of television are comics who parody and satirize the recognizable figures of the day. The ridiculing of celebrities by celebrity comics confirms the culture of celebrity. It validates the targets as sufficiently important to merit parody in the selfsame medium that creates the comedians' continuing celebrity.

The ordinary carnival might be interrupted by exceptional, brief periods of cessation following dramatic moments of tragedy, such as the death of a national leader or a horrific terrorist incident. Following the death of Princess Diana in Britain and the destruction of the World Trade Center in the United States, it was deemed inappropriate to show humorous programmes on television for a short period. Such brief moments of collective seriousness are a reversal of those brief collective carnivals that interrupted the serious ordinariness of former times. The difference is that these modern moments of collective seriousness are irregular, unforeseen, sudden events that are experienced as moments that should not happen. They are not built into the yearly calendar.

One might ask what is the ideological relation between the continual carnival of fun and the social system in which it is created. The question is a big one. In general terms, such a constant carnival fits well with the economic system of contemporary capitalism that constantly has to revolutionize itself. Companies that wish to profit in the so-called 'market-place' must demonstrate the sort of elasticity that Bergson believed to be essential for the progress of social life. Nothing can remain stationary. Production processes, marketing systems and the products themselves must constantly be updated. The consumer must be left in a continual state of desire, ready to discard the products of last year in order to purchase the latest items. What is outdated should be mocked, at least until it is sufficiently outdated that it can be re-branded as the latest 'retro' look. Advertisements will depict the person who lacks the advertised product as a somewhat ridiculous figure. The commercial climate demands enterprise, irreverence and a willingness of experiment. Those who have failed to keep pace with the market and those who have failed to update their possessions through continual expenditure should be mocked into showing the commercially desirable elasticity.

In this cultural climate few would wish to appear stuffy, old-fashioned and, heaven forbid, puritan. If there is an element of 'infantilism' in this culture, then this is manifested in the way that the position of the naughty child is far more comfortable and desirable than that of the humourless, disciplinarian parent. Everyone, except the young, should be youthful. The wrinkles of age are to be removed by special products and, even if they cannot be, it is still desirable to remain 'young at heart'. Even the most powerful politicians can slip easily into the position of youthful naughtiness. George W. Bush, as President of the United States, spoke at a dinner in honour of the conservative intellectual William Buckley. He recalled their time together at Yale University: 'We go back a long way and have a lot in common. Bill wrote a book at Yale. And I read one' (Vulliamy, 2003). It would not go down well, if the modern politician were to reverse the joke, claiming to have written a book while someone else only managed to read one. These are not Platonic times. The attractive quality is naughtiness, not haughtiness.

Critics on the left can find themselves in a difficult position with regard to humour, as apparently rebellious humour fulfils conservative functions. Where conformity to the 'market' dictates constant revolution, the conformists can appear to have radical jokes. Today, many of the big controversies about comedians going too far are not about left-wing comedians. In some respects, it is the left that tries to insist upon codes of speech, pointing out that it is unacceptable to use traditional terms for describing those with physical disabilities, non-heterosexual preferences and foreign citizenship. In these circumstances, conventional comedians can easily adopt the position of being daring rebels, uttering the unutterable, speaking with the frankness of the traditional carnivalesque fool, and transgressing the restrictive codes of respectability. They can appear as the naughty children resisting the orthodoxy of humourless authorities. And if the violation is not too blatant, the temptation to join with the mockery of social restriction is all the more seductive. It's only a joke. You've got to laugh. You've got to ... but the pleasure is unforced.

Comically, this can put the left on the defensive. For years, the left has been told that the right is fundamentally humourless. It has been easy to associate the right with the old puritanical traditions. But today the right can have some of the best and naughtiest jokes. Who can mock the President for his illiteracy, when he does so himself to the applause of the rich and powerful? There is, of course, still space for further pointed mockery, as the filmmaker and author Michael Moore has demonstrated so effectively. But shocking moves can also come from elsewhere. Radio 'shock-jocks' have established large followings in the United States by their willingness to offend for the sake of laughter. No topic seems beyond their mockery. They are the cheeky boys (and occasionally cheeky girls) defying all conventions, especially those of liberal sensitivity. They can accrue fame and fortune in the process. Again and again, they will claim to be defying 'political correctness', as if such a claim validated their humour and their persona as naughty rebels.

At the time of writing, an established, politically conservative American comedian, famous for his ethnic jokes, is touring Britain. His show is being advertised under the title of 'Politically Incorrect'. Publicists presumably anticipate audiences being drawn by the prospect of daring, but conservatively safe, rebellion against restrictive codes. By contrast, a progressive radio station, Air America Radio, has been formed to counter the influence of the shock-jocks and right-wing talk hosts. Apparently the station has not been successful. It simply is not funny enough. One observer has commented that it is 'much easier to jeer at those seeking compassion for others than vice versa' (Anthony, 2004: 5). As Bergson recognized, the very act of jeering requires a lack of compassion, an anaesthesia of the heart.

If it is true that left-wing comedy can operate at a disadvantage, then this is not a technical problem. Nor is the problem that left-wing comedians are insufficiently humorous, or that the right-wing has stolen the best gags. The problem may not lie in the humour itself but in the assumptions that it is morally desirable to be funny and that rebelliously experienced humour is rebellious in effect. Marx did not believe that the working classes needed to be led by cadres of radical comics. Yet, his writings contain an abundance of humour. There is more biting wit in the opening paragraphs of *The German Ideology* than most philosophers produce in a lifetime of writing. Marx's bursts of wit did not undermine the seriousness of his message. Serious politics by its nature is serious. In a culture of fun such seriousness can operate at a disadvantage. The radical can resemble the unwelcome puritan guest, who in former days sought to reduce the levity of every social occasion. The eventual departure of such a guest will be followed by a huge sigh of relief and a burst of laughter.

The goal of criticism is neither to increase seriousness at the expense of laughter, nor vice versa. It is not as if the two are in opposition, so that a gain in one by necessity requires a diminution of the other, as if there are predetermined amounts of serious and humorous nervous energy. The previous argument has stressed that humour and seriousness are necessarily linked. The world of serious meaning requires the disciplinary use of mockery. In return, mockery can be turned rebelliously against seriousness. Neither move is intrinsically meritorious. As Freud's analysis stressed, the outward form of humour can serve different tendentious purposes. The morality comes not from the humour itself but from the purposes to which it is put.

Marcuse in *Eros and Civilization* (1972) described the movement of history as being 'a dialectic of civilization'. He was referring to the constant oscillation between freedom and necessity, pleasure and duty, and, above all, the dialectic between love and aggression. To this might be added the dialectic of humour and seriousness, laughter and unlaughter. The point about such a dialectic is that it is never finally resolved in favour of one or other of the opposing terms. Each needs the other for its existence, even as they struggle for momentary supremacy. A similar dialectic underwrites Bergson's account of the battle between the inelasticity of the body and the vitality of the spirit. Humour, in this vision, was a weapon of the spirit against the body. But, of course, it cannot break free from the body. Quite apart from anything else, it requires the bodily reaction of laughter, whose own iterated movements represent the sort of bodily inelasticity that, according to Bergson, humour seeks to discipline.

So, humour and seriousness remain inextricably linked. Neither can abolish the other without abolishing itself – or without threatening the social order. It serves little point to look forward to a utopia that will only know laughter. A utopia of laughter and laughter alone cannot be a place of humour. Instead, there must be a continual movement between laughter and seriousness, without a final resting place on one side or another. Within particular contexts, which are marked by a conventionally defined end-point, there can be a last moment of humour or seriousness. Some stand-up comedians in the age of variety theatre would reserve their best, most trusted jokes until last, so they could leave the stage amid appreciative laughter. Others would end their act with a seriously delivered, sentimental song. Serious books analyzing humour, just like the comic variety acts of the past, must also have an ending. Some theorists, such as Peter Berger or Simon Critchley, write in praise of the human genius for humour. They like to finish on an up-beat note. Others don't.

References

Adamson, J. (1973) *Groucho, Harpo, Chico and Sometimes Zeppo*. London: W.H. Allen.

Addison, J. (1711) *The Spectator*, 47, 24 April.

Addison, J. (1965) *The Spectator*, ed. D.F. Bond. Oxford: Clarendon Press.

Akenside, M. (1810) *The Pleasures of Imagination: A New Edition*. London: T. Cadell and W. Davies.

Allsop, D. (1997) *Kicking in the Wind: The Real Life Drama of a Small-Town Football Club*. London: Headline.

Amada, G. (1993) 'The role of humour in a college mental health program', in W.F. Fry and W.A. Salameh (eds), *Advances in Humour and Psychotherapy*. Sarasota, FL: Professional Resource Exchange.

Andreski, S. (1971) *Herbert Spencer*. London: Nelson.

Anonymous (1963) *Joe Miller's Jests or the Wit's Vade-Mecum* (1739) New York: Dover.

Anthony, A. (2004) 'Why does the devil have all the best gags?', The *Guardian* G2, 15 April, 5.

Apte, M.L. (1983) 'Humour research, methodology and theory in anthropology', in P.E. McGhee and J.H. Goldstein (eds), *Handbook of Humour Research*. New York: Springer-Verlag.

Apter, M.J. (1982) *The Experience of Motivation*. London: Academic Press.

Apter, M.J. (1982b) '"Fawlty Towers": a reversal theory analysis of a popular comedy series', *Journal of Popular Culture*, 16, 128–38.

Aristophanes (1973) *The Clouds*, in *Lysistrata, The Acharnians, The Clouds*. Harmondsworth: Penguin.

Aristotle (1909) *Rhetoric*. Cambridge: Cambridge University Press.

Aristotle (1926) *The Nicomachean Ethics*. London: William Heinemann.

Aristotle (1963) *The Poetics*. London: Dent.

Aristotle (1968) *On the Parts of Animals*. London: Loeb Classical Library.

Attardo, S. (1993) 'Violation of conversational maxims and cooperation: the case of jokes', *Journal of Pragmatics*, 19, 537–58.

Attardo, S. (2000) 'Irony as relevant inappropriateness', *Journal of Pragmatics*, 32, 793–826.

Attardo, S. and Raskin, V. (1991) 'Script theory revis(it)ed: joke similarity and joke representation model', *Humor*, 4, 293–347.

Aubrey, J. (1999) 'The Brief Life: An abstract of John Aubrey's notes', in T. Hobbes *Human Nature and De Corpore Politico*. Oxford: Oxford University Press.

Audi, R. (ed.) (1995) *Cambridge Dictionary of Philosophy*. Cambridge: Cambridge University Press

Austin, G. (1806) *Chironomia: or a Treatise on Rhetorical Delivery*. London: T. Cadell and W. Davies.

Bacon, F. ([1625] 1902) *The Essays*. London: J.M. Dent.

Bain, A. (1865) *The Emotions and the Will*, 2nd edn. London: Longmans, Green and Co.

Bain, A. (1868a) *The Senses and the Intellect*, 3rd edn. London: Longmans, Green and Co.

Bain, A. (1868b) *Mental and Moral Science*. Longmans, Green and Co.

Bain, A. (1877) *English Composition and Rhetoric*. London: Longmans, Green and Co.

Bain, A. (1879) *Education as a Science*. London: C. Kegan Paul and Co.

Bain, A. (1882) *J.S. Mill: A Criticism*. London: Longmans, Green and Co.

Bain, A. (1899) *The Emotions and the Will*, 3rd edn. London: Longmans, Green and Co.

Bain, A. (1904) *Autobiography*. London: Longmans, Green and Co.

Bakhtin, M. (1981) *The Dialogic Imagination*. Austin, TX: University of Texas.

Bakhtin, M. (1986) *Speech Genres and Other Late Essays*. Austin, TX: University of Texas.

Banerji, C. and Donald, D. (1999) *Gillray Observed*. Cambridge: Cambridge University Press.

Barsoux, J.-L. (1993) *Funny Business: Humour, Management and Business Culture.* London: Cassell and Co.

Barthes, R. (1982) 'Inaugural lecture, Collège de France', in R. Barthes, *Selected Writings.* London: Collins.

Bauman, Z. (1995) *Life in Fragments.* Oxford: Blackwell.

Beattie, J. (1779) 'Essay on Laughter and Ludicrous Composition', in J. Beattie *Essays: On Poetry and Music.* London: E. and C. Dilly; Edinburgh: W. Creech. (facsmile edition: London: Routledge/Thoemmes Press, 1996).

Beattie, J. (1783) 'The theory of language', in J. Beattie, *Dissertations Moral and Critical.* Dublin: Exshaw, Walker, Beatty, White, Byrne, Cash and McKenzie.

Beck, C.T. (1997) 'Humour in nursing practice: a phenomenological study', *International Journal of Nursing Studies*, 34, 346–52.

Beck, U. (1992) *Risk Society: Towards a New Modernity.* London: Sage.

Bell, M.B. and Gardner, M. (eds) (1998) *Bakhtin and the Human Sciences.* London: Sage.

Bennett, M. (1989) 'Children's self-attribution of embarrassment', *British Journal of Developmental Psychology*, 7, 207–17.

Bennett, M. and Gillingham, K. (1991) 'The role of self-focused attentions in children's attributions of social emotions to the self', *Journal of Genetic Psychology*, 152, 303–9.

Benton, G. (1988) 'The origins of the political joke', in C. Powell and G.E.C. Paton (eds), *Humour in Society: Resistance and Control.* Basingstoke: Macmillan.

Bergen, D. (1998) 'Development of the sense of humour', in W. Ruch (ed.), *The Sense of Humour: Explorations of a Personality Characteristic.* Berlin: Mouton de Gruyter.

Berger, P.L. (1997) *Redeeming Laughter: The Comic Dimension of Human Experience.* Berlin/New York: Walter de Gruyter.

Berger, P.L. and Luckmann, T. (1967) *The Social Construction of Reality.* London: Allen Lane.

Bergson, H. (1900) *Le rire: essai sur la signification du comique.* Paris: Félix Alcan.

Bergson, H. (1911a) *Laughter: An Essay on the Meaning of the Comic.* London: Macmillan and Co.

Bergson, H. (1911b) *Creative Evolution.* New York: Henry Holt.

Bergson, H. (1911c) *Matter and Memory.* London: Swan Sonnenschein and Co.

Bergson, H. (1913) *Time and Free Will: An Essay on the Immediate Data of Consciousness.* London: George Allen.

Bergson, H. (1920) *Mind-Energy: Lectures and Essays.* London: Macmillan and Co.

Bergson, H. (1946) *The Creative Mind.* New York: Citadel Press.

Billig, M. (1996) *Arguing and Thinking.* Cambridge: Cambridge University Press.

Billig, M. (1998) 'Dialogic repression and the Oedipus Complex: reinterpreting the Little Hans case', *Culture and Psychology*, 4, 11–47.

Billig, M. (1999) *Freudian Repression: Conversation Creating the Unconscious.* Cambridge: Cambridge University Press.

Billig, M. (2000) 'Freud's different versions of forgetting "Signorelli": rhetoric and repression', *International Journal of Psychoanalysis*, 81, 483–98.

Billig, M. (2001) 'Humour and hatred: the racist jokes of the Ku Klux Klan', *Discourse and Society*, 12, 267–89.

Billig, M. (2005) 'Violent racist jokes: an analysis of extreme racist humour', in M. Pickering and S. Lockyer (eds), *Beyond a Joke.* London: Macmillan.

Billig, M., Condor, S., Edwards, D., Gane, M., Middleton, D. and Radley, A.R. (1988) *Ideological Dilemmas: A Social Psychology of Everyday Thinking.* London: Sage.

Bilmes, J. (1987) 'The concept of preference in conversation analysis', *Language in Society*, 17, 161–87.

Boskin, J. (1987) 'The complicity of humour: the life and death of Sambo', in J. Morreall (ed.), *The Philosophy of Laughter and Humour.* Albany, NY: State University of New York Press.

Boswell, J. (1950) *London Journal, 1762–1763.* London: William Heinemann.

Bowne, B.P. (1912) *Kant and Spencer.* Boston: Houghton Mifflin.

Boxer, D. and Cortés-Conde, F. (1997) 'From bonding to biting: conversational joking and identity play', *Journal of Pragmatics*, 27, 275–94.

Boyle, G.J. and Joss-Reid, J.M. (2004) 'Relationship of humour to health: a psychometric investigation', *British Journal of Health Psychology*, 9, 51–66.

Bremner, J. (1997) 'Jokes, jokers and jokebooks in Ancient Greece', in J. Bremner and H. Roodenburg (eds), *A Cultural History of Humour*. Cambridge: Polity.

Brown, J. (1751) *Essays on the Characteristics*. London: C. Davis.

Brown, P. and Levinson, S.C. (1987) *Politeness: Some Universals in Language Use*. Cambridge: Cambridge University Press.

Burke, P. (1993) *The Art of Conversation*. Ithaca, NY: Cornell University Press.

Buss, A.H. (1980) *Self-Consciousness and Social Anxiety*. San Francisco: W.H. Freeman.

Campbell G. ([1776] 1856) *The Philosophy of Rhetoric*. New York: Harper and Brothers.

Carpenter, W.B. (1879) *Principles of Mental Physiology*, 5th edn. London: Kegan Paul.

Carver, C.S., Lehman, J.M. and Antoni, M.H. (2003) 'Dispositional pessimism predicts illness-related disruption of social and recreational activities amongst breast cancer patients', *Journal of Personality and Social Psychology*, 84, 813–21.

Caudron, S. (1992) 'Humour is healthy in the workplace', *Personnel Journal*, 71, 63–8.

Chapman, R. (2001) '"Am I doing it right?": A discursive analysis of cancer narratives', unpublished PhD thesis, Loughborough University.

Chevalier, J. (1928) *Henri Bergson*. London: Rider and Co.

Clancy, P.M. (1986) 'The acquisition of communicative style in Japanese', in B.B. Schieffelin and E. Ochs (eds), *Language Socialization across Cultures*. Cambridge: Cambridge University Press.

Cohen, E. (1953) *Human Behaviour in the Concentration Camp*. New York: Grosset and Dunlap.

Cohen, T. (1999) *Jokes: Philosophical Thoughts on Joking Matters*. Chicago: University of Chicago.

Colley, L. (1992) *Britons: Forging the Nation 1707–1837*. New Haven, CT: Yale University Press.

Conte, Y. (1998) *Serious Laughter: Live a Happier, Healthier, More Productive Life*. Amsterdam: Berwick Publishing.

Coser, L. (2003) 'Functionalism', in W. Outhwaite (ed.), *The Blackwell Dictionary of Modern Social Thought*. Oxford: Blackwell.

Coupland, J. (1996) 'Dating advertisements: discourses of the commodified self', *Discourse and Society*, 7, 187–207.

Coupland, N. and Coupland, J. (2001) 'Language, ageing and agism', in W.P. Robinson and H. Giles (eds), *The New Handbook of Language and Social Psychology*. Chichester: John Wiley.

Crews, F. (1995) *The Memory Wars: Freud's Legacy in Dispute*. New York: New York Review.

Crews, F. (ed.) (1998) *Unauthorized Freud: Doubters Confront a Legend*. New York: Penguin.

Critchley, S. (2002) *On Humour*. London: Routledge.

Crozier, W.R. (2001) 'Blushing and the exposed self: Darwin revisited', *Journal for the Theory of Social Behaviour*, 31, 61–72.

Crozier, W.R. and Dimmock, P.S. (1999) 'Name-calling and nicknames in a sample of primary school children', *British Journal of Educational Psychology*, 69, 505–16.

Danner, D.D., Snowdon, D.A. and Friesen, W.V. (2001) 'Positive emotions in early life and longevity: findings from the nun study', *Journal of Personality and Social Psychology*, 80, 804–13.

Darwin, C. ([1872] 1896) *The Expression of the Emotions in Man and Animals*. New York: D. Appleton.

Davies, C. (1990) *Ethnic Humour around the World*. Bloomington, IN: Indiana University Press.

Davies, C. (1998) 'The dog that didn't bark in the night: a new sociological approach to the cross-cultural study of humour', in W. Ruch (ed.), *The Sense of Humour*. Berlin: Mouton de Gruyter.

Deleuze, G. (1988) *Bergsonism*. New York: Zone Books.

Diogenes Laertius (1972) *The Lives and Views of Eminent Philosophers*. London: Loeb Classical Library.

Donald, D. (1996) *The Age of Caricature: Satirical Prints in the Reign of George III*. New Haven, CT: Yale University Press.

Drew, P. (1987) 'Po-faced receipt of teases', *Linguistics*, 25, 219–53.

Dugas, L. (1902) *Psychologie du rire*. Paris: Félix Alcan.

Duncan, D. (1908) *The Life and Letters of Herbert Spencer*. London: Methuen.

Dundes A. (1987) *Cracking Jokes: Studies of Sick Humour Cycles and Stereotypes*. Berkeley, CA.: Ten Speed Press.

Dunn, J. (1988) *The Beginnings of Social Understanding*. Oxford: Blackwell.

Du Pré, A. (1998) *Humour and the Healing Arts*. Mahwah, NJ: Lawrence Erlbaum.

Edelman, M. (1977) *Political Language*. New York: Academic Press.

Eder, D. (1990) 'Serious and playful disputes: variations in conflict talk among female adolescents', in A.D. Grimshaw (ed.), *Conflict Talk*. Cambridge: Cambridge University Press.

Edmonds, D. and Eidinow, J. (2001) *Wittgenstein's Poker: The Story of a Ten Minute Argument between Two Great Philosophers*. London: Faber and Faber.

Edwards, D. (1997) *Discourse and Cognition*. London: Sage.

Edwards, D. and Potter, J. (1993) *Discursive Psychology*. London: Sage.

Eisenberg, A.R. (1986) 'Teasing: verbal play in two Mexicano homes', in B.B. Schieffelin and E. Ochs (eds), *Language Socialization across Cultures*. Cambridge: Cambridge University Press.

Ekman, P. (1984) 'Expression and the nature of emotion', in K.S. Scherer and P. Ekman (eds), *Approaches to Emotion*. Hillsdale, NJ: Erlbaum.

Ekman, P. (1992) 'An argument for basic emotions', *Cognition and Emotions*, 6, 169–200

Epictetus (1910) *The Moral Discourses*. London: J.M. Dent.

Erwin, E. (1996) *A Final Accounting: Philosophical and Empirical Issues in Freudian Psychology*. Cambridge, MA: MIT Press.

Fairclough, N. (2003) '"Political correctness": the politics of culture and language', *Discourse and Society*, 14, 17–28.

Ferguson, A. ([1767] 1966) *An Essay on the History of Civil Society*. Edinburgh: Edinburgh University Press.

Ferrand, L. and Nicolas, S. (2000) 'L'œuvre de Ribot à travers les sommaires de ses ouvrages', *Psychologie et Histoire*, 1, 82–130.

Ferris, P. (1997) *Dr Freud: A Life*. London: Sinclair-Stevenson.

Feuer, A.C. (ed.) (1977) *Tehillim, with a Commentary Anthologized from Talmudic, Midrashic and Rabbinic Sources*. New York: Mesorah.

Fife, G. (1999) *Tour de France: The History, the Legend, the Riders*. Edinburgh: Mainstream.

Figgou, E. (2002) 'Social psychological and lay understandings of prejudice, racism and discrimination: an exploration of their dilemmatic aspects', unpublished PhD thesis, Lancaster University.

Fine, G.A. (1983) 'Sociological approaches to the study of humor', in P.E. McGee and J.H. Goldstein (eds), *Handbook of Humor Research*, vol. 1. New York: Springer.

Forbes, W. (1824) *An Account of the Life and Writings of James Beattie*. London: W. Baynes and Son.

Forrester, J. (1991) *The Seductions of Psychoanalysis*. Cambridge: Cambridge University Press.

Fotheringham, W. (2003) *Put Me Back on My Bike: In Search of Tom Simpson*. London: Yellow Jersey Press.

Franzoi, S.L. (2000) *Social Psychology*, 2nd edn. Boston: McGraw-Hill.

Fredrickson, B.L. (1998) 'What good are positive emotions?', *Review of General Psychology*, 2, 300–19.

Fredrickson, B.L. (2000) 'Cultivating positive emotions to optimize health and well-being', *Prevention and Treatment*, 3, http://journals.apa.org/prevention/volume3/toc-mar07-00.html

Fredrickson, B.L. (2003) 'The value of positive emotions', *American Scientist*, 91, 330–5.

Fredrickson, B.L. and Branigan, C. (2005) 'Positive emotions broaden the scope of attention and thought-action repertoires', *Cognition and Emotion*, 20, 313–332.

Fredrickson, B.L. and Joiner, T. (2002) 'Positive emotions trigger upward spirals toward emotional well-being', *Psychological Science*, 13, 172–5.

Fredrickson, B.L. Tugade, M.M., Waugh, C.E. and Larkin, G. (2003) 'What good are positive emotions in crises? A prospective study of resilience and emotions following the terrorist attacks on the United States on September 11th, 2001', *Journal of Personality and Social Psychology*, 84, 365–76.

Freud, S. ([1900] 1990) *The Interpretation of Dreams*, Penguin Freud Library, vol. 4. Harmondsworth: Penguin.

Freud, S. ([1901] 1975) *The Psychopathology of Everyday Life*, Penguin Freud Library, vol. 5. Harmondsworth: Penguin.

Freud, S. ([1905a] 1977) 'Three essays on the theory of sexuality', in *On Sexuality*, Penguin Freud Library, vol. 7. Harmondsworth: Penguin.

Freud, S. ([1905b] 1991) *Jokes and their Relation to the Unconscious*, Penguin Freud Library, vol. 6. Harmondsworth: Penguin.

Freud, S. ([1909] 1990) 'Analysis of a phobia in a five-year-old boy ("Little Hans")', in *Case Histories 1*, Penguin Freud Library, vol. 8. Harmondsworth: Penguin.

Freud, S. ([1913] 1990) 'Totem and taboo', in *The Origins of Religion*, Penguin Freud Library, vol. 13. Harmondsworth: Penguin.

Freud, S. ([1914] 1993) 'On the history of the psychoanalytic movement', in *Historical and Expository Works*, Penguin Freud Library, vol. 15. Harmondsworth: Penguin.

Freud, S. ([1920] 1991) 'Beyond the pleasure principle', in *On Metapsychology*, Penguin Freud Library, vol. 11. Harmondsworth: Penguin.

Freud, S. ([1921] 1985) 'Group psychology and the analysis of the ego', in *Civilization, Society and Religion*, Penguin Freud Library, vol. 12. Harmondsworth: Penguin.

Freud, S. ([1925a] 1993) 'An autobiographical study', in *Historical and Expository Works*, Penguin Freud Library, vol. 15. Harmondsworth: Penguin.

Freud, S. ([1925b] 1993) 'Resistances to psychoanalysis', in *Historical and Expository Works*, Penguin Freud Library, vol. 15. Harmondsworth: Penguin.

Freud, S. ([1927] 1990) 'Humour', in *Art and Literature*, Penguin Freud Library, vol. 14. Harmondsworth: Penguin.

Freud, S. ([1930] 1987) 'Civilization and its discontents', in *Civilization, Society and Religion*, Penguin Freud Library, vol. 12. Harmondsworth: Penguin.

Freud, S. (1985) *The Complete Letters of Sigmund Freud to Wilhelm Fliess, 1887–1904*, ed. by J.M. Masson. Cambridge, MA.: Harvard University Press.

Freud, S. (1993) '"Wir und der Tod": a previously unpublished version of a paper given by Sigmund Freud on the attitude towards death', in D. Meghnagi (ed.), *Freud and Judaism*. London: Karnac Books.

Freud, S. and Breuer, J. ([1895] 1991) *Studies on Hysteria*, Penguin Freud Library, vol. 3. Harmondsworth: Penguin.

Fry, W.F. (1987) 'Introduction', in W.F. Fry and W.A. Salameh (eds), *Handbook of Humour and Psychotherapy*. Sarasota, FL: Professional Resource Exchange.

Fry, W.F. and Salameh, W. (eds) (1993) *Advances in Humour and Psychotherapy*. Sarasota, FL: Professional Resource Exchange.

Garfinkel, H. (1967) *Studies in Ethnomethodology*. New York: Prentice Hall.

Gay, P. (1995) *Freud: A Life for our Time*. London: Papermac.

Gergen, K.J. (1991) *The Saturated Self*. New York: Basic Books.

Giddens, A. (1991) *Modernity and Self-Identity*. Cambridge: Polity Press.

Giora, R. (1991) 'On the cognitive aspects of the joke', *Journal of Pragmatics*, 16, 463–85.

Goffman, E. (1967) *Interaction Ritual*. New York: Pantheon Books.

Goffman, E. (1981) *Forms of Talk*. Philadelphia, PA: University of Pennsylvania.

Gombrich, E.H. and Kris, E. (1940) *Caricature*. Harmondsworth: Penguin.

Graham, E., Papa, M. and Brooks, G. (1992) 'Functions of humour in conversation: conceptualization and measurement', *Western Journal of Communication*, 56, 161–83.

Grice, H.P. (1975) 'Logic and conversation', in P. Cole (ed.), *Syntax and Semantics*, vol. 9. New

York: Academic Press.

Grinstein, A. (1990) *Freud at the Crossroads*. Madison, CT: International Universities Press.

Gruner, R. (1997) *The Game of Humour: A Comprehensive Theory of Why We Laugh*. New Brunswick, NJ: Transaction.

Gundelach, P. (2000) 'Joking relationships and national identity in Scandinavia', *Acta Sociologica*, 43, 113–23.

Gurjeva, L. (2001) 'James Sully and scientific psychology 1880s–1910', in G. Bunn, A.D. Lovie and G.D. Richards (eds), *Psychology in Britain*. Leicester: British Psychological Society.

Hageseth III, C. (1988) *A Laughing Place: The Art and Psychology of Positive Humour in Love and Adversity*. Fort Collins, CO: Berwick.

Hartley D. ([1749] 1834) *Observations on Man, his Frame, his Duty, and his Expectations*. London: Thomas Tegg

Hay, J. (2000) 'Functions of humour in the conversations of men and women', *Journal of Pragmatics*, 32, 709–42.

Hazlitt, W. (1987) 'Lectures on English comic writers', in J. Morreall (ed.), *The Philosophy of Laughter and Humour*. Albany, NY: New York State University Press.

Hepburn, A. (1997) 'Teachers and secondary school bullying: a postmodern discourse analysis', *Discourse and Society*, 8, 27–48.

Hepburn, A. (2000) 'Power lines: Derrida, discursive psychology and the management of accusations of teacher bullying', *British Journal of Social Psychology*, 39, 605–28.

Heritage, J. (1984) *Garfinkel and Ethnomethodology*. Cambridge: Polity Press.

Hervey, G.H. (1854) *The Rhetoric of Conversation*. New York: Harper and Brothers.

Herzog, T.R. (1999) 'Gender differences in humour revisited', *Humor*, 12, 411–23.

Herzog, T.R. and Bush, B.A. (1994) 'The prediction of preference for sick humour', *Humor*, 7, 323–40.

Herzog, T.R. and Karafa, J.A. (1998) 'Preferences for sick versus nonsick humour', *Humor*, 11, 291–312.

Heuscher, J.E. (1993) 'Kirkegaard's humour and its implications for indirect humorous communication in psychotherapy', in W.F. Fry and W.A. Salameh (eds), *Advances in Humour and Psychotherapy*. Sarasota, FL: Professional Resource Exchange.

Hill, D. (1966) *Fashionable Contrasts: Caricatures* by James Gillray. London: Phaidon.

Hitler A. (1988) *Hitler's Table Talk*. Oxford: Oxford University Press.

Hobbes, T. (1996) *Leviathan*. Cambridge: Cambridge University Press.

Hobbes, T. (1999) *Human Nature and De Corpore Politico*. Oxford: Oxford University Press.

Höffding H. (1892) *Outlines of Psychology*. London: Macmillan.

Hogarth, W. (1955) *The Analysis of Beauty* (1753) Oxford: Clarendon Press.

Holmes, J. (2000) 'Politeness, power and provocation: how humour functions in the workplace', *Discourse Studies*, 2, 159–85.

Holmes, J. and Marra, M. (2002) 'Having a laugh at work: how humour contributes to workplace culture', *Journal of Pragmatics*, 34, 1683–710.

Holtgraves, T. (2001) 'Politeness', in W.P. Robinson and H. Giles (eds), *The New Handbook of Language and Social Psychology*. Chichester: John Wiley.

Husband, C. (1988) 'Racist humour and racist ideology in British television or I laughed till you cried', in C. Powell and G.E.C. Paton (eds), *Humour in Society*. Basingstoke: Macmillan.

Hutcheson, F. (1758) *Thoughts on Laughter*. Glasgow: Robert and Andrew. (facsimile edition, Bristol: Thoemmes, 1989).

Hutcheson, F. ([1775] 1969) *A System of Moral Philosophy*. Hildersheim: Georg Olms.

Imahori, T.T. and Cupach, W.R. (1994) 'A cross-cultural comparison of the interpretation and management of race: United States American and Japanese responses to embarrassing predicaments', *International Journal of Intercultural Relations*, 18, 193–219.

James, C.L.R. (1964) *Beyond a Boundary*. London: Sportsmans Books Club.

James, W. (1890) *The Principles of Psychology*. London: Macmillan.

James, W. (1909) *A Pluralistic Universe*. London: Longmans, Green and Co.

James, W. (1911) *Memories and Studies*. London: Longmans, Green and Co.

Jaret, C. (1999) 'Attitudes of Whites and Blacks towards ethnic humour: a comparison', *Humor*, 12, 385–409.

Jarrett, D. (1976) *England in the Age of Hogarth*. St. Albans: Paladin.

Jefferson, G. (1984) 'On the organization of laughter in talk about troubles', in M. Atkinson and J. Heritage (eds), *Structures of Social Action*. Cambridge: Cambridge University Press.

Jefferson, G. (1985) 'An exercise in the transcription and analysis of laughter', in T. A. van Dijk (ed.), *Handbook of Discourse Analysis*, vol. 3. London: Academic Press.

Johnson, K.E. and Marvis, C.B. (1997) 'First steps in the emergence of verbal humour: a case study', *Infant Behaviour and Development*, 20, 187–96.

Johnson, S., Culpeper, J. and Suhr, S. (2003) 'From "Politically Correct Councillors" to "Blairite Nonsense": discourses of "political correctness" in three British newspapers', *Discourse and Society*, 14, 29–47.

Jones, E. (1964) *The Life and Work of Sigmund Freud*. Harmondsworth: Penguin.

Kames, Lord (Henry Home) ([1762] 1854) *Elements of Criticism*. New York: F.J. Huntington and Mason Brothers.

Katriel, T. (1986) *Talking Straight: Dugri Speech in Israeli Sabra Culture*. Cambridge: Cambridge University Press.

Kelly, F.D. and Osborne, D. (1999) 'Ego states and preferences for humour', *Psychological Reports*, 85, 1031–9.

Keltner, D. (1995) 'Signs of appeasement: evidence for the distinct displays of embarrassment, amusement and shame', *Journal of Personality and Social Psychology*, 68, 441–54.

Keltner, D., Young, R.C., Heerey, E.A., Oemig, C. and Monarch, N.D. (1998) 'Teasing in hierarchical and intimate relations', *Journal of Personality and Social Psychology*, 75, 1231–47.

Kitzinger, C. (2000) 'How to resist an idiom', *Research on Language and Social Interaction*, 32, 121–54.

Klein, A. (1989) *The Healing Power: Techniques for Getting through Loss, Setbacks, Upsets, Disappointments, Difficulties, Trials, Tribulations and All That Not-So-Funny Stuff*. New York: J.P. Tarcher.

Klein, A. (1998) *The Courage to Laugh: Humour, Hope, and Healing in the Face of Death and Dying*. New York: J.P. Tarcher.

Koestler, A. (1964) *The Act of Creation*. London: Hutchinson.

Koffka, K. (1928) *The Growth of the Mind*. London: Kegan Paul, Trench, Trubner.

Kotthoff, H. (1999) 'Gender and joking: on the complexities of women's image politics in humorous narratives', *Journal of Pragmatics*, 32, 55–80.

Kotthoff, H. (2003) 'Responding to irony in different contexts: on cognition in conversation', *Journal of Pragmatics*, 35, 1387–411.

Kuhlman, T.L. (1985) 'A study of salience and motivational theories of humour', *Journal of Personality and Social Psychology*, 49, 281–6.

Lambourne, L. (1983) *An Introduction to Caricature*. London: Her Majesty's Stationery Office.

Lampert, M.D. and Ervin-Tripp, S. M. (1998) 'Exploring paradigms: the study of gender and sense of humour near the end of the 20th century', in W. Ruch (ed.), *The Sense of Humour: Explorations of a Personality Characteristic*. Berlin: Mouton de Gruyter.

LaRoche, L. (1998) *Relax – You May Only Have a Few Minutes Left: Using the Power of Humour to Overcome Stress in Life and Work*. New York: Villard Books.

Lefcourt, H.M. (2001) *Humour: The Psychology of Living Buoyantly*. New York: Kluwer Academic/Plenum.

Legman, G. (1969) *Rationale of the Dirty Joke: An Analysis of Sexual Humour*. London: Jonathan Cape.

Le Roy, E. (1913) *A New Philosophy: Henri Bergson*. London: Williams and Norgate.

Levesque, G. (1973) *Bergson: Vie et mort de l'homme et de dieu*. Paris: Les Éditions du Cerf.

Lewis, P. (1997) 'The killing jokes of the American eighties', *Humor*, 10, 251–83.

Locke, J. ([1690] 1964) *An Essay Concerning Human Understanding*. London: Dent.

Lockyer, S. and Pickering, M. (2001) 'Dear shit-shovellers: humour, censure and the discourse of complaint', *Discourse and Society*, 12, 633–52.

Macmillan, M. (1997) *Freud Evaluated: The Completed Arc*. Cambridge, MA: MIT Press.

Maher, M. (1993) 'Humour in substance abuse treatment', in W.F. Fry and W.A. Salameh (eds), *Advances in Humour and Psychotherapy*. Sarasota, FL: Professional Resource Exchange.

Manstead, A.S.R. and Semin, G.R. (1981) 'Social transgressions, social perspectives and social emotionality', *Motivation and Emotion*, 5, 249–61.

Marcus, D.K. and Miller, R.S. (1999) 'The perception of "live" embarrassment: a social relations analysis of class presentations', *Cognition and Emotion*, 13, 105–17.

Marcuse, H. (1972) *Eros and Civilisation*. London: Abacus.

Martin, R.A. (2001) 'Humour, laughter and physical health: methodological issues and research findings', *Psychological Bulletin*, 127, 504–19.

McDougall, W. (1923) *An Outline of Psychology*. London: Methuen.

McGhee, P.E. (1983) 'Humour development: Toward a life span approach', in P.E. McGhee and J.H. Goldstein (eds), *Handbook of Humour Research*. New York: Springer-Verlag.

McNamara, P. (1996) 'Bergson's "Matter and Memory" and modern selectionist theories of memory', *Brain and Cognition*, 30, 215–31.

Mead, G.H. (1962) *Mind, Self and Society*. Chicago: University of Chicago Press.

Melucci, A. (1996) *The Playing Self*. Cambridge: Cambridge University Press.

Meredith, G. (1897) *An Essay on Comedy*. Westminster: Archibald Constable.

Merryman, R. (2003) 'The Tramp was something within me', *Guardian Review*, Nov. 1, 16–17.

Metts, S. and Cupach, W.R. (1989) 'Situational influence on the use of remedial strategies in embarrassing predicaments', *Communication Monographs*, 56, 151–62.

Middleton, D. and Brown, S.D. (2005) *The Social Psychology of Experience*. London: Sage.

Miller, P. (1986) 'Teasing as language socialization and verbal play in a white working-class community', in B.B. Schieffelin and E. Ochs (eds), *Language Socialization across Cultures*. Cambridge: Cambridge University Press.

Miller, R.S. (1987) 'Empathic embarrassment: situational and personal determinants of reactions to the embarrassment of another', *Journal of Personality and Social Psychology*, 53, 1061–9.

Miller, R.S. (1992) 'The nature and severity of self-reported embarrassing circumstances', *Personality and Social Psychology Bulletin*, 18, 190–8.

Miller, R.S. (1996) *Embarrassment*. New York: Guildford Press.

Miller, R.S. and Tangney, J.P. (1994) 'Differentiating embarrassment and shame', *Journal of Social and Clinical Psychology*, 13, 273–87.

Mindess, H., Miller, C., Turek, J., Bender, A. and Corbin, S. (1985) *The Antioch Humour Test*. New York: Avon Books.

Modigliani, A. (1968) 'Embarrassment and embarrassability', *Sociometry*, 31, 313–26.

Moerman, M. (1988) *Talking Culture: Ethnography and Conversation Analysis*. Philadelphia. PA: University of Pennsylvania Press.

Monk, R. (1997) *Bertrand Russell*. London: Vintage.

Morreall, J. (1983) *Taking Laughter Seriously*. Albany, NY: State University of New York Press.

Morreall, J. (1987) 'Introduction', in J. Morreall (ed.) *The Philosophy of Laughter and Humour*. Albany, NY: State University of New York Press.

Morreall, J. (1997) *Humour Works*. Amherst, MA.: HRD Press.

Mosak, H. and Maniacci, M. (1993) 'An "Adlerian" approach to humour and psychotherapy', in W.F. Fry and W.A. Salameh (eds), *Advances in Humour and Psychotherapy*. Sarasota, FL: Professional Resource Exchange.

Mulkay, M. (1988) *On Humour*. Cambridge: Polity Press.

Nevo, O. (1998) 'Do Jews in Israel still laugh at themselves?' In A. Ziv (ed.), *Jewish Humour*. New Brunswick, NJ: Transaction.

Nicolas, S. and Murray, D.J. (2000) 'Le fondateur de la psychologie "scientifique" française: Théodule Ribot (1839–1916)', *Psychologie et Histoire*, 1, 1–42.

Nofsinger, R.E. (1993) *Everyday Conversation*. Newbury Park, CA: Sage.

Norrick, N.R. (1993) *Conversational Joking*. Bloomington, IN: Indiana University Press.

Norrick, N.R. (2003) 'Issues in conversational joking', *Journal of Pragmatics*, 35, 1333–59.

Oring, E. (1984) *The Jokes of Sigmund Freud: A Study in Humour and Jewish Identity*. Philadelphia, PA: University of Pennsylvania Press.

Oring, E. (1989) 'Between jokes and tales: on the nature of punch lines', *Humor*, 2, 349–64.

Parkinson, B. (1995) *Ideas and Realities of Emotion*. London: Routledge.

Parrott, W.G. and Harré, R. (1996) 'Embarrassment and the threat to character', in R, Harré and W.G. Parrott (eds), *The Emotions*. London: Sage.

Parrott, W.G. and Smith, S.F. (1991) 'Embarrassment: actual vs typical cases, classical vs. proto-typical representations', *Cognition and Emotion*, 5, 467–88.

Peale, N.V. (1987) *You Can If You Think You Can*. New York: Simon and Schuster.

Peale, N.V. (1990) *Six Attitudes for Winners*. Wheaton, IL: Tyndale House.

Peale, N.V. (1996a) *Tough-Minded Optimist*. New York: Ballantine Books.

Peale, N.V. (1996b) *Power of Positive Thinking*. New York: Ballantine Books.

Pearsall, R. (1975) *Collapse of Stout Party: Victorian Wit and Humour*. London: Weidenfeld and Nicolson.

Peterson, C. (2000) 'The future of optimism', *American Psychologist*, 55, 44–55.

Piddington, R. (1933) *The Psychology of Laughter: A Study in Social Adaptation*. London: Figurehead.

Plato (1925) 'Philebus', in *The Statesman and Philebus*. London: William Heinemann.

Plato (1974) *The Republic*. Harmondsworth: Penguin.

Plato (1982) 'Meno', in *Protagoras and Meno*. Harmondsworth: Penguin.

Pomerantz, A. (1984) 'Agreeing and disagreeing with assessments: some features of pre-ferred/dispreferred turn shapes', in J.M. Atkinson and J. Heritage (eds), *Structures of Social Action*. Cambridge: Cambridge University Press.

Popper, K. (1984) *The Open Society and its Enemies* vol. 2. London: Routledge.

Potter, J. (1996) *Representing Reality*. London: Sage.

Provine, R.R. (2000) *Laughter: A Scientific Investigation*. London: Faber and Faber.

Psathas, G. (1995) *Conversation Analysis*. London: Sage.

Raskin, V. (1985) *Semantic Mechanisms of Humor*. Dordrecht: Reidel

Raskin, V. (1998) 'The sense of humour and the truth', in W. Ruch (ed.), *The Sense of Humor*. Berlin: Mouton de Gruyter.

Reik, T. (1956) *The Search Within*. New York: Farrar, Straus and Cudahy.

Reik, T. (1962) *Jewish Wit*. New York: Gamut Press.

Retzinger, S. (1991) *Violent Emotions*. Newbury Park: Sage.

Ribot, T. (1870) *La psychologie anglaise*. Paris: Ladrange.

Ribot, T. (1897) *The Psychology of the Emotions*. London: Walter Scott.

Rizzo, S. (2000) *Becoming a Humour Being: The Power to Choose a Better Way*. Lindenhurst: Full Circle Publishing.

Rogoff, B. (1990) *Apprenticeship in Thinking: Cognitive Development in Social Context*. New York: Oxford University Press.

Rosenbaum, R. (1998) *Explaining Hitler: The Search for the Origins of his Evil*. London: Papermac.

Ruch, W. (ed.) (1988) *The Sense of Humour*. Berlin: Mouton de Gruyter.

Ruhe, A. and Paul, N.M. (1914) *Henri Bergson: An Account of his Life and Philosophy*. London: Macmillan.

Sabini, J. (1992) *Social Psychology*. New York: W.W. Norton.

Sabini, J., Siepmann, M., Stein, J. and Meyerowitz, M. (2000) 'Who is embarrassed by what?', *Cognition and Emotion*, 14, 213–40.

Sacks, H. (1992) *Lectures on Conversation*, vol. 2. Oxford: Blackwell.

Salameh, W.A. (1993) 'Introduction: on therapeutic icons and therapeutic personae', in W.F. Fry and W.A. Salameh (eds), *Advances in Humour and Psychotherapy*. Sarasota, FL: Professional Resource Exchange.

Salovey, P., Rothman, A.J., Detweiler, J.B. and Steward, W.T. (2000) 'Emotional states and phys-ical health', *American Psychologist*, 55, 110–21.

Sartre, J.P. (1948) *Portrait of the Anti-Semite*. London: Secker and Warburg.

Scheff, T.J. (1990) *Microsociology: Discourse, Emotion and Social Structure*. Chicago: University of Chicago Press.

Scheff, T.J. (1994) *Bloody Revenge: Emotions, Nationalism and War*. Boulder, CO: Westview Press.

Scheff, T.J. (1997) *Emotions, the Social Bond, and Human Reality*. Cambridge: Cambridge University Press.

Scheff, T.J. (2000) 'Shame and the social bond: a sociological theory', *Sociological Theory*, 18, 84–99.

Schieffelin, B.B. (1986) 'Teasing and shaming in Kaluli children's interactions', in B.B. Schieffelin and E. Ochs (eds), *Language Socialization across Cultures*. Cambridge: Cambridge University Press.

Schieffelin, B.B. (1990) *The Give and Take of Everyday Life: Language Socialization of Kaluli Children*. Cambridge: Cambridge University Press.

Schieffelin, B.B. and Ochs, E. (eds) (1986) *Language Socialization across Cultures*. Cambridge: Cambridge University Press.

Schimel, J.L. (1993) 'Reflections on the function of humour in psychotherapy, especially with adolescents', in W.F. Fry and W.A. Salameh (eds), *Advances in Humour and Psychotherapy*. Sarasota, FL: Professional Resource Exchange.

Schopenhauer, A. (1987) 'The World as Will and Idea (1819): extracts from Book 1', in J. Morreall (ed.), *The Philosophy of Laughter and Humour*. Albany, NY: New York State University Press.

Screech, M.A. (1997) *Laughter at the Foot of the Cross*. London: Allen Lane.

Seligman, M.E.P. (1990) *Learned Optimism: How to Change your Mind and your Life*. New York: Knopf.

Seligman, M.E.P. (2002a) 'Positive psychology, positive prevention and positive therapy', in C.R. Snyder and S. Lopez (eds) *Handbook of Positive Psychology*. Oxford: Oxford University Press.

Seligman, M.E.P. (2002b) 'Positive clinical psychology', in L.G. Aspinwall and U.M. Staudinger (eds), *A Psychology of Human Strengths*. Washington, DC: American Psychological Association.

Seligman, M.E.P. and Csikszentmihalyi, M. (2000) 'Positive psychology: an introduction', *American Psychologist*, 55, 5–14.

Shaftesbury, Third Earl ([1711] 1999) *Characteristics of Men, Manners, Opinions, Times*. Cambridge: Cambridge University Press.

Shapiro, J.P., Baumeister, R.F. and Kessler, J.W. (1991) 'A 3-component model of children's teasing: aggression, humour and ambiguity', *Journal of Social and Clinical Psychology*, 10: 459–72.

Sharkey, W.F. (1992) 'Use and response to intentional embarrassment', *Communication Studies*, 43, 257–75.

Simpson, R. (1994) *Sir John Tenniel: Aspects of his Work*. London: Associated University Press.

Smiles, S. (1882) *Self-Help*. London: John Murray.

Smith, P.K. (ed.) (1999) *The Nature of School Bullying*. London: Routledge.

Smith, P.K. and Sharp, S. (eds) (1994) *School Bullying: Insights and Perspectives*. London: Routledge.

Smith, S. (1864) *Elementary Sketches of Moral Philosophy: Delivered at the Royal Institution in the Years 1804, 1805 and 1806*. New York: Harper and Brothers.

Speier, H. (1998) 'Wit and politics: an essay on laughter', *American Journal of Sociology*, 103, 1352–401.

Spencer, H. (1851) *Social Statics*. London: John Chapman.

Spencer, H. (1861) *Education: Intellectual, Moral and Physical*. London: G. Manwaring.

Spencer, H. (1864a) 'The physiology of laughter', in H. Spencer, *Essays: Scientific, Political and Speculative* (Second Series). New York: D. Appleton.

Spencer, H. (1864b) 'Bain on the emotions and the will', in H. Spencer, *Essays: Scientific, Political and Speculative* (Second Series). New York: D. Appleton

Spencer, H. (1864c) *First Principles of a New System of Philosophy*. New York: D. Appleton.

Spencer, H. (1881) *The Principles of Psychology*, 3rd edn. London: Williams and Norgate.

Spencer, H. (1893) *The Inadequacy of 'Natural Selection'*. New York: D. Appleton.

Spencer, H. (1897) *The Study of Sociology* (1873). London: Kegan Paul, Trench, Trübner.

Spencer, H. (1904) *An Autobiography*. London: Williams and Norgate.

Sperber, D. and Wilson, D. (1986) *Relevance: Communication and Cognition*. Oxford: Basil Blackwell.

Steadman, R. (1979) *Sigmund Freud*. London: Paddington Press.

Stewart, D. ([1792] 1814) *Elements of the Philosophy of the Human Mind*. London: T. Cadell and W. Davies.

Stewart, D. ([1793] 1808) *Outlines of Moral Philosophy*. Edinburgh: William Creech.

Strachey, J. (1991) 'Editor's introduction', in S. Freud, *Jokes and their Relation to the Unconscious*, Penguin Freud Library, vol. 6. Harmondsworth: Penguin.

Strachey, L. (1928) *Queen Victoria*. London: Chatto and Windus.

Strack, F., Martin, L.L. and Stepper, S. (1988) 'Inhibiting and facilitating conditions of the human smile: a non-obtrusive test of the facial feedback hypothesis', *Journal of Personality and Social Psychology*, 54, 768–77.

Sullivan, E. (2000) 'Gallows humour in social work practice: an issue for supervision and reflexivity', *Practice*, 12 (2), 45–54.

Sully, J. (1895) *Studies of Childhood*. London: Longmans, Green and Co.

Sully, J. (1902) *An Essay on Laughter*. London: Longmans, Green and Co.

Sully, J. (1918) *My Life and Friends: A Psychologist's Memories*. London: T. Fisher Unwin.

Sultanoff, S.M. (1999) 'Where has all my humour gone; long time passing…Humour from children to adults', *Therapeutic Humor*, 13(4), 2.

Surkis, A.A. (1993) 'Humour in relation to obsessive-compulsive processes', in W.F. Fry and W.A. Salameh (eds), *Advances in Humour and Psychotherapy*. Sarasota, FL: Professional Resource Exchange.

Sutherland, J. (ed.) (1987) *The Oxford Book of Literary Anecdotes*. Oxford: Oxford University Press.

Swales, P.J. (1982) 'Freud, Minna Bernays and the conquest of Rome: new light on the origins of psychoanalysis', *New American Review*, 1, 1–23.

Swales, P.J. (2003) 'Freud, death and sexual pleasures: on the psychical mechanism of Dr. Sigm. Freud', *Arc de Cercle*, 1, 5–74.

Swearingen, J. (1991) *Rhetoric and Irony*. New York: Oxford University Press.

Swift, J. (1909a) 'A Complete Collection of Genteel and Ingenious Conversation – in three dialogues', in J. Swift, *A Tale of the Tub and Other Satires*. London: J.M. Dent.

Swift, J. (1909b) 'Hints towards an essay on conversation', in J. Swift, *A Tale of the Tub and Other Satires*. London: J.M. Dent.

Tangney, J.P. (1992) 'Situation determinants of shame and guilt in young adulthood', *Personality and Social Psychology Bulletin*, 18, 199–206.

Tangney, J.P., Miller, R.S., Flicker, L. and Barlow, D.H. (1996) 'Are shame, guilt and embarrassment distinct emotions?', *Journal of Personality and Social Psychology*, 70, 1256–69.

Tangney, J.P., Niedenthal, P.M., Covert, M.V. and Barlow, D.H. (1998) 'Are shame and guilt related to distinct self-discrepancies? A test of Higgins's (1987) hypotheses', *Journal of Personality and Social Psychology*, 75, 256–68.

Tannen, D. (1989) *Talking Voices*. Cambridge: Cambridge University Press.

Tave, S.M. (1960) *The Amiable Humorist: A Study in the Comic Theory and Criticism of the Eighteenth and Early Nineteenth Centuries*. Cambridge: University of Chicago Press.

Taylor, S.E. and Brown, J.D. (1994) 'Positive illusions and well-being revisited: separating fact from fiction', *Psychological Bulletin*, 116, 21–7.

Taylor, S.E. (1991) *Positive Illusions: Creative Self-Deception and the Healthy Mind*. New York: Basic Books.

Terasahjo, T. and Salmivalli, C. (2003) '"She is not actually bullied". The discourse of harassment in student groups', *Aggressive Behaviour*, 29, 134–54.

Timpanero, S. (1985) *The Freudian Slip*. London: New Let Books.

Turnbull, C.M. (1972) *The Mountain People*. New York: Simon and Schuster.

Uglow, J. (1997) *Hogarth: A Life and a World*. London: Faber and Faber.

Vaid, J., Hull, R., Heredia, R., Gerkens, D. and Martinez, F. (2003) 'Getting a joke: the time course of meaning activation in verbal humour' *Journal of Pragmatics*, 35, 1431–49.

Valentine, E. (1999) 'The founding of the Psychological Laboratory, University College, London: "Dear Galton...Yours truly, J. Sully"', *History of Psychology*, 2, 204–18.

Van Giffen, K. and Maher, K.M. (1995) 'Memorable humorous incidents: gender themes and setting effects', *Humor*, 8, 39–50.

Vilaythong, A., Arnau, R.C., Rosen, D.H. and Mascaro, N. (2003) 'Humour and hope: can humour increase hope?' *Humor*, 16, 79–89.

Voltaire (n.d.) *Philosophical Dictionary*. London: E. Truelove.

Vulliamy, E. (2003) 'The President rides out', *Observer Review*, January 26, 1–2.

Wade, N.J. (2001) 'The Bains of psychology', *Perception*, 30, 777–83.

Watson-Gegeo, K.A. and Gegeo, D.W. (1986) 'Calling-out and repeating routines in Kwara'ae children's language socialization', in B.B. Schieffelin and E. Ochs (eds), *Language Socialization across Cultures*. Cambridge: Cambridge University Press.

Webster, R. (1996) *Why Freud Was Wrong*. Harmondsworth: Penguin.

Weininger, O. ([1903] 1906) *Sex and Character*. London: William Heinemann.

Whately, R. (1860) *Elements of Rhetoric*. London: John W. Parker.

Wickberg, D. (1998) *The Senses of Humour*. Ithaca, NY: Cornell University Press.

Wierzbicka, A. (1995) 'Emotion and facial expression: a semantic approach', *Culture and Psychology*, 1, 227–58.

Wilkes, A.L. and Wade, N.J. (1997) 'Bain on neural networks', *Brain and Cognition*, 33, 295–305.

Wilkinson, S. and Kitzinger, C. (2000) 'Thinking differently about thinking positive: a discursive approach to cancer patients' talk', *Social Science and Medicine*, 50, 797–811.

Wistrich, R.S. (1989) *The Jews of Vienna in the Age of Franz Joseph*. Oxford: Oxford University Press.

Wolf, M.P. (2002) 'A grasshopper walks into a bar: the role of humour in normativity', *Journal for the Theory of Social Behaviour*, 32, 330–43.

Wyer, R.S. Jnr and Collins, J.E. (1992) 'A theory of humour elicitation', *Psychological Review*, 99, 663–88.

Xenophon (1910) 'Symposium, or Banquet', in A.D. Lindsay (ed.), *Socratic Discourses by Plato and Xenophon*. London: J.M. Dent.

Yedes, J. (1996) 'Playful teasing: kiddin' on the square', *Discourse and Society*, 7, 417–38.

Young, R.M. (1990) 'Herbert Spencer and inevitable progress', in G. Marsden (ed.), *Victorian Values*. London: Longman.

Zijderveld, A.C. (1982) *Reality in a Looking-Glass: Rationality through an Analysis of Traditional Folly*. London: Routledge and Kegan Paul.

Zillman, D. (1983) 'Disparagement humor', in P.E. McGee and J.H. Goldstein (eds) *Handbook of Humor Research*, vol. 1. New York: Springer.

Ziv, A. (ed.) (1998) *Jewish Humour*. New Brunswick, NJ: Transaction.

Name Index

Subject Index